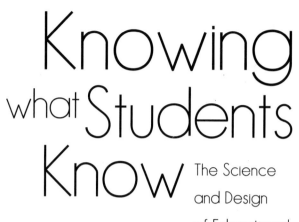

Knowing what Students Know

The Science
and Design
of Educational
Assessment

Committee on the Foundations of Assessment

James W. Pellegrino, Naomi Chudowsky, and Robert Glaser, *editors*

Board on Testing and Assessment

Center for Education

Division of Behavioral and Social Sciences and Education

National Research Council

NATIONAL ACADEMY PRESS
Washington, DC

NATIONAL ACADEMY PRESS • 2101 Constitution Avenue N.W. • Washington, DC 20418

NOTICE: The project that is the subject of this report was approved by the Governing Board of the National Research Council, whose members are drawn from the councils of the National Academy of Sciences, the National Academy of Engineering, and the Institute of Medicine. The members of the committee responsible for the report were chosen for their special competences and with regard for appropriate balance.

This study was supported by Grant No. REC-9722707 between the National Academy of Sciences and the U.S. National Science Foundation. Any opinions, findings, conclusions, or recommendations expressed in this publication are those of the author(s) and do not necessarily reflect the views of the organizations or agencies that provided support for the project.

Library of Congress Cataloging-in-Publication Data

Knowing what students know : the science and design of educational assessment / Committee on the Foundations of Assessment, Center for Education, Division on Behavioral and Social Sciences and Education, National Research Council ; James Pellegrino, Naomi Chudowsky, and Robert Glaser, editors.
    p. cm
Includes bibliographical references and index.
ISBN 0-309-07272-7
   1. Educational tests and measurements—United States—Design and construction. 2. Cognitive learning theory. I. Pellegrino, James W. II. Chudowsky, Naomi. III. Glaser, Robert, 1921- IV. National Research Council (U.S.). Division of Behavioral and Social Sciences and Education. Committee on the Foundations of Assessment.
LB3051.K59 2001
31.26′1—dc21   2001003876

Additional copies of this report are available from National Academy Press, 2101 Constitution Avenue, N.W., Lockbox 285, Washington, DC 20055; (800) 624-6242 or (202) 334-3313 (in the Washington metropolitan area); Internet, http://www.nap.edu

Suggested citation: National Research Council. 2001. *Knowing what students know: The science and design of educational assessment.* Committee on the Foundations of Assessment. Pelligrino, J., Chudowsky, N., and Glaser, R., editors. Board on Testing and Assessment, Center for Education. Division of Behavioral and Social Sciences and Education. Washington, DC: National Academy Press.

Printed in the United States of America

THE NATIONAL ACADEMIES

National Academy of Sciences
National Academy of Engineering
Institute of Medicine
National Research Council

The **National Academy of Sciences** is a private, nonprofit, self-perpetuating society of distinguished scholars engaged in scientific and engineering research, dedicated to the furtherance of science and technology and to their use for the general welfare. Upon the authority of the charter granted to it by the Congress in 1863, the Academy has a mandate that requires it to advise the federal government on scientific and technical matters. Dr. Bruce M. Alberts is president of the National Academy of Sciences.

The **National Academy of Engineering** was established in 1964, under the charter of the National Academy of Sciences, as a parallel organization of outstanding engineers. It is autonomous in its administration and in the selection of its members, sharing with the National Academy of Sciences the responsibility for advising the federal government. The National Academy of Engineering also sponsors engineering programs aimed at meeting national needs, encourages education and research, and recognizes the superior achievements of engineers. Dr. Wm. A. Wulf is president of the National Academy of Engineering.

The **Institute of Medicine** was established in 1970 by the National Academy of Sciences to secure the services of eminent members of appropriate professions in the examination of policy matters pertaining to the health of the public. The Institute acts under the responsibility given to the National Academy of Sciences by its congressional charter to be an adviser to the federal government and, upon its own initiative, to identify issues of medical care, research, and education. Dr. Kenneth I. Shine is president of the Institute of Medicine.

The **National Research Council** was organized by the National Academy of Sciences in 1916 to associate the broad community of science and technology with the Academy's purposes of furthering knowledge and advising the federal government. Functioning in accordance with general policies determined by the Academy, the Council has become the principal operating agency of both the National Academy of Sciences and the National Academy of Engineering in providing services to the government, the public, and the scientific and engineering communities. The Council is administered jointly by both Academies and the Institute of Medicine. Dr. Bruce M. Alberts and Dr. Wm. A. Wulf are chairman and vice chairman, respectively, of the National Research Council.

COMMITTEE ON THE FOUNDATIONS OF ASSESSMENT

James W. Pellegrino *(Co-chair)*, Peabody College of Education, Vanderbilt University

Robert Glaser *(Co-chair)*, Learning Research and Development Center, University of Pittsburgh

Eva L. Baker, The Center for the Study of Evaluation, University of California, Los Angeles

Gail P. Baxter, Educational Testing Service, Princeton, New Jersey

Paul J. Black, School of Education, King's College, London, England

Christopher L. Dede, Graduate School of Education, Harvard University

Kadriye Ercikan, School of Education, University of British Columbia

Louis M. Gomez, School of Education, Northwestern University

Earl B. Hunt, Department of Psychology, University of Washington

David Klahr, Department of Psychology, Carnegie Mellon University

Richard Lehrer, School of Education, University of Wisconsin

Robert J. Mislevy, School of Education, University of Maryland

Willie Pearson, Jr., Department of Sociology, Wake Forest University

Edward A. Silver, School of Education, University of Michigan

Richard F. Thompson, Department of Psychology, University of Southern California

Richard K. Wagner, Department of Psychology, Florida State University

Mark R. Wilson, School of Education, University of California, Berkeley

Naomi Chudowsky, *Study Director*
Tina Winters, *Research Assistant*
M. Jane Phillips, *Senior Project Assistant*

Acknowledgments

The work of the Committee on the Foundations of Assessment benefited tremendously from the contributions and good will of many people, and the committee is grateful for their support.

First, we wish to acknowledge the sponsor, the National Science Foundation (NSF). Special thanks go to Larry Suter, who was instrumental in getting the project off the ground and who provided enthusiastic support throughout. We also appreciate the support and valuable input of Elizabeth VanderPutten, Janice Earle, Nora Sabelli, and Eric Hamilton at NSF, as well as Eamonn Kelly, now at George Mason University.

The committee was aided greatly by individuals who participated in a series of information-gathering workshops held in conjunction with several of the committee meetings. We valued the opportunity to hear from a diverse group of researchers and practitioners about the complex issues involved in designing and implementing new forms of assessment.

We wish to make special note of Robbie Case from Stanford University and the Ontario Institute for Studies in Education, who deeply influenced this study. Robbie shared with us his powerful ideas about children's conceptual development and the implications for assessment and educational equity. Several aspects of his thinking and published work can be found referenced throughout this report. In every respect he was a gentleman and a scholar. His untimely death in 2000 deeply saddened the members of the committee on both a personal and a professional level. His passing represents a major loss for the fields of psychological and educational research.

A number of researchers working at the intersection of cognition and assessment took time to share their work and ideas with the committee, including Drew Gitomer of the Educational Testing Service, Irvin Katz of George Mason University, Jim Minstrell of A.C.T. Systems for Education, Kurt

VanLehn of the Learning Research and Development Center at the University of Pittsburgh, Ken Koedinger of Carnegie Mellon Univeristy, Barbara White and John Frederiksen of the University of California at Berkeley, and Jim Greeno of Stanford University. The committee discussed the beliefs and theories of learning underlying some innovative large-scale assessments with Phil Daro of the New Standards Project, Steven Leinwand of the Connecticut State Department of Education, Hugh Burkhardt and Sandy Wilcox of the Mathematics Assessment Resource Service, and Carol Myford of the Educational Testing Service. We also heard from teachers who have used various assessment programs in their classrooms. We thank Guy Mauldin of Science Hill High School, Johnson City, Tennessee; Elizabeth Jones of Walnut Elementary School, Lansing, Michigan; Margaret Davis, Westminster Schools, Atlanta, Georgia; Ramona Muniz, Roosevelt Middle School, San Francisco, California; Cherrie Jones, Alice Carlson Applied Learning Center, Fort Worth, Texas; and Suzanna Loper of the Educational Testing Service, Oakland, CA.

Several individuals discussed special considerations related to disadvantaged students and the design of new forms of assessment. They included Bill Trent of the University of Illinois, Urbana-Champaign, Shirley Malcom of the American Association for the Advancement of Science, Sharon Lewis of the Council of Great City Schools, and Louisa Moats of the National Institute of Child Health and Human Development. Developmental psychologists Susan Goldin-Meadow of the University of Chicago, Robert Siegler of Carnegie Mellon University, and Micki Chi of the Learning Research and Development Center at the University of Pittsburgh discussed research methodologies from their discipline that may have application to educational assessment. A number of researchers helped the committee explore the future role of technology in assessment, including Randy Bennett of the Educational Testing Service, Amy Bruckman of the Georgia Institute of Technology, Walter Kintsch of the University of Colorado, Paul Horwitz of The Concord Consortium, and Gregory Leazer of the University of California at Los Angeles. Lorraine McDonnell of the University of California at Santa Barbara, James Kadamus of the New York State Department of Education, and James Gray of the Dorchester Public Schools in Maryland provided valuable policy perspectives on the prospects for a new science of assessment.

The committee was provided excellent input on advances in statistics and measurement by Steven Raudenbush from the University of Michigan and Brian Junker from Carnegie Mellon University. Their presentations, as well as Brian's commissioned review of statistical methods that are potentially useful for cognitively based assessment, greatly informed our discussions. Linda Steinberg of the Educational Testing Service and Geoff Masters of the Australian Council for Educational Research shared state-of-the-art work on assessment design.

A number of other education researchers provided reactions and synthesizing remarks at the various workshops. They included Bob Linn of the University of Colorado, Rich Shavelson of Stanford University, David Berliner of Arizona State University, Barbara Means of SRI International, Ed Haertel of Stanford University, Goodwin Liu of the U.S. Department of Education, and Nora Sabelli of NSF.

The Board on Testing and Assessment, the unit within the National Research Council (NRC) that launched this study, was instrumental in shaping this project and in providing general guidance and support along the way. Many board members have been mentioned above as participants in the committee's work.

We are especially grateful to several consultants to the project, including Nancy Kober and Robert Rothman, who helped with the writing of this report and provided invaluable assistance in thinking about the organization and presentation of ideas. Rona Briere's skillful editing brought further clarity to our ideas.

Within the NRC, a number of individuals supported the project. Michael Feuer, Director of the Center for Education, conceptualized the project and provided good humor and support along the way. Pasquale DeVito, recently appointed Director of the Board on Testing and Assessment, enthusiastically supported us during the final stages of the project. Patricia Morison offered a great deal of wisdom, advice, and encouragement throughout, and Judy Koenig lent us her substantive knowledge of psychometrics whenever needed. Kirsten Sampson Snyder and Genie Grohman expertly maneuvered us through the NRC review process.

The committee expresses particular gratitude to members of the NRC project staff for contributing their intellectual and organizational skills throughout the study. Three deserve particular recognition. Naomi Chudowsky, the project's study director, was a pleasure to work with and brought incredible talents and expertise to the project. She tirelessly assisted the committee in many ways—serving as a valuable source of information about assessment issues and testing programs; organizing and synthesizing the committee's work; keeping the committee moving forward through its deliberations and the report drafting process; and providing energy, enthusiasm, and exceptional good humor throughout. Her attention to detail while simultaneously helping the committee focus on the bigger picture was a major asset in the creation of the final report. Naomi was assisted by Tina Winters, who provided exceptional research support and adeptly handled preparation of the manuscript. Jane Phillips expertly managed the finances and arranged the meetings for the project, always ensuring that the committee's work proceeded smoothly.

This report has been reviewed in draft form by individuals chosen for their diverse perspectives and technical expertise, in accordance with procedures approved by the NRC's Report Review Committee. The purpose of this independent review is to provide candid and critical comments that will assist the institution in making its published report as sound as possible and to ensure that the report meets institutional standards for objectivity, evidence, and responsiveness to the study charge. The review comments and draft manuscript remain confidential to protect the integrity of the deliberative process. We wish to thank the following individuals for their review of this report: James Greeno, Stanford University; Sharon Griffin, Clark University; Suzanne Lane, University of Pittsburgh; Alan Lesgold, University of Pittsburgh; Marcia C. Linn, University of California, Berkeley; Michael I. Posner, Cornell University; Catherine E. Snow, Harvard University; Norman L. Webb, University of Wisconsin; and Sheldon H. White, Harvard University.

Although the reviewers listed above have provided many constructive comments and suggestions, they were not asked to endorse the conclusions or recommendations nor did they see the final draft of the report before its release. The review of this report was overseen by Lauress Wise, Human Resources Research Organization, and Lyle V. Jones, University of North Carolina, Chapel Hill. Appointed by the National Research Council, they were responsible for making certain that an independent examination of this report was carried out in accordance with institutional procedures and that all review comments were carefully considered. Responsibility for the final content of this report rests entirely with the authoring committee and the institution.

Finally, we would like to sincerely thank all of the committee members, who generously contributed their time and intellectual efforts to this project. A study of the scientific foundations of assessment represents an extraordinary challenge, requiring coverage of an exceedingly broad array of complex topics and issues. We were faced with the task of defining the nature of the problem to be studied and solved and then charting a path through a rather ill-defined solution space. Throughout the process, the committee members displayed an extraordinary ability to tolerate ambiguity as we navigated through a vast space of issues and possible answers, at times seemingly without a compass. Simultaneously, they showed a remarkable commitment to learning from each others' expertise and from the many individuals who shared their knowledge with the group. It has been noted before that the idea of eighteen "experts" collaborating to write a book on any topic, let alone educational assessment, is an absurdity. And yet were it not for the collective expertise, thoughtfulness, and good will of all the committee members, this report and its consensual substantive messages would not have been developed. It has been a professionally stimulating and personally gratifying experience to work with the members of the committee and everyone at the NRC associated with this effort.

Jim Pellegrino, *Co-chair*
Bob Glaser, *Co-chair*

Preface

In recent years, the National Research Council (NRC), through its Board on Testing and Assessment (BOTA), has explored some of today's most pressing and complex issues in educational assessment. Several NRC committees have examined the role and appropriate uses of assessment in standards-based reform, a movement that is reshaping education throughout the country. For example, committees have studied the impact and uses of tests with high stakes for students, approaches for assessing students with disabilities in a standards-based system, and issues related to proposed voluntary national tests. In the process of carrying out this work, the board and its committees have delved into fundamental questions about educational assessment, such as what its purposes are; which kinds of knowledge and skills should be assessed; how well current assessments, such as the National Assessment of Educational Progress, are fulfilling the various demands placed on them; and which new developments hold promise for improving assessment.

At roughly the same time, other NRC committees have been exploring equally compelling issues related to human cognition and learning. A 1998 report entitled *Preventing Reading Difficulties in Young Children* consolidates current research findings on how students learn to read and which approaches are most effective for reading instruction. Most recently, the NRC Committee on Developments in the Science of Learning examined findings from cognitive science that have advanced understanding of how people think and learn. The 1999 report of that committee, *How People Learn*, not only summarizes major changes in conceptions about learning, but also examines the implications of these changes for designing effective teaching and learning environments.

As these multiple committees were progressing with their work, some

NRC staff and members of BOTA decided this would be an ideal time to address a long-standing issue noted by numerous researchers interested in problems of educational assessment: the need to bring together advances in assessment and in the understanding of human learning. Each of these disciplines had produced a body of knowledge that could enrich the other. In fact, some scholars and practitioners were already applying findings from cognitive science in the development of innovative methods of assessment. Although these efforts were generally small-scale or experimental, they pointed to exciting possibilities.

Accordingly, the board proposed that an NRC committee be formed to review advances in the cognitive and measurement sciences, as well as early work done in the intersection between the two disciplines, and to consider the implications for reshaping educational assessment. In one sense, this work would be a natural extension of the conclusions and recommendations of *How People Learn*. In another sense, it would follow through on a desire expressed by many of those involved in the board's activities to revisit the foundations of assessment—to explore developments in the underlying science and philosophy of assessment that could have significant implications for the long term, but were often glossed over in the short term because of more urgent demands. The National Science Foundation (NSF), recognizing the importance and timeliness of such a study, agreed to sponsor this new NRC effort.

The Committee on the Foundations of Assessment was convened in January 1998 by the NRC with support from NSF. The committee comprised eighteen experts from the fields of cognitive and developmental psychology, neuroscience, testing and measurement, learning technologies, mathematics and science education, and education policy with diverse perspectives on educational assessment.

During its 3-year study, the committee held nine multi-day meetings to conduct its deliberations and five workshops to gather information about promising assessment research and practice. At the workshops, numerous invited presenters shared with the committee members their cutting-edge work on the following topics: (1) assessment practices that are based on cognitive principles and are being successfully implemented in schools and classrooms, (2) new statistical models with promise for use in assessing a broad range of cognitive performances, (3) programs that engage students in self- and peer assessment, (4) innovative technologies for learning and assessment, (5) cognitively based instructional intervention programs, and (6) policy perspectives on new forms of assessment. This report presents the findings and recommendations that resulted from the committee's deliberations.

Contents

Part III
Assessment Design and Use:
Principles, Practices, and Future Directions

Part IV
Conclusion

Knowing
what Students
Know
The Science
and Design
of Educational
Assessment

Executive Summary

Educational assessment seeks to determine how well students are learning and is an integral part of the quest for improved education. It provides feedback to students, educators, parents, policy makers, and the public about the effectiveness of educational services. With the movement over the past two decades toward setting challenging academic standards and measuring students' progress in meeting those standards, educational assessment is playing a greater role in decision making than ever before. In turn, education stakeholders are questioning whether current large-scale assessment practices are yielding the most useful kinds of information for informing and improving education. Meanwhile, classroom assessments, which have the potential to enhance instruction and learning, are not being used to their fullest potential.

Advances in the cognitive and measurement sciences make this an opportune time to rethink the fundamental scientific principles and philosophical assumptions serving as the foundations for current approaches to assessment. Advances in the cognitive sciences have broadened the conception of those aspects of learning that are most important to assess, and advances in measurement have expanded the capability to interpret more complex forms of evidence derived from student performance.

The Committee on the Foundations of Assessment, supported by the National Science Foundation, was established to review and synthesize advances in the cognitive sciences and measurement and to explore their implications for improving educational assessment. At the heart of the committee's work was the critical importance of developing new kinds of educational assessments that better serve the goal of equity. Needed are classroom and large-scale assessments that help all students learn and succeed in school by making as clear as possible to them, their teachers, and other education stakeholders the nature of their accomplishments and the progress of their learning.

CONCLUSIONS

The Nature of Assessment and Reasoning from Evidence

This report addresses assessments used in both classroom and large-scale contexts for three broad purposes: to assist learning, to measure individual achievement, and to evaluate programs. The purpose of an assessment determines priorities, and the context of use imposes constraints on the design. *Thus it is essential to recognize that one type of assessment does not fit all.*

Often a single assessment is used for multiple purposes; in general, however, the more purposes a single assessment aims to serve, the more each purpose will be compromised. For instance, many state tests are used for both individual and program assessment purposes. This is not necessarily a problem, as long as assessment designers and users recognize the compromises and trade-offs such use entails.

Although assessments used in various contexts and for differing purposes often look quite different, they share certain common principles. One such principle is that assessment is always a process of reasoning from evidence. By its very nature, moreover, assessment is imprecise to some degree. Assessment results are only estimates of what a person knows and can do.

Every assessment, regardless of its purpose, rests on three pillars: a model of how students represent knowledge and develop competence in the subject domain, tasks or situations that allow one to observe students' performance, and an interpretation method for drawing inferences from the performance evidence thus obtained. In the context of large-scale assessment, the interpretation method is usually a statistical model that characterizes expected data patterns, given varying levels of student competence. In less formal classroom assessment, the interpretation is often made by the teacher using an intuitive or qualitative rather than formal statistical model.

Three foundational elements, comprising what is referred to in this report as the "assessment triangle," underlie all assessments. *These three elements—cognition, observation, and interpretation—must be explicitly connected and designed as a coordinated whole.* If not, the meaningfulness of inferences drawn from the assessment will be compromised.

The central problem addressed by this report is that most widely used assessments of academic achievement are based on highly restrictive beliefs about learning and competence not fully in keeping with current knowledge about human cognition and learning. Likewise, the observation and interpretation elements underlying most current assessments were created to fit prior conceptions of learning and need enhancement to support the kinds of inferences people now want to draw about student achievement. *A model of cognition and learning should serve as the cornerstone of the assessment design process. This model should be based on the best available understanding of how students represent knowledge and develop competence in the domain.*

The model of learning can serve as a unifying element—a nucleus that brings cohesion to curriculum, instruction, and assessment. This cohesive function is a crucial one because *educational assessment does not exist in isolation, but must be aligned with curriculum and instruction if it is to support learning.*

Finally, aspects of learning that are assessed and emphasized in the classroom should ideally be consistent with (though not necessarily the same as) the aspects of learning targeted by large-scale assessments. In reality, however, these two forms of assessment are often out of alignment. The result can be conflict and frustration for both teachers and learners. *Thus there is a need for better alignment among assessments used for different purposes and in different contexts.*

Advances in the Sciences of Thinking and Learning

Contemporary theories of learning and knowing emphasize the way knowledge is represented, organized, and processed in the mind. Emphasis is also given to social dimensions of learning, including social and participatory practices that support knowing and understanding. This body of knowledge strongly implies that *assessment practices need to move beyond a focus on component skills and discrete bits of knowledge to encompass the more complex aspects of student achievement.*

Among the fundamental elements of cognition is the mind's cognitive architecture, which includes working or short-term memory, a highly limited system, and long-term memory, a virtually limitless store of knowledge. What matters in most situations is how well one can evoke the knowledge stored in long-term memory and use it to reason efficiently about current information and problems. *Therefore, within the normal range of cognitive abilities, estimates of how people organize information in long-term memory are likely to be more important than estimates of working memory capacity.*

Understanding the contents of long-term memory is especially critical for determining what people know; how they know it; and how they are able to use that knowledge to answer questions, solve problems, and engage in additional learning. While the contents include both general and specific knowledge, much of what one knows is domain- and task-specific and organized into structures known as schemas. Assessments should evaluate what schemas an individual has and under what circumstances he or she regards the information as relevant. This evaluation should include how a person organizes acquired information, encompassing both strategies for problem solving and ways of chunking relevant information into manageable units.

The importance of evaluating knowledge structures comes from research on expertise. *Studies of expert-novice differences in subject domains illuminate critical features of proficiency that should be the targets for assessment.* Experts in a subject domain typically organize factual and procedural knowledge into schemas that support pattern recognition and the rapid retrieval and application of knowledge.

One of the most important aspects of cognition is metacognition—the process of reflecting on and directing one's own thinking. Metacognition is crucial to effective thinking and problem solving and is one of the hallmarks of expertise in specific areas of knowledge and skill. Experts use metacognitive strategies for monitoring understanding during problem solving and for performing self-correction. *Assessment should therefore attempt to determine whether an individual has good metacognitive skills.*

Not all children learn in the same way and follow the same paths to competence. Children's problem-solving strategies become more effective over time and with practice, but the growth process is not a simple, uniform progression, nor is there movement directly from erroneous to optimal solution strategies. *Assessments should focus on identifying the specific strategies children are using for problem solving, giving particular consideration to where those strategies fall on a developmental continuum of efficiency and appropriateness for a particular domain of knowledge and skill.*

Children have rich intuitive knowledge of their world that undergoes significant change as they mature. Learning entails the transformation of naive understanding into more complete and accurate comprehension, and assessment can be used as a tool to facilitate this process. To this end, *assessments, especially those conducted in the context of classroom instruction, should focus on making students' thinking visible to both their teachers and themselves so that instructional strategies can be selected to support an appropriate course for future learning.*

Practice and feedback are critical aspects of the development of skill and expertise. *One of the most important roles for assessment is the provision of timely and informative feedback to students during instruction and learning so that their practice of a skill and its subsequent acquisition will be effective and efficient.*

As a function of context, knowledge frequently develops in a highly contextualized and inflexible form, and often does not transfer very effectively. Transfer depends on the development of an explicit understanding of when to apply what has been learned. *Assessments of academic achievement need to consider carefully the knowledge and skills required to understand and answer a question or solve a problem, including the context in which it is presented, and whether an assessment task or situation is functioning as a test of near, far, or zero transfer.*

Much of what humans learn is acquired through discourse and interaction with others. Thus, knowledge is often embedded in particular social and cultural contexts, including the context of the classroom, and it encompasses understandings about the meaning of specific practices such as asking and answering questions. *Assessments need to examine how well students engage in communicative practices appropriate to a domain of knowledge and skill, what they understand about those practices, and how well they use the tools appropriate to that domain.*

Models of cognition and learning provide a basis for the design and implementation of theory-driven instructional and assessment practices. Such programs and practices already exist and have been used productively in certain curricular areas. However, the vast majority of what is known has yet to be applied to the design of assessments for classroom or external evaluation purposes. *Further work is therefore needed on translating what is already known in cognitive science to assessment practice, as well as on developing additional cognitive analyses of domain-specific knowledge and expertise.*

Many highly effective tools exist for probing and modeling a person's knowledge and for examining the contents and contexts of learning. *The methods used in cognitive science to design tasks, observe and analyze cognition, and draw inferences about what a person knows are applicable to many of the challenges of designing effective educational assessments.*

Contributions of Measurement and Statistical Modeling to Assessment

Advances in methods of educational measurement include the development of formal measurement (psychometric) models, which represent a particular form of reasoning from evidence. These models provide explicit, formal rules for integrating the many pieces of information drawn from assessment tasks. *Certain kinds of assessment applications require the capabilities of formal statistical models for the interpretation element of the assessment triangle.* These tend to be applications with one or more of the following features: high stakes, distant users (i.e., assessment interpreters without day-to-day interaction with the students), complex models of learning, and large volumes of data.

Measurement models currently available can support the kinds of inferences that cognitive science suggests are important to pursue. In particular, it is now possible to characterize student achievement in terms of multiple aspects of proficiency, rather than a single score; chart students' progress over time, instead of simply measuring performance at a particular point in time; deal with multiple paths or alternative methods of valued performance; model, monitor, and improve judgments on the basis of informed evaluations; and model performance not only at the level of students, but also at the levels of groups, classes, schools, and states.

Nonetheless, *many of the newer models and methods are not widely used because they are not easily understood or packaged in accessible ways for those without a strong technical background.* Technology offers the possibility of addressing this shortcoming. For instance, building statistical models into technology-based learning environments for use in classrooms enables teachers to employ more complex tasks, capture and replay students' performances, share exemplars of competent performance, and in the process gain critical information about student competence.

Much hard work remains to focus psychometric model building on the critical features of models of cognition and learning and on observations that reveal meaningful cognitive processes in a particular domain. If anything, the task has become more difficult because an additional step is now required—determining in tandem the inferences that must be drawn, the observations needed, the tasks that will provide them, and the statistical models that will express the necessary patterns most efficiently. Therefore, *having a broad array of models available does not mean that the measurement model problem has been solved.* The long-standing tradition of leaving scientists, educators, task designers, and psychometricians each to their own realms represents perhaps the most serious barrier to progress.

Implications of the New Foundations for Assessment Design

The design of high-quality classroom and large-scale assessments is a complex process that involves numerous components best characterized as iterative and interdependent, rather than linear and sequential. A design decision made at a later stage can affect one occurring earlier in the process. As a result, assessment developers must often revisit their choices and refine their designs.

One of the main features that distinguishes the committee's proposed approach to assessment design from current approaches is the central role of a model of cognition and learning, as emphasized above. This model may be fine-grained and very elaborate or more coarsely grained, depending on the purpose of the assessment, but it should always be based on empirical studies of learners in a domain. Ideally, the model will also provide a developmental perspective, showing typical ways in which learners progress toward competence.

Another essential feature of good assessment design is an interpretation model that fits the model of cognition and learning. Just as sophisticated interpretation techniques used with assessment tasks based on impoverished models of learning will produce limited information about student competence, assessments based on a contemporary, detailed understanding of how students learn will not yield all the information they otherwise might if the statistical tools available to interpret the data, or the data themselves, are not sufficient for the task. *Observations, which include assessment tasks along with the criteria for evaluating students' responses, must be carefully designed to elicit the knowledge and cognitive processes that the model of learning suggests are most important for competence in the domain.* The interpretation model must incorporate this evidence in the results in a manner consistent with the model of learning.

Validation that tasks tap relevant knowledge and cognitive processes, often lacking in assessment development, is another essential aspect of the development effort. Starting with hypotheses about the cognitive demands of a task, a variety of research techniques, such as interviews, having students think aloud as they work problems, and analysis of errors, can be used to analyze the mental processes of examinees during task performance. Conducting such analyses early in the assessment development process can help ensure that assessments do, in fact, measure what they are intended to measure.

Well-delineated descriptions of learning in the domain are key to being able to communicate effectively about the nature of student performance. *Although reporting of results occurs at the end of an assessment cycle, assessments must be designed from the outset to ensure that reporting of the desired types of information will be possible.* The ways in which people learn the subject matter, as well as different types or levels of competence, should be displayed and made as recognizable as possible to educators, students, and the public.

Fairness is a key issue in educational assessment. *One way of addressing fairness in assessment is to take into account examinees' histories of instruction—or opportunities to learn the material being tested—when designing assessments and interpreting students' responses.* Ways of drawing such conditional inferences have been tried mainly on a small scale, but hold promise for tackling persistent issues of equity in testing.

Some examples of assessments that approximate the above features already exist. They are illustrative of the new approach to assessment the committee advocates, and they suggest principles for the design of new assessments that can better serve the goals of learning.

Assessment in Practice

Guiding the committee's work were the premises that (1) something important should be learned from every assessment situation, and (2) the information gained should ultimately help improve learning. The power of classroom assessment resides in its close connections to instruction and teachers' knowledge of their students' instructional histories. Large-scale, standardized assessments can communicate across time and place, but by so constraining the content and timeliness of the message that they often have limited utility in the classroom. *Thus the contrast between classroom and large-scale assessments arises from the different purposes they serve and contexts in which they are used.* Certain trade-offs are an inescapable aspect of assessment design.

Students will learn more if instruction and assessment are integrally related. *In the classroom, providing students with information about particular qualities of their work and about what they can do to improve is crucial for maximizing learning.* It is in the context of classroom assessment that theories of cognition and learning can be particularly helpful by providing a picture of intermediary states of student understanding on the pathway from novice to competent performer in a subject domain.

Findings from cognitive research cannot always be translated directly or easily into classroom practice. Most effective are programs that interpret the findings from cognitive research in ways that are useful for teachers. Teachers need theoretical training, as well as practical training and assessment tools, to be able to implement formative assessment effectively in their classrooms.

Large-scale assessments are further removed from instruction, but can still benefit learning if well designed and properly used. Substantially more valid and useful inferences could be drawn from such assessments if the principles set forth in this report were applied during the design process.

Large-scale assessments not only serve as a means for reporting on student achievement, but also reflect aspects of academic competence societies consider worthy of recognition and reward. *Thus large-scale assessments can provide worthwhile targets for educators and students to pursue.* Whereas teaching directly to the items on a test is not desirable, teaching to the theory of cognition and learning that underlies an assessment can provide positive direction for instruction.

To derive real benefits from the merger of cognitive and measurement theory in large-scale assessment, it will be necessary to devise ways of covering a broad range of competencies and capturing rich information about the nature of student understanding. *Indeed, to fully capitalize on the new foundations described in this report will require substantial changes in the way large-scale assessment is approached and relaxation of some of the constraints that currently drive large-scale assessment practices.* Alternatives to on-demand, census testing are available. If individual student scores are needed, broader sampling of the domain can be achieved by extracting evidence of student performance from classroom work produced during the course of instruction. If the primary purpose of the assessment is program evaluation, the constraint of having to produce reliable individual student scores can be relaxed, and population sampling can be useful.

For classroom or large-scale assessment to be effective, students must understand and share the goals for learning. Students learn more when they understand (and even participate in developing) the criteria by which their work will be evaluated, and when they engage in peer and self-assessment during which they apply those criteria. These practices develop students' metacognitive abilities, which, as emphasized above, are necessary for effective learning.

The current educational assessment environment in the United States assigns much greater value and credibility to external, large-scale assessments of individuals and programs than to classroom assessment designed to assist learning. The investment of money, instructional time, research, and development for large-scale testing far outweighs that for effective classroom assessment. *More of the research, development, and training investment must be shifted toward the classroom, where teaching and learning occur.*

A vision for the future is that assessments at all levels—from classroom to state—will work together in a system that is comprehensive, coherent, and continuous. In such a system, assessments would provide a variety of evidence to support educational decision making. Assessment at all levels would be linked back to the same underlying model of student learning and would provide indications of student growth over time.

Information Technologies: Opportunities for Advancing Educational Assessment

Information technologies are helping to remove some of the constraints that have limited assessment practice in the past. Assessment tasks no longer need be confined to paper-and-pencil formats, and the entire burden of classroom assessment no longer need fall on the teacher. At the same time, *technology will not in and of itself improve educational assessment.* Improved methods of assessment require a design process that connects the three elements of the assessment triangle to ensure that the theory of cognition, the observations, and the interpretation process work together to support the intended inferences. Fortunately, there exist multiple examples of technology tools and applications that enhance the linkages among cognition, observation, and interpretation.

Some of the most intriguing applications of technology extend the nature of the problems that can be presented and the knowledge and cognitive processes that can be assessed. By enriching task environments through the use of multimedia, interactivity, and control over the stimulus display, it is possible to assess a much wider array of cognitive competencies than has heretofore been feasible. New capabilities enabled by technology include directly assessing problem-solving skills, making visible sequences of actions taken by learners in solving problems, and modeling and simulating complex reasoning tasks. Technology also makes possible data collection on concept organization and other aspects of students' knowledge structures, as well as representations of their participation in discussions and group projects. *A significant contribution of technology has been to the design of systems for implementing sophisticated classroom-based formative assessment practices.* Technology-based systems have been developed to support individualized instruction by extracting key features of learners' responses, analyzing patterns of correct and incorrect reasoning, and providing rapid and informative feedback to both student and teacher.

A major change in education has resulted from the influence of technology on what is taught and how. Schools are placing more emphasis on teaching critical content in greater depth. Examples include the teaching of advanced thinking and reasoning skills within a discipline through the use of technology-mediated projects involving long-term inquiry. Such projects often integrate content and learning across disciplines, as well as integrate assessment with curriculum and instruction in powerful ways.

A possibility for the future arises from the projected growth across curricular areas of technology-based assessment embedded in instructional settings. Increased availability of such systems could make it possible to pursue balanced designs representing a more coordinated and coherent assessment system. Information from such assessments could possibly be used for multiple purposes, including the audit function associated with many existing external assessments.

Finally, *technology holds great promise for enhancing educational assessment at multiple levels of practice, but its use for this purpose also raises issues of utility, practicality, cost, equity, and privacy.* These issues will need to be addressed as technology applications in education and assessment continue to expand, evolve, and converge.

RECOMMENDATIONS FOR RESEARCH, POLICY, AND PRACTICE

Like groups before us, the committee recognizes that the bridge between research and practice takes time to build and that research and practice must proceed interactively. It is unlikely that insights gained from current or new knowledge about cognition, learning, and measurement will be sufficient by themselves to bring about transformations in assessment such as those described in this report. Research and practice need to be connected more directly through the building of a cumulative knowledge base that serves both sets of interests. In the context of this study, that knowledge base would focus on the development and use of theory-based assessment. Furthermore, it is essential to recognize that research impacts practice indirectly through the influence of the existing knowledge base on four important mediating arenas: instructional materials, teacher education and professional development, education policies, and public opinion and media coverage. By influencing each of these arenas, an expanding knowledge base on the principles and practices of effective assessment can help change educational practice. And the study of changes in practice, in turn, can help in further developing the knowledge base.

The recommendations presented below collectively form a proposed research and development agenda for expanding the knowledge base on the integration of cognition and measurement, and encompass the implications of such a knowledge base for each of the four mediating arenas that directly influence educational practice. Before turning to this agenda, we offer two guidelines for how future work should proceed:

• **The committee advocates increased and sustained multidisciplinary collaboration around theoretical and practical matters of assessment.** We apply this precept not only to the collaboration between researchers in the cognitive and measurement sciences, but also to the collaboration of these groups with teachers, curriculum specialists, and assessment developers.

• **The committee urges individuals in multiple communities, from research through practice and policy, to consider the conceptual scheme and language used in this report as a guide for stimulating further thinking and discussion about the many issues associated with the productive use of assessments in education.** The assessment triangle provides a conceptual framework for principled thinking about the assumptions and foundations underlying an assessment.

Recommendations for Research

Recommendation 1: Accumulated knowledge and ongoing advances from the merger of the cognitive and measurement sciences should be synthesized and made available in usable forms to multiple educational constituencies. These constituencies include educational researchers, test developers, curriculum specialists, teachers, and policy makers.

Recommendation 2: Funding should be provided for a major program of research, guided by a synthesis of cognitive and measure-

ment principles, focused on the design of assessments that yield more valid and fair inferences about student achievement. This research should be conducted collaboratively by multidisciplinary teams comprising both researchers and practitioners. A priority should be the development of models of cognition and learning that can serve as the basis for assessment design for all areas of the school curriculum. Research on how students learn subject matter should be conducted in actual educational settings and with groups of learners representative of the diversity of the student population to be assessed. Research on new statistical measurement models and their applicability should be tied to modern theories of cognition and learning. Work should be undertaken to better understand the fit between various types of cognitive theories and measurement models to determine which combinations work best together. Research on assessment design should include exploration of systematic and fair methods for taking into account aspects of examinees' instructional background when interpreting their responses to assessment tasks. This research should encompass careful examination of the possible consequences of such adaptations in high-stakes assessment contexts.

Recommendation 3: Research should be conducted to explore how new forms of assessment can be made practical for use in classroom and large-scale contexts and how various new forms of assessment affect student learning, teacher practice, and educational decision making. This research should also explore how teachers can be assisted in integrating new forms of assessment into their instructional practices. It is particularly important that such work be done in close collaboration with practicing teachers who have varying backgrounds and levels of teaching experience. The research should encompass ways in which school structures (e.g., length of time of classes, class size, and opportunity for teachers to work together) affect the feasibility of implementing new types of assessments and their effectiveness.

Recommendation 4: Funding should be provided for in-depth analyses of the critical elements (cognition, observation, and interpretation) underlying the design of existing assessments that have attempted to integrate cognitive and measurement principles (including the multiple examples presented in this report). This work should also focus on better understanding the impact of such exemplars on student learning, teaching practice, and educational decision making.

Recommendation 5: Federal agencies and private-sector organizations concerned with issues of assessment should support the establishment of multidisciplinary discourse communities. The purpose of such discourse would be to facilitate cross-fertilization of ideas among researchers and assessment developers working at the intersection of cognitive theory and educational measurement.

Recommendations for Policy and Practice

Recommendation 6: Developers of assessment instruments for classroom or large-scale use should pay explicit attention to all three elements of the assessment triangle (cognition, observation, and interpretation) and their coordination. All three elements should be based on modern knowledge of how students learn and how such learning is best measured. Considerable time and effort should be devoted to a theory-driven design and validation process before assessments are put into operational use.

Recommendation 7: Developers of educational curricula and classroom assessments should create tools that will enable teachers to implement high-quality instructional and assessment practices, consistent with modern understanding of how students learn and how such learning can be measured. Assessments and supporting instructional materials should interpret the findings from cognitive research in ways that are useful for teachers. Developers are urged to take advantage of the opportunities afforded by technology to assess what students are learning at fine levels of detail, with appropriate frequency, and in ways that are tightly integrated with instruction.

Recommendation 8: Large-scale assessments should sample the broad range of competencies and forms of student understanding that research shows are important aspects of student learning. A variety of matrix sampling, curriculum-embedded, and other assessment approaches should be used to cover the breadth of cognitive competencies that are the goals of learning in a domain of the curriculum. Large-scale assessment tools and supporting instructional materials should be developed so that clear learning goals and landmark performances along the way to competence are shared with teachers, students, and other education stakeholders. The knowledge and skills to be assessed and the criteria for judging the desired outcomes should be clearly specified and available to all potential examinees and other concerned individuals. Assessment developers should pursue new ways of reporting assessment results that convey important differences in performance at various levels of competence in ways that are clear to different users, including educators, parents, and students.

Recommendation 9: Instruction in how students learn and how learning can be assessed should be a major component of teacher preservice and professional development programs. This training should be linked to actual experience in classrooms in assessing and interpreting the development of student competence. To ensure that this occurs, state and national standards for teacher licensure and program accreditation should include specific requirements focused on the proper integration of learning and assessment in teachers' educational experience.

Recommendation 10: Policy makers are urged to recognize the limitations of current assessments, and to support the development of new systems of multiple assessments that would improve their ability to make decisions about education programs and the allocation of resources. Important decisions about individuals should not be based on a single test score. Policy makers should instead invest in the development of assessment systems that use multiple measures of student performance, particularly when high stakes are attached to the results. Assessments at the classroom and large-scale levels should grow out of a shared knowledge base about the nature of learning. Policy makers should support efforts to achieve such coherence. Policy makers should also promote the development of assessment systems that measure the growth or progress of students and the education system over time and that support multilevel analyses of the influences responsible for such change.

Recommendation 11: The balance of mandates and resources should be shifted from an emphasis on external forms of assessment to an increased emphasis on classroom formative assessment designed to assist learning.

Recommendation 12: Programs for providing information to the public on the role of assessment in improving learning and on contemporary approaches to assessment should be developed in cooperation with the media. Efforts should be made to foster public understanding of the basic principles of appropriate test interpretation and use.

Part I

Overview and Background

1

Rethinking the Foundations of Assessment

The time is right to rethink the fundamental scientific principles and philosophical assumptions that underlie current approaches to educational assessment. These approaches have been in place for decades and have served a number of purposes quite well. But the world has changed substantially since those approaches were first developed, and the foundations on which they were built may not support the newer purposes to which assessments may be put. Moreover, advances in the understanding and measurement of learning bring new assumptions into play and offer the potential for a much richer and more coherent set of assessment practices. In this volume, the Committee on the Foundations of Assessment outlines these new understandings and proposes a new approach to assessment.

CHARGE TO THE COMMITTEE

The Committee on the Foundations of Assessment was convened in January 1998 by the National Research Council (NRC) with support from the National Science Foundation. The committee's charge was to review and synthesize advances in the cognitive sciences and to explore their implications for improving educational assessment in general and assessment of science and mathematics education in particular. The committee was also charged with evaluating the extent to which evolving assessment practices in U.S. schools were derived from research on cognition and learning, as well as helping to improve public understanding of current and emerging assessment practices and uses. The committee approached these three objectives as interconnected themes rather than as separate tasks.

SCOPE OF THE STUDY

The committee considered the implications of advances in the cognitive and measurement sciences for both classroom and large-scale assessment. Consistent with its charge, the committee focused primarily on assessment in science and mathematics education. Although new concepts of assessment could easily apply to other disciplines, science and mathematics hold particular promise for rethinking assessment because of the substantial body of important research and design work already done in these disciplines. Because science and mathematics also have a major impact on the nation's technological and economic progress, they have been primary targets for education reform at the national and state levels, as well as a focus of concern in international comparative studies. Furthermore, there are persistent disparities among ethnic, geographic, and socioeconomic groups in access to quality K-12 science and mathematics instruction. Black, Hispanic, and Native American youth continue to lag far behind Whites and Asians in the amount of coursework taken in these subjects and in levels of achievement; this gap negatively affects their access to certain careers and workforce skills. Better assessment, curriculum, and instruction could help educators diagnose the needs of at-risk students and tailor improvements to meet those needs.

The committee also focused on the assessment of school achievement, or the outcomes of schooling, and gave less emphasis to predictive tests (such as college selection tests) that are intended to project how successful an individual will be in a future situation. We had several reasons for this emphasis. First, when one considers the use of assessments at the classroom, district, state, and national levels in any given year, it is clear that the assessment of academic achievement is far more extensive than predictive testing. Second, many advances in cognitive science have already been applied to the study and design of predictive instruments, such as assessments of aptitude or ability. Much less effort has been expended on the application of advances in the cognitive and measurement sciences to issues of assessing academic content knowledge, including the use of such information to aid teaching and learning. Finally, the committee believed that the principles and practices uncovered through a focus on the assessment of academic achievement would generally apply also to what we view as the more circumscribed case of predictive testing.

Our hope is that by reviewing advances in the sciences of how people learn and how such learning can be measured, and by suggesting steps for future research and development, this report will help lay the foundation for a significant leap forward in the field of assessment. The committee envisions a new generation of educational assessments that better serve the goal of equity. Needed are assessments that help all students learn and succeed in school by making as clear as possible the nature of their accomplishments and the progress of their learning.

CONTEXT

In this first chapter we embed the discussion of classroom and large-scale assessment in a broader context by considering the social, technological, and educational setting in which it operates. The discussion of context is organized around four broad themes:

- Any assessment is based on three interconnected elements or foundations: the aspects of achievement that are to be assessed (cognition), the tasks used to collect evidence about students' achievement (observation), and the methods used to analyze the evidence resulting from the tasks (interpretation). To understand and improve educational assessment, the principles and beliefs underlying each of these elements, as well as their interrelationships, must be made explicit.
- Recent developments in society and technology are transforming people's ideas about the competencies students should develop. At the same time, education policy makers are attempting to respond to many of the societal changes by redefining what all students should learn. These trends have profound implications for assessment.
- Existing assessments are the product of prior theories of learning and measurement. While adherence to these theories has contributed to the enduring strengths of these assessments, it has also contributed to some of their limitations and impeded progress in assessment design.
- Alternative conceptions of learning and measurement now exist that offer the possibility to establish new foundations for enhanced assessment practices that can better support learning.

The following subsections elaborate on each of these themes in turn. Some of the key terms used in the discussion and throughout this report are defined in Box 1-1.

The Significance of Foundations

From teachers' informal quizzes to nationally administered standardized tests, assessments have long been an integral part of the educational process. Educational assessments assist teachers, students, and parents in determining how well students are learning. They help teachers understand how to adapt instruction on the basis of evidence of student learning. They help principals and superintendents document the progress of individual stu-

BOX 1-1   Some Terminology Used in This Report

The *cognitive sciences* encompass a spectrum of researchers and theorists from diverse fields—including psychology, linguistics, computer science, anthropology, and neuroscience—who use a variety of approaches to study and understand the workings of human minds as they function individually and in groups. The common ground is that the central subject of inquiry is *cognition,* which includes the mental processes and contents of thought involved in attention, perception, memory, reasoning, problem solving, and communication. These processes are studied as they occur in real time and as they contribute to the acquisition, organization, and use of knowledge.

The terms *educational measurement, assessment,* and *testing* are used almost interchangeably in the research literature to refer to a process by which educators use students' responses to specially created or naturally occurring stimuli to draw inferences about the students' knowledge and skills (Popham, 2000). All of these terms are used in this report, but we often opt for the term "assessment" instead of "test" to denote a more comprehensive set of means for eliciting evidence of student performance than the traditional paper-and-pencil, multiple-choice instruments often associated with the word "test."

dents, classrooms, and schools. And they help policy makers and the public gauge the effectiveness of educational systems.

Every educational assessment, whether used in the classroom or large-scale context, is based on a set of scientific principles and philosophical assumptions, or *foundations* as they are termed in this report. First, every assessment is grounded in a conception or theory about how people learn, what they know, and how knowledge and understanding progress over time. Second, each assessment embodies certain assumptions about which kinds of observations, or tasks, are most likely to elicit demonstrations of important knowledge and skills from students. Third, every assessment is premised on certain assumptions about how best to interpret the evidence from the observations to draw meaningful inferences about what students know and can do. These three cornerstones of assessment are discussed and further developed with examples throughout this report.

The foundations influence all aspects of an assessment's design and use, including content, format, scoring, reporting, and use of the results. Even though these fundamental principles are sometimes more implicit than explicit, they are still influential. In fact, it is often the tacit nature of the foundations and the failure to question basic assumptions that creates conflicts about the meaning and value of assessment results.

Advances in the study of thinking and learning (cognitive science) and in the field of measurement (psychometrics) have stimulated people to think in new ways about how students learn and what they know, what is therefore worth assessing, and how to obtain useful information about student competencies. Numerous researchers interested in problems of educational assessment have argued that, if brought together, advances in the cognitive and measurement sciences could provide a powerful basis for refashioning educational assessment (e.g., Baker, 1997; Glaser and Silver, 1994; Messick, 1984; Mislevy, 1994; National Academy of Education, 1996; Nichols, 1994; National Research Council [NRC], 1999b; Pellegrino, Baxter, and Glaser, 1999; Snow and Lohman, 1989; Wilson and Adams, 1996). Indeed, the merger could be mutually beneficial, with the potential to catalyze further advances in both fields.

Such developments, if vigorously pursued, could have significant long-term implications for the field of assessment and for education in general. Unfortunately, the theoretical foundations of assessment seldom receive explicit attention during most discussions about testing policy and practice. Short-term issues of implementation, test use, or score interpretation tend to take precedence, especially in the context of many large-scale testing programs (NRC, 1999b). It is interesting to note, however, that some of today's most pressing issues, such as whether current assessments for accountability encourage effective teaching and learning, ultimately rest on an analysis of the fundamental beliefs about how people learn and how to measure such learning that underlie current practices. For many reasons, the present climate offers an opportune time to rethink these theoretical underpinnings of assessment, particularly in an atmosphere, such as that surrounding the committee's deliberations, not charged with the polarities and politics that often envelop discussions of the technical merits of specific testing programs and practices.

Changing Expectations for Learning

Major societal, economic, and technological changes have transformed public conceptions about the kinds of knowledge and skills schools should teach and assessments should measure (Secretary's Commission on Achieving Necessary Skills, 1991). These developments have sparked widespread debate and activity in the field of assessment. The efforts under way in every state to reform education policy and practice through the implementation of higher standards for students and teachers have focused to a large extent on assessment, resulting in a major increase in the amount of testing and in the emphasis placed on its results (Education Week, 1999). The following subsections briefly review these trends, which are changing expectations for student learning and the assessment of that learning.

Societal, Economic, and Technological Changes

Societal, economic, and technological changes are transforming the world of work. The workforce is becoming more diverse, boundaries between jobs are blurring, and work is being structured in more varying ways (NRC, 1999a). This restructuring often increases the skills workers need to do their jobs. For example, many manufacturing plants are introducing sophisticated information technologies and training employees to participate in work teams (Appelbaum, Bailey, Berg, and Kalleberg, 2000). Reflecting these transformations in work, jobs requiring specialized skills and postsecondary education are expected to grow more quickly than other types of jobs in the coming years (Bureau of Labor Statistics, 2000).

To succeed in this increasingly competitive economy, all students, not just a few, must learn how to communicate, to think and reason effectively, to solve complex problems, to work with multidimensional data and sophisticated representations, to make judgments about the accuracy of masses of information, to collaborate in diverse teams, and to demonstrate self-motivation (Barley and Orr, 1997; NRC, 1999a, 2001). As the U.S. economy continues its transformation from manufacturing to services and, within services, to an "information economy," many more jobs are requiring higher-level skills than in the past. Many routine tasks are now automated through the use of information technology, decreasing the demand for workers to perform them. Conversely, the demand for workers with high-level cognitive skills has grown as a result of the increased use of information technology in the workplace (Bresnahan, Brynjolfsson, and Hitt, 1999). For example, organizations have become dependent upon quick e-mail interactions instead of slow iterations of memoranda and replies. Individuals not prepared to be quickly but effectively reflective are at a disadvantage in such an environment.

Technology is also influencing curriculum, changing what and how students are learning, with implications for the types of competencies that should be assessed. New information and communications technologies present students with opportunities to apply complex content and skills that are difficult to tap through traditional instruction. In the Weather Visualizer program, for example, students use sophisticated computer tools to observe complex weather data and construct their own weather forecasts (Edelson, Gordon, and Pea, 1999).

These changes mean that more is being demanded of all aspects of education, including assessment. Assessments must tap a broader range of competencies than in the past. They must capture the more complex skills and deeper content knowledge reflected in new expectations for learning. They must accurately measure higher levels of achievement while also providing meaningful information about students who still perform below expectations. All of these trends are being played out on a large scale in the drive to set challenging standards for student learning.

An Era of Higher Standards and High-Stakes Tests

Assessment has been greatly influenced by the movement during the past two decades aimed at raising educational quality by setting challenging academic standards. At the national level, professional associations of subject matter specialists have developed widely disseminated standards outlining the content knowledge, skills, and procedures schools should teach in mathematics, science, and other areas. These efforts include, among others, the mathematics standards developed by the National Council of Teachers of Mathematics (2000), the science standards developed by the NRC (1996), and the standards in several subjects developed by New Standards (e.g., New Standards™, 1997), a privately funded organization.

In addition, virtually every state and many large school districts have standards in place outlining what all students should know and be able to do in core subjects. These standards are intended to guide both practice and policy at the state and district levels, including the development of large-scale assessments of student performance. The process of developing and implementing standards at the national and local levels has advanced public dialogue and furthered professional consensus about the kinds of knowledge and skills that are important for students to learn at various stages of their education. Many of the standards developed by states, school districts, and professional groups emphasize that it is important for students not only to attain a deep understanding of the content of various subjects, but also to develop the sophisticated thinking skills necessary to perform competently in these disciplines.

By emphasizing problem solving and inquiry, many of the mathematics and science standards underscore the idea that students learn best when they are actively engaged in learning. Several of the standards also stress the need for students to build coherent structures of knowledge and be able to apply that knowledge in much the same manner as people who work in a particular discipline. For instance, the national science standards (NRC, 1996) state:

> Learning science is something students do, not something that is done to them. In learning science, students describe objects and events, ask questions, organize knowledge, construct explanations of natural phenomena, test those explanations in many different ways, and communicate their ideas to others. . . . Students establish connections between their current

knowledge of science and the scientific knowledge found in many sources; they apply science content to new questions; they engage in problem solving, planning, and group discussions; and they experience assessments that are consistent with an active approach to learning. (p. 20)

In these respects, the standards represent an important start toward incorporating findings from cognitive research about the nature of knowledge and expertise into curriculum and instruction. Standards vary widely, however, and some have fallen short of their intentions. For example, some state standards are too vague to be useful blueprints for instruction or assessment. Others call upon students to learn a broad range of content rather than focusing in depth on the most central concepts and methods of a particular discipline, and some standards are so detailed that the big ideas are lost or buried (American Federation of Teachers, 1999; Finn, Petrilli, and Vanourek, 1998).

State standards, whatever their quality, have significantly shaped classroom practices and exerted a major impact on assessment. Indeed, assessment is pivotal to standards-based reforms because it is the primary means of measuring progress toward attainment of the standards and of holding students, teachers, and administrators accountable for improvement over time. This accountability, in turn, is expected to create incentives for modifying and improving performance.

Without doubt, the standards movement has increased the amount of testing in K-12 schools and raised the consequences, expectations, and controversies attached to test results. To implement standards-based reforms, many states have put in place new tests in multiple curriculum areas and/or implemented tests at additional grade levels. Currently, 48 states have statewide testing programs, compared with 39 in 1996, and many school districts also have their own local testing programs (in addition to the range of classroom tests teachers regularly administer). As a result of this increased emphasis on assessment as an instrument of reform, the amount of spending on large-scale testing has doubled in the past 4 years, from $165 million in 1996 to $330 million in 2000 (Achieve, 2000).

Moreover, states and school districts have increasingly attached high stakes to test results. Scores on assessments are being used to make decisions about whether students advance to the next grade or graduate from high school, which students receive special services, how teachers and administrators are evaluated, how resources are allocated, and whether schools are eligible for various rewards or subject to sanctions or intervention by the district or state. These efforts have particular implications for equity if and when certain groups are disproportionately affected by the policies. As a result, the courts are paying greater attention to assessment results, and lawsuits are under way in several states that seek to use measures of educational quality to determine whether they are fulfilling their responsibility to provide all students with an adequate education (NRC, 1999c).

Although periodic testing is a critical part of any education reform, some of the movement toward increased testing may be fueled by a misguided assumption that more frequent testing, in and of itself, will improve education. At the same time, criticism of test policies may be predicated on an equally misguided assumption that testing, in and of itself, is responsible for most of the problems in education. A more realistic view is to address education problems not by stepping up the amount of testing or abandoning assessments entirely, but rather by refashioning assessments to meet current and future needs for quality information. However, it must be recognized that even very well-designed assessments cannot by themselves improve learning. Improvements in learning will depend on how well assessment, curriculum, and instruction are aligned and reinforce a common set of learning goals, and on whether instruction shifts in response to the information gained from assessments.

With so much depending on large-scale assessment results, it is more crucial than ever that the scores be reliable in a technical sense and that the inferences drawn from the results be valid and fair. It is just as important, however, that the assessments actually measure the kinds of competencies students need to develop to keep pace with the societal, economic, and technological changes discussed above, and that they promote the kinds of teaching and learning that effectively build those competencies. By these criteria, the heavy demands placed on many current assessments generally exceed their capabilities.

Impact of Prior Theories of Learning and Measurement

Current assessment practices are the cumulative product of theories of learning and models of measurement that were developed to fulfill the social and educational needs of a different time. This evolutionary process is described in more detail in Chapters 3 and 4. As Mislevy (1993, p. 19) has noted, "It is only a slight exaggeration to describe the test theory that dominates educational measurement today as the application of 20th century statistics to 19th century psychology." Although the core concepts of prior theories and models are still useful for certain purposes, they need to be augmented or supplanted to deal with newer assessment needs.

Early standardized tests were developed at a time when enrollments in public schools were burgeoning, and administrators sought tools to help them educate the rapidly growing student populations more efficiently. As described in *Testing in American Schools* (U.S. Congress, Office of Technology Assessment, 1992), the first reported standardized written achievement exam was administered in Massachusetts in the mid-19th century and intended to serve two purposes: to enable external authorities to monitor school systems and to make it possible to classify children in pursuit of more efficient learning. Thus it was believed that the same tests used to monitor the effectiveness of schools in accomplishing their missions could be used to sort students according to their general ability levels and provide schooling according to need. Yet significant problems have arisen in the history of assessment when it has been assumed that tests designed to evaluate the effectiveness of programs and schools can be used to make judgments about individual students. (Ways in which the purpose of an assessment should influence its design are discussed in Chapter 2 and more fully in Chapter 6.) At the same time, some educators also sought to use tests to equalize opportunity by opening up to individuals with high ability or achievement an educational system previously dominated by those with social connections—that is, to establish an educational meritocracy (Lemann, 1999). The achievement gaps that continue to persist suggest that the goal of equal educational opportunity has yet to be achieved.

Some aspects of current assessment systems are linked to earlier theories that assumed individuals have basically fixed dispositions to behave in certain ways across diverse situations. According to such a view, school achievement is perceived as a set of general proficiencies (e.g., mathematics ability) that remain relatively stable over situations and time.

Current assessments are also derived from early theories that characterize learning as a step-by-step accumulation of facts, procedures, definitions, and other discrete bits of knowledge and skill. Thus, the assessments tend to include items of factual and procedural knowledge that are relatively circumscribed in content and format and can be responded to in a short amount of time. These test items are typically treated as independent, discrete entities sampled from a larger universe of equally good questions. It is further assumed that these independent items can be accumulated or aggregated in various ways to produce overall scores.

Limitations of Current Assessments

The most common kinds of educational tests do a reasonable job with certain functions of testing, such as measuring knowledge of basic facts and procedures and producing overall estimates of proficiency for an area of the curriculum. But both their strengths and limitations are a product of their adherence to theories of learning and measurement that fail to capture the breadth and richness of knowledge and cognition. The limitations of these theories also compromise the usefulness of the assessments. The growing reliance on tests for making important decisions and for improving educational outcomes has called attention to some of their more serious limitations.

One set of concerns relates to whether the most widely used assessments effectively capture the kinds of complex knowledge and skills that are emphasized in contemporary standards and deemed essential for success in the information-based economy described above (Resnick and Resnick, 1992; Rothman, Slattery, Vranek, and Resnick, in press). Traditional tests do not focus on many aspects of cognition that research indicates are important, and they are not structured to capture critical differences in students' levels of understanding. For example, important aspects of learning not adequately tapped by current assessments include students' organization of knowledge, problem representations, use of strategies, self-monitoring skills, and individual contributions to group problem solving (Glaser, Linn, and Bohrnstedt, 1997; NRC, 1999b).

The limits on the kinds of competencies currently being assessed also raise questions about the validity of the inferences one can draw from the results. If scores go up on a test that measures a relatively narrow range of knowledge and skills, does that mean student learning has improved, or has instruction simply adapted to a constrained set of outcomes? If there is explicit "teaching to the test," at what cost do such gains in test scores accrue relative to acquiring other aspects of knowledge and skill that are valued in today's society? This is a point of considerable current controversy (Klein, Hamilton, McCaffrey, and Stecher, 2000; Koretz and Barron, 1998; Linn, 2000).

A second issue concerns the usefulness of current assessments for improving teaching and learning—the ultimate goal of education reforms. On the whole, most current large-scale tests provide very limited information that teachers and educational administrators can use to identify why students do not perform well or to modify the conditions of instruction in ways likely to improve student achievement. The most widely used state and district assessments provide only general information about where a student stands relative to peers (for example, that the student scored at the 45th percentile) or whether the student has performed poorly or well in certain domains (for example, that the student performs "below basic in mathematics"). Such tests do not reveal whether students are using misguided strategies to solve problems or fail to understand key concepts within the subject matter being tested. They do not show whether a student is advancing toward competence or is stuck at a partial understanding of a topic that could seriously impede future learning. Indeed, it is entirely possible that a student could answer certain types of test questions correctly and still lack the most basic understanding of the situation being tested, as a teacher would quickly learn by asking the student to explain the answer (see Box 1-2). In short, many current assessments do not offer strong clues as to the types of educational interventions that would improve learners' performance, or even provide information on precisely where the students' strengths and weaknesses lie.

A third limitation relates to the static nature of many current assessments. Most assessments provide "snapshots" of achievement at particular points in time, but they do not capture the progression of students' concep-

BOX 1-2   Rethinking the Best Ways to Assess Competence

Consider the following two assessment situations:

Assessment #1

Question: What was the date of the battle of the Spanish Armada?
Answer: 1588 [correct].
Question: What can you tell me about what this meant?
Answer: Not much. It was one of the dates I memorized for the exam. Want to hear the others?

Assessment #2

Question: What was the date of the battle of the Spanish Armada?
Answer: It must have been around 1590.
Question: Why do you say that?
Answer: I know the English began to settle in Virginia just after 1600, not sure of the exact date. They wouldn't have dared start overseas explorations if Spain still had control of the seas. It would take a little while to get expeditions organized, so England must have gained naval supremacy somewhere in the late 1500s.

Most people would agree that the second student showed a better understanding of the Age of Colonization than the first, but too many examinations would assign the first student a better score. When assessing knowledge, one needs to understand how the student connects pieces of knowledge to one another. Once this is known, the teacher may want to improve the connections, showing the student how to expand his or her knowledge.

tual understanding over time, which is at the heart of learning. This limitation exists largely because most current modes of assessment lack an underlying theoretical framework of how student understanding in a content domain develops over the course of instruction, and predominant measurement methods are not designed to capture such growth.

A fourth and persistent set of concerns relates to fairness and equity. Much attention has been given to the issue of test bias, particularly whether differences occur in the performance of various groups for reasons that are irrelevant to the competency the test is intended to measure (Cole and Moss, 1993). Standardized tests items are subjected to judgmental and technical reviews to monitor for this kind of bias. The use of assessments for high-stakes decisions raises additional questions about fairness (NRC, 1999c). If the assessments are not aligned with what students are being taught, it is not fair to base promotion or rewards on the results, especially if less advantaged students are harmed disproportionately by the outcome. If current assessments do not effectively measure the impact of instruction or fail to capture important skills and knowledge, how can educators interpret and address gaps in student achievement?

One of the main goals of current reforms is to improve learning for low-achieving students. If this goal is to be accomplished, assessment must give students, teachers, and other stakeholders information they can use to improve learning and inform instructional decisions for individuals and groups, especially those not performing at high levels. To be sure, assessments by themselves do not cause or cure inequities in education; indeed, many of the causes of such inequities are beyond the scope of the education system itself. However, when assessment fails to provide information that can enhance learning, it leaves educators ill equipped to close achievement gaps.

While concerns associated with large-scale tests have received considerable attention, particularly in recent years, the classroom assessments commonly used by teachers also are often limited in the information they provide. Just as large-scale tests have relied on an incomplete set of ideas about learning, so, too, have the kinds of assessments teachers regularly administer in their classrooms. Often, teachers adhere to assessment formats and scoring practices found in large-scale tests. This can be traced largely to teacher education programs and professional development experiences that have for the most part failed to equip teachers with contemporary knowledge about learning and assessment, especially the knowledge needed to develop tasks that would elicit students' thinking skills or make it possible to assess their growth and progress toward competence (Cizek, 2000; Dwyer, 1998).

Alternative Assessment Practices

Standards-based reform continues to stimulate research and development on assessment as people seek to design better approaches for measuring valued knowledge and skills. States and school districts have made major investments to better align tests with standards and to develop alternative approaches for assessing knowledge and skills not well captured by most current tests. Teachers have been offered professional development opportunities focusing on the development and scoring of new state assessment instruments more closely aligned with curricular and instructional practices. Nowhere has this confluence of activity been more evident than in the area of "performance assessment" (Council of Chief State School Officers, 1999;

Linn, Baker, and Dunbar, 1991; National Center for Education Statistics, 1996; U.S. Congress, Office of Technology Assessment, 1992).

The quest for alternatives to traditional assessment modes has led many states to pursue approaches that include the use of more open-ended tasks that call upon students to apply their knowledge and skills to create a product or solve a problem. Performance assessment represents one such effort to address some of the limitations of traditional assessments. Performance assessment, an enduring concept (e.g., Lindquist, 1951) that attracted renewed attention during the 1990s, requires students to perform more "authentic" tasks that involve the application of combined knowledge and skills in the context of an actual project. Even with such alternative formats, however, there has been a constant gravitation toward familiar methods of interpreting student performance. For example, Baxter and Glaser (1998) analyzed a range of current performance assessments in science and often found mismatches between the intentions of the developers and what the tasks and associated scoring rubrics actually measured. Particularly distressing was the observation that some performance tasks did not engage students in the complex thinking processes intended.

As a result of these limitations, the growing interest in performance assessment was followed by a recognition that it is not the hoped-for panacea, especially in light of the costs, feasibility, and psychometric concerns associated with the use of such measures (Mehrens, 1998; National Center for Education Statistics, 1996). The cumulative work on performance assessment serves as a reminder that the key question is whether an assessment, whatever its format, is founded on a solid model of learning and whether it will provide teachers and students with information about what students know that can be used for meaningful instructional guidance.

Simply put, steps have been taken to improve assessment, but a significant leap forward needs to occur to equip students, parents, teachers, and policy makers with information that can help them make appropriate decisions about teaching practices and educational policies that will assist learning. Fortunately, the elements of change that could produce such an advance are already present within the cognitive and measurement sciences.

Assessment Based on Contemporary Foundations

Several decades of research in the cognitive sciences has advanced the knowledge base about how children develop understanding, how people reason and build structures of knowledge, which thinking processes are associated with competent performance, and how knowledge is shaped by social context. These findings, presented in Chapter 3, suggest directions for revamping assessment to provide better information about students' levels of understanding, their thinking strategies, and the nature of their misunderstandings.

During this same period, there have been significant developments in measurement methods and theory. As presented in Chapter 4, a wide array of statistical measurement methods is currently available to support the kinds of inferences that cognitive research suggests are important to draw when measuring student achievement.

In this report we describe examples of some initial and promising attempts to capitalize on these advances. However, these efforts have been limited in scale and have not yet coalesced around a set of guiding principles. In addition to discerning those principles, it is necessary to undertake more research and development to move the most promising ideas and prototypes into the varied and unpredictable learning environments found in diverse classrooms embedded within complex educational systems and policy structures.

In pursuing new forms of assessment, it is important to remember that assessment is a system composed of the three interconnected elements discussed earlier—cognition, observation, and interpretation—and that assessments function within a larger system of curriculum, instruction, and assessment. Radically changing one of these elements and not the others runs the risk of producing an incoherent system. All of the elements and how they interrelate must be considered together.

Moreover, while new forms of assessment could address some of the limitations described above and give teachers, administrators, and policy makers tools to help them improve schooling, it is important to note that tests by themselves do not improve teaching and learning, regardless of how effective they are at providing information about student competencies. Many factors affect instruction and learning, including the quality of the curriculum, the experience and skills of teachers, and the support students receive outside of class. It is also essential to keep in mind that any assessment operates within constraints, and these constraints can limit its ability to provide useful information. For example, such factors as the amount of money available for developing an assessment and the amount of instructional time available for its administration or scoring can restrict the types of tasks used for the assessment and thus the evidence it can provide about student learning. In addition, classroom factors such as class size and opportunity for teachers to interact with one another can affect teachers' ability to profit from the information that is derived. Thus while new assessments can enhance the available information about student competencies, their full potential can be realized only by removing such constraints.

That potential is significant. Assessments that inform teachers about the nature of student learning can help them provide better feedback to students, which in turn can enhance learning (Black and Wiliam, 1998). Assessments based on theories of how competence develops across grade levels in a curriculum domain could provide more valid measures of growth and the value added by teachers and schools.

Assessments based on current cognitive principles and measurement theories could also enhance community dialogue about goals for student learning and indicators of achievement at various grade levels and in different subject areas. Comparisons based on attainment of worthwhile learning goals, rather than normative descriptions of how students perform, could enhance the public's understanding of educational quality. New forms of assessment could also help provide descriptive and accurate information about the nature of achievement in a subject area and patterns of students' strengths and weaknesses that would be more useful than existing data for guiding policy decisions and reform efforts.

Issues of fairness and equity must be central concerns in any effort to develop new forms of assessment. Relevant to these issues is a substantial body of research on the social and cultural dimensions of cognition and learning (discussed in Chapter 3). To improve the fairness of assessment, it must be recognized that cultural practices equip students differently to participate in the discourse structures that are often unique to testing contexts. It is all too easy to conclude that some cultural groups are deficient in academic competence, when the differences can instead be attributable to cultural variations in the ways students interpret the meaning, information demands, and activity of taking tests (Steele, 1995, 1997). These sorts of differences need to be studied and taken into account when designing and interpreting the results of assessments. If well-designed and used, new models of assessment could not only measure student achievement more fairly, but also promote more equitable opportunity to learn by providing better-quality information about the impact of educational interventions on children. More informative classroom assessments could result in earlier identification of learning problems and interventions for children at risk, rather than waiting for results from large-scale assessments to signal problems. Students with disabilities could also benefit from this approach. At the same time, it will be necessary for educators and researchers to monitor the effects of their practices continually to ensure that new assessments do not exacerbate existing inequalities. While there are many reasons to question the fairness of current testing practices, it would be misguided to implement new assessment approaches and assume that they promote fairness and equity without validating such presumptions.

ISSUES AND CHALLENGES

The key issues that emerge from the themes discussed above strongly suggest that it is appropriate and necessary to rethink the scientific principles and philosophical assumptions that serve as the foundations of educational assessment. Doing so will provide new ways of understanding and approaching these issues and finding solutions to the assessment challenges they pose.

- Expectations about what all students should learn—and, by implication, what they should be tested on—have changed in response to social, economic, and technological changes and as a result of the standards-based reform movement. All students are now expected to demonstrate the kinds of reasoning and problem-solving abilities once expected of only a minority of young people. Assessments are needed to gauge these aspects of student competence.

- Standards-based reform has increased both the amount of testing and the stakes attached to test results. This development has placed more pressure on current assessment systems than they were meant to bear and has highlighted some of their limitations.

- Current assessment systems are the cumulative product of various prior theories of learning and methods of measurement. Although some of these foundations are still useful for certain functions of testing, change is needed. Assessment systems need to evolve to keep pace with developments in the sciences of learning and measurement and to achieve the learning goals pursued by reformers.

- Four decades of research in the cognitive sciences has advanced the knowledge base about how children develop understanding, how people reason and build structures of knowledge, which thinking processes are associated with competent performance, and how knowledge is shaped by social context. These findings suggest directions for revamping assessment to enable more valid and fair inferences about students' levels of understanding, their thinking strategies, and the nature of their misunderstandings.

- Developments in the science and technology of assessment have made available a variety of measurement methods and statistical models that could be used to design assessments capable of better capturing the complexity of cognition and learning.

- A science of assessment that brought together cognitive principles and highly developed measurement models could address some of the limitations of current assessments and yield a number of benefits for students, teachers, and the educational system as a whole. Effort must be made to study what can be accomplished through programs of sustained assessment design and implementation based on current scientific knowledge.

- At the same time, it is important to recognize that any assessment operates within the constraints of the larger education system. The ability of new forms of assessment to function to their fullest potential can be impeded by constraints such as limited resources and time for assessment; large class sizes and little time for teachers to interact; and misalignment among curriculum, instruction, and assessment. The influences of such factors can not be ignored but must be incorporated into the process of assessment reform.

Education reform will be difficult to achieve if educators continue to carry the weight of practices designed for times past. New methods of assessment can begin to drive changes in curriculum, teaching, and learning that support patterns of human cognitive growth and prepare people for dignified lives, workplace competence, and social development.

STRUCTURE OF THIS REPORT

This report addresses many of the conceptual issues and pragmatic challenges noted above. It is divided into four parts, as detailed below. Part I consists of this chapter and Chapter 2, which provides background on the purposes and nature of assessment and introduces key concepts used throughout the report.

Part II, consisting of Chapters 3 and 4, explains how expanding knowledge in the fields of human cognition and measurement can form the foundations for an improved approach to assessment. Chapter 3 reviews contemporary understanding of how people learn, focusing on findings that have implications for improving educational assessment. The discussion addresses the way knowledge is represented and organized in the mind, the characteristics of expertise in a discipline and the development of that expertise, and the influence of cultural and social factors on learning. Chapter 4 describes current measurement methods, both familiar and new, and why they evolved. It explores how the broad array of existing methods can be used to develop a new generation of assessments that can provide better evidence of students' understanding and cognitive processes.

Part III, consisting of Chapters 5, 6, and 7, sets forth principles for designing and using assessments based on advances in cognitive and measurement theories. Chapter 5 describes features of a new approach to assessment design based on a synthesis of cognitive and measurement principles; existing and innovative assessment examples are used to illustrate the application of the general design principles to different assessment purposes and contexts. The discussion focuses on how current educational testing guidelines and practice could be improved by making stronger connections between advances in cognitive and measurement theories. Chapter 6 addresses contrasts and design trade-offs between classroom and large-scale assessment, and explores how assessments can be designed and used in each context to improve student learning. Opportunities for enhancing the synergy between classroom and large-scale assessment are also addressed. Chapter 7 considers the role of technology in transforming both the kinds of learning that should be assessed and the assessment methods used. The chapter includes examples of technological tools that illustrate new uses for assessment and highlights some issues that need to be considered as technology becomes more important in education.

Chapters 2 through 7 open with a listing of the themes used to organize the discussion that follows. Each of these chapters ends with a set of conclusions based on the findings and analysis presented under those themes.

Part IV, Chapter 8, proposes a research and development agenda for expanding the knowledge base on the integration of cognition and measurement. It also considers the avenues through which the growing knowledge base is most likely to have an impact on actual assessment practice.

With five themes, this chapter reviews the purposes and nature of educational assessment and its role in the educational system.

- Educational assessments are used in classroom and large-scale policy contexts for multiple purposes. This report addresses assessments used for three broad purposes: to assist learning, to measure individual achievement, and to evaluate programs. The purpose of an assessment determines priorities, and the context of use imposes constraints on the design.
- Although an assessment intended to help teachers plan the next set of lessons may look far different from one used by state administrators to gauge the effectiveness of school mathematics programs, certain common principles underlie all assessments. One such principle is that, by its very nature, assessment is imprecise to some degree. Assessment results are estimates, based on samples of knowledge and performance drawn from the much larger universe of everything a person knows and can do.
- Assessment is a process of reasoning from evidence. Because one cannot directly perceive students' mental processes, one must rely on less direct methods to make judgments about what they know.
- As discussed in Chapter 1, every assessment is based on three interconnected elements: a theory of what students know and how they develop competence in a subject domain (cognition); tasks or situations used to collect evidence about student performance (observation); and a method for drawing inferences from those observations (interpretation). These three elements can serve as a framework for thinking about the foundations of assessment and their interrelationships.
- Assessment does not exist in isolation, but must be closely aligned with the goals of curriculum and instruction. A model of how students learn, based on cognitive findings and educational research, can serve as a unifying element that lends cohesion to curriculum, instruction, and assessment.

2

The Nature of Assessment and Reasoning from Evidence

PURPOSES OF ASSESSMENT

This report focuses on the assessment of school learning, also referred to as the assessment of school *achievement*. The assessment of achievement is often contrasted with the assessment of *aptitude* (ability), which has the purpose of predicting performance in some future situation. An example is the use of the SAT I to predict college performance. This type of assessment is not the focus of this report, although many of the theoretical underpinnings discussed here apply to assessments used for any purpose.

Assessments of school learning provide information to help educators, policy makers, students, and parents make decisions. The specific purposes for which an assessment will be used are an important consideration in all phases of its design. For example, assessments used by teachers in classrooms to assist learning may need to provide more detailed information than assessments whose results will be used by state policy makers. The following subsections address issues of purpose and use by examining three broad purposes served by assessments in classroom and large-scale contexts: assisting learning, measuring individual student achievement, and evaluating programs.

Assessment to Assist Learning

In the classroom context, effective teachers use various forms of assessment to inform day-to-day and month-to-month decisions about next steps for instruction, to give students feedback about their progress, and to motivate students. One familiar type of classroom assessment is a teacher-made quiz, but assessment also includes more informal methods for determining how students are progressing in their learning, such as classroom projects, feedback from computer-assisted instruction, classroom observation, written work, homework, and conversations with and among students—all interpreted by the teacher in light of additional information about the students, the schooling context, and the content being studied.

In this report, these situations are referred to as *assessment to assist learning,* or *formative assessment.* These assessments provide specific information about students' strengths and difficulties with learning. For example, statistics teachers need to know more than the fact that a student does not understand probability; they need to know the details of this misunderstanding, such as the student's tendency to confuse conditional and compound probability. Teachers can use information from these types of assessment to adapt their instruction to meet students' needs, which may be difficult to anticipate and are likely to vary from one student to another. Students can use this information to determine which skills and knowledge they need to study further and what adjustments in their thinking they need to make.

A recent review (Black and Wiliam, 1998) revealed that classroom-based formative assessment, when appropriately used, can positively affect learning. According to the results of this review, students learn more when they receive feedback about particular qualities of their work, along with advice on what they can do to improve. They also benefit from training in self-assessment, which helps them understand the main goals of the instruction and determine what they need to do to achieve. But these practices are rare, and classroom assessment is often weak. The development of good classroom assessments places significant demands on the teacher. Teachers must have tools and other supports if they are to implement high-quality assessments efficiently and use the resulting information effectively.

Assessment of Individual Achievement

Another type of assessment used to make decisions about individuals is that conducted to help determine whether a student has attained a certain level of competency after completing a particular phase of education, whether it be a classroom unit or 12 years of schooling. In this report, this is referred to as *assessment of individual achievement,* or *summative assessment.*[1]

Some of the most familiar forms of summative assessment are those used by classroom teachers, such as end-of-unit tests and letter grades assigned when a course is finished. Large-scale assessments—which are administered at the direction of users external to the classroom—also provide

---

[1]The committee recognizes that all assessment is in a sense "formative" in that it is intended to provide feedback to the system to inform next steps for learning. For a more nuanced discussion of the formative-summative distinction, see Scriven (1991).

information about the attainment of individual students, as well as comparative information about how one individual performs relative to others. This information may be used by state- or district-level administrators, teachers, parents, students, potential employers, and the general public. Because large-scale assessments are typically given only once a year and involve a time lag between testing and availability of results, the results seldom provide information that can be used to help teachers or students make day-to-day or month-to-month decisions about teaching and learning.

As described in the National Research Council (NRC) report *High Stakes* (1999a), policy makers see large-scale assessments of student achievement as one of their most powerful levers for influencing what happens in local schools and classrooms. Increasingly, assessments are viewed as a way not only to measure performance, but also to change it, by encouraging teachers and students to modify their practices. Assessment programs are being used to focus public attention on educational concerns; to change curriculum, instruction, and teaching practices; and to motivate educators and students to work harder and achieve at higher levels (Haertel, 1999; Linn, 2000).

A trend that merits particular attention is the growing use of state assessments to make high-stakes decisions about individual students, teachers, and schools. In 1998, 18 states required students to pass an exam before receiving a high school diploma, and 8 of these states also used assessment results to make decisions about student promotion or retention in grade (Council of Chief State School Officers, 1999). When stakes are high, it is particularly important that the inferences drawn from an assessment be *valid, reliable,* and *fair* (American Educational Research Association, American Psychological Association, and National Council on Measurement in Education, 1999; NRC, 1999a). Validity refers to the degree to which evidence and theory support the interpretations of assessment scores. Reliability denotes the consistency of an assessment's results when the assessment procedure is repeated on a population of individuals or groups. And fairness encompasses a broad range of interconnected issues, including absence of bias in the assessment tasks, equitable treatment of all examinees in the assessment process, opportunity to learn the material being assessed, and comparable validity (if test scores underestimate or overestimate the competencies of members of a particular group, the assessment is considered unfair). Moreover, even when these criteria for assessment are met, care must be taken not to extend the results to reach conclusions not supported by the evidence. For example, a teacher whose students have higher test scores is not necessarily better than one whose students have lower scores. The quality of inputs—such as the entry characteristics of students or educational resources available—must also be considered. Too often, high-stakes assessments are used to make decisions that are inappropriate in light of the limitations discussed above.

Assessment to Evaluate Programs

Another common purpose of assessment is to help policy makers formulate judgments about the quality and effectiveness of educational programs and institutions (these assessments also fall under the category of summative assessment). Assessments are used increasingly to make high-stakes decisions not only about individuals, but also about institutions. For instance, public reporting of state assessment results by school and district can influence the judgments of parents and taxpayers about their schools. In addition, many states provide financial or other rewards to schools in which performance increases and impose sanctions—including closing schools—when performance declines. Just as with individuals, the quality of the measure is of critical importance in the validity of these decisions.

The National Assessment of Educational Progress (NAEP), a national program begun in 1969 to measure broad trends in the achievement of U.S. students, is used for program evaluation in broad terms. Also known as "the nation's report card," NAEP is administered periodically in core academic subjects to students at certain ages. The NAEP assessment items are not designed to match any particular curriculum, but rather to reflect national consensus about what students should know and be able to do. Since 1990, NAEP results have also been available for participating states, providing them with an independent source of information about how their students are achieving relative to the nation as a whole.

As with evaluating teachers, care must be taken not to extend the results of assessments at a particular school to reach conclusions not supported by the evidence. For example, a school whose students have higher test scores is not necessarily better than one whose students have lower test scores. As in judging teacher performance, the quality of inputs—such as the entry characteristics of students or educational resources available—must also be considered.

Reflections on the Purposes of Assessment

Several important points should be made about the purposes of assessment. Note that all of the issues introduced briefly below are discussed more fully in Chapter 6.

First, many of the cognitive and measurement principles set forth in this report apply to the design of assessments for all three purposes discussed above. At the same time, it is important to emphasize that one type of assessment does not fit all. The purpose of an assessment determines priorities, and the context of use imposes constraints on the design. Often a single assessment will be used for multiple purposes. For instance, many state tests are used for both individual and program assessment purposes. In general, however, the more purposes a single assessment aims to serve, the more each purpose will be compromised. This is not necessarily a problem as long as the assessment designers and users recognize the compromises and trade-offs involved.

Second, U.S. society generally places greater value on large-scale than on classroom assessment. A significant industry and an extensive research literature have grown up around large-scale tests; by contrast, teachers have tended to fend for themselves in developing assessments for classroom use. The good news is that researchers are paying more attention to the potential benefits of well-designed classroom assessments for improving learning (e.g., Falk, 2000; NRC, 2001; Niyogi, 1995; Pellegrino, Baxter, and Glaser, 1999; Shepard, 2000; Stiggins, 1997; Wiggins, 1998). Moreover, national standards in science and mathematics recognize this type of assessment as a fundamental part of teaching and learning (National Council of Teachers of Mathematics [NCTM], 2000; NRC, 1996). This report describes ways in which substantially more valid and useful inferences could be drawn from large-scale assessments. Also emphasized is the significant potential for advances in the cognitive and measurement sciences to improve classroom assessment. Powerful theories and tools are now available that enable deep and frequent assessment of student understanding during the course of instruction.

Third, there is a need for better alignment among the various purposes of assessment. Ideally, teachers' goals for learning should be consistent with those of large-scale assessments and vice versa. In reality, however, this is often not the case. Black and Wiliam (1998, p. 59) emphasize that a major problem to be addressed relates to "the possible confusions and tensions, both for teachers and learners, between the formative and summative purposes which their work might have to serve . . . if an optimum balance is not sought, formative work will always be insecure because of the threat of renewed dominance by the summative." The contrast between classroom and large-scale assessments arises from the different purposes they serve and contexts in which they are used. To guide instruction and monitor its effects, teachers need information intimately connected to what their students are studying, and they interpret this evidence in light of everything else they know about their students and their instruction. The power of classroom assessment resides in these connections. Yet precisely because they are individualized, neither the rationale nor the results of the typical classroom assessments are easy to communicate beyond the classroom. Standardized assessments do communicate efficiently across time and place— but by so constraining the content and timeliness of the message that they often have little utility in the classroom. Most would agree that there is a need for both classroom and large-scale assessments in the educational system; one challenge is to make stronger connections between the two so they work together to support a common set of learning goals. Needed are systems of assessments, consisting of both classroom and large-scale components, that provide a variety of evidence to inform and support educational decision making.

PRECISION AND IMPRECISION IN ASSESSMENT

Assessments serve a vital role in providing information to help students, parents, teachers, administrators, and policy makers reach decisions. Sophisticated statistical methods have been developed to enhance the accuracy of assessments and describe precisely their margins of error. But the heightened, and possibly exaggerated, attention paid to standardized testing in the U.S. educational system can overshadow the essential point that even assessments meeting the highest technical requirements are still, by their nature, imprecise to some degree. As noted earlier, an assessment result is an *estimate*, based on samples of knowledge and performance from the much larger universe of everything a person knows and can do. Although assessment can provide valuable information about a student's competence, scores may nevertheless vary for reasons unrelated to achievement, such as the specific content being assessed, the particular format of the assessment items, the timing and conditions for administering the assessment, or the health of the student on that particular day.

Educators assess students to learn about what they know and can do, but assessments do not offer a direct pipeline into a student's mind. Assessing educational outcomes is not as straightforward as measuring height or weight; the attributes to be measured are mental representations and processes that are not outwardly visible. One must therefore draw inferences about what students know and can do on the basis of what one sees them say, do, or make in a handful of particular situations. What a student knows and what one observes a student doing are not the same thing. The two can be connected only through a chain of inference, which involves reasoning from what one knows and observes to form explanations, conclusions, or predictions, as discussed in the following section. Assessment users always reason in the presence of uncertainty; as a result, the information produced by an assessment is typically incomplete, inconclusive, and amenable to more than one explanation.

ASSESSMENT AS A PROCESS OF REASONING FROM EVIDENCE

An assessment is a tool designed to observe students' behavior and produce data that can be used to draw reasonable inferences about what students know. In this report, the process of collecting evidence to support the types of inferences one wants to draw is referred to as *reasoning from evidence* (Mislevy, 1994, 1996). This chain of reasoning about student learning characterizes all assessments, from classroom quizzes and standardized achievement tests, to computerized tutoring programs, to the conversation a student has with her teacher as they work through an experiment.

People reason from evidence every day about any number of decisions, small and large. When leaving the house in the morning, for example, one does not know with certainty that it is going to rain, but may reasonably decide to take an umbrella on the basis of such evidence as the morning weather report and the clouds in the sky.

The first question in the assessment reasoning process is "evidence about what?" *Data* become *evidence* in an analytic problem only when one has established their relevance to a conjecture being considered (Schum, 1987, p. 16). Data do not provide their own meaning; their value as evidence can arise only through some interpretational framework. What a person perceives visually, for example, depends not only on the data she receives as photons of light striking her retinas, but also on what she thinks she might see. In the present context, educational assessments provide data such as written essays, marks on answer sheets, presentations of projects, or students' explanations of their problem solutions. These data become evidence only with respect to conjectures about how students acquire knowledge and skill.

Assessment comes down to which types of evidence or observations are available to help reason about the examinee's competence. What one believes about the nature of learning will affect the kinds of assessment data sought and the chain of inferences drawn. Cognitive researchers, for example, would seek evidence about how learners approach problems, including what they understand about why they are being asked to solve these problems, as well as the strategies they then use for solution. Assessment also depends on which tools are available to make sense of the evidence. Measurement science offers various methods for using available evidence to make determinations about the competencies of learners. For example, some assessments use probabilistic models to handle sampling or to communicate uncertainty. The chain of reasoning determines what to look for in what students say, do, or produce and why it constitutes evidence about what they know and can do.

The methods and practices of familiar tests and test theory are special cases of reasoning from evidence. Their evolution has been channeled by the kinds of inferences teachers and other assessment users have wanted to draw, shaped by the ways people have thought about learning and schooling, and constrained by the technologies that have been available to gather and use assessment data. The same underlying principles of reasoning from evidence that led to classical test theory can support inference in a broader universe of assessments, including those based on cognitive theory.

THE ASSESSMENT TRIANGLE

The process of reasoning from evidence can be portrayed as a triad referred to throughout this report as the *assessment triangle.* As shown in Figure 2-1, the corners of the triangle represent the three key elements underlying any assessment noted earlier: a model of student *cognition* and learning in the domain, a set of beliefs about the kinds of *observations* that will provide evidence of students' competencies, and an *interpretation* process for making sense of the evidence.

These three elements, which are discussed in detail below, may be explicit or implicit, but an assessment cannot be designed and implemented without some consideration of each. The three are represented as corners of a triangle because each is connected to and dependent on the other two. A major tenet of this report is that for an assessment to be effective, the three elements must be in synchrony. The assessment triangle provides a useful framework for analyzing current assessment or designing future ones.

Cognition

The *cognition* corner of the triangle refers to a theory or set of beliefs about how students represent knowledge and develop competence in a subject domain (e.g., fractions). In any particular assessment application, a theory of learning in the domain is needed to identify the set of knowledge and skills that is important to measure for the task at hand, whether that be characterizing the competencies students have acquired thus far or guiding instruction to increase learning.

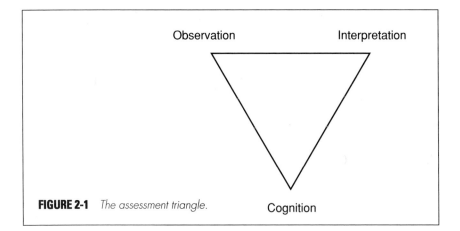

FIGURE 2-1 *The assessment triangle.*

In this report we argue that assessment will be most effective if the designer (in many cases the teacher) starts with such an explicit and clearly conceptualized cognitive model of learning. This model should reflect the most scientifically credible understanding of typical ways in which learners represent knowledge and develop expertise in a domain. These findings should derive from cognitive and educational research about how people learn, as well as the experience of expert teachers (Webb, 1992). As scientific understanding of learning evolves, the cognitive underpinnings of assessment should change accordingly. Our use of the term "cognition" is not meant to imply that the theory must necessarily come from a single cognitive research perspective. As discussed in Chapter 3, theories of student learning and understanding can take different forms and encompass several levels and types of knowledge representation that include social and contextual components.

Depending on the purpose for an assessment, one might distinguish from one to hundreds of aspects of student competence to be sampled. These *targets of inference* for a given assessment will be a subset of the larger theory of how people learn the subject matter. Targets for assessment could be expressed in terms of numbers, categories, or some mix; they might be conceived as persisting over long periods of time or apt to change at the next problem step. They might concern tendencies in behavior, conceptions of phenomena, available strategies, or levels of development. For instance, at one extreme, verbal and quantitative ability are the only two variables in the cognitive framework that underlies the SAT I. In this case, the purpose is to rank order examinees in relation to their general verbal and quantitative abilities, so a more detailed theory may not be necessary.

More detailed cognitive models of learning can be used by teachers to diagnose particular difficulties students are having in a specific domain of the curriculum. For instance, on the basis of research with learners, developmental psychologist Robert Siegler (1998) has identified rules (both correct and erroneous) learners appear to use to solve problems in various mathematical and scientific domains. The example presented in Box 2-1 is a cognitive model of the rules learners use to solve balance-scale problems.

Below we continue to use the balance-scale problem to illustrate the observation and interpretation elements of the triangle. But first it should be noted that the cognitive model underlying performance on this set of problems is more straightforward than would be the case if one were trying to model performance on less structured problems. Furthermore, additional analyses of children's reasoning with the balance scale and in other domains of problem solving have provided more dynamic and complex accounts of the understandings children have and develop about these kinds of systems (see, e.g., Goldman, Pellegrino and Mertz, 1988; Schauble, 1990; Siegler and Crowley, 1991). This point raises an issue of practicality. Assessment design

BOX 2-1   Example of a Cognitive Model of Learning for Assessing Children's Problem-Solving Rules

Siegler (1976) examined how people develop an understanding of the components underlying the principle of torque in balance-scale problems. He presented children of different ages with the type of balance scale shown below, which includes a fulcrum and an arm that can rotate around it. The arm can tip left or right or remain level, depending on how weights (metal disks with holes in them) are arranged on the pegs on each side of the fulcrum. However, a lever (not shown in the figure) is typically set to hold the arm motionless. The child's task is to predict which (if either) side would go down if the lever were released.

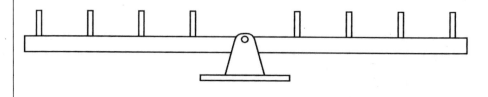

Two variables influence the outcome: (1) the amount of weight on each side of the fulcrum and (2) the distance of the weight from the fulcrum. Thus the keys to solving such problems are to attend to both of the relevant dimensions and to combine them appropriately by using the multiplicative relationship of weight times distance. On the basis of his research, together with the known tendency of young

need not take into account every subtlety and complexity about learning in a domain that has been uncovered by cognitive research. Instead, what is being proposed in this report is that assessment design be based on a representation or approximation of cognition that is both consistent with a richer psychological perspective and at a level of detail sufficient to accomplish the job of assessment. Any model of learning underlying an assessment will be a simplification of what is going on in the mind of the examinee and in the social situation within which the assessment takes place. As described and illustrated more fully in Chapter 5, the point of basing assessment on a cognitive model is to focus the assessment on those competencies that are most important to measure in light of the desired inferences about student learning.

Finally, if the goal of basing assessment on an appropriate model of learning is to be realized, cognitive models will need to be developed for a broader range of the curriculum. Currently, cognition and learning are con-

children to focus on a single relevant dimension, Siegler developed the following cognitive model, which incorporates four different rules children use to solve such problems:

Rule I—If the weight is the same on both sides, predict that the scale will balance. If the weight differs, predict that the side with more weight will go down.

Rule II—If one side has more weight, predict that it will go down. If the weights on the two sides are equal, choose the side with the greater distance (i.e., the side that has the weight farther from the fulcrum).

Rule III—If both weight and distance are equal, predict that the scale will balance. If one side has more weight or distance, and the two sides are equal on the other dimension, predict that the side with the greater value on the unequal dimension will go down. If one side has more weight and the other side more distance, muddle through or guess.

Rule IV—Proceed as in Rule III unless one side has more weight and the other more distance. In that case, calculate torques by multiplying weight times distance on each side. Then predict that the side with the greater torque will go down.

SOURCE: Siegler (1976, p. 482). Used by permission of Academic Press.

siderably better understood in some domains, such as physics and reading, than in others, such as history and chemistry. Moreover, the models developed by cognitive scientists will need to be recast in ways that are easily understood and readily usable by assessment developers and teachers.

Observation

Every assessment is also based on a set of beliefs about the kinds of tasks or situations that will prompt students to say, do, or create something that demonstrates important knowledge and skills. The tasks to which students are asked to respond on an assessment are not arbitrary. They must be carefully designed to provide evidence that is linked to the cognitive model of learning and to support the kinds of inferences and decisions that will be based on the assessment results.

The *observation* corner of the assessment triangle represents a description or set of specifications for assessment tasks that will elicit illuminating responses from students. In a tutoring session, for example, the observation framework describes what the learner says and does, does not say and do, or says or does with specific kinds of support or scaffolding. In a formal assessment, the observation model describes examinee products, such as written or oral responses or the choice of a distractor for multiple choice items. In assessment, one has the opportunity to structure some small corner of the world to make observations. The assessment designer can use this capability to maximize the value of the data collected, as seen through the lens of the underlying beliefs about how students learn in the domain.

For example, on the basis of the cognitive model presented in Box 2-1, Siegler (1976) designed situations to observe which rules, if any, describe how a child is solving balance-scale problems. Asking children how they solved the problems might appear to be the simplest strategy, but Siegler believed that answers to such questions could either overestimate or underestimate children's knowledge. The answers would give a misleadingly positive impression if children simply repeated information they had heard at home or in school, whereas the answers would give a misleadingly negative impression if children were too inarticulate to communicate knowledge they in fact possessed. In light of these considerations, Siegler formulated an observation method that he called the *rule assessment method* to determine which rule a given child is using (see Box 2-2).

The tasks selected for observation should be developed with the purpose of the assessment in mind. The same rich and demanding performance task that provides invaluable information to a teacher about his tenth-grade class—because he knows they have been studying transmission genetics for the past 6 weeks—could prove impenetrable and worthless for assessing the knowledge of the vast majority of students across the nation. Large-scale assessments generally collect the same kind of evidence for all examinees; thus observations cannot be closely tied to the specific instruction a given student has recently experienced.

Interpretation

Every assessment is based on certain assumptions and models for interpreting the evidence collected from observations. The *interpretation* corner of the triangle encompasses all the methods and tools used to reason from fallible observations. It expresses how the observations derived from a set of assessment tasks constitute evidence about the knowledge and skills being assessed. In the context of large-scale assessment, the interpretation method is usually a statistical model, which is a characterization or summarization of patterns one would expect to see in the data given varying levels of student

BOX 2-2   Methods for Observing Children's Rules for Solving Balance-Scale Problems

Below are descriptions of the kinds of problems Siegler (1976) crafted to observe which rules children are using to solve balance-scale problems. Children
who use different rules produce different patterns of responses to these six problems:

1. *Balance problems*—The same configuration of weights on pegs on each side
of the fulcrum.

2. *Weight problems*—Unequal amounts of weights, equidistant from the
fulcrum.

3. *Distance problems*—Equal amounts of weights, different distances from the
fulcrum.

4. *Conflict-weight problems*—One side with more weight, the other side with
its weight farther from the fulcrum, and the side with more weight goes down.

5. *Conflict-distance problems*—One side with more weight, the other side with
more distance, and the side with more distance goes down.

6. *Conflict-balance problems*—The usual conflict between weight and distance,
and the two sides balance.

SOURCE: Siegler (1976).   Used by permission of Academic Press.

competency. In the context of classroom assessment, the interpretation is
often made less formally by the teacher, and is usually based on an intuitive
or qualitative model rather than a formal statistical one.

Returning to the example of Siegler's balance-scale problems, one example of an interpretation method is presented in Box 2-3. In this example
the interpretation framework specifies patterns of response to the six problems and the corresponding rule, if any, that one can infer a student is using.

Relationships Among the Three Vertices of the Assessment Triangle

A crucial point is that each of the three elements of the assessment
triangle not only must make sense on its own, but also must connect to
each of the other two elements in a meaningful way to lead to an effective
assessment and sound inferences.

BOX 2-3 Interpreting Observations of Student Performance on Balance-Scale Problems

Siegler (1976) describes how children who use the different rules described in Box 2-1 will produce different patterns of response to the problems presented in Box 2-2. For instance, children using Rule I would be expected to predict correctly on balance, weight, and conflict-weight problems and incorrectly on the other three problem types. Children using Rule II would behave similarly, except that they would answer correctly on distance problems. The figure below shows the predicted percentage of correct answers on each problem type for children using each of the four rules.

	RULE			
PROBLEM TYPE	I	II	III	IV
Balance	100	100	100	100
Weight	100	100	100	100
Distance	0 (Should say "Balance")	100	100	100
Conflict-Weight	100	100	33 (Chance Responding)	100
Conflict-Distance	0 (Should say "Right Down")	0 (Should say "Right Down")	33 (Chance Responding)	100
Conflict-Balance	0 (Should say "Right Down")	0 (Should say "Right Down")	33 (Chance Responding)	100

In a study of 5- to 17-year-olds solving balance-scale problems, Siegler found that more than 80 percent used one of the four rules consistently; the other 20 percent produced less consistent patterns of responses that did not match perfectly any of the above profiles. This finding may reflect an intermediate or transitional state of responding, which would not be unexpected in children's development.

SOURCE: Siegler (1976, p. 486). Used by permission of Academic Press.

Connections Between Cognition and Observation. A cognitive theory of how people develop competence in a domain provides clues about the types of situations that will elicit evidence about that competence. Conversely, a well-developed knowledge base about the properties and affordances of tasks—what does and does not work to reveal what students know and can do—helps the assessment designer anticipate the types of knowledge and skills likely to be elicited by tasks with certain features. When the knowledge derived from both perspectives is combined, relevant information about student performance is more likely to be collected through assessment tasks.

Connections Between Cognition and Interpretation. A cognitive theory of how people develop competence in a domain also provides clues about the types of interpretation methods that are appropriate for transforming the data about student performance into assessment results. The cognitive theory suggests aspects of knowledge and skills by which we want to characterize students. Conversely, a familiarity with available measurement models provides a set of experience-tested methods for handling thorny and often subtle issues of evidence.

Connections Between Observation and Interpretation. Knowing the possibilities and limitations of various interpretation models helps in designing a set of observations that is at once effective and efficient for the task at hand. The interpretation model expresses how the observations from a given task constitute evidence about the performance being assessed as it bears on the targeted knowledge. It is only sensible to look for evidence one knows how to reason from or interpret.

Thus to have an effective assessment, all three vertices of the triangle must work together in synchrony. It will almost certainly be necessary for developers to go around the assessment triangle several times, looking for mismatches and refining the elements to achieve consistency. The interdependent relationships among cognition, observation, and interpretation in the assessment design process are further elaborated and illustrated throughout this report.

ASSESSMENT, CURRICULUM, AND INSTRUCTION: COGNITION AT THE CORE

Assessment is not an isolated part of the education system. What is measured and how the information is used depend to a great extent on the curriculum that is taught and the instructional methods used. Viewed from the other perspective, assessment has a strong effect on both curriculum and instruction.

Curriculum consists of the knowledge and skills in subject areas that teachers teach and students learn. The curriculum generally encompasses a scope or breadth of content in a given subject area and a sequence for learning. The standards discussed in Chapter 1 outline the goals of learning, whereas curriculum sets forth the more specific means to be used to achieve those ends. *Instruction* refers to methods of teaching and the learning activities used to help students master the content and objectives specified by a curriculum. Instruction encompasses the activities of both teachers and students. It can be carried out by a variety of methods, sequences of activities, and topic orders. *Assessment* is the means used to measure the outcomes of education and the achievement of students with regard to important competencies. As discussed earlier, assessment may include both formal methods, such as large-scale state assessments, or less formal classroom-based procedures, such as quizzes, class projects, and teacher questioning.

A precept of educational practice is the need for alignment among curriculum, instruction, and assessment (e.g., NCTM, 1995; Webb, 1997). Alignment, in this sense, means that the three functions are directed toward the same ends and reinforce each other rather than working at cross-purposes. Ideally, an assessment should measure what students are actually being taught, and what is actually being taught should parallel the curriculum one wants students to learn. If any of the functions is not well synchronized, it will disrupt the balance and skew the educational process. Assessment results will be misleading, or instruction will be ineffective. Alignment is difficult to achieve, however. Often what is lacking is a central theory around which the three functions can be coordinated.

Decisions about assessment, curriculum, and instruction are further complicated by actions taken at different levels of the educational system, including the classroom, the school or district, and the state. Each of these levels has different needs, and each uses assessment data in varied ways for somewhat different purposes. Each also plays a role in making decisions and setting policies for assessment, curriculum, and instruction, although the locus of power shifts depending on the type of decision involved. Some of these actions emanate from the top down, while others arise from the bottom up. States generally exert considerable influence over curriculum, while classroom teachers have more latitude in instruction. States tend to determine policies on assessment for program evaluation, while teachers have greater control over assessment for learning. This situation means that adjustments must continually be made among assessment, curriculum, and instruction not only horizontally, within the same level (such as within school districts), but also vertically across levels. For example, a change in state curriculum policy will require adjustments in assessment and instruction at all levels.

Realizing the new approach to assessment set forth in this report will depend on making compatible changes in curriculum and instruction. As with assessment, most current approaches to curriculum and instruction are based on theories that have not kept pace with modern knowledge of how people learn (NRC, 1999b; Shepard, 2000). The committee believes that alignment among assessment, curriculum, and instruction could be better achieved if all three were derived from a shared knowledge base about cognition and learning in the subject domain. The model of learning would provide the central bonding principle, serving as a nucleus around which the three functions would revolve. Without such a central core, and under pressure to prepare students for high-stakes accountability tests, teachers may feel compelled to move back and forth between instruction and assessment and teach directly to the items on a test. This approach can result in an undesirable narrowing of the curriculum and a limiting of learning outcomes. Such problems can be ameliorated if, instead, decisions about both instruction and assessment are guided by a model of learning in the domain. Although current curriculum, instruction, and assessment are designed on the basis of implicit conceptions of learning, those conceptions tend to be fragmented, outdated, and not clearly delineated. Instead, the committee contends that the cognitive underpinnings should be made explicit and public, and they should represent the best available scientific understanding of how people learn.

CONCLUSIONS

This report addresses assessments used in both classroom and large-scale contexts for three broad purposes: to assist learning, to measure individual achievement, and to evaluate programs. The purpose of an assessment determines priorities, and the context of use imposes constraints on the design. *Thus it is essential to recognize that one type of assessment does not fit all.*

Often a single assessment is used for multiple purposes; in general, however, the more purposes a single assessment aims to serve, the more each purpose will be compromised. For instance, many state tests are used for both individual and program assessment purposes. This is not necessarily a problem, as long as assessment designers and users recognize the compromises and trade-offs such use entails.

Although assessments used in various contexts and for differing purposes often look quite different, they share certain common principles. One such principle is that assessment is always a process of reasoning from evidence. By its very nature, moreover, assessment is imprecise to some degree. Assessment results are only estimates of what a person knows and can do.

Every assessment, regardless of its purpose, rests on three pillars: a model of how students represent knowledge and develop competence in the subject domain, tasks or situations that allow one to observe students' performance, and an interpretation method for drawing inferences from the performance evidence thus obtained. In the context of large-scale assessment, the interpretation method is usually a statistical model that characterizes expected data patterns, given varying levels of student competence. In less formal classroom assessment, the interpretation is often made by the teacher using an intuitive or qualitative rather than formal statistical model.

Three foundational elements, comprising what is referred to in this report as the "assessment triangle," underlie all assessments. *These three elements—cognition, observation, and interpretation—must be explicitly connected and designed as a coordinated whole.* If not, the meaningfulness of inferences drawn from the assessment will be compromised.

The central problem addressed by this report is that most widely used assessments of academic achievement are based on highly restrictive beliefs about learning and competence not fully in keeping with current knowledge about human cognition and learning. Likewise, the observation and interpretation elements underlying most current assessments were created to fit prior conceptions of learning and need enhancement to support the kinds of inferences people now want to draw about student achievement. *A cognitive model of learning should serve as the cornerstone of the assessment design process. This model should be based on the best available understanding of how students represent knowledge and develop competence in the domain.*

The model of learning can serve as a unifying element—a nucleus that brings cohesion to curriculum, instruction, and assessment. This cohesive function is a crucial one because *educational assessment does not exist in isolation, but must be aligned with curriculum and instruction if it is to support learning.*

Finally, aspects of learning that are assessed and emphasized in the classroom should ideally be consistent with (though not necessarily the same as) the aspects of learning targeted by large-scale assessments. In reality, however, these two forms of assessment are often out of alignment. The result can be conflict and frustration for both teachers and learners. *Thus there is a need for better alignment among assessments used for different purposes and in different contexts.*

Part II

The Scientific Foundations of Assessment

INTRODUCTION

The scientific basis for rethinking the foundations of assessment comes from two disciplines: cognitive science and educational measurement. The following two chapters review developments in these disciplines over the last several decades that have important implications for the design and use of educational assessments. The committee presents these developments side by side because they form the necessary and complementary foundations of the science and design of educational assessment. Modern knowledge, theories, models, and methods from these two fields provide the underpinnings of a scientifically credible and principled approach to assessment.

Chapter 3 summarizes findings from cognitive science about how people think and learn. With reference to the assessment triangle introduced in Chapter 2, cognitive research provides the scientific basis for the central model of cognition and learning that informs the assessment design, or the *cognition* vertex of the triangle. Cognitive research suggests the important aspects of learning about which one would want to draw inferences when measuring student achievement. It also helps determine the design of the *observation* corner of the triangle by suggesting the types of situations or tasks that will elicit evidence from students to support the desired inferences. Four decades of theory and research on human cognition, learning, and development has provided powerful insights into how students represent knowledge and develop competence in specific domains, as well as how tasks and situations can be designed to provide evidence for inferences about what students know and can do.

Chapter 4 summarizes the contributions that the discipline of educational measurement (psychometrics) can make to a new approach to assessment. Measurement models are statistical examples of the *interpretation* corner of the assessment triangle. They provide the statistical tools that make it possible to integrate the myriad of information obtained from the tasks of an assessment to formulate assessment results (inferences about student competencies). In most current forms of assessment, the measurement models are relatively simple, enabling inferences about students' general proficiency levels and relative rankings. But just as there have been advances in the sciences of cognition and learning, there have been significant developments in methods of measurement over the last several decades. A wide array of newer models and methods are available that can better capture the complexities of learning as it is now understood.

Taken together, developments from the sciences of cognition and measurement should serve as the scientific foundations of assessment. The knowledge accumulated in these fields can guide the determination of what observations it is sensible to undertake and what sense can be made of those observations when measuring student achievement.

Five themes are the focus for the discussion of advances in the sciences of thinking and learning in this chapter:

- Theories of learning and knowing have expanded substantially over the last 100 years. We briefly describe those shifts and their impact on assessment practices.
- Current understanding of the nature of learning and knowledge details various fundamental components of the structures, processes, and contents of the human mind. Consideration is given to each of these components and their significance for understanding and assessing human knowledge and performance.
- A hallmark of contemporary cognitive science is the study of how expertise is acquired in particular subject domains. The features of expertise are considered, together with research on the acquisition of expertise. We also examine those aspects of children's development and learning that relate to the acquisition of subject matter expertise and that have implications for instruction and assessment.
- Empirically based models of student knowledge and learning have been developed for multiple curricular areas. Examples are provided of detailed models that have been directly employed to support innovative instructional and assessment practices in specific academic domains.
- The cognitive sciences are founded on rigorous empirical study of both simple and complex forms of cognition. Various methods of observation and inference used in the cognitive sciences to probe the nature of thinking are discussed because of their relevance to issues regarding the design of assessment tasks and methods of inference about what students know.

3

Advances in the Sciences of Thinking and Learning

In the latter part of the 20th century, study of the human mind generated considerable insight into one of the most powerful questions of science: How do people think and learn? Evidence from a variety of disciplines—cognitive psychology, developmental psychology, computer science, anthropology, linguistics, and neuroscience, in particular—has advanced our understanding of such matters as how knowledge is organized in the mind; how children develop conceptual understanding; how people acquire expertise in specific subjects and domains of work; how participation in various forms of practice and community shapes understanding; and what happens in the physical structures of the brain during the processes of learning, storing, and retrieving information. Over the same time period, research in mathematics and science education has advanced greatly. In the 1999 volume *How People Learn*, the National Research Council (NRC) describes numerous findings from the research on learning and analyzes their implications for instruction. This chapter focuses on those findings that have the greatest implications for improving the assessment of school learning.

EXPANDING VIEWS OF THE NATURE OF KNOWING AND LEARNING

In the quest to understand the human mind, thinkers through the centuries have engaged in reflection and speculation; developed theories and philosophies of elegance and genius; conducted arrays of scientific experiments; and produced great works of art and literature—all testaments to the powers of the very entity they were investigating. Over a century ago, scientists began to study thinking and learning in a more systematic way, taking early steps toward what we now call the cognitive sciences. During the first few decades of the 20th century, researchers focused on such matters as the nature of general intellectual ability and its distribution in the population. In the 1930s, scholars started emphasizing such issues as the laws governing stimulus-and-response associations in learning. Beginning in the 1960s, advances in fields as diverse as linguistics, computer science, and neuroscience offered provocative new perspectives on human development and powerful new technologies for observing behavior and brain functions. The result during the past 40 years has been an outpouring of scientific research on the mind and brain—a "cognitive revolution" as some have termed it. With richer and more varied evidence in hand, researchers have refined earlier theories or developed new ones to explain the nature of knowing and learning.

As described by Greeno, Pearson and Schoenfeld (1996b), four perspectives are particularly significant in the history of research and theory regarding the nature of the human mind: the *differential, behaviorist, cognitive,* and *situative* perspectives. Most current tests, and indeed many aspects of the science of educational measurement, have theoretical roots in the differential and behaviorist traditions. The more recent perspectives—the cognitive and the situative—are not well reflected in traditional assessments but have influenced several recent innovations in the design and use of educational assessments. These four perspectives, summarized below, are not mutually exclusive. Rather, they emphasize different aspects of knowing and learning with differing implications for what should be assessed and how the assessment process should be transacted (see e.g., Greeno, Collins, and Resnick, 1996a; Greeno et al., 1996b).

The Differential Perspective

The differential perspective focuses mainly on the nature of individual differences in what people know and in their potential for learning. The roots of research within this tradition go back to the start of the 20th century. "Mental tests" were developed to discriminate among children who were more or less suited to succeed in the compulsory school environment that had recently been instituted in France (Binet and Simon, 1980). The construction and composition of such tests was a very practical matter: tasks were chosen to represent a variety of basic knowledge and cognitive skills that children of a given age could be expected to have acquired. Inclusion of a task in the assessment was based on the how well it discriminated among children within and across various age ranges. A more abstract approach to theorizing about the capacities of the mind arose, however, from the practice of constructing mental tests and administering them to samples of children and adults. Theories of intelligence and mental ability emerged that were based entirely on analyses of the patterns of correlation among test scores. To pursue such work, elaborate statistical machinery was developed for determining the separate factors that define the structure of intellect (Carroll, 1993).

At the core of this approach to studying the mind is the concept that individuals differ in their mental capacities and that these differences define stable mental traits—aspects of knowledge, skill, and intellectual competence—that can be measured. It is presumed that different individuals possess these traits in differing amounts, as measured by their performance on sample tasks that make up a test. Specific traits or mental abilities are inferred when the pattern of scores shows consistent relationships across different situations.

The differential perspective was developed largely to assess aspects of intelligence or cognitive ability that were separate from the processes and content of academic learning. However, the methods used in devising aptitude tests and ranking individuals were adopted directly in the design of "standardized" academic achievement tests that were initially developed during the first half of the century. In fact, the logic of measurement was quite compatible with assumptions about knowing and learning that existed within the behaviorist perspective that came to dominate much of research and theory on learning during the middle of the century.

The Behaviorist Perspective

Behaviorist theories became popular during the 1930s (e.g., Hull, 1943; Skinner, 1938), about the same time that theories of individual differences in intellectual abilities and the mental testing movement were maturing. In some ways the two perspectives are complementary. In the behaviorist view, knowledge is the organized accumulation of stimulus-response associations that serve as the components of skills. Learning is the process by which one acquires those associations and skills (Thorndike, 1931). People learn by acquiring simple components of a skill, then acquiring more complicated units that combine or differentiate the simpler ones. Stimulus-response associations can be strengthened by reinforcement or weakened by inattention. When people are motivated by rewards, punishments, or other (mainly extrinsic) factors, they attend to relevant aspects of a situation, and this favors the formation of new associations and skills.

A rich and detailed body of research and theory on learning and performance has arisen within the behaviorist perspective, including important work on the strengthening of stimulus-response associations as a consequence of reinforcement or feedback. Many behavioral laws and principles that apply to human learning and performance are derived from work within this perspective. In fact, many of the elements of current cognitive theories of knowledge and skill acquisition are more elaborate versions of stimulus-response associative theory. Missing from this perspective, however, is any treatment of the underlying structures or representations of mental events and processes and the richness of thought and language.

The influence of associationist and behaviorist theories can easily be discerned in curriculum and instructional methods that present tasks in sequence, from simple to complex, and that seek to ensure that students learn prerequisite skills before moving on to more complex ones. Many common assessments of academic achievement have also been shaped by behaviorist theory. Within this perspective, a domain of knowledge can be analyzed in terms of the component information, skills, and procedures to be acquired. One can then construct tests containing samples of items or assessment situations that represent significant knowledge in that domain. A person's performance on such a test indicates the extent to which he or she has mastered the domain.

The Cognitive Perspective

Cognitive theories focus on how people develop structures of knowledge, including the concepts associated with a subject matter discipline (or domain of knowledge) and procedures for reasoning and solving problems. The field of cognitive psychology has focused on how knowledge is encoded, stored, organized in complex networks, and retrieved, and how different types of internal representations are created as people learn about a domain (NRC, 1999). One major tenet of cognitive theory is that learners actively construct their understanding by trying to connect new information with their prior knowledge.

In cognitive theory, knowing means more than the accumulation of factual information and routine procedures; it means being able to integrate knowledge, skills, and procedures in ways that are useful for interpreting situations and solving problems. Thus, instruction should not emphasize basic information and skills as ends in themselves, but as resources for more meaningful activities. As Wiggins (1989) points out, children learn soccer not just by practicing dribbling, passing, and shooting, but also by actually playing in soccer games.

Whereas the differential and behaviorist approaches focus on how much knowledge someone has, cognitive theory also emphasizes what type of knowledge someone has. An important purpose of assessment is not only to determine what people know, but also to assess how, when, and whether they use what they know. This information is difficult to capture in traditional tests, which typically focus on how many items examinees answer correctly or incorrectly, with no information being provided about how they derive those answers or how well they understand the underlying concepts. Assessment of cognitive structures and reasoning processes generally requires more complex tasks that reveal information about thinking patterns, reasoning strategies, and growth in understanding over time. As noted later in this chapter and subsequently in this report, researchers and educators have made a start toward developing assessments based on cognitive theories. These assessments rely on detailed models of the goals and processes involved in mental performances such as solving problems, reading, and reasoning.

The Situative Perspective

The situative perspective, also sometimes referred to as the sociocultural perspective, grew out of concerns with the cognitive perspective's nearly exclusive focus on individual thinking and learning. Instead of viewing thought as individual response to task structures and goals, the situative perspective describes behavior at a different level of analysis, one oriented toward practical activity and context. Context refers to engagement in particular forms of practice and community. The fundamental unit of analysis in these accounts is *mediated activity*, a person's or group's activity mediated by cultural artifacts, such as tools and language (Wertsch, 1998). In this view, one learns to participate in the practices, goals, and habits of mind of a particular community. A community can be any purposeful group, large or small, from the global society of professional physicists, for example, to a local book club or school.

This view encompasses both individual and collective activity. One of its distinguishing characteristics is attention to the artifacts generated and used by people to shape the nature of cognitive activity. Hence, from a traditional cognitive perspective, reading is a series of symbolic manipulations that result in comprehension of text. In both contrast and complement, from the perspective of mediated activity, reading is a social practice rooted in the development of writing as a model for speech (Olson, 1996). So, for example, how parents introduce children to reading or how home language supports language as text can play an important role in helping children view reading as a form of communication and sense making.

The situative perspective proposes that every assessment is at least in part a measure of the degree to which one can participate in a form of practice. Hence, taking a multiple-choice test is a form of practice. Some students, by virtue of their histories, inclinations, or interests, may be better prepared than others to participate effectively in this practice. The implication is that simple assumptions about these or any other forms of assessment as indicators of knowledge-in-the-head seem untenable. Moreover, opportunities to participate in even deceptively simple practices may provide important preparation for current assessments. A good example is dinnertime conversations that encourage children to weave narratives, hold and defend positions, and otherwise articulate points of view. These forms of cultural capital are not evenly distributed among the population of test takers.

Most current testing practices are not a good match with the situative perspective. Traditional testing presents abstract situations, removed from the actual contexts in which people typically use the knowledge being tested. From a situative perspective, there is no reason to expect that people's performance in the abstract testing situation adequately reflects how well they would participate in organized, cumulative activities that may hold greater meaning for them.

From the situative standpoint, assessment means observing and analyzing how students use knowledge, skills, and processes to participate in the real work of a community. For example, to assess performance in mathematics, one might look at how productively students find and use information resources; how clearly they formulate and support arguments and hypotheses; how well they initiate, explain, and discuss in a group; and whether they apply their conceptual knowledge and skills according to the standards of the discipline.

Points of Convergence

Although we have emphasized the differences among the four perspectives, there are many ways in which they overlap and are complementary. The remainder of this chapter provides an overview of contemporary understanding of knowing and learning that has resulted from the evolution of these perspectives and that includes components of all four. Aspects of the most recent theoretical perspectives are particularly critical for understanding and assessing what people know. For example, both the individual development of knowledge emphasized by the cognitive approach and the social practices of learning emphasized by the situative approach are important aspects of education (Anderson, Greeno, Reder, and Simon, 2000; Cobb, 1998).

The cognitive perspective can help teachers diagnose an individual student's level of conceptual understanding, while the situative perspective can orient them toward patterns of participation that are important to knowing in a domain. For example, individuals learn to reason in science by crafting and using forms of notation or inscription that help represent the natural world. Crafting these forms of inscription can be viewed as being situated within a particular (and even peculiar) form of practice—modeling—into which students need to be initiated. But modeling practices can also be profitably viewed within a framework of goals and cognitive processes that govern conceptual development (Lehrer, Schauble, Carpenter and Penner, 2000; Roth and McGinn, 1998).

he cognitive perspective informs the design and development of tasks
〜mote conceptual development for particular elements of knowledge,
〜eas the situative perspective informs a view of the larger purposes and
〜ices in which these elements will come to participate. Likewise, the
〜itive perspective can help teachers focus on the conceptual structures
〜nodes of reasoning a student still needs to develop, while the situative
〜〜ective can aid them in organizing fruitful participatory activities and
〜room discourse to support that learning.

〜oth perspectives imply that assessment practices need to move beyond
〜〜cus on individual skills and discrete bits of knowledge that characterizes the earlier associative and behavioral perspectives. They must expand
to encompass issues involving the organization and processing of knowledge, including participatory practices that support knowing and understanding and the embedding of knowledge in social contexts.

FUNDAMENTAL COMPONENTS OF COGNITION

How does the human mind process information? What kinds of "units"
does it process? How do individuals monitor and direct their own thinking?
Major theoretical advances have come from research on these types of questions. As it has developed over time, cognitive theory has dealt with thought
at two different levels. The first focuses on the mind's information processing capabilities, generally considered to comprise capacities independent of
specific knowledge. The second level focuses on issues of representation,
addressing how people organize the specific knowledge associated with
mastering various domains of human endeavor, including academic content.
The following subsections deal with each of these levels in turn and their
respective implications for educational assessment.

Components of Cognitive Architecture

One of the chief theoretical advances to emerge from cognitive research
is the notion of *cognitive architecture*—the information processing system
that determines the flow of information and how it is acquired, stored, represented, revised, and accessed in the mind. The main components of this
architecture are working memory and long-term memory. Research has identified the distinguishing characteristics of these two types of memory and the
mechanisms by which they interact with each other.

Working Memory

Working memory, sometimes referred to as *short-term memory*, is what
people use to process and act on information immediately before them

(Baddeley, 1986). Working memory is a conscious system that receives input from memory buffers associated with the various sensory systems. There is also considerable evidence that working memory can receive input from the long-term memory system.

The key variable for working memory is capacity—how much information it can hold at any given time. Controlled (also defined as conscious) human thought involves ordering and rearranging ideas in working memory and is consequently restricted by finite capacity. The ubiquitous sign "Do not talk to the bus driver" has good psychological justification.

Working memory has assumed an important role in studies of human intelligence. For example, modern theories of intelligence distinguish between *fluid intelligence*, which corresponds roughly to the ability to solve new and unusual problems, and *crystallized intelligence*, or the ability to bring previously acquired information to bear on a current problem (Carroll, 1993; Horn and Noll, 1994; Hunt, 1995). Several studies (e.g., Kyllonen and Christal, 1990) have shown that measures of fluid intelligence are closely related to measures of working memory capacity. Carpenter, Just, and Shell (1990) show why this is the case with their detailed analysis of the information processing demands imposed on examinees by Raven's Progressive Matrix Test, one of the best examples of tests of fluid intelligence. The authors developed a computer simulation model for item solution and showed that as working memory capacity increased, it was easier to keep track of the solution strategy, as well as elements of the different rules used for specific problems. This led in turn to a higher probability of solving more difficult items containing complex rule structures. Other research on inductive reasoning tasks frequently associated with fluid intelligence has similarly pointed to the importance of working memory capacity in solution accuracy and in age differences in performance (e.g., Holzman, Pellegrino, and Glaser, 1983; Mulholland, Pellegrino, and Glaser, 1980).

This is not to suggest that the needs of educational assessment could be met by the wholesale development of tests of working memory capacity. There is a simple argument against this: the effectiveness of an information system in dealing with a specific problem depends not only on the system's capacity to handle information in the abstract, but also on how the information has been coded into the system.

Early theories of cognitive architecture viewed working memory as something analogous to a limited physical container that held the items a person was actively thinking about at a given time. The capacity of working memory was thought to form an outer boundary for the human cognitive system, with variations according to task and among individuals. This was the position taken in one of the first papers emerging from the cognitive revolution—George Miller's (1956) famous "Magic Number Seven" argument, which maintains that people can readily remember seven numbers or unrelated items (plus or minus two either way), but cannot easily process more than that.

Subsequent research developed an enriched concept of working memory to explain the large variations in capacity that were being measured among different people and different contexts, and that appeared to be caused by the interaction between prior knowledge and encoding. According to this concept, people extend the limits of working memory by organizing disparate bits of information into "chunks" (Simon, 1974), or groupings that make sense to them. Using chunks, working memory can evoke from long-term memory items of highly variable depth and connectivity.

Simply stated, working memory refers to the currently active portion of long-term memory. But there are limits to such activity, and these limits are governed primarily by how information is organized. Although few people can remember a randomly generated string of 16 digits, anyone with a slight knowledge of American history is likely to be able to recall the string 1492-1776-1865-1945. Similarly, while a child from a village in a developing country would be unlikely to remember all nine letters in the following string—AOL-IBM-USA—most middle-class American children would have no trouble doing so. But to conclude from such a test that the American children had more working memory capacity than their developing-country counterparts would be quite wrong. This is just one example of an important concept: namely, that knowledge stored in long-term memory can have a profound effect on what appears, at first glance, to be the capacity constraint of working memory.

Recent theoretical work has further extended notions about working memory by viewing it not as a "place" in the cognitive system, but as a kind of cognitive energy level that exists in limited amounts, with individual variations (Miyake, Just, and Carpenter, 1994). In this view, people tend to perform worse when they try to do two tasks at once because they must allocate a limited amount of processing capacity to two processes simultaneously. Thus, performance differences on any task may derive not only from individual differences in prior knowledge, but also from individual differences in both the amount and allocation or management of cognitive resources (Just, Carpenter, and Keller, 1996). Moreover, people may vary widely in their conscious or unconscious control of these allocation processes.

Long-Term Memory

Long-term memory contains two distinct types of information—semantic information about "the way the world is" and procedural information about "how things are done." Several theoretical models have been developed to characterize how information is represented in long-term memory. At present the two leading models are production systems and connectionist networks (also called parallel distributed processing or PDP systems). Under the production system model, cognitive states are represented in terms of the activation of specific "production rules," which are stated as condition-action pairs. Under the PDP model, cognitive states are represented as patterns of activation or inhibition in a network of neuronlike elements.

At a global level, these two models share some important common features and processes. Both rely on the association of contexts with actions or facts, and both treat long-term memory as the source of information that not only defines facts and procedures, but also indicates how to access them (see Klahr and MacWhinney, 1998, for a comparison of production and PDP systems). The production system model has the added advantage of being very useful for constructing "intelligent tutors"—computerized learning systems, described later in this chapter, that have promising applications to instruction and assessment in several domains.

Unlike working memory, long-term memory is, for all practical purposes, an effectively limitless store of information. It therefore makes sense to try to move the burden of problem solving from working to long-term memory. What matters most in learning situations is not the capacity of working memory—although that is a factor in speed of processing—but how well one can evoke the knowledge stored in long-term memory and use it to reason efficiently about information and problems in the present.

Cognitive Architecture and Brain Research

In addition to examining the information processing capacities of individuals, studies of human cognition have been broadened to include analysis of mind-brain relations. This topic has become of increasing interest to both scientists and the public, especially with the appearance of powerful new techniques for unobtrusively probing brain function such as positron-emission tomography (PET) scans and functional magnetic resonance imaging (fMRI). Research in cognitive neuroscience has been expanding rapidly and has led to the development and refinement of various brain-based theories of cognitive functioning. These theories deal with the relationships of brain structure and function to various aspects of the cognitive architecture and the processes of reasoning and learning. Brain-based research has convincingly demonstrated that experience can alter brain states, and it is highly likely that, conversely, brain states play an important role in the potential for learning (NRC, 1999).

Several discoveries in cognitive neuroscience are relevant to an understanding of learning, memory, and cognitive processing, and reinforce many of the conclusions about the nature of cognition and thinking derived from behavioral research. Some of the more important topics addressed by this research, such as hemispheric specialization and environmental effects on brain development, are discussed in Annex 3-1 at the end of this chapter. As noted in that discussion, these discoveries point to the need for caution so as not to overstate and overgeneralize current findings of neuroscience to derive direct implications for educational and assessment practices.

Contents of Memory

Contemporary theories also characterize the types of cognitive content that are processed by the architecture of the mind. The nature of this content is extremely critical for understanding how people answer questions and solve problems, and how they differ in this regard as a function of the conditions of instruction and learning.

There is an important distinction in cognitive content between domain-general knowledge, which is applicable to a range of situations, and domain-specific knowledge, which is relevant to a particular problem area. In science education, for example, the understanding that unconfounded experiments are at the heart of good experimental design is considered domain-general knowledge (Chen and Klahr, 1999) because the logic underlying this idea extends into all realms of experimental science. In contrast, an understanding of the underlying principles of kinetics or inorganic chemistry, for example, constitutes domain-specific knowledge, often accompanied by local theories and particular types of notation. Similarly, in the area of cognitive development, the general understanding that things can be organized according to a hierarchy is a type of domain-general knowledge, while an understanding of how to classify dinosaurs is domain-specific (Chi and Koeske, 1983).

Domain-General Knowledge and Problem-Solving Processes

Cognitive researchers have studied in depth the domain-general procedures for solving problems known as *weak methods*. Newell and Simon (1972) identify a set of such procedures, including hill climbing; means-ends analysis; analogy; and, as a last resort, trial and error. Problem solvers use these weak methods to constrain what would otherwise be very large search spaces when they are solving novel problems. Because the weak methods, by definition, are not tied to any specific context, they may reveal (and predict) people's underlying ability to solve problems in a wide range of novel situations. In that sense, they can be viewed as the types of processes that are frequently assessed by general aptitude tests such as the SAT I.

In most domains of instruction, however, learners are expected to use *strong methods*: relatively specific algorithms, particular to the domain, that will make it possible to solve problems efficiently. Strong methods, when available, make it possible to find solutions with little or no searching. For example, someone who knows the calculus finds the maximum of a function by applying a known algorithm (taking the derivative and setting it equal to zero). To continue the assessment analogy, strong methods are often measured by such tests as the SAT II. Paradoxically, although one of the hallmarks of expertise is access to a vast store of strong methods in a particular domain, both children and scientists fall back on their repertoire of weak methods when faced with truly novel problems (Klahr and Simon, 1999).

Schemas and the Organization of Knowledge

Although weak methods remain the last resort when one is faced with novel situations, people generally strive to interpret situations so that they can apply *schemas*—previously learned and somewhat specialized techniques (i.e., strong methods) for organizing knowledge in memory in ways that are useful for solving problems. Schemas help people interpret complex data by weaving them into sensible patterns. A schema may be as simple as "Thirty days hath September" or more complex, such as the structure of a chemical formula. Schemas help move the burden of thinking from working memory to long-term memory. They enable competent performers to recognize situations as instances of problems they already know how to solve; to represent such problems accurately, according to their meaning and underlying principles; and to know which strategies to use to solve them.

This idea has a very old history. In fact, the term *schema* was introduced more than 50 years ago to describe techniques people use to reconstruct stories from a few, partially remembered cues (Bartlett, 1932). The modern study of problem solving has carried this idea much further. Cheng and Holyoak's (1985) study of schematic problem solving in logic is a good example. It is well known that people have a good deal of trouble with the implication relationship, often confusing "A implies B" with the biconditional relationship "A implies B, and B implies A" (Wason and Johnson-Laird, 1972). Cheng and Holyoak showed that people are quite capable of solving an implication problem if it is rephrased as a narrative schema that means something to them. An example is the "permission schema," in which doing A implies that one has received permission to do B; to cite a specific case, "Drinking alcoholic beverages openly implies that one is of a legal age to do so." Cheng and Holyoak pointed out that college students who have trouble dealing with abstract A implies B relationships have no trouble understanding implication when it is recast in the context of "permission to drink."

The existence of problem-solving schemas has been demonstrated in a wide variety of contexts. For instance, Siegler and colleagues have shown that schoolchildren learn progressively more complicated (and more accurate) schemas for dealing with a variety of situations, such as balance-scale problems (Siegler, 1976) (see Boxes 2-1, 2-2, and 2-3 in Chapter 2) and simple addition (Siegler and Crowley, 1991). Marshall (1995) developed a computer-aided instruction program that reinforces correct schematic problem solving in elementary arithmetic. Finally, Lopez, Atran, Coley, and Medin (1997) showed that different cultures differentially encourage certain types of schemas. In reasoning about animals, American college students tend to resort to taxonomic schemas, in which animals are related by dint of possessing common features (and indirectly, having certain genetic relationships). In contrast, the Itzaj Maya, a jungle-dwelling group in Guatemala, are more likely to reason by emphasizing ecological relationships. It is not that the Americans are unaware of ecological relations or the Maya are unaware of feature possession. Rather, each group has adopted its own schema for generalizing from an observed characteristic of one animal to a presumed characteristic of another. In each case, however, the schema has particular value for the individuals operating within a given culture.

Extensive research shows that the ways students represent the information given in a mathematics or science problem or in a text that they read depends on the organization of their existing knowledge. As learning occurs, increasingly well-structured and qualitatively different organizations of knowledge develop. These structures enable individuals to build a representation or mental model that guides problem solution and further learning, avoid trial-and-error solution strategies, and formulate analogies and draw inferences that readily result in new learning and effective problem solving (Glaser and Baxter, 1999). The impact of schematic knowledge is powerfully demonstrated by research on the nature of expertise as described below.

Implications for Assessment

Although we have discussed aspects of cognition at a rather general level thus far, it is possible to draw implications for assessment practice. Most of these implications relate to which memory system one might need to engage to accomplish different purposes, as well as the care needed to disentangle the mutual effects and interactions of the two systems.

For example, it can be argued that estimates of what people have stored in long-term memory and how they have organized that information are likely to be more important than estimates of working memory capacity in most instances of educational assessment. The latter estimates may be useful in two circumstances: first, when the focus of concern is a person's capacity to deal with new and rapidly occurring situations, and second, when one is assessing individuals below the normal range and is interested in a potential indicator of the limits of a person's academic learning proficiency. However, such assessments must be carefully designed to minimize the potential advantages of using knowledge previously stored in long-term memory.

To estimate a person's knowledge and problem-solving ability in familiar fields, however, it is necessary to know which domain-specific problem-solving schemas people have and when they use them. Assessments should evaluate what information people have and under what circumstances they see that information as relevant. This evaluation should include how a person organizes acquired information, encompassing both strategies for problem solving and ways of chunking relevant information into manageable units. There is a further caveat, however, about such assessments. Assessment results that are intended to measure knowledge and procedures in long-term memory may, in fact, be modulated by individual differences in the processing capacity of working memory. This can occur when testing situations have properties that inadvertently place extra demands on working memory, such as keeping track of response options or large amounts of information while answering a question.

THE NATURE OF SUBJECT-MATTER EXPERTISE

In addition to expanding our understanding of thinking and learning in general, cognitive research conducted over the past four decades has generated a vast body of knowledge about how people learn the content and procedures of specific subject domains. Researchers have probed deeply the nature of expertise and how people acquire large bodies of knowledge over long periods of time. Studies have revealed much about the kinds of mental structures that support problem solving and learning in various domains ranging from chess to physics, what it means to develop expertise in a domain, and how the thinking of experts differs from that of novices.

The notion of expertise is inextricably linked with subject-matter domains: experts must have expertise in *something*. Research on how people develop expertise has provided considerable insight into the nature of thinking and problem solving. Although every child cannot be expected to become an expert in a given domain, findings from cognitive science about the nature of expertise can shed light on what successful learning looks like and guide the development of effective instruction and assessment.

Knowledge Organization: Expert-Novice Differences

What distinguishes expert from novice performers is not simply general mental abilities, such as memory or fluid intelligence, or general problem-solving strategies. Experts have acquired extensive stores of knowledge and skill in a particular domain. But perhaps most significant, their minds have organized this knowledge in ways that make it more retrievable and useful.

In fields ranging from medicine to music, studies of expertise have shown repeatedly that experts commit to long-term memory large banks of well-organized facts and procedures, particularly deep, specialized knowledge of their subject matter (Chi, Glaser, and Rees, 1982; Chi and Koeske, 1983). Most important, they have efficiently coded and organized this information into well-connected schemas. These methods of encoding and organizing help experts interpret new information and notice features and meaningful patterns of information that might be overlooked by less competent learners. These schemas also enable experts, when confronted with a problem, to retrieve the relevant aspects of their knowledge.

Of particular interest to researchers is the way experts encode, or chunk, information into meaningful units based on common underlying features or functions. Doing so effectively moves the burden of thought from the limited capacity of working memory to long-term memory. Experts can represent problems accurately according to their underlying principles, and they quickly know when to apply various procedures and strategies to solve them. They then go on to derive solutions by manipulating those meaningful units. For example, chess experts encode midgame situations in terms of meaningful clusters of pieces (Chase and Simon, 1973), as illustrated in Box 3-1.

One of the best demonstrations of the differences between expert and novice knowledge structures comes from physics. When presented with problems in mechanics, expert physicists recode them in terms of the basic principles of physics as illustrated in Box 3-2. For example, when presented with a problem involving balancing a cart on an inclined plane, the expert physicist sees the problem as an example of a balance-of-forces problem, while the novice is more likely to view it as being specific to carts and inclined planes (Chi, Feltovich, and Glaser, 1981; Larkin, McDermott, Simon, and Simon, 1980).

The knowledge that experts have cannot be reduced to sets of isolated facts or propositions. Rather, their knowledge has been encoded in a way that closely links it with the contexts and conditions for its use. An example of this observation is provided in Box 3-3 which illustrates the ways in which the physics knowledge of novices and experts is structured. Differences in what is known and how it is represented give rise to the types of responses shown in Box 3-2. Because the knowledge of experts is "conditionalized" in the manner illustrated in Box 3-3, they do not have to search through the vast repertoire of everything they know when confronted with a problem. Instead, they can readily activate and retrieve the subset of their knowledge that is relevant to the task at hand (Glaser, 1992; Larkin et al., 1980). These and other related findings suggest that teachers should place more emphasis on the conditions for applying the facts or procedures being taught, and that assessment should address whether students know when, where, and how to use their knowledge.

BOX 3-1   Meaningful Units as Encoded by Chess Experts

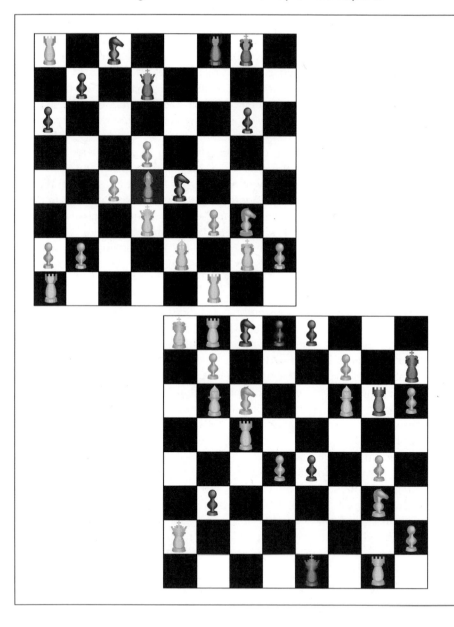

In one study a chess master, a Class A player (good but not a master), and a novice were given 5 seconds to view a chess board as of the middle of a chess game, as in the examples shown.

After 5 seconds the board was covered, and each participant attempted to reconstruct the positions observed on another board. This procedure was repeated for multiple trials until every participant had received a perfect score. On the first trial, the master player correctly placed many more pieces than the Class A player, who in turn placed more than the novice: 16, 8, and 4, respectively.

However, these results occurred only when the chess pieces were arranged in configurations that conformed to meaningful games of chess. When the pieces were randomized and presented for 5 seconds, the recall of the chess master and Class A player was the same as that of the novice—all placed from 2 to 3 pieces correctly. Data over trials for valid middle-game positions and random board positions are shown below.

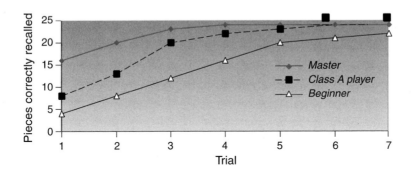

SOURCE: Adapted from Chase and Simon (1973) and NRC (1999).

BOX 3-2 Sorting of Physics Problems

Novices' explanations for their grouping of two problems

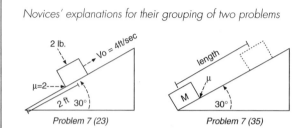

Problem 7 (23)   Problem 7 (35)

Explanations

Novice 1: These deal with blocks on an inclined plane.

Novice 5: Inclined plane problems, coefficient of friction.

Novice 6: Blocks on inclined planes with angles.

Experts' explanations for their grouping of two problems

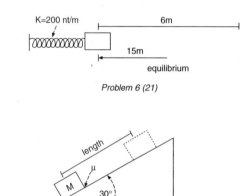

Problem 6 (21)

Problem 7 (35)

Explanations

Expert 2: Conservation of energy.

Expert 3: Work-theory theorem. They are all straightforward problems.

Expert 4: These can be done from energy considerations. Either you should know the principle of conservation of energy, or work is lost somewhere.

Above is an example of the sorting of physics problems performed by novices and experts. Each picture shown represents a diagram that can be drawn from the storyline of a physics problem taken from an introductory physics textbook. The novices and experts in this study were asked to categorize many such problems on the basis of similarity of solution. A marked contrast can be noted in the experts' and novices' categorization schemes. Novices tend to categorize physics problems as being solved similarly if they "look the same" (that is, share the same surface features), whereas experts categorize according to the major principle that could be applied to solve the problems.

SOURCE: Adapted from Chi, Feltovich, and Glaser (1981, p. 67) and NRC (1999).

BOX 3-3   Novices' and Experts' Schemas of Inclined Planes

Some studies of experts and novices in physics have explored the organization of their knowledge structures. Chi, Glaser, and Rees (1982) found that novices' schemas of an inclined plane contain primarily surface features, whereas experts' schemas connect the notion of an inclined plane with the laws of physics and the conditions under which the laws are applicable.

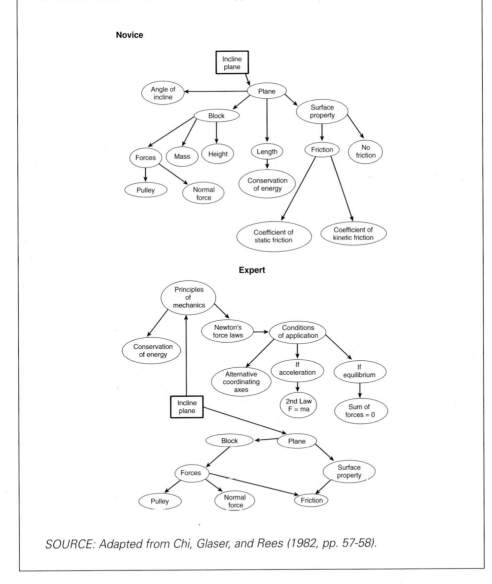

SOURCE: Adapted from Chi, Glaser, and Rees (1982, pp. 57-58).

The Importance of Metacognition

In his book on unified theories of cognition, Newell (1990) points out that there are two layers of problem solving—applying a strategy to the problem at hand, and selecting and monitoring that strategy. Good problem solving, Newell observed, often depends as much on the selection and monitoring of a strategy as on its execution. The term *metacognition* (literally "thinking about thinking") is commonly used to refer to the selection and monitoring processes, as well as to more general activities of reflecting on and directing one's own thinking.

Experts have strong metacognitive skills (Hatano, 1990). They monitor their problem solving, question limitations in their knowledge, and avoid overly simplistic interpretations of a problem. In the course of learning and problem solving, experts display certain kinds of regulatory performance, such as knowing when to apply a procedure or rule, predicting the correctness or outcomes of an action, planning ahead, and efficiently apportioning cognitive resources and time. This capability for self-regulation and self-instruction enables advanced learners to profit a great deal from work and practice by themselves and in group efforts.

Metacognition depends on two things: knowing one's mental capabilities and being able to step back from problem-solving activities to evaluate one's progress. Consider the familiar situation of forgetting the name of a person to whom one was introduced only a few minutes ago. There are simple metacognitive tricks for avoiding this situation, including asking the person for a business card and then reading it immediately instead of putting it in one's pocket. Metacognition is crucial to effective thinking and competent performance. Studies of metacognition have shown that people who monitor their own understanding during the learning phase of an experiment show better recall performance when their memories are tested (Nelson, 1996). Similar metacognitive strategies distinguish stronger from less competent learners. Strong learners can explain which strategies they used to solve a problem and why, while less competent students monitor their own thinking sporadically and ineffectively and offer incomplete explanations (Chi, Bassok, Lewis, Reiman, and Glaser, 1989; Chi and VanLehn, 1991). Good problem solvers will try another strategy if one is not working, while poor problem solvers will hold to a strategy long after it has failed. Likewise, good writers will think about how a hypothetical audience might read their work and revise parts that do not convey their meaning (Hayes and Flower, 1986).

There is ample evidence that metacognition develops over the school years; for example, older children are better than younger ones at planning for tasks they are asked to do (Karmiloff-Smith, 1979). Metacognitive skills can also be taught. For example, people can learn mental devices that help them stay on task, monitor their own progress, reflect on their strengths and weaknesses, and self-correct errors. It is important to note, however, that the teaching of metacognitive skills is often best accomplished in specific content areas since the ability to monitor one's understanding is closely tied to domain-specific knowledge and expertise (NRC, 1999).

Implications for Assessment

Studies of expert-novice differences in subject domains illuminate critical features of proficiency that should be the targets for assessment. The study of expertise reinforces the point made earlier about the importance of assessing the nature of the knowledge that an individual has in long-term memory. Experts in a subject domain have extensive factual and procedural knowledge, and they typically organize that knowledge into schemas that support pattern recognition and the rapid retrieval and application of knowledge.

As noted above, one of the most important aspects of cognition is metacognition—the process of reflecting on and directing one's own thinking. Metacognition is crucial to effective thinking and problem solving and is one of the hallmarks of expertise in specific areas of knowledge and skill. Experts use metacognitive strategies for monitoring understanding during problem solving and for performing self-correction. Assessment of knowledge and skill in any given academic domain should therefore attempt to determine whether an individual has good metacognitive skills.

THE DEVELOPMENT OF EXPERTISE

Studies of expertise have helped define the characteristics of knowledge and thought at stages of advanced learning and practice. As a complement to such work, considerable effort has also been expended on understanding the characteristics of people and of the learning situations they encounter that foster the development of expertise. Much of what we know about the development of expertise has come from studies of children as they acquire competence in many areas of intellectual endeavor, including the learning of school subject matter.

In this section we consider various critical issues related to learning and the development of expertise. We begin with a consideration of young children's predisposition to learn, and how this and other characteristics of children and instructional settings impact the development of expertise. We close with a discussion of the important role of social context in defining expertise and supporting its development.

Predisposition to Learn

From a cognitive standpoint, *development* and *learning* are not the same thing. Some types of knowledge are universally acquired in the course of normal development, while other types are learned only with the intervention of deliberate teaching (which includes teaching by any means, such as apprenticeship, formal schooling, or self-study). For example, all normal children learn to walk whether or not their caretakers make any special efforts to teach them to do so, but most do not learn to ride a bicycle or play the piano without intervention.

Infants and young children appear to be predisposed to learn rapidly and readily in some domains, including language, number, and notions of physical and biological causality. Infants who are only 3 or 4 months old, for example, have been shown to understand certain concepts about the physical world, such as the idea that inanimate objects need to be propelled in order to move (Massey and Gelman, 1988).

Young children have a natural interest in numbers and will seek out number information. Studies of surprise and searching behaviors among infants suggest that 5-month-olds will react when an item is surreptitiously added to or subtracted from the number of items they expected to see (Starkey, 1992; Wynn, 1990, 1992). By the time children are 3 or 4 years old, they have an implicit understanding of certain rudimentary principles for counting, adding, and subtracting cardinal numbers. Gelman and Gallistel (1978) studied number concepts in preschoolers by making a hand puppet count a row of objects in correct, incorrect, or unusual ways; the majority of 3- and 4-year-olds could detect important counting errors, such as violations of the principles of one-to-one correspondence (only one number tag per item and one item per tag) or cardinality (the last ordinal tag represents the value).

Thus in mathematics, the fundamentals of ordinality and cardinality appear to develop in all normal human infants without instruction. In contrast, however, such concepts as mathematical notation, algebra, and Cartesian graphing representations must be taught. Similarly, the basics of speech and language comprehension emerge naturally from millions of years of evolution, whereas mastery of the alphabetic code necessary for reading typically requires explicit instruction and long periods of practice (Geary, 1995).

Even though young children lack experience and knowledge, they have the ability to reason adeptly with what knowledge they do have. Children are curious and natural problem solvers, and will try to solve problems presented to them and persist in doing so because they want to understand (Gelman and Gallistel, 1978; Piaget, 1978). Children can also be deliberate, self-directed, and strategic about learning things they are not predisposed to attend to, but they need adult guidance to develop strategies of intentional learning. Much of what we want to assess in educational contexts is the product of such deliberate learning.

Multiple Paths of Learning

Not all children come to school ready to learn in the same way, nor do they follow the same avenues of growth and change. Rather, children acquire new procedures slowly and along multiple paths. This contradicts earlier notions, inspired by Piaget's work (e.g., 1952), that cognitive development progresses in one direction through a rigid set of stages, each involving radically different cognitive schemes. Although children's strategies for solving problems generally become more effective with age and experience, the growth process is not a simple progression. When presented with the same arithmetic problem two days in a row, for instance, the same child may apply different strategies to solve it (Siegler and Crowley, 1991).

With respect to assessment, one of the most important findings from detailed observations of children's learning behavior is that children do not move simply and directly from an erroneous to an optimal solution strategy (Kaiser, Proffitt, and McCloskey, 1985). Instead, they may exhibit several different but locally or partially correct strategies (Fay and Klahr, 1996). They also may use less-advanced strategies even after demonstrating that they know more-advanced ones, and the process of acquiring and consolidating robust and efficient strategies may be quite protracted, extending across many weeks and hundreds of problems (Siegler, 1998). These studies have found, moreover, that short-term transition strategies frequently precede more lasting approaches and that generalization of new approaches often occurs very slowly. Studies of computational abilities in children indicate that the processes children use to solve problems change with practice and that some children invent more efficient strategies than those they are taught. Box 3-4 provides examples of the types of strategies children often use for solving simple arithmetic problems and how their use of strategies can be studied.

Development of knowledge not only is variable as noted above, but also is constituted within particular contexts and situations, an observation that reflects an "interactionist" perspective on development (Newcombe and Huttenlocher, 2000). Accordingly, assessment of children's development in school contexts should include attention to the nature of classroom cultures and the practices they promote, as well as to individual variation. For example, the kinds of expectations established in a classroom for what counts as a mathematical explanation affect the kinds of strategies and explanations children pursue (Ball and Bass, in press; Cobb and McClain, in press). To illustrate, in classrooms where teachers value mathematical generalization, even young children (first and second graders) develop informal proofs and related mathematical means to grapple with the mathematically important idea of "knowing for sure" (Lehrer et al., 1998; Strom, Kemeny, Lehrer and Forman, in press). Given a grounding in what it takes to know "for sure,"

BOX 3-4 Studying Children's Strategies for Simple Addition

Children who are learning to add two numbers but no longer count on their fingers often use various mental counting strategies to answer addition problems (Resnick, 1989). Those who have not learned their "number facts" to the point where they can quickly retrieve them typically use the following strategies, which increase in developmental sophistication and cognitive demands as learning progresses:

- The **sum** strategy—counting up to the first number and counting on from the second number to obtain the sum.
- The **count-on** strategy—setting one's counter at the first number in the problem and counting on an amount equal to the second number to obtain the sum.
- The **min** strategy—setting one's counter to the larger of the two numbers and then counting on an amount equal to the smaller number to obtain the sum.

To gather evidence about the strategies being used, researchers directly observe children and also measure how long it takes them to solve addition problems that vary systematically across the three important properties of such problems (total sum, size of the first addend, and size of the minimum addend). For example, children might be asked to solve the following three problems: What is 6 + 4? What is 3 + 5? What is 2 + 9? The amount of time it takes children to solve these problems depends on what strategy they are using. Using the sum strategy, the second problem should be solved most rapidly, followed by the first, then the third. Using the count-on strategy, the first problem should solved most quickly, then the second, then the third. Using the min strategy, the third problem should be solved soonest, followed by the second, then the first.

Mathematical models of the actual times it takes children to respond are compared with models of predicted times to determine how well the data fit any given strategy. Interestingly, as children become more competent in adding single-digit numbers, they tend to use a mixture of strategies, from counting to direct retrieval.

SOURCE: Siegler and Crowley (1991).

young children can also come to appreciate some of the differences between mathematical and scientific generalization (Lehrer and Schauble, 2000).

It is not likely that children will spontaneously develop appreciation of the epistemic grounds of proof and related forms of mathematical argument in the absence of a classroom culture that values and promotes them. Hence, to assess whether children can or cannot reason about appropriate forms of argument assumes participation in classrooms that support these forms of disciplinary inquiry, as well as individual development of the skills needed to generate and sustain such participation.

Role of Prior Knowledge

Studies such as those referred to in the above discussion of children's development and learning, as well as many others, have shown that far from being the blank slates theorists once imagined, children have rich intuitive knowledge that undergoes significant change as they grow older (Case, 1992; Case and Okamoto, 1996; Griffin, Case, and Siegler, 1994). A child's store of knowledge can range from broad knowledge widely shared by people in a society to narrow bodies of knowledge about dinosaurs, vehicles, or anything else in which a child is interested. Long before they enter school, children also develop theories to organize what they see around them. Some of these theories are on the right track, some are only partially correct, while still others contain serious misconceptions.

When children are exposed to new knowledge, they attempt to reconcile it with what they think they already know. Often they will need to reevaluate and perhaps revise their existing understanding. The process works both ways: children also apply prior knowledge to make judgments about the accuracy of new information. From this perspective, learning entails more than simply filling minds with information; it requires the transformation of naive understanding into more complete and accurate comprehension.

In many cases, children's naive conceptions can provide a good foundation for future learning. For example, background knowledge about the world at large helps early readers comprehend what they are reading; a child can determine whether a word makes sense in terms of his or her existing knowledge of the topic or prior notions of narrative. In other cases, misconceptions can form an impediment to learning that must be directly addressed. For example, some children have been found to reconcile their preconception that the earth is flat with adult claims that it is a sphere by imagining a round earth to be shaped like a pancake (Vosniadou and Brewer, 1992). This construction of a new understanding is guided by a model of the earth that helps the child explain how people can stand or walk on its surface. Similarly, many young children have difficulty giving up the notion that one-eighth is greater than one-fourth, because 8 is more than 4 (Gelman and Gallistel, 1978). If children were blank slates, telling them that the earth is round or that one-fourth is greater than one-eighth would be adequate. But since they already have ideas about the earth and about numbers, those ideas must be directly addressed if they are to be transformed or expanded.

Drawing out and working with existing understandings is important for learners of all ages. Numerous experiments have demonstrated the persistence of a preexisting naïve understanding even after a new model that contradicts it has been taught. Despite training to the contrary, students at a variety of ages persist in their belief that seasons are caused by the earth's distance from the sun rather than by its tilt (Harvard-Smithsonian Center for Astrophysics, 1987), or that an object that has been tossed in the air is being acted upon by both the force of gravity and the force of the hand that tossed it (Clement, 1982). For the scientific to replace the naive understanding, students must reveal the latter and have the opportunity to see where it falls short.

For the reasons just noted, considerable effort has been expended on characterizing the naive conceptions and partially formed schemas that characterize various stages of learning, from novice through increasing levels of expertise. For instance, there are highly detailed descriptions of the common types of misconceptions held by learners in algebra, geometry, physics, and other fields (e.g., Driver, Squires, Rushworth, and Wood-Robinson, 1994; Gabel, 1994; Minstrell, 2000). Knowing the ways in which students are likely to err in their thinking and problem solving can help teachers structure lessons and provide feedback. Such knowledge has also served as a basis for intelligent tutoring systems (discussed further below). As illustrated in subsequent chapters, there are descriptions as well of typical progressions in student understanding of particular domains, such as number sense, functions, and physics. As we show in Chapter 5, such work demonstrates the value of carefully describing students' incomplete understandings and of building on them to help students develop a more sophisticated grasp of the domain.

Practice and Feedback

Every domain of knowledge and skill has its own body of concepts, factual content, procedures, and other items that together constitute the knowledge of that field. In many domains, including areas of mathematics and science, this knowledge is complex and multifaceted, requiring sustained effort and focused instruction to master. Developing deep knowledge of a domain such as that exhibited by experts, along with conditions for its use, takes time and focus and requires opportunities for practice with feedback.

Whether considering the acquisition of some highly specific piece of knowledge or skill, such as the process of adding two numbers, or some larger schema for solving a mathematics or physics problem, certain laws of skill acquisition always apply. The first of these is the *power law of practice:* acquiring skill takes time, often requiring hundreds or thousands of instances of practice in retrieving a piece of information or executing a procedure. This law operates across a broad range of tasks, from typing on a keyboard to solving geometry problems (Rosenbloom and Newell, 1987). Data consistent with this law are illustrated in Figure 3-1. According to the power law of practice, the speed and accuracy of performing a simple or complex cognitive operation increases in a systematic nonlinear fashion over successive attempts. This pattern is characterized by an initial rapid improvement in performance, followed by subsequent and continuous improvements that accrue at a slower and slower rate. As shown in Figure 3-1, this relationship is linear if plotted in a log-log space.

The power law of practice is fully consistent with theories of cognitive skill acquisition according to which individuals go through different stages in acquiring the specific knowledge associated with a given cognitive skill (e.g., Anderson, 1982). Early on in this process, performance requires effort because it is heavily dependent on the limitations of working memory. Individuals must create a representation of the task they are supposed to perform, and they often verbally mediate or "talk their way through" the task while it is being executed. Once the components of the skill are well represented in long-term memory, the heavy reliance on working memory and the problems associated with its limited capacity can be bypassed. As a consequence, exercise of the skill can become fluent and then automatic. In the latter case, the skill requires very little conscious monitoring, and thus mental capacity is available to focus on other matters. An example of this pattern is the process of learning to read. Children can better focus on the meaning of what they are reading after they have mastered the process of decoding words. Another example is learning multicolumn addition. It is more difficult to metacognitively monitor and keep track of the overall procedure if one must compute sums by counting rather than by directly retrieving a number fact from memory. Evidence indicates that with each repetition of a cognitive skill—as in accessing a concept in long-term memory from a printed word, retrieving an addition fact, or applying a schema for solving differential equations—some additional knowledge strengthening occurs that produces the continual small improvements illustrated in Figure 3-1.

Practice, however, is not enough to ensure that a skill will be acquired. The conditions of practice are also important. The second major law of skill acquisition involves *knowledge of results.* Individuals acquire a skill much more rapidly if they receive feedback about the correctness of what they

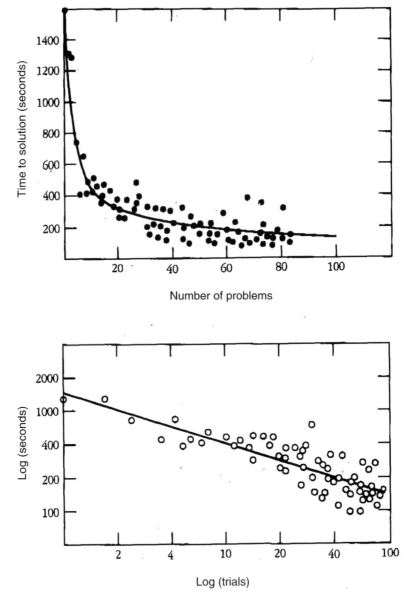

FIGURE 3-1 *Skill Acquisition Curves.*
SOURCE: Anderson (1990, p. 262). Used with permission from Worth Publishers.

have done. If incorrect, they need to know the nature of their mistake. It was demonstrated long ago that practice without feedback produces little learning (Thorndike, 1931). One of the persistent dilemmas in education is that students often spend time practicing incorrect skills with little or no feedback. Furthermore, the feedback they ultimately receive is often neither timely nor informative. For the less capable student, unguided practice (e.g., homework in mathematics) can be practice in doing tasks incorrectly. As discussed in Chapter 6, one of the most important roles for assessment is the provision of timely and informative feedback to students during instruction and learning so that their practice of a skill and its subsequent acquisition will be effective and efficient.

Transfer of Knowledge

A critical aspect of expertise is the ability to extend the knowledge and skills one has developed beyond the limited contexts in which they were acquired. Yet research suggests that knowledge does not transfer very readily (Bjork and Richardson-Klavhen, 1989; Carraher, 1986; Cognition and Technology Group at Vanderbilt, 1997; Lave, 1988). Contemporary studies have generally discredited the old idea of "mental exercise"—the notion that learning Latin, for example, improves learning in other subjects. More to the point, learning to solve a mathematics problem in school may not mean that the learner can solve a problem of the same type in another context.

Insights about learning and transfer have come from studies of situations in which people have failed to use information that, in some sense, they are known to have. Bassok and Holyoak (1989) showed, for example, that physics students who had studied the use of certain mathematical forms in the context of physics did not recognize that the same equations could be applied to solve problems in economics. On the other hand, mathematics students who had studied the same mathematical forms in several different contexts, but not economics, could apply the equations to economics problems.

A body of literature has clarified the principles for structuring learning so that people will be better able to use what they have learned in new settings. If knowledge is to be transferred successfully, practice and feedback need to take a certain form. Learners must develop an understanding of when (under what conditions) it is appropriate to apply what they have learned. Recognition plays an important role here. Indeed, one of the major differences between novices and experts is that experts can recognize novel situations as minor variants of situations for which they already know how to apply strong methods. Transfer is also more likely to occur when the person understands the underlying principles of what was learned. The models children develop to represent a problem mentally and the fluency with which they can move back and forth among representations are other important dimensions that can be enhanced through instruction. For example, children need to understand how one problem is both similar to and different from other problems.

The Role of Social Context

Much of what humans learn is acquired through discourse and interactions with others. For example, science, mathematics, and other domains are often shaped by collaborative work among peers. Through such interactions, individuals build communities of practice, test their own theories, and build on the learning of others. For example, those who are still using a naive strategy can learn by observing others who have figured out a more productive one. This situation contrasts with many school situations, in which students are often required to work independently. Yet the display and modeling of cognitive competence through group participation and social interaction is an important mechanism for the internalization of knowledge and skill in individuals.

An example of the importance of social context can be found in the work of Ochs, Jacoby, and Gonzalez (1994). They studied the activities of a physics laboratory research group whose members included a senior physicist, a postdoctoral researcher, technical staff, and predoctoral students. They found that workers' contributions to the laboratory depended significantly on their participatory skills in a collaborative setting—being able to formulate and understand questions and problems, develop arguments, and contribute to the construction of shared meanings and conclusions.

Even apparently individual cognitive acts, such as classifying colors or trees, are often mediated by tools and practice. Goodwin's (2000) study of archaeologists suggests that classifying the color of a sample of dirt involves a juxtaposition of tools (the Munsell color chart) and particular practices, such as the sampling scheme. The chart arranges color into an ordered grid that can be scanned repeatedly, and cognitive acts such as these are coordinated with practices such as spraying the dirt with water, which creates a consistent environment for viewing. Tools and activity are coordinated among individuals as well, resulting in an apparently self-evident judgment, but upon closer inspection, it becomes clear that these apparently mundane judgments rely on multiple forms and layers of mediation. Similarly, Medin, Lynch, and Coley (1997) examined the classification of trees by experts from different fields of practice (e.g., university botanists and landscape architects). Here, too, classifications were influenced by the goals and contexts of these different forms of practice, so that there were substantial disagreements about how to characterize some of the specimens observed by the experts involved in the study. Cognition was again mediated by culturally specific practice.

Studies such as these suggest that much knowledge is embedded within systems of representation, discourse, and physical activity. Moreover, communities of practices are sites for developing identity—one is what one practices, to some extent. This view of knowledge can be compared with that which underlies standard test-taking practice, whereby knowledge is regarded as disembodied and incorporeal. Testing for individual knowledge captures only a small portion of the skills actually used in many learning communities.

School is just one of the many contexts that can support learning. A number of studies have analyzed the use of mathematical reasoning skills in workplace and other everyday contexts (Lave, 1988; Ochs, Jacoby, and Gonzalez, 1994). One such study found that workers who packed crates in a warehouse applied sophisticated mathematical reasoning in their heads to make the most efficient use of storage space, even though they might not have been able to solve the same problem expressed as a standard numerical equation. The rewards and meaning people derive from becoming deeply involved in a community can provide a strong motive to learn.

Hull, Jury, Ziv, and Schultz (1994) studied literacy practices in an electronics assembly plant where work teams were responsible for evaluating and representing their own performance. Although team members had varying fluency in English, the researchers observed that all members actively participated in the evaluation and representation processes, and used texts and graphs to assess and represent their accomplishments. This situation suggests that reading, writing, quantitative reasoning, and other cognitive abilities are strongly integrated in most environments, rather than being separated into discrete aspects of knowledge. Tests that provide separate scores may therefore be inadequate for capturing some kinds of integrated abilities that people need and use on the job.

Studies of the social context of learning show that in a responsive social setting, learners can adopt the criteria for competence they see in others and then use this information to judge and perfect the adequacy of their own performance. Shared performance promotes a sense of goal orientation as learning becomes attuned to the constraints and resources of the environment. In the context of school, students also develop facility in giving and accepting help (and stimulation) from others. Social contexts for learning make the thinking of the learner apparent to teachers and other students so it can be examined, questioned, and built upon as part of constructive learning.

Impact of Cultural Norms and Student Beliefs

It is obvious that children from different backgrounds and cultures bring differing prior knowledge and resources to learning. Strong supports for learning exist in every culture, but some kinds of cultural resources may be better recognized or rewarded in the typical school setting. There are cultural variations in communication styles, for example, that may affect how a child interacts with adults in the typical U.S. school environment (Heath, 1981, 1983; Ochs and Schieffelin, 1984; Rogoff, 1990; Ward, 1971). Similarly, cultural attitudes about cooperation, as opposed to independent work, can affect the degree of support students provide for each other's learning (Treisman, 1990). It is important for educators and others to take these kinds of differences into account in making judgments about student competence and in facilitating the acquisition of knowledge and skill.

The beliefs students hold about learning are another social dimension that can significantly affect learning and performance (e.g., Dweck and Legitt, 1988). For example, many students believe, on the basis of their typical classroom and homework assignments, that any mathematics problem can be solved in 5 minutes or less, and if they cannot find a solution in that time, they will give up. Many young people and adults also believe that talent in mathematics and science is innate, which gives them little incentive to persist if they do not understand something in these subjects immediately. Conversely, people who believe they are capable of making sense of unfamiliar things often succeed because they invest more sustained effort in doing so.

Box 3-5 lists several common beliefs about mathematics derived from classroom studies, international comparisons, and responses on National Assessment of Educational Progress (NAEP) questionnaires. Experiences at home and school shape students' beliefs, including many of those shown in Box 3-5. For example, if mathematics is presented by the teacher as a set of rules to be applied, students may come to believe that "knowing" mathematics means remembering which rule to apply when a question is asked (usually the rule the teacher last demonstrated), and that comprehending the concepts that undergird the question is too difficult for ordinary students. In contrast, when teachers structure mathematics lessons so that important principles are apparent as students work through the procedures, students are more likely to develop deeper understanding and become independent and thoughtful problem solvers (Lampert, 1986).

Implications for Assessment

Knowledge of children's learning and the development of expertise clearly indicates that assessment practices should focus on making students' thinking visible to themselves and others by drawing out their current under-

BOX 3-5   Typical Student Beliefs About the Nature of Mathematics

- Mathematical talent is innate—"either you have it or you don't,"—and effort doesn't make much of a difference.
- Mathematics problems have one and only one right answer.
- There is only one correct way to solve any mathematics problem—usually the rule the teacher has most recently demonstrated to the class.
- Ordinary students cannot expect to understand mathematics; they expect simply to memorize it and to apply what they have learned mechanically and without understanding.
- Mathematics is a solitary activity, done by individuals in isolation.
- Students who have understood the mathematics they have studied will be able to solve any assigned problem in 5 minutes or less.
- The mathematics learned in school has little or nothing to do with the real world.
- Formal proof is irrelevant to processes of discovery or invention.

SOURCE: Greeno, Pearson, and Schoenfeld. (1996b, p. 20).

standing so that instructional strategies can be selected to support an appropriate course for future learning. In particular, assessment practices should focus on identifying the preconceptions children bring to learning settings, as well as the specific strategies they are using for problem solving. Particular consideration needs to be given to where children's knowledge and strategies fall on a developmental continuum of sophistication, appropriateness, and efficiency for a particular domain of knowledge and skill.

Practice and feedback are critical aspects of the development of skill and expertise. One of the most important roles for assessment is the provision of timely and informative feedback to students during instruction and learning so that their practice of a skill and its subsequent acquisition will be effective and efficient.

As a function of context, knowledge frequently develops in a highly contextualized and inflexible form, and often does not transfer very effectively. Transfer depends on the development of an explicit understanding of when to apply what has been learned. Assessments of academic achievement need to consider carefully the knowledge and skills required to understand and answer a question or solve a problem, including the context in which it is presented, and whether an assessment task or situation is functioning as a test of near, far, or zero transfer.

Knowledge is often embedded in particular social and cultural contexts, including the context of the classroom, and it encompasses understandings about the meaning of specific practices such as question asking and answering. Assessments need to examine how well students engage in communicative practices appropriate to a domain of knowledge and skill, what they understand about those practices, and how well they use the tools appropriate to that domain.

By considering context and development as co-emerging, school-based assessment can be directed toward the intersection of classroom contexts and individual cognition. Equitable assessment, then, relies on the creation of opportunities for growth and development. Without systematic attention to opportunity, the results of assessment simply recapitulate existing patterns of distribution of resources, both financial and social. Questions must therefore be raised about the validity of inferences that can be drawn from assessments of individual student achievement, using criteria for reasoning and argumentation defined in mathematics and science standards documents. It is uncertain what can be inferred in the absence of clear documentation of students' opportunities to participate in forms of practice valued by disciplines such as mathematics and science—an issue that is addressed later in this volume.

INTEGRATION OF MODELS OF COGNITION AND LEARNING WITH INSTRUCTION AND ASSESSMENT

By building on findings about cognition, learning, and the development of expertise, researchers have produced models to describe the thinking processes, reasoning strategies, and conceptual understandings of students at various stages of competency. This work has tended to focus on the nature of knowledge and performance in specific domains of mathematics, science, or history. These models can be used to diagnose student understanding, determine next steps in instruction, and design assessments (Baker, 1997).

Detailed models of cognition and learning in specific curricular areas can be used to formulate a set of criteria that are valuable for evaluating the progress of any individual or group, as well as for informing teaching and learning. In other words, a well-developed and empirically validated model of thinking and learning in an academic domain can be used to design and select assessment tasks that support the analysis of various kinds of student performance. Such a model can also serve as the basis for rubrics for evaluating and scoring pupils' work, with discriminating features of expertise defining the specific targets of assessment. Ideally, models will highlight the main determinants of and obstacles to learning and include descriptions of students' conceptual progressions as they develop competence and expertise.

Selected yet powerful examples of such models currently exist and demonstrate how cognitive theory can be applied to issues of curriculum, instruction, and assessment. Some integrate instruction and assessment and make it possible to assess students continuously as they work on problems. The following are three examples of attempts at such integration.

Intelligent Tutoring

Some of the most productive research in cognitive science comes from efforts to understand thinking in a domain in enough detail to craft computerized systems known as intelligent tutors. These systems show that it is possible to assess components of students' knowledge while they are working on problems on line. In principle, intelligent tutors could be used for assessment in a wide range of well-structured knowledge domains.

The intelligent tutors developed by Anderson and colleagues (Anderson, Boyle, Corbett, and Lewis, 1990) and VanLehn and Martin (1998) represent a well-developed integration of multiple methods of observation and inference about cognition. To design such tutors, these researchers have developed highly specific descriptions of thinking about school subjects typically taught at the secondary level, such as geometry, algebra, and physics. As further discussed in the next section, their task analysis and model-building efforts incorporate information from reaction-time measures, strategy diagnosis, eye-movement analysis, and knowledge assessment. The importance of their cognitive task analyses cannot be overstated. As Newell and Simon (1972, p. 8) point out, "If performance is not well understood, it is somewhat premature to study learning," and it would certainly be premature to design complex instructional systems that attempt to integrate instruction and assessment to support student learning.

For instance, the systems designed by Anderson's group seamlessly integrate specific cognitive objectives, such as being able to solve a certain kind of algebraic equation, with individualized assessment of student errors, or "bugs," and specific instructional steps to remediate those bugs. When a student makes a mistake, the system provides advice and remediation to correct the error. Studies suggest that when individuals work with these tutors, there is a relatively direct relationship between the assessment of student learning and the research-based model of student thinking. On average, students learn more with the system than with traditional instruction (Koedinger and Anderson, 1999). Intelligent tutoring systems are discussed in more detail in subsequent chapters.

Models of Learning Arithmetic

Researchers have conducted a broad range of inquiries about the cognitive foundations of arithmetic, beginning with infants' sense of number and culminating in the arithmetic basis of algebra. Particularly intriguing from the standpoint of cognitive theory are children's skills in reasoning about arithmetic word problems. Researchers generally attempt to account for problem difficulty, transitions in children's solution strategies, and errors. For example, children find the first of the following two problems easier than the second:

1. Joe has 5 marbles. Then Tom gives him 6 more marbles. How many marbles does he have now?
2. Melissa has 5 pieces of candy. Elaine gives her some more pieces of candy. Now Melissa has 11 pieces of candy. How many pieces of candy did Elaine give her?

Carpenter and Moser (1982) and Steffe (1970) attribute the relative difficulty of these problems to their semantic structure. Both problems involve actions, which makes them generally easier for children to solve than nonaction problems. But the second problem is more difficult than the first because it includes an unknown change quantity, and children have difficulty imagining actions that involve combinations of unspecified quantities. Unlike adults, children perceive the problems not as involving different operators (e.g., $5 + 6 = ?$ and $11 - 5 = ?$), but as variants of combining sets (e.g., $5 + 6 = ?$ and $5 + ? = 11$). Thus it is somewhat more difficult for them to invoke a simple counting strategy to solve the second problem. In contrast, the first can be solved quite easily by counting all the marbles.

Other researchers have supplemented these accounts by building explicit models of student knowledge and cognitive processes. For example, Riley, Greeno and Heller (1983) accounted for differences in problem difficulty by appealing to problem schemas that differentiate among problem types. Under this theory, certain problem schemas are activated by the semantic structure of word problems. Once activated, the schemas invoke associated strategies, such as finding differences between sets. The Riley, Greeno and Heller (1983) model was subsequently augmented by Kintsch and Greeno (1985) to include natural language processing of the problems. A somewhat different set of assumptions guided Briars and Larkin (1984), who assumed that children would use concrete objects, such as teddy bears or chips, to model the relations evident in the semantic structure of a problem. This model predicted that children could solve a wide range of problems, including those typically thought of as multiplication or division, if they could "directly model" (e.g., represent) sets and their relations with counters. This prediction was subsequently confirmed (Carpenter, Ansell, Franke, and Fennema, 1993).

Carpenter, Fennema, and Franke (1996) propose that teachers who understand children's thinking about arithmetic would be in a better position to craft more effective mathematics instruction. Their approach, called *cognitively guided instruction*, borrows from work in cognitive science to characterize the semantic structure of word problems, as well as the strategies children typically use to solve them. Cognitively guided instruction explicitly recasts this work as a coarse-grained model of student thinking that can easily be understood and used by teachers. The model allows teachers to recognize and react to ongoing events as they unfold during the course of instruction. In a sense, the work of Carpenter and colleagues suggests that teachers use this model to support continuous assessment in the classroom so that instruction can be modified frequently as needed. More detail about how this model is used in classroom practice is provided in Chapter 6.

Debugging of Computer Programs

Klahr and Carver (1988) analyzed the kinds of knowledge and reasoning skills required for students to write and debug a basic graphics design program in LOGO (a simple computer language). Beginning students were asked to write a program for drawing a house with windows and doors. Since first attempts usually involve errors (bugs), students had to learn how to debug their programs. This process involves several steps: (1) noticing and describing the discrepancies between the actual and the intended drawing, (2) considering which commands might have bugs ("buggy commands"), (3) creating a mapping between the descriptions of discrepancies and the potentially buggy commands, and (4) examining specific commands to see whether any of them was the culprit.

The investigators formulated these steps as a series of explicit rules, or "productions," each consisting of a condition (noting, for example, whether there was a discrepancy in the orientation of the drawing) and an action (checking the values on all of the program's "turn" commands). They wrote a debugging program, or model, based on these rules, then ran simulations to see how well the model could simulate the performance of students at two different levels of programming knowledge. When the model was set to simulate a student who had a high level of knowledge about the structure of computer programs, it quickly converged on the buggy command; when it simulated a student who lacked this knowledge, the model painstakingly examined a much greater number of possible culprits. The simulation paths followed by these two variants of the model were consistent with the behavior of real students having different levels of programming knowledge.

The model not only provided a rough assessment instrument that could reveal whether students had and used knowledge about program structure, but also served as a set of cognitive objectives in the form of a highly detailed group of productions that could guide instruction and assessment. Klahr and Carver also devised a process for teaching children both the productions and the reasons why they were useful and efficient. The instruction combined explaining to students, posting visual examples of mappings, and engaging children in practice with increasingly subtle bugs. Students achieved the goals of this instruction and were able to transfer these skills to another, nonprogramming procedure, such as written instructions for following a map or recipe. This example shows how characterization of cognitive objectives in the form of productions can provide powerful guidance for instruction and assessment, even when the teaching and assessment methods are fairly conventional.

Implications for Assessment

The preceding three examples are representative of the many cases in which a connection between theories of cognition and learning and the processes of instruction and assessment has been forged. Efforts such as these seek to provide clearer benchmarks of student thinking so that teachers can understand what preceded and is likely to follow the student performance they observe in their classrooms. Having good formative benchmarks helps channel teachers' attention toward important components and landmarks of thinking. These types of programs therefore emphasize ongoing classroom assessment as an integral part of teaching practice, while still allowing teachers the flexibility to decide which kinds of assistance from their repertoires of informed practice will best achieve the learning goals. Thus the effectiveness of assessment based on cognitive theory rests on a bedrock of informed professional practice.

There are several other examples in the literature in which cognitive principles have been applied to instruction and assessment. Some are not as tightly linked to a highly explicit underlying model of cognition. Marshall's (1995) schematic problem-solving system for teaching elementary school mathematics is an example. Others, discussed more fully later in this report, include Hunt and Minstrell's (1996) DIAGNOSER and White and Fredcriksen's (1998) Thinkertools programs for teaching high school and middle school science, respectively. Records of students' interactions with these programs are a rich source of information about which strategies students use, how well they are able to recognize and repair flawed strategies, and in which situations they see particular knowledge as relevant. As discussed later in this report, efforts such as these provide a foundation for exploring new methods of assessment that can enhance the processes of learning and teaching.

Without question, important work remains to be done to develop models for areas of the curriculum as it now exists and as it will change with the advent of powerful technology-based learning environments (see Chapter 7). In most domains, including many parts of the science and mathematics curricula, research has not produced descriptions as detailed or robust as some of the examples mentioned in this chapter and elsewhere throughout this report. More extensive research should eventually produce models of progression in learning in many domains beyond mathematics and science. Ultimately, it may be necessary to develop as many models as there are disciplines in the curriculum or domains within a discipline.

METHODS OF OBSERVATION AND INFERENCE

We close this presentation of advances in the sciences of thinking and learning with a discussion of some of the methods of observation and inference that underlie our current understanding of cognition. We describe these methods for two reasons. The first is to illustrate the types of scientific methods on which the findings in this chapter are based. The second is to suggest connections between methods of educational assessment and the methods used by cognitive researchers to uncover students' content knowledge and cognitive processes.

To accomplish the goal of understanding cognition and learning, cognitive scientists have developed a variety of methods and tools for evaluating people's knowledge structures and mental processes as they reason and solve problems and for studying what infants and young children know and can do. These methods are linked to a general approach of theory development and testing identical in its overall logic to our earlier discussion in Chapter 2 of the three elements of the assessment triangle—cognition, observation, and interpretation—and their interrelationships. For instance, many detailed studies of human cognition begin with the development of a theoretical model (or models) of the knowledge structures and cognitive processes that characterize people at different levels of competence. Researchers then design tasks for people to perform in order to test the model, carefully selecting those tasks that maximize the possibility of discriminating among competing models or hypotheses. Data from observations of individuals performing various tasks are then evaluated using a logical and/or statistical scheme to determine how well the evidence fits a given model.

This method of reasoning from data about underlying cognitive processes and knowledge structures has been applied to both simple and complex performances. As illustrated earlier in Box 3-4, it is possible to obtain a highly accurate and detailed picture of how children are approaching problems—using correct or incorrect, taught or invented strategies—by such formal analysis. As the simple addition example in Box 3-4 illustrates, hypothesized models of underlying cognitive activities lead researchers to collect rich data sets that can be used to test hypotheses about both the process and progress of students' learning. Such models can also provide a foundation for interpreting evidence derived using other data gathering and analysis techniques. Some of the most useful techniques, including reaction-time studies, computational modeling and simulations, analysis of protocols, microgenetic analysis, and ethnographic analysis, are described below.

Reaction-Time Studies

As illustrated for the case of simple addition problems, one method of evaluating cognitive processes is to measure and analyze the amount of time people spend on various phases or components of a given task. Data from these analyses can be highly informative when interpreted according to a model of cognitive processes. With an appropriately chosen set of problems, researchers can determine which of several potential strategies or approaches the problem solver is using. This general approach has been used for a wide variety of tasks, varying in complexity from simple addition and subtraction problems for children (e.g., Siegler, 1998) to complex multimove puzzles (Klahr and Robinson, 1981).

MacLeod, Hunt, and Mathews (1978), for example, used reaction-time profiles to determine whether people used imagery to solve simple verbally presented problems. More recently, Hunt, Streissguth, Kerr, and Olson (1995) used a combined measure of reaction time and accuracy to show that children whose mothers had used alcohol during pregnancy displayed tendencies to be impulsive in problem-solving behavior. This observation, which took less than an hour to make, was consistent with observations made by classroom teachers over a period of months. (It may be noted that the children were 14 years old at the time of testing, so the method may have isolated the effect of a drug taken 15 years prior to testing.)

Eye-movement tracking, a specialized technique for studying reaction times and other key behaviors, has received virtually no attention in the assessment literature. By using what is now relatively inexpensive equipment capable of detecting the direction of a person's gaze while he or she is engaged in a task, psychologists can gather data about the sequence and duration of eye fixations. This information can then be combined with the results of cognitive analysis to infer—quite precisely, in many cases—which of several strategies is being used. Such analyses can yield insights into differences between experts and novices in a range of domains, from playing chess to operating a modern airliner. This approach provides a "window on the mind" that complements and augments other, more traditional ways of investigating cognitive and perceptual processes. It has been applied quite effectively in studies ranging from an analysis of strategies used to take well-known intelligence and aptitude tests (e.g., Dillon, 1985; Just and Carpenter, 1992) to analyses of strategies used to process and comprehend sentences (Just and Carpenter, 1992) and even of how students interact with a computer-based cognitive tutor (Anderson and Gluck, 2001).

Computational Modeling and Simulation

For many aspects of cognition that unfold over periods of time greater than a few seconds, methods such as the analysis of reaction-time data are less effective. The processes of cognition may be extremely complex, involving multiple mental operations, and they may be highly dependent on the contents of long-term memory. To study such situations, researchers often develop a detailed model of the knowledge structures and processing steps used to perform a particular task or solve some problem. Many such models are developed as formal computer models that embody a variety of assumptions about the nature of the cognitive architecture and the form in which knowledge is represented in the mind. It is common for these models to be written in the language of *production systems* containing explicit statements about what people know when they perform a task and the sequence of mental events that occur as the task is performed. Such models are not arbitrary because they are developed from observations and logical analysis of task demands. Most important, they are tested by examining the quality of the fit between results obtained from the simulation and actual human performance. The approach has been used in a wide variety of domains, from young children's understanding of how balance scales work (Klahr and Siegler, 1978), to high schoolers' learning of geometry (Anderson and Boyle, 1985), to adults' performance on text editing (Singley and Anderson, 1988) and spatial navigation (Anderson, Kushmerick, and Lebiere, 1993), to the solution of intelligence test problems such as Raven's Matrices (Carpenter et al., 1990).

Analysis of Protocols

Rich sources of information about the thinking process are offered by records of what people say as they go about solving a problem. These reports, referred to as *concurrent verbal protocols*, offer a window on the fleeting contents of working memory. An example is a person's string of utterances while solving a mental arithmetic problem; these comments might refer to partial and temporary results or to the goals and subgoals the person generates during the episode. What a person says, however, should not be viewed as a reliable description of the underlying cognitive strategies being used to solve the problem. That information remains to be discovered by researchers who analyze the protocol. (See Ericsson and Simon, 1984, for an elaboration of this fundamental point.)

Verbal reports have been used effectively with a range of age groups, starting as early as kindergarten (Klahr and Robinson, 1981). Inter-rater reliabilities are often in the 0.6-0.7 range, depending on the complexity of the report and the training of the people who interpret it. There is a substantial trade-off between the reliability and richness of the record. Also, the analysis of verbal reports is extremely labor-intensive.

An equally rich but potentially more problematic source of data is the analysis of verbal interactions when two or more people work on a series of problems (Okada and Simon, 1997; Palincsar and Magnusson, 2001; Teasley, 1995). Obvious difficulties arise when these data are used to evaluate individual performance. However, the communicative demands of group problem solving may reveal certain kinds of knowledge that might otherwise not easily be assessed. Although it might be difficult to apply group problem-solving situations to large-scale assessment, it could be informative to ask individuals to respond to—or interpret others' responses to—such multiple-player contexts. Indeed, several studies of cognitive development have used the technique of asking children to explain why another child responded erroneously to a question (Siegler, in press). These probes often yield highly diagnostic information about how well the child doing the explaining understands a domain.

Microgenetic Analysis

An increasingly refined and popular method of investigating cognitive development is *microgenetic analysis*.[1] In this kind of fine-grained analysis, researchers closely observe people at densely spaced time intervals to view minute processes that could be obscured during less-frequent and less-detailed assessments. The properties of microgenetic analysis include (1) observations that span as much as possible of the period during which rapid change in competence occurs; (2) a density of observations within this period that is high relative to the rate of change in the phenomenon; and (3) observations that are examined on an intensive, trial-by-trial basis, with the goal of understanding the process of change in detail. Microgenetic observations may span weeks or months and hundreds of problems. The process

---

[1]This terminology is an artifact of Piaget's view of his own focus of research as "genetic epistemology," with "genetic" meaning simply growth over the life span. The method has no particular connection to or implications for the role of genetics in cognitive development. It could just as well be dubbed "microtemporal analysis" or "microdevelopmental analysis."

has been likened to high-speed stroboscopic photography of a drop of water forming and falling from a spigot or the famous photograph of a drop of milk splashing into a shallow dish of milk. The finer temporal grain reveals phenomena that would not be seen at normal speeds, thereby indicating new underlying processes. (See Siegler and Crowley [1991] for an extensive discussion of the method.)

Investigators have examined such issues as a child's development of concepts, with the goal of identifying when the child first used a new strategy, what the experience was like, what led to its discovery, and how it was generalized beyond its individual use. Research by Alibali and Goldin-Meadow (1993), for instance, suggests that a child's gestures can be indicators of cognitive change; a mismatch between gesture and speech often indicates a point at which a child is poised to make a transition in understanding. As in the case of reaction-time measures, gestures provide yet another potential window on the mind.

Ethnographic Analysis

Long used by anthropologists and other social scientists to study cultural practices and social patterns, ethnographic analyses have also proven useful for analyzing cognitive processes. These techniques are aimed at gathering rich information about the day-to-day experiences of a community and its individual members. They have been used to study cognitive performance in many different settings, including classrooms, workplaces, and other environments. In the ethnographic approach, researchers immerse themselves in a particular situation to obtain a sense of its characteristics and its people. They make detailed observations and records of people engaging in normal tasks. They may also use interviews, surveys, videotape recordings, or other methods to elicit qualitative information. This approach has been adapted by cognitive scientists to conduct what Dunbar (1999) calls "in vivo" studies of complex, situated, scientific problem solving in contexts such as world-class research laboratories.

Implications for Assessment

Many highly effective tools exist for probing and modeling a person's knowledge and for examining the contents and contexts of learning. Some of these methods, such as tracking of eye movements and computational modeling, rely on sophisticated technology, while others, such as close observation of what problem solvers say and do over meaningful periods of time, are outgrowths of more traditional and lower-technology modes of research. Although several of these techniques have been designed for use in laboratory studies with one person at a time, they could potentially be modified to meet the more demanding constraints of everyday assessment, especially assessment in the context of classrooms.

More generally, the methods used in cognitive science to design tasks linked to underlying models of knowledge and cognitive processing, observe and analyze cognitive performance, and draw inferences about what a person knows are directly applicable to many of the challenges involved in educational assessment. Furthermore, these methods can be used across a variety of assessment contexts and purposes. As developed in subsequent chapters of this report, the crux of the assessment process is the integration of empirically based models of student learning and cognition with methods for designing tasks and carefully observing student performance, and with procedures for interpreting the meaning of those observations. In the next chapter we look at how these three elements come together in the many situations in which a statistical method is needed to help interpret the observational data.

CONCLUSIONS

Contemporary theories of learning and knowing emphasize the way knowledge is represented, organized, and processed in the mind. Emphasis is also given to social dimensions of learning, including social and participatory practices that support knowing and understanding. This body of knowledge strongly implies that *assessment practices need to move beyond a focus on component skills and discrete bits of knowledge to encompass the more complex aspects of student achievement.*

Among the fundamental elements of cognition is the mind's cognitive architecture, which includes working or short-term memory, a highly limited system, and long-term memory, a virtually limitless store of knowledge. What matters in most situations is how well one can evoke the knowledge stored in long-term memory and use it to reason efficiently about current information and problems. *Therefore, within the normal range of cognitive abilities, estimates of how people organize information in long-term memory are likely to be more important than estimates of working memory capacity.*

Understanding the contents of long-term memory is especially critical for determining what people know; how they know it; and how they are able to use that knowledge to answer questions, solve problems, and engage in additional learning. While the contents include both general and specific knowledge, much of what one knows is domain- and task-specific and organized into structures known as schemas. Assessments should evaluate what schemas an individual has and under what circumstances he or she regards the information as relevant. This evaluation should include how a person organizes acquired information, encompassing both strategies for problem solving and ways of chunking relevant information into manageable units.

The importance of evaluating knowledge structures comes from research on expertise. *Studies of expert-novice differences in subject domains illuminate critical features of proficiency that should be the targets for assessment.* Experts in a subject domain typically organize factual and procedural knowledge into schemas that support pattern recognition and the rapid retrieval and application of knowledge.

One of the most important aspects of cognition is metacognition—the process of reflecting on and directing one's own thinking. Metacognition is crucial to effective thinking and problem solving and is one of the hallmarks of expertise in specific areas of knowledge and skill. Experts use metacognitive strategies for monitoring understanding during problem solving and for performing self-correction. *Assessment should therefore attempt to determine whether an individual has good metacognitive skills.*

Not all children learn in the same way and follow the same paths to competence. Children's problem-solving strategies become more effective over time and with practice, but the growth process is not a simple, uniform progression, nor is there movement directly from erroneous to optimal solution strategies. *Assessments should focus on identifying the specific strategies children are using for problem solving, giving particular consideration to where those strategies fall on a developmental continuum of efficiency and appropriateness for a particular domain of knowledge and skill.*

Children have rich intuitive knowledge of their world that undergoes significant change as they mature. Learning entails the transformation of naive understanding into more complete and accurate comprehension, and assessment can be used as a tool to facilitate this process. To this end, *assessments, especially those conducted in the context of classroom instruction, should focus on making students' thinking visible to both their teachers and themselves so that instructional strategies can be selected to support an appropriate course for future learning.*

Practice and feedback are critical aspects of the development of skill and expertise. *One of the most important roles for assessment is the provision of timely and informative feedback to students during instruction and learning so that their practice of a skill and its subsequent acquisition will be effective and efficient.*

As a function of context, knowledge frequently develops in a highly contextualized and inflexible form, and often does not transfer very effectively. Transfer depends on the development of an explicit understanding of when to apply what has been learned. *Assessments of academic achievement need to consider carefully the knowledge and skills required to understand and answer a question or solve a problem, including the context in which it is presented, and whether an assessment task or situation is functioning as a test of near, far, or zero transfer.*

Much of what humans learn is acquired through discourse and interaction with others. Thus, knowledge is often embedded in particular social and cultural contexts, including the context of the classroom, and it encompasses understandings about the meaning of specific practices such as asking and answering questions. *Assessments need to examine how well students engage in communicative practices appropriate to a domain of knowledge and skill, what they understand about those practices, and how well they use the tools appropriate to that domain.*

Models of cognition and learning provide a basis for the design and implementation of theory-driven instructional and assessment practices. Such programs and practices already exist and have been used productively in certain curricular areas. However, the vast majority of what is known has yet to be applied to the design of assessments for classroom or external evaluation purposes. *Further work is therefore needed on translating what is already known in cognitive science to assessment practice, as well as on developing additional cognitive analyses of domain-specific knowledge and expertise.*

Many highly effective tools exist for probing and modeling a person's knowledge and for examining the contents and contexts of learning. *The methods used in cognitive science to design tasks, observe and analyze cognition, and draw inferences about what a person knows are applicable to many of the challenges of designing effective educational assessments.*

ANNEX 3-1: COGNITION AND BRAIN SCIENCE

There is an ever-increasing amount of information about how the brain develops and processes information and how this is linked to various aspects of cognition, development, and learning. Here we briefly consider two areas of special concern—hemispheric specialization and the effects of enriched environments on brain development—because of the way they have been treated in the popular literature, especially as regards educational practices.

Hemispheric Specialization: Realities and Myths

The notion that the left and right hemispheres of the brain serve specialized functions emerged some years ago from studies of people whose speech was impaired after damage to the left hemisphere. A study by Sperry (1984) of split-brain humans popularized this notion. Essentially, these studies indicated that in most humans, the right hemisphere has become specialized for spatial and synthetic tasks and the left for verbal, analytic, and sequential tasks. Careful laboratory studies of normal humans show clear hemispheric advantages in reaction times when information such as words or spatial objects is presented to only one hemisphere or the other (Hellige, 1993; Springer and Deutsch, 1993).

Brain imaging studies reveal extraordinary degrees of hemispheric specialization (Thompson, 2000). Spatial navigation involves the right hippocampus; attention shift involves the right parietal lobe; attention processes also involve the right anterior cingulate gyrus and right anterior medial frontal lobe; and visual attention processes also activate areas in the left cerebellum. Verbal short-term memory involves the left parietal and frontal areas; spatial short-term memory involves the right parietal, occipital, and frontal areas and the superior frontal sulcus bilaterally; and face working memory predominantly involves the left precentral sulcus, the left middle frontal gyrus, and the left inferior frontal gyrus. The left prefrontal cortex is more involved in retrieval of information from semantic memory, whereas the right prefrontal cortex is more involved in episodic memory retrieval.

In short, hemispheric specialization is the norm for cognitive processes. But from an educational standpoint, this is of little consequence. While there may be some educational implications, those claimed most often (e.g., that a teacher should address the left and right hemispheres separately) are ill founded. In normal humans, the two hemispheres communicate seamlessly. Information projected to one hemisphere is immediately transferred to the other as needed. During most cognitive operations, both hemispheres are activated.

Enriched Environments and Brain Development: Realities and Myths

Another strand of neuroscientific research has examined the effects of enriched environments on the development of the brain and behavior (Greenough, 1976). Various studies have concluded that rats raised together in a complex environment ("rich" rats) have a significantly thicker cerebral cortex and many more dendritic spines (synapses) on their cortical neurons than rats raised alone in plain cages. Similar results have been found with monkeys. Enhanced cortical development can occur in adult rats, but in rich rats it regresses if the animals are placed in poor environments. Rich rats also perform better than poor rats on learning tasks, but we do not yet know whether the cortical changes relate to learning experiences per se or to other processes, such as arousal.

There is a major problem, however, in the way this literature has been interpreted and applied to humans, such that parents believe they should expose their infants to super-rich environments filled with bells, whistles, and moving objects. A particular example of this phenomenon is the attention given to "the Mozart effect" (see Annex Box 3-1). In fact, the animal literature suggests that the effects of a rich environment on brain development are simply the effects of a normal environment; the abnormal condition is isolation, resulting in impaired development, as is seen with children raised in extreme isolation.

Indeed, wild rats and laboratory rats raised in semiwild environments (which may be rich in stress) have the same cortical development as rich rats. Thus, the available evidence suggests that the normal environment provided by caring parents or other caregivers is sufficient for normal brain development.

A common misconception is that the brain grows in spurts and is particularly sensitive to specific educational procedures at these critical growth times. This is not the case. Critical periods—periods in development during which brain systems are especially vulnerable—are indeed real, as demonstrated by the literature on visual deprivation. These periods are important, however, only in abnormal or extreme circumstances. Nor is it true that no new nerve cells form after birth. Studies in rats indicate that particular learn-

ANNEX BOX 3-1   **The Mozart Effect**

Several years ago, great excitement arose over a report published in *Nature* that claimed listening to the music of Mozart enhanced intellectual performance, increasing IQ by the equivalent of 8 to 9 points as measured by portions of the Stanford-Binet Intelligence Scale (Rauscher, Shaw, and Ky, 1993). Dubbed "the Mozart effect," this claim was widely disseminated by the popular media. Articles encouraged parents to play classical music to infants and children and even to listen to such music during pregnancy. Companies responded by selling Mozart effect kits including tapes and players. (An aspect of the *Nature* account overlooked by the media is that the Mozart effect is reported to last about 10 to 15 minutes.) The authors of the *Nature* report subsequently offered a neurophysiological rationale for their claim (Rauscher, Shaw, and Ky, 1995). This rationale essentially held that exposure to complex musical compositions excites cortical firing patterns similar to those used in spatial-temporal reasoning, so that performance on spatial-temporal tasks is positively affected.

Several groups attempted to replicate the Mozart effect, with consistently negative results (Carstens, Huskins, and Hounshell, 1995; Kenealy and Monsef, 1994; Newman et al., 1995; Steele, Ball, and Runk, 1997;. In a careful study, Steele, Bass and Crook (1999) precisely replicated the conditions described by Rauscher and Shaw as critical. Yet the results were entirely negative, even though subjects were

ing experiences can enhance the proliferation of new neurons, specifically, the hippocampal dentate gyrus used in hippocampal-dependent tasks.

Implications

In general, applications of brain-based theories to education and assessment are relatively limited at this time, though that may not be the case in the future. As Bruer (1997, 1999) and others have noted, brain research by itself currently provides limited guidance for understanding or modifying complex higher-order cognitive processes. Although neuroimaging or neurophysiological measures may reveal limits to cognitive abilities at the behavioral level, in most cases additional understanding and cognitive theory are necessary to translate these observations into instructional and assessment practices. Rushing to conclusions about the educational implications

"significantly happier" listening to silence or Mozart than they were listening to a control piece of postmodern music by Philip Glass. One recent report (Nantais and Schellenberg, 1999) indicates a very slight but significant improvement in performance after listening to music by Mozart and Schubert as compared with silence. When listening to Mozart was compared with listening to a story, however, no effect was observed, a finding that negates the brain model. Mood appeared to be the critical variable in this study.

Why did the Mozart effect receive so much media play, particularly when the effect, if it exists at all, lasts only minutes? One might speculate that this was the case in part because the initial positive result was published in *Nature*, a journal routinely viewed by the media as being highly prestigious in science. Another factor, no doubt, is that exposing one's child to music appears to be an easy way of making her or him smarter—much easier than reading to the child regularly. Moreover, the so-called neurophysiological rationale provided for the effect probably enhanced its scientific credibility in the eyes of the media. Actually, this rationale is not neurophysiological at all: there is no evidence whatsoever to support the argument that music excites cortical firing patterns similar to those used in spatial-temporal tasks.

of neuroscientific observations could lead to misguided instructional practices, as illustrated by reactions to press reports of the Mozart effect.

The exceptions are limited to situations in which cognitive capacities are far below the normal range. For example, the design of a rehabilitation program following brain damage may indeed benefit from neuroimaging or neurophysiological measures. A less extreme example is emergent neural imaging research on dyslexia (see Annex Box 3-2, above). At present, however, both the theoretical basis and the methodology for applying these

ANNEX BOX 3-2 **Neural Bases of Dyslexia**

Recent studies using brain imaging techniques suggest that dyslexia is in some degree due to specific abnormalities in the way the brain processes visual and verbal language information (see Thompson, 2000). Guenevere Eden and associates at the National Institute of Mental Health used functional magnetic resonance imaging (fMRI) to examine the extent of brain activation in area V5/MT—an area particularly involved in the perception of movement—in response to moving stimuli in dyslexic men and normal control subjects. The control group showed substantial activation in this area, while the dyslexic subjects did not. In contrast, presenting the subjects with stationary patterns resulted in equivalent activations in other visuocortical areas in each group. A key point here is that area V5/MT is a part of the magnocellular visual system, which is critical to normal perception of motion. Perceptual studies suggest that dyslexics are deficient in motion detection.

A study at the National Institute on Aging used positron emission tomography (PET) to study the degree of activation of the angular gyrus, relative to occipital regions, during reading in normal and dyslexic men. In the normal subjects, there was a strong correlation between activation (i.e., increased blood flow) in the angular gyrus and occipital regions. In the dyslexic group, by contrast, there appeared to be a disconnection between the angular gyrus and the occipital regions; there was no correlation between changes in blood flow in the two regions. Additional PET studies of reading tasks (Shaywitz et al., 2000) also found striking differences between dyslexic and nondyslexic subjects in the degree of activation of different brain areas.

Studies conducted by Merzenich, Tallal, and colleagues showed that

measures to education or training within the normal range remain to be developed. Even in situations in which methods from neuroscience can be used to diagnose learning needs—for example, in imaging diagnosis of dyslexia—behavioral methods are much simpler to use.

children who have trouble understanding spoken language have major deficits in their ability to recognize some rapidly successive phonetic elements in speech and similar impairments in detecting rapid changes in nonspeech sounds. The investigators trained a group of these children in computer "games" designed to cause improvement in auditory temporal processing skills. Following 8 to 16 hours of training over a 20-day period, the children improved markedly in their ability to recognize fast sequences of speech stimuli. In fact, their language was notably enhanced. (See Buonomano and Merzenich [1998] and Fitch, Miller, and Tallal [1997] for extensive discussion of issues of brain plasticity and language, and Merzenich et al. [1996] and Tallal et al. [1996] for initial findings on their procedures for treating language-learning-impaired children.) This appears to be one of the few cases in which basic neuroscience knowledge has led to an effective treatment for a learning disorder.*

---

* The conventional view of dyslexia is that the children have speech-specific deficits in phonological representation rather than in auditory temporal processing. This view finds considerable support in the literature. For example, Mody, Studdert-Kennedy, and Brady (1997) studied groups of second-grade children who were good and poor readers, matched for age and intelligence. The children were selected to differ on a temporal task used by Tallal as diagnostic (e.g., / ba / - / da / temporal order judgement task). The children were tested on several auditory tasks, including rapid changes in nonspeech sine wave analogues of speech sounds. The results supported the view that the perceptual problem for these poor readers was confusion between phonetically similar, though phonologically contrastive, syllables rather than difficulty in perceiving rapid auditory spectral changes, i.e., speech-specific rather than general auditory deficits. There are, of course, procedural differences between this and other studies supporting the phonological hypothesis and studies supporting the auditory perception hypothesis. Nonetheless, the work by Tallal and Merzenich offers a possible example of how basic research in neuroscience may have practical application to learning in a particular disadvantaged group.

Using three themes, this chapter reviews broad categories of formal measurement models and the principles of reasoning from evidence that underlie them:

- Formal measurement models are a particular form of reasoning from evidence. They provide explicit, formal rules for how to integrate the many pieces of information that may be relevant to a particular inference. Effectively, they are statistical examples of ways to articulate the relationships between the cognition and observation elements of the assessment triangle described in Chapter 2. The current array of psychometric models and methods is the result of an evolutionary progression shaped, in part, by changes in the kinds of inferences teachers and policy makers want to draw, the ways people have thought about learning and schooling, and the technologies that have been available for gathering and using test data.

- Work on measurement models has progressed from (1) developing models that are intended to measure general proficiency and/or to rank examinees (referred to here as *standard* models); to (2) adding enhancements to a standard psychometric model to make it more consistent with changing conceptions of learning, cognition, and curricular emphasis; to (3) incorporating cognitive elements, including a model of learning and curriculum directly into psychometric models as parameters; to (4) creating a family of models that are adaptable to a broad range of contexts. Each model and adaptation has its particular uses, strengths, and limitations.

- Measurement models now exist that can address specific aspects of cognition. An example is the choice of problem-solving strategies and the strategy changes that occur from person to person, from task to task for an individual, and within a task for an individual. Developments in statistical methods have made it possible to create and work with models more flexibly than in the past, opening the door to a wider array of assessment data and uses. To do so, however, requires closer attention to the interplay between the statistical and cognitive aspects of assessment than has been customary.

4

Contributions of Measurement and Statistical Modeling to Assessment

Over the past century, scientists have sought to bring objectivity, rigor, consistency, and efficiency to the process of assessment by developing a range of formal theories, models, practices, and statistical methods for deriving and interpreting test data. Considerable progress has been made in the field of measurement, traditionally referred to as "psychometrics." The measurement models in use today include some very sophisticated options, but they have had surprisingly little impact on the everyday practice of educational assessment. The problem lies not so much with the range of measurement models available, but with the outdated conceptions of learning and observation that underlie most widely used assessments. Further, existing models and methods may appear to be more rigid than they actually are because they have long been associated with certain familiar kinds of test formats and with conceptions of student learning that emphasize general proficiency or ranking.

Findings from cognitive research suggest that new kinds of inferences are needed about students and how they acquire knowledge and skills if assessments are to be used to track and guide student learning. Advances in technology offer ways to capture, store, and communicate the multitude of things one can observe students say, do, and make. At issue is how to harness the relevant information to serve as evidence for the new kinds of inferences that cognitive research suggests are important for informing and improving learning. An important emphasis of this chapter is that currently available measurement methods could yield richer inferences about student knowledge if they were linked with contemporary theories of cognition and learning.[1]

---

[1]This chapter draws, in part, on a paper commissioned by the committee and written by Brian Junker (1999) that describes some statistical models and computational methods that may

FORMAL MEASUREMENT MODELS AS A FORM OF REASONING FROM EVIDENCE

As discussed in Chapter 2, assessment is a process of drawing reasonable inferences about what students know on the basis of evidence derived from observations of what they say, do, or make in selected situations. To this end, the three elements of the assessment triangle—cognition, observation, and interpretation—must be well coordinated. In this chapter, the three elements are defined more specifically, using terminology from the field of measurement: the aspects of cognition and learning that are the targets for the assessment are referred to as the *construct* or *construct variables*, observation is referred to as the *observation model*, and interpretation is discussed in terms of formal statistical methods referred to as *measurement models*.

The methods and practices of standard test theory constitute a special type of reasoning from evidence. The field of psychometrics has focused on how best to gather, synthesize, and communicate evidence of student understanding in an explicit and formal way. As explained below, psychometric models are based on a probabilistic approach to reasoning. From this perspective, a statistical model is developed to characterize the patterns believed most likely to emerge in the data for students at varying levels of competence. When there are large masses of evidence to be interpreted and/or when the interpretations are complex, the complexity of these models can increase accordingly.

Humans have remarkable abilities to evaluate and summarize information, but remarkable limitations as well. Formal probability-based models for assessment were developed to overcome some of these limitations, especially for assessment purposes that (1) involve high stakes; (2) are not limited to a specific context, such as one classroom; or (3) do not require immediate information. Formal measurement models allow one to draw meaning from quantities of data far more vast than a person can grasp at once and to express the degree of uncertainty associated with one's conclusions. In other words, a measurement model is a framework for communicating with others how the evidence in observations can be used to inform the inferences one wants to draw about learner characteristics that are embodied in the construct variables. Further, measurement models allow people to avoid reasoning errors that appear to be hard-wired into the human mind, such as biases associated with preconceptions or with the representativeness or recency of information (Kahneman, Slovic, and Tversky, 1982).

---

be useful for cognitively informed assessment. Junker's paper reviews some of the measurement models in more technical detail than is provided in this chapter and can be found at <http://www.sat.cmu.edu/~brian/nrc/cfa/>. [March 2, 2001].

Reasoning Principles and Formal Measurement Models

Those involved in educational and psychological measurement must deal with a number of issues that arise when one assumes a probabilistic relationship between the observations made of a learner and the learner's underlying cognitive constructs. The essential idea is that statistical models can be developed to predict the probability that people will behave in certain ways in assessment situations, and that evidence derived from observing these behaviors can be used to draw inferences about students' knowledge, skills, and strategies (which are not directly observable).[2] In assessment, aspects of students' knowledge, skills, and strategies that cannot be directly observed play the role of "that which is to be explained"—generally referred to as "cognition" in Chapter 2 and more specifically as the "construct" in this chapter. The constructs are called "latent" because they are not directly observable. The things students say and do constitute the evidence used in this explanation—the observation element of the assessment triangle.

In broad terms, the construct is seen as "causing" the observations, although generally this causation is probabilistic in nature (that is, the constructs determine the probability of a certain response, not the response itself). More technically there are two elements of probability-based measurement models: (1) unobservable latent constructs and (2) observations or observable variables, which are, for instance, students' scores on a test intended to measure the given construct. The nature of the construct variables depends partly on the structure and psychology of the subject domain and partly on the purpose of assessment. The nature of the observations is determined by the kinds of things students might say or do in various situations to provide evidence about their values with respect to the construct. Figure 4-1 shows how the construct is related to the observations. (In the figure, the latent construct is denoted θ [theta] and the observables x.) Note that although the latent construct causes the observations, one needs to go the other way when one draws inferences—back from the observations to their antecedents.

Other variables are also needed to specify the formal model of the observations; these are generally called *item parameters*. The central idea of probability models is that these unknown constructs and item parameters do not determine the specifics of what occurs, but they do determine the probability associated with various possible results. For example, a coin might be expected to land as heads and as tails an approximately equal number of

---

[2]This idea dates back to Spearman's (1904) early work and was extended by Wright's (1934) path analyses, Lazarsfeld's (1950) latent class models, item response theory (Lawley, 1943), and structural equations modeling with measurement error (e.g., Jöreskog and Sörbom, 1979).

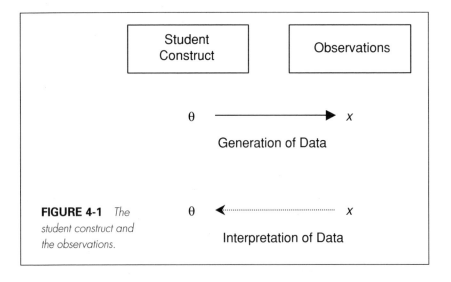

FIGURE 4-1 *The student construct and the observations.*

times. That is, the probability of heads is the same as the probability of tails. However, this does not mean that in ten actual coin tosses these exact probabilities will be observed.

The notion of "telling stories that match up with what we see" corresponds to the technical concept of *conditional independence* in formal probability-based reasoning. Conditional independence means that any systematic relationships among multiple observations are due entirely to the unobservable construct variables they tap. This is a property of mathematical probability models, not necessarily of any particular situation in the real world. Assessors choose where, in the real world, they wish to focus their attention. This includes what situation they want to explore and what properties of that situation are most important to manipulate. They then decide how to build a model or "approximation" that connects the construct variables to the specific observations. The level of unobservable constructs corresponds to "the story" people tell, and it is ultimately expressed in terms of important patterns and principles of knowledge in the cognitive domain under investigation. The level of observations represents the specifics from which evidence is derived about the unobservable level. Informally, conditional independence expresses the decision about what aspects of the situation are built into one's story and what is ignored.

Psychometric models are particular instances of this kind of reasoning. The most familiar measurement models evolved to help in "constructing stories" that were useful in situations characterized by various psychological perspectives on learning, for particular educational purposes, with certain recurring forms of evidence. The following sections describe some of these models, explaining how these stories have grown and adapted to handle the increasingly complex demands of assessment. Knowing the history of these adaptations may help in dealing with new demands from more complex models of learning and the types of stories we would now like to be able to tell in many educational contexts.

The BEAR Assessment System

An example of the relationships among the conception of learning, the observations, and the interpretation model is provided by the Berkeley Evaluation and Assessment Research (BEAR) Center (Wilson and Sloane, 2000). The BEAR assessment system was designed to correspond to a middle school science curriculum called Issues, Evidence and You (IEY) (Science Education for Public Understanding Program, 1995). We use this assessment as a running example to illustrate various points throughout this chapter.

The conception of cognition and learning underlying IEY is not based on a specific theory from cognitive research; rather it is based on pedagogic content knowledge, that is, teachers' knowledge of how students learn specific types of content. Nevertheless, the BEAR example illustrates many of the principles that the committee is setting forth, including the need to pay attention to all three vertices of the assessment triangle and how they fit together.

The IEY curriculum developers have conceptualized the learner as progressing along five *progress variables* that organize what students are to learn into five topic areas and a progression of concepts and skills (see Box 4-1). The BEAR assessment system is based on the same set of progress variables. A progress variable focuses on progression or growth. Learning is conceptualized not simply as a matter of acquiring more knowledge and skills, but as progressing toward higher levels of competence as new knowledge is linked to existing knowledge, and deeper understandings are developed from and take the place of earlier understandings. The concepts of ordered levels of understanding and direction are fundamental: in any given area, it is assumed that learning can be described and mapped as progress in the direction of qualitatively richer knowledge, higher-order skills, and deeper understandings. Progress variables are derived in part from professional opinion about what constitutes higher and lower levels of performance or competence, but are also informed by empirical research on how students respond or perform in practice. They provide qualitatively interpreted frames of reference for particular areas of learning and permit students' levels of achievement to be interpreted in terms of the kinds of knowledge, skills, and understandings typically associated with those levels. They also allow individual and group achievements to be interpreted with respect to the achievements of other learners. The order of the activities intended to take

BOX 4-1 Progress Variables from the Issues, Evidence and You (IEY) Curriculum

Designing and Conducting Investigations—designing a scientific experiment, performing laboratory procedures to collect data, recording and organizing data, and analyzing and interpreting the results of an experiment.

Evidence and Trade-offs—identifying objective scientific evidence, as well as evaluating the advantages and disadvantages of different possible solutions to a problem on the basis of the available evidence.

Understanding Concepts—understanding scientific concepts (such as properties and interactions of materials, energy, or thresholds) in order to apply the relevant scientific concepts to the solution of problems.

Communicating Scientific Information—effectively, and free of technical errors, organizing and presenting results of an experiment or explaining the process of gathering evidence and weighing trade-offs in selecting a solution to a problem.

Group Interaction—developing skill in collaborating with teammates to complete a task (such as a laboratory experiment), sharing the work of the activity, and contributing ideas to generate solutions to a given problem.

SOURCE: Roberts, Wilson, and Draney (1997, p. 8). Used with permission of the authors.

students through the progress variables is specified in a *blueprint*—a table showing an overview of all course activities, indicating where assessment tasks are located and to which variables they relate.

During IEY instruction, students carry out laboratory exercises and investigations in structured quadruples, work on projects in pairs, and then create reports and respond to assessment questions on their own. Observations of student performance consist of *assessment tasks* (which are embedded in the instructional program, and each of which has direct links to the progress variables) and *link tests* (which are composed of short-answer items also linked to the progress variables). Recording of teacher judgments about students' work is aided by *scoring guides*—criteria unique to each progress variable that are used for assessing levels of student performance and interpreting student work (an example is provided in Table 4-1 for the Evidence and Trade-offs variable). These are augmented with *exemplars*—samples of actual student work illustrating performance at each score level for all assessment tasks.

The interpretation of these judgments is carried out using *progress maps*— graphic displays used to record the progress of each student on particular progress variables over the course of the year. The statistical underpinning for these maps is a multidimensional item response model (explained later); the learning underpinning is the set of progress variables. An example of a BEAR progress map is shown in Box 4-2. Teacher and student involvement in the assessment system is motivated and structured through *assessment moderation*—a process by which groups of teachers and students reach consensus on standards of student performance and discuss the implications of assessment results for subsequent learning and instruction (Roberts, Sloane, and Wilson, 1996).

To summarize, the BEAR assessment system as applied in the IEY curriculum embodies the assessment triangle as follows. The conception of learning consists of the five progress variables mentioned above. Students are helped in improving along these variables by the IEY instructional materials, including the assessments. The observations are the scores teachers assign to student work on the embedded assessment tasks and the link tests. The interpretation model is formally a multidimensional item response model (discussed later in this chapter) that underlies the progress maps; however, its meaning is elaborated through the exemplars and through the teacher's knowledge about the specific responses a student gave on various items.

STANDARD PSYCHOMETRIC MODELS

Currently, standard measurement models focus on a situation in which the observations are in the form of a number of items with discrete, ordered response categories (such as the categories from an IEY scoring guide illustrated in Table 4-1) and in which the construct is a single continuous variable (such as one of the IEY progress variables described in Box 4-1). For example, a standardized achievement test is typically composed of many (usually dichotomous[3]) items that are often all linked substantively in some way to a common construct variable, such as mathematics achievement. The construct is thought of as a continuous unobservable (latent) characteristic

---

[3]That is, the items can be scored into just two categories, e.g., either right or wrong.

TABLE 4-1 Sample Scoring Guide for the BEAR Assessment

Evidence and Trade-offs (ET) Variable

Score	Using Evidence:	Using Evidence to Make Trade-offs:
	Response uses objective reason(s) based on relevant evidence to support choice.	Response recognizes multiple perspectives of issue and explains each perspective using objective reasons, supported by evidence, in order to make choice.
4	Response accomplishes Level 3 AND goes beyond in some significant way, such as questioning or justifying the source, validity, and/or quantity of evidence.	Response accomplishes Level 3 AND goes beyond in some significant way, such as suggesting additional evidence beyond the activity that would further influence choices in specific ways, OR questioning the source, validity, and/or quantity of evidence and explaining how it influences choice.
3	Response provides major objective reasons AND supports each with relevant and accurate evidence.	Response discusses at least two perspectives of issue AND provides objective reasons, supported by relevant and accurate evidence, for each perspective.
2	Response provides some objective reasons AND some supporting evidence, BUT at least one reason is missing and/or part of the evidence is incomplete.	Response states at least one perspective of issue AND provides some objective reasons using some relevant evidence, BUT reasons are incomplete and/or part of the evidence is missing; OR only one complete and accurate perspective has been provided.
1	Response provides only subjective reasons (opinions) for choice and/or uses inaccurate or irrelevant evidence from the activity.	Response states at least one perspective of issue BUT only provides subjective reasons and/or uses inaccurate or irrelevant evidence.
0	No response; illegible response; response offers no reasons AND no evidence to support choice made.	No response; illegible response; response lacks reasons AND offers no evidence to support decision made.
X	Student had no opportunity to respond.	

SOURCE: Roberts, Wilson, and Draney (1997, p. 9). Used with permission of the authors.

of the learner, representing relatively more or less of the competency that is common to the set of items and their responses. This can be summarized graphically as in Figure 4-2, where the latent construct variable θ (represented inside an oval shape in the figure to denote that it is unobservable) is thought of as potentially varying continuously from minus infinity to plus

BOX 4-2 Example of a BEAR Progress Map

Below is an example of one of the types of progress maps produced by the BEAR assessment program. This particular example is called a "conference map" and is created by the GradeMap software (Wilson, Draney and Kennedy, 1999). This map shows the "current estimate" of where a student is on four of the IEY progress variables (the variable Group Interaction is not yet calibrated). The estimate is expressed in terms of a series of levels that are identified as segments of the continua (e.g., "Incorrect," "Advanced") and are specified in greater detail in the scoring guide for each progress variable. Additional examples of BEAR maps are provided later in this chapter.

File

Name: Brown, Amy

	Designing and Conducting Investigations	Evidence and Tradeoffs	Understanding Concepts	Communicating Scientific Information
4 - Advanced				
3 - Correct	*		*	*
2 - Incomplete		*		
1 - Incorrect				
0 - Off Task				
To improve your performance, you can:	Think about the limits of your investigation Identify possible alternative procedures Think of new data displays Explain any unexpected results Think about additional investigations you could do	Be sure to include all major reasons for your choice Make sure you find all of the important evidence Make sure you've described at least two complete and accurate perspectives	Think about other ways you could use the scientific information Think about other scientific information that might be helpful Think about possible limitations of the scientific information provided	Think of creative things you could add to your work to make it stand out, such as extra charts or pictures that are not required, use of color in graphs and charts, special labels, and so on

SOURCE: Wilson, Draney, and Kennedy (2001). Used with permission of the authors.

infinity. The assessment items are shown in boxes (to denote that they are observed variables), and the arrows show that the construct "causes" the observations. Although not shown in the figure, each observed response consists of a component that statisticians generally call "error." Note that error in this context means something quite different from its usual educational sense—it means merely that the component is not modeled (i.e., not attributable to the construct θ).

The representation in Figure 4-2 corresponds to a class of measurement models called *item response models,* which are discussed below. First, how-

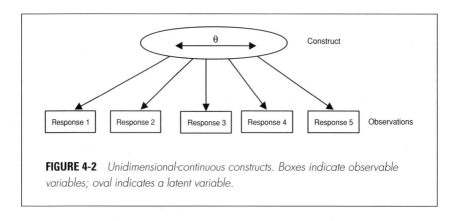

FIGURE 4-2   *Unidimensional-continuous constructs. Boxes indicate observable variables; oval indicates a latent variable.*

ever, some methods that emerged earlier in the evolution of measurement models are described.

Classical Test Theory

Early studies of student testing and retesting led to the conclusion that although no tests were perfectly consistent, some gave more consistent results than others. Classical test theory (CTT) was developed initially by Spearman (1904) as a way to explain certain of these variations in consistency (expressed most often in terms of the well-known *reliability* index). In CTT, the construct is represented as a single continuous variable, but certain simplifications were necessary to allow use of the statistical methods available at that time. The observation model is simplified to focus only on the sum of the responses with the individual item responses being omitted (see Figure 4-3). For example, if a CTT measurement model were used in the BEAR example, it would take the sum of the student scores on a set of assessment tasks as the observed score. The measurement model, sometimes referred to as a "true-score model," simply expresses that the true score (θ) arises from an observed score (x) plus error (e). The reliability is then the ratio of the variance of the true score to the variance of the observed score. This type of model may be sufficient when one is interested only in a single aspect of student achievement (the total score) and when tests are considered only as a whole. Scores obtained using CTT modeling are usually translated into percentiles for norm-referenced interpretation and for comparison with other tests.

The simple assumptions of CTT have been used to develop a very large superstructure of concepts and measurement tools, including reliability indices, standard error estimation formulae, and test equating practices used to link scores on one test with those on another. CTT modeling does not allow

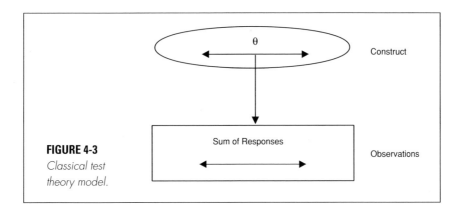

FIGURE 4-3

Classical test theory model.

the simultaneous assessment of multiple aspects of examinee competence and does not address problems that arise whenever separate parts of a test need to be studied or manipulated. Formally, CTT does not include components that allow interpretation of scores based on subsets of items in the test. Historically, CTT has been the principal tool of formal assessments, and in part because of its great simplicity, it has been applied to assessments of virtually every type. Because of serious practical limitations, however, other theories—such as generalizability theory, item response modeling, and factor analysis—were developed to enable study of aspects of items.

Generalizability Theory

The purpose of generalizability theory (often referred to as G-theory) is to make it possible to examine how different aspects of observations—such as using different raters, using different types of items, or testing on different occasions—can affect the dependability of scores (Brennan, 1983; Cronbach, Gleser, Nanda, and Rajaratnam, 1972). In G-theory, the construct is again characterized as a single continuous variable. However, the observation can include design choices, such as the number of types of tasks, the number of raters, and the uses of scores from different raters (see Figure 4-4). These are commonly called *facets*[4] of measurement. Facets can be treated as fixed or random. When they are treated as random, the observed elements in the facet are considered to be a random sample from the universe of all possible elements in the facet. For instance, if the set of tasks included on a test were

---

[4]The term "facets" used in this sense is not to be confused with the facets-based instruction and assessment program (Hunt and Minstrell, 1994; Minstrell, 2000) referred to in Chapters 3, 5, 6, and 7.

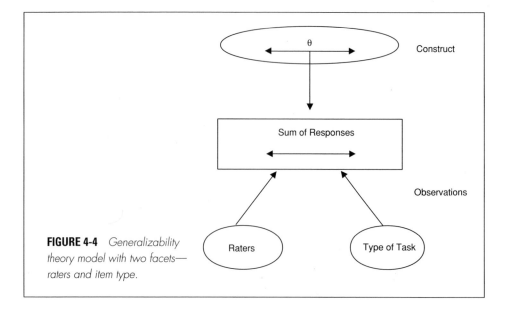

FIGURE 4-4 *Generalizability theory model with two facets— raters and item type.*

treated as a random facet, it would be considered a random sample of all possible tasks generated under the same rules to measure the construct, and the results of the g-study would be considered to generalize to that universe of tasks. When facets are treated as fixed, the results are considered to generalize only to the elements of the facet in the study. Using the same example, if the set of tasks were treated as fixed, the results would generalize only to the tasks at hand (see Kreft and De Leeuw, 1998, for a discussion of this and other usages of the terms "random" and" fixed").

In practice, researchers carry out a g-study to ascertain how different facets affect the reliability (generalizability) of scores. This information can then guide decisions about how to design sound situations for making observations—for example, whether to average across raters, add more tasks, or test on more than one occasion. To illustrate, in the BEAR assessment, a g-study could be carried out to see which type of assessment—embedded tasks or link items—contributed more to reliability. Such a study could also be used to examine whether teachers were as consistent as external raters. Generalizability models offer two powerful practical advantages. First, they allow one to characterize how the conditions under which the observations were made affect the reliability of the evidence. Second, this information is expressed in terms that allow one to project from the current assessment design to other potential designs.

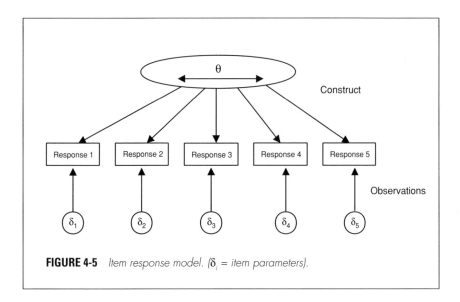

FIGURE 4-5 *Item response model. (δ_i = item parameters).*

Item Response Modeling

Perhaps the most important shortcoming of both CTT and G-theory is that examinee characteristics and test characteristics cannot be separated; each can be interpreted only in the specific context of the other. An examinee's achievement level is defined only in terms of a particular test. When the test is "difficult," the examinee will appear to have low achievement; when the test is "easy," the examinee will appear to have high achievement. Whether an item is difficult or easy depends on the ability of the examinees being measured, and the ability of the examinees depends on whether the test items are difficult or easy.

Item response modeling (IRM) was developed to enable comparisons among examinees who take different tests and among items whose parameters are estimated using different groups of examinees (Lord and Novick, 1968; Lord, 1980). Furthermore, with IRM it is possible to predict the properties of a test from the properties of the items of which it is composed. In IRM, the construct model is still represented as a single continuous variable, but the observation model is expressed in terms of the items (as in Figure 4-5). The model is usually written as an equation relating the probability of a

---

[5]The original units of the IRM, called "logits," are usually transformed to other units that are thought to be more easily understood by the nontechnical person (e.g., to avoid negative numbers).

certain response to an item in terms of student and item parameters. The student parameter (same as the latent construct θ) indicates level of proficiency, ability, achievement, or sometimes attitude. The student parameter is usually translated into a scaled score[5] for interpretation. The item parameters express, in a mathematical equation, characteristics of the item that are believed to be important in determining the probabilities of observing different response categories. Examples include (1) how "difficult" it is to get an item correct; (2) the extent to which an item differentiates between students who are high and low on the latent construct (sometimes called an item "discrimination" parameter); and (3) other complications, such as how guessing or rater harshness might influence the result. (Note that IRMs that assume an a priori discrimination parameter have particular characteristics and are generally dubbed "Rasch" models in honor of George Rasch [Rasch, 1960]). Most applications of IRM use unidimensional models, which assume that there is only one construct that determines student responses. Indeed, if one is interested primarily in measuring a single main characteristic of a student, this is a good place to start. However, IRMs can also be formulated for multidimensional contexts (discussed below).

Formal components of IRM have been developed to help diagnose test and item quality. For instance, person and item fit indices help identify items that do not appear to work well and persons for whom the items do not appear to work well.

As an example of how IRM can be used, consider the map of student progress for the variable Designing and Conducting Investigations displayed in Figure 4-6. Here, the successive scores on this variable (similar to the levels in Table 4-1) are indicated by the categories in the far right-hand column (the "criterion zones") and by the corresponding bands across the map. As students move "up" the map, they progress to higher levels of performance. The ability to express the student construct and item parameters on the same scale is one of the most useful and intuitive features of IRM, allowing one to interpret the student's rise in performance over time as an increased probability of receiving higher scores (corresponding to higher qualitative levels of performance) on the items and link items. Although hidden in this image of the results, the underlying foundation of this map (i.e., the unconfounding of item difficulty and student change) is based on a technical manipulation of the item parameters that would not be possible with a CTT approach.

As with CTT, with IRM one can still tell a story about a student's proficiency with regard to the latent construct. One can now, additionally, talk about what tends to happen with specific items, as expressed by their item parameters. This formulation allows for observation situations in which different students can respond to different items, as in computerized adaptive testing and matrix-sampling designs of the type used in the National Assessment of Educational Progress (NAEP).

| File | | | | | | | | | | | |

Combined DCI ET UC CSI GI

Performance Map for: Brown, Amy   Designing & Conducting Investigations (DCI)

Pre-Anch	Water				Materials Science			Energy		Post-Tests	SEPUP Score	Criterion Zones
	1-12	13-20	21-28	Link 1	29-38	39-46	Link 2	47-58	Link 3			
											1950	
											1900	
											1850	
											1800	Level 4
											1750	
											1700	
											1650	
											1600	Level 3
											1550	
											1500	
											1450	Level 2
											1400	
											1350	
											1300	Level 1
											1250	
											1200	
											1150	
											1100	Level 0
											1050	

FIGURE 4-6 *Example of a performance map for the Designing and Conducting Investigations variable.*
SOURCE: Wilson, Draney, and Kennedy (2001). Used with permission of the authors.

Figure 4-5 can also be used to portray a one-dimensional *factor analysis*, although, in its traditional formulation, factor analysis differs somewhat from IRM. Like IRM, unidimensional factor analysis models the relationship between a latent construct or factor (e.g., mathematics computation skill) and observable manifestations of the construct (e.g., scores on tests of mathematics computation). With traditional factor analysis, the relationship between an observed variable and the factor is called a "factor loading." Factor loadings correspond to item discrimination parameters in IRM. In factor analysis, the observable variables are strictly continuous rather than ordered categories as in IRM. This latter feature implies that the "items" in factor analysis might better be thought of as sums from subsets of more basic items. More recent formulations relax these limitations.

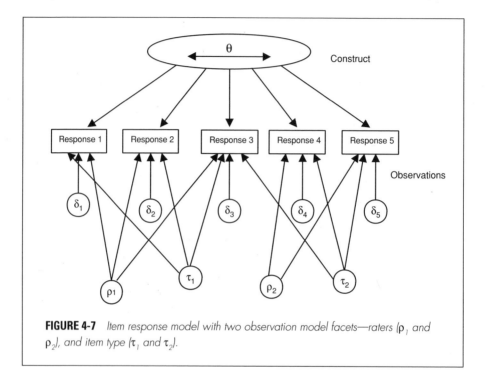

FIGURE 4-7   *Item response model with two observation model facets—raters (ρ_1 and ρ_2), and item type (τ_1 and τ_2).*

Similar to ways in which G-theory has extended CTT, elements of the observations, such as raters and item features, can be added to the basic item response framework (see Figure 4-7) in what might be called *faceted* IRMs. Examples of facets are (1) different raters, (2) different testing conditions, and (3) different ways to communicate the items. One foundational difference is that in IRMs the items are generally considered fixed, whereas in G-theory they are most often considered random. That is, in G-theory the items are considered random samples from the universe of all possible similarly generated items measuring the particular construct. In practice very few tests are constructed in a way that would allow the items to be truly considered a random sampling from an item population.

Latent Class Models

In the measurement approaches described thus far, the latent construct has been assumed to be a continuous variable. In contrast, some of the research on learning described in Chapter 3 suggests that achievement in certain domains of the curriculum might better be characterized in the form of discrete classes or types of understanding. That is, rather than assuming that each student lies somewhere on a continuum, one could assume that the student belongs to one of a number of categories or classes. Models based on this approach are called *latent class models*. The classes themselves can be considered *ordered* or *unordered*. When the classes are ordered, there is an analogy with the continuum models: each latent class can be viewed as a point on the continuum (see Figure 4-8). When the classes are unordered, that analogy breaks down, and the situation can be represented by deleting the ">" signs in Figure 4-8.

An argument could be made for using latent classes in the BEAR example discussed earlier. If one assumed that a student's responses are "caused" by being in ordered latent classes corresponding to the successive scores in the Designing and Conducting Investigations scoring guide, one could construct something like the progress map in Figure 4-6, although the vertical dimension would lose its metric and become a set of four categories. For interpretation purposes, this map would probably be just about as useful as the current one.

One might ask, which assumption is right—continuous or discrete? The determining factor should be how useful the measurement model is in reflecting the nature of achievement in the domain, not whether the continuous or the categorical assumption is "the right one." In fact, there have been cases in which both the continuous and discrete models have been fit reasonably well to the same dataset (see, e.g., Haertel, 1990). The important question is, given the decisions one has to make and the nature of cognition and learning in the domain, which approach provides the most interpretable information? Investigating this question may indeed reveal that one approach is better than the other for that particular purpose, but this finding does not answer the more general question.

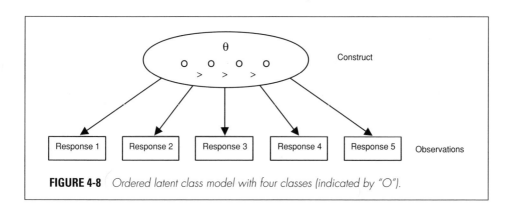

FIGURE 4-8 *Ordered latent class model with four classes (indicated by "O").*

Multiattribute Models

Each of the four general classes of models described above—classical, generalizability, item response, and latent class—can be extended to incorporate more than one attribute of the student. Doing so allows for connections to a richer substantive theory and educationally more complex interpretations. In *multidimensional IRM,* observations are hypothesized to correspond to multiple constructs (Reckase, 1972; Sympson, 1978). For instance, performance on mathematics word problems might be attributable to proficiency in both mathematics and reading. In the IEY example above, the progress of students on four progress variables in the domain of science was mapped and monitored (see Box 4-2, above). Note that in this example, one might have analyzed the results separately for each of the progress variables and obtained four independent IRM estimations of the student and item parameters, sometimes referred to as a consecutive approach (Adams, Wilson, and Wang, 1997).

There are both measurement and educational reasons for using a multidimensional model. In measurement terms, if one is interested, for example, in finding the correlation among the latent constructs, a multidimensional model allows one to make an unbiased estimate of this correlation, whereas the consecutive approach produces smaller correlations than it should. Educationally dense longitudinal data such as those needed for the IEY maps can be difficult to obtain and manage: individual students may miss out on specific tasks, and teachers may not use tasks or entire activities in their instruction. In such a situation, multidimensional models can be used to bolster sparse results by using information from one dimension to estimate performance on another. This is a valuable use and one on which the BEAR assessment system designers decided to capitalize. This profile allows differential performance and interpretation on each of the single dimensions of IEY Science, at both the individual and group levels. A diagram illustrating a two-dimensional IRM is shown in Figure 4-9. The curved line indicates that the two dimensions may be correlated. Note that for clarity, extra facets have not been included in this diagram, but that can be routinely done. Multidimensional factor analysis can be represented by the same diagram. Among true-score models, *multivariate G-theory* allows multiple attributes. Latent class models may also be extended to include multiple attributes, both ordered and unordered. Figures analogous to Figure 4-9 could easily be generated to depict these extended models.

MODELS OF CHANGE AND GROWTH

The measurement models considered thus far have all been models of status, that is, methods for taking single snapshots of student achievement in

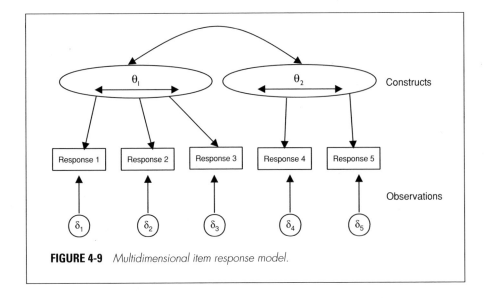

FIGURE 4-9 *Multidimensional item response model.*

time. Status measures are important in many assessment situations, but in an educational setting it is also important to track and monitor student change over time. One way to do this is to repeatedly record status measures at different times and to directly interpret patterns in those measures. This approach is not the same, however, as explicitly modeling changes in performance.

The account that follows should make clear that quite flexible and complex formal models of growth and change are available to complement the status models described in the previous section. Use of these models is currently limited by their relative newness and the statistical sophistication they demand of the user. More important, however, growth models require the existence of longitudinal data systems that can be used for measuring growth. In fact, as the following IEY example shows, monitoring of growth can take place without the use of any formal growth model.

The IEY maps are examples of repeated status measures; in particular see the map of student progress in Figure 4-6. Although a complex statistical model lies behind the measures of status recorded on that map, no overall model of growth was used to arrive at the map for each individual. Each map is simply a record of the different estimates for each student over time. For many assessment applications, especially when previous work has not established expectations for patterns of growth, this may be the most useful approach. The constraints on the use of a growth or change perspective tend to be due not to a lack of applicable models, but to the difficulties of collecting, organizing, and maintaining data that would allow one to display these sorts of maps.

However, models of change or growth can be added to the status models described above. That is, when it is important to focus on modeling change or growth in the stories one builds, one can formally include a framework for doing so in the statistical models employed. The formal modeling of such change adds a hierarchical level to the construct. Specifically, one level of the construct is a theory for the status measurement of a student at a particular time, and a second level is the theory of how students tend to change over time. Higher levels of analysis can also be added, such as how classrooms or schools change over time. This can be done with each of the three types of models described above—true-score models (e.g., CTT), models with continuous latent variables (e.g., IRM), and models with discrete latent variables (e.g., latent class analysis).

True-Score Modeling of Change

One can incorporate change into a true-score framework by modeling changes in performance over time. Often, simple polynomial models (e.g., linear, quadratic) are used, but other formulations may be preferable under certain circumstances. Effectively, data for each individual are grouped together, the point in time when each observation was made is recorded, and a linear or other model is fitted to each individual. This approach is termed "slopes as outcomes" (Burstein, 1980) or, more generally, "varying coefficients" (Kreft and De Leeuw, 1998), since it examines the relationship between performance on the outcome variable and the timing of the observation. Such an approach seeks to determine the change in the outcome variable associated with a given unit change in time.

For example, one might be interested in the variation in particular students' scores on an attitude scale, administered several times over a year when a new curriculum was being tried. Figure 4-10 shows three different families of linear models, where x = time; y = attitude, and each line represents a different student's trajectory. The first panel would model a situation in which students began with differing attitudes and changed in unison as the year progressed. The second panel would model a situation in which all students began with the same attitude, but their attitudes changed at different rates throughout the year, all in the same general direction. The third panel would model a situation in which both initial status and rates of change varied from student to student.

A different formulation would see these individual students as "random"; that is, they would be regarded as a sample that represents some population, and the model would then be termed a "random coefficients" model. Figure 4-11 shows a presentation equivalent to that in Figure 4-10

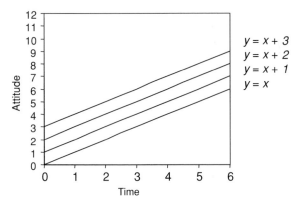

$y = x + 3$
$y = x + 2$
$y = x + 1$
$y = x$

Four regression lines, varying in intercept

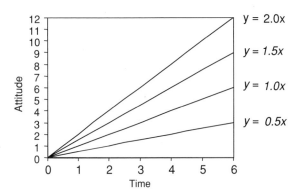

$y = 2.0x$

$y = 1.5x$

$y = 1.0x$

$y = 0.5x$

Four regression lines, varying in slope

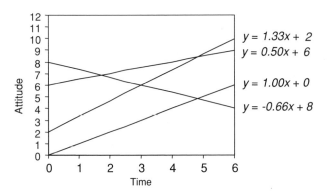

$y = 1.33x + 2$
$y = 0.50x + 6$

$y = 1.00x + 0$

$y = -0.66x + 8$

Four regression lines, varying in intercept and slope

FIGURE 4-10   *Families of linear models: "slopes as outcomes." Adapted from Kreft and De Leeuw (1998, pp. 36-37).*

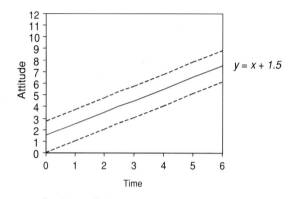

Random coefficient solution with random intercept

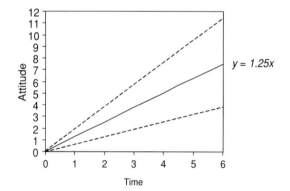

Random coefficient solution with random slope

FIGURE 4-11 *Families of linear models: "random coefficients." Adapted from Kreft and De Leeuw (1998, pp. 40-41).*

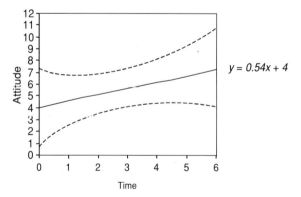

under the random coefficients model. In this case, only a single solid line is shown, expressing the general tendency inferred for the population; two dashed lines on either side express the variation observed around that general tendency. Here the interpretation of results would focus on (1) the general tendency and (2) the variation around that general tendency. For example, it might be found in the attitude example that students tended to improve their attitudes throughout the year (slope of general tendency is up), but that the variation was such that some students still had negative growth (see the third panel of Figure 4-11).

With random coefficients models, the next step is to investigate whether certain conditions—such as students' scores on an entry test or different variants of the educational program—affect the slope or its variability. For example, students who score higher on the entry test (presumably those who are better prepared for the curriculum) might be found to improve their attitude more quickly than those who score lower, or it might be found that students who are given better feedback tend to have greater gains. With students clustered within classrooms, classrooms within schools, and schools within higher levels of organization, further hierarchical levels of the models can be added to investigate within- and across-level effects that correspond to a wide variety of instructional, organizational, and policy issues. Several software packages have been developed to implement these approaches, the most prominent probably being hierarchical linear modeling (HLM) (Bryk and Raudenbush, 1992) and MLn (Goldstein, Rasbash, Plewis, and Draper, 1998).

Modeling of Change in Continuous Latent Variables

There are a number of approaches that extend the above ideas into the continuous latent variables domain. One such approach is to modify the true-score approaches to incorporate measurement error; an example is the "V-known" option in the HLM software (Raudenbush, Bryk, and Congdon, 1999), which makes it possible to include the standard error of measurement of latent variable estimates as input to the analysis. Another approach is structural equation modeling (SEM) (Willet and Sayer, 1994; Muthen and Khoo, 1998). Here each time point is regarded as a separate factor, and thereafter, all the tools and techniques of SEM are available for modeling. Software packages with quite generalized modeling capabilities (e.g., LISREL, M-Plus) are available that can incorporate growth and change features into SEM. The limitation of this approach is that the assignment of time points as factors means that the data need to be structured with (not too many) fixed time points. This pattern, called time-structured data (Bock, 1979), is common in planned studies, but may be difficult to impose on many forms of educational data, especially those close to the classroom.

IRMs that address these issues have also been proposed. Fischer (1995) has developed models that focus on uniform group change (analogous to that in the first panel of Figure 4-10) by adding parameters to the observation model. Embretson (1996) has proposed more complex models of change that span both student and observation models. These models were built expressly for contexts for which there is an explicit cognitive theory involving conditional dependence among the responses. All of the approaches mentioned thus far have been unidimensional in the student model. IRMs that incorporate both a multidimensional and a hierarchical student model have been implemented in the ConQuest software (referred to as "multidimensional latent regression") (Wu, Adams, and Wilson, 1998).

Modeling of Change in Discrete Latent Variables

When the latent construct(s) is best represented by classes rather than by a continuum, it makes sense to examine the probabilities of individuals moving from one latent class to another over time. One way to do this is with a latent Markov model, the application of which within psychological studies has been termed latent transition analysis. For example, Collins and Wugalter (1992) expressed the mathematics learning theory of Rock and Pollack-Ohls (1987) as in Figure 4-12. This is a five-attribute model with just two latent classes ("has ability" and "does not have ability") for each attribute (note that only the "has ability" latent classes are represented here by the circles). The arrows indicate that under this model, the learning of mathematical skills takes place in a forward direction only. More complex relationships can also be modeled. Quite general software packages for implementing these models are available, such as LCAG (Hagenaars and Luijkx, 1990) and PANMARK (van de Pol, Langeheine, and de Jong, 1989).

INCORPORATION OF COGNITIVE ELEMENTS IN EXISTING MEASUREMENT MODELS

The array of models described in the previous section represents a formidable toolkit for current psychometrics. These models can be applied in many educational and psychological settings to disentangle systematic effects and errors and to aid in their interpretation. However, there is considerable dissatisfaction with this standard set of approaches, especially among cognitive psychologists, but also among educational reformers. This dissatisfaction is due in part to the dominance of the older, simpler, and more widely known parts of the toolkit—for example, models for dichotomous (right-wrong) responses over those for polytomous responses (e.g., constructed response items scored into several ordered categories), models for continuous attributes over those for discrete attributes, and single-attribute

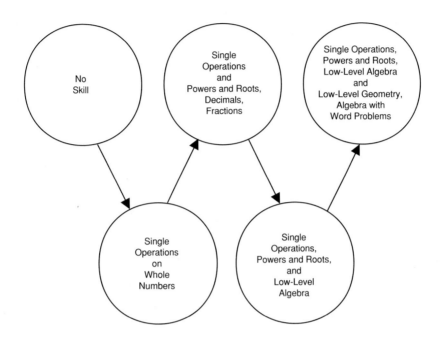

FIGURE 4-12 *A stage-sequential dynamic latent variable exhibiting cumulative monotonic development.*
SOURCE: Collins and Wugalter (1992, p.135). Reprinted by permission of Lawrence Erlbaum Associates.

over multiattribute models. If some of the less common models in the toolkit were more widely utilized, much of the dissatisfaction might well disappear. However, this is probably not a sufficient response to the criticisms. For example, Wolf, Bixby, Glenn, and Gardner (1991) present a strong argument for the following needs:

> If we are able to design tasks and modes of data collection that permit us to change the data we collect about student performance, we will have still another task in front of us. This is the redesign or invention of educational psychometrics capable of answering the much-changed questions of educational achievement. In place of ranks, we will want to establish a developmentally ordered series of accomplishments. First . . . we are opening up the possibility of multiple paths to excellence. . . . Second, if we indeed value clinical judgment and a diversity of opinions among appraisers (such as certainly occurs in professional settings and post secondary education), we will have to revise our notions of high-agreement reliability as a cardinal symptom of a useful and viable approach to scoring student performance. . . . Third, we will have to break step with the drive to arrive

at a single, summary statistic for student performance. . . . After all, it is critical to know that a student can arrive at an idea but cannot organize her or his writing or cannot use the resources of language in any but the most conventional and boring ways. . . . Finally, we have to consider different units of analysis . . . because so much of learning occurs either in social situations or in conjunction with tools or resources, we need to consider what performance looks like in those more complex units. (pp. 63-64)

Although a single statement could not be expected to outline all possible needs, the list provided here is challenging and instructive. Much of this agenda could be accomplished now, with the measurement tools already available. For example, the second call—for the "valuing of diversity of opinions among appraisers"—could be incorporated through the use of rater facets in the observations model (see Figure 4-4, above). And the third call—for something beyond "a single, summary statistic for student performance"—could be addressed using multidimensional item response models or, more broadly, the range of multiattribute models (as in Figure 4-7, above). Other parts of this agenda are less easily satisfied. Below we discuss some ways in which statistical approaches have been augmented to address the types of issues raised in the Wolf et al. agenda.

Progress Maps: Making Numbers More Interpretable

Wolf et al. call for a "developmentally ordered series of accomplishments" which could be regarded as a prompt to apply an ordered latent class approach; indeed, some see this as the only possible interpretation. Yet while there have been explications of that approach, this has not been a common usage. What has been attempted more frequently is enhancement of the continuous approaches to incorporate a developmental perspective. This approach, dubbed *developmental assessment* by Masters, Adams, and Wilson (1990), is based on the seminal work of Wright using the Rasch model and its extensions (Wright and Masters, 1982). In this approach, an attempt is made to construct a framework for describing and monitoring progress that is larger and more important than any particular test or method of collecting evidence of student achievement. A simple analogy is the scale for measuring weight. This scale, marked out in ounces and pounds, is a framework that is more important and "true" than any particular measuring instrument. Different instruments (e.g., bathroom scales, kitchen scales) can be constructed and used to measure weight against this more general reporting framework. This is done by developing a "criterion-referenced" interpretation of the scale (Glaser, 1963).

Under the "norm-referenced" testing tradition, each test instrument has a special importance. Students' performances are interpreted in terms of the performances of other students on that same test.[6] In developmental assessment, the theory of developing knowledge, skills, and understandings is of central importance. The particular instruments (approaches to assembling evidence) are of transient and secondary importance, and serve only to provide information relative to that psychological scale or theory. The frameworks for describing and monitoring progress are often referred to as *progress maps* (see the above example in Figure 4-6), and go by many other names including *progress variables, developmental continua, progressions of developing competence,* and *profile strands.* What these frameworks have in common is an attempt to capture in words and examples what it means to make progress or to improve in an area of learning.

An important feature of a developmental framework is that it provides a substantive basis for monitoring student progress over time. It also provides teachers, parents, and administrators with a shared understanding of the nature of development across the years of school and a basis for monitoring individual progress from year to year. A further advantage of a developmental framework or progress map is that it provides a frame of reference for setting standards of performance (i.e., desired or expected levels of achievement). An example of how results may be reported for an individual student at the classroom level, taken from the First Steps Developmental Continuum (West Australian Ministry of Education, 1991), is presented in Box 4-3.

Note that while the example in Box 4-3 illustrates change over time, no formal measurement model of growth was involved in the estimation, only a model of status repeated several times. These broad levels of development are based on the estimated locations of items on an item response scale. An example in the area of arithmetic, from the Keymath Diagnostic Arithmetic Test (Connolly, Nachtman, and Pritchett, 1972), is shown in Box 4-4. An example of the use of progress maps at the national level is given in Box 4-5. This map is an example of using information available beyond the formal statistical model to make the results more useful and interpretable. In contexts where interpretation of results is relatively more important than formal statistical tests of parameters, this sort of approach may be very useful.

Enhancement Through Diagnostics

Another fairly common type of enhancement in educational applications is the incorporation of diagnostic indices into measurement models to add richer interpretations. For example, as noted above, the call for something beyond "a single, summary statistic for student performance" could be addressed using multidimensional IRMs; this assumes, however, that the

---

[6]See Chapter 5 for discussion of norm-referenced vs. criterion-referenced testing.

BOX 4-3   Reporting Individual Achievement in Spelling

Pictured below is a developmental continuum that has been constructed as a map for monitoring children's developing competence in spelling. Five broad levels of spelling development, labeled "Preliminary Spelling" to "Independent Spelling" are shown. On the left of the figure, one child's estimated levels of spelling attainment on four occasions are shown. Each estimate has been dated to show the child's progress as a speller over time.

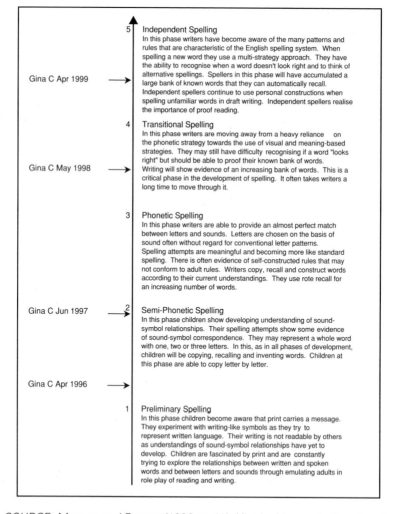

SOURCE: Masters and Forster (1996, p. 41). Used with permission of authors.

THE NATIONAL ACADEMIES PRESS

Publisher for The National Academies

National Academy of Sciences • National Academy of Engineering • Institute of Medicine • National Research Council

Visit our web site at **www.nap.edu**

THE NATIONAL ACADEMIES
Advisers to the Nation on Science, Engineering, and Medicine

Use the form on the reverse of this card to order additional copies, or order online and receive a 10% discount.

(Customers in North America Only)

and Design of Educational Assessment

PLEASE SEND ME:

Qty.	Code	Title	Price
	STKRNO	**Knowing What Students Know**	$39.95

Use this card to order additional copies of **Knowing What Students Know**.
All orders must be prepaid. Please add $4.50 for shipping and handling for
the first copy ordered and $0.95 for each additional copy. If you live in CA,
DC, FL, MD, MO, TX, CT, NY or Canada, add applicable sales tax or GST.
Prices apply only in the United States, Canada, and Mexico and are subject to
change without notice.

Subtotal
Shipping
Tax
Total

__ I am enclosing a U.S. check or money order.

__ Please charge my VISA/MasterCard/American Express account.

Number: _____

Expiration date: _____

Signature: _____

Please print.

Name _____

Address _____

City _____ State _____ Zip Code _____

FOUR EASY WAYS TO ORDER

- **Electronically:** Order from our secure website at: www.nap.edu
- **By phone:** Call toll-free 1-888-624-8422 or (202) 334-3313 or call your favorite bookstore.
- **By fax:** Copy the order card and fax to (202) 334-2451.
- **By mail:** Return this card with your payment to NATIONAL ACADEMIES PRESS, 500 Fifth St., NW, Lockbox 285, Washington, DC 20055.

Quantity Discounts: 5-24 copies, 15%; 25-499 copies, 25%. To be eligible for a discount, all copies must be shipped and billed to one address.

All international customers please contact National Academies Press for export prices and ordering information.

7272

BOX 4-4 **Keymath Diagnostic Arithmetic Test**

Here the range for successive grades is shown on the left side of the figure. Shown on the right are arithmetic tasks that are typically learned during that year. That is, tasks in each band are examples of tasks that the average student in that grade probably could *not* complete correctly at the beginning of the year, but probably could do by the end of the year.

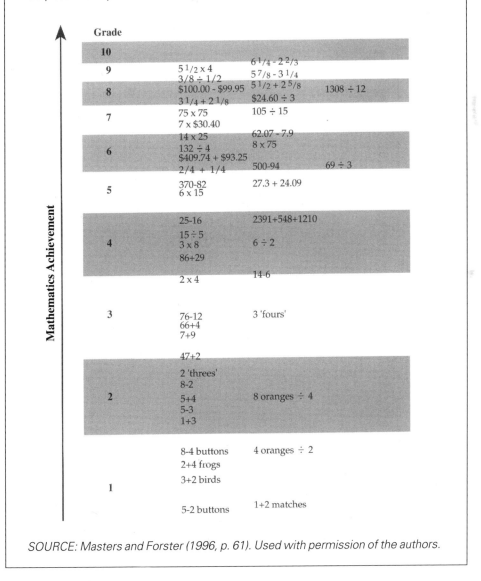

SOURCE: Masters and Forster (1996, p. 61). Used with permission of the authors.

BOX 4-5   Map of Writing Achievement at the National Level

The figures below illustrate the use of progress maps to depict changes in development over time, applied in this case to writing achievement at the national level. In the right panel, one can see broad bands in the spell-

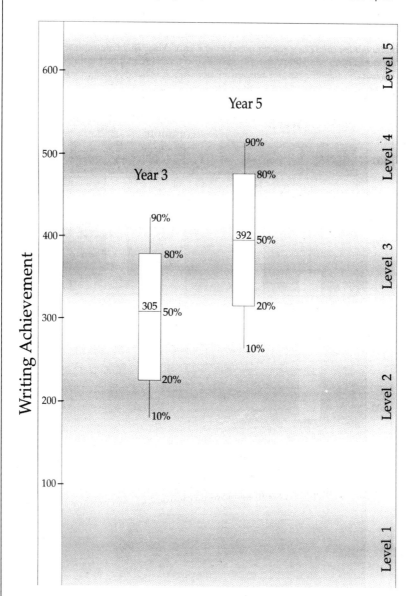

ing portion of the writing achievement continuum. In the left panel are "box and whisker" plots representing student achievement as found in a national survey of Australian school students.

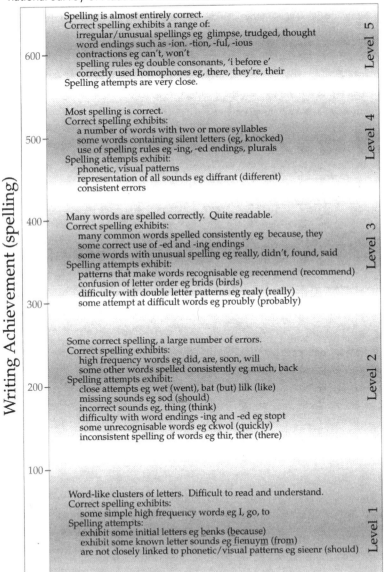

Writing Achievement (spelling)

Level 5 (≈600)
Spelling is almost entirely correct.
Correct spelling exhibits a range of:
    irregular/unusual spellings eg glimpse, trudged, thought
    word endings such as -ion. -tion, -ful, -ious
    contractions eg can't, won't
    spelling rules eg double consonants, 'i before e'
    correctly used homophones eg, there, they're, their
Spelling attempts are very close.

Level 4 (≈500)
Most spelling is correct.
Correct spelling exhibits:
    a number of words with two or more syllables
    some words containing silent letters (eg, knocked)
    use of spelling rules eg -ing, -ed endings, plurals
Spelling attempts exhibit:
    phonetic, visual patterns
    representation of all sounds eg diffrant (different)
    consistent errors

Level 3 (≈400–300)
Many words are spelled correctly. Quite readable.
Correct spelling exhibits:
    many common words spelled consistently eg because, they
    some correct use of -ed and -ing endings
    some words with unusual spelling eg really, didn't, found, said
Spelling attempts exhibit:
    patterns that make words recognisable eg recenmend (recommend)
    confusion of letter order eg brids (birds)
    difficulty with double letter patterns eg realy (really)
    some attempt at difficult words eg proubly (probably)

Level 2 (≈200)
Some correct spelling, a large number of errors.
Correct spelling exhibits:
    high frequency words eg did, are, soon, will
    some other words spelled consistently eg much, back
Spelling attempts exhibit:
    close attempts eg wet (went), bat (but), lilk (like)
    missing sounds eg sod (should)
    incorrect sounds eg, thing (think)
    difficulty with word endings -ing and -ed eg stopt
    some unrecognisable words eg ckwol (quickly)
    inconsistent spelling of words eg thir, ther (there)

(100)

Level 1
Word-like clusters of letters. Difficult to read and understand.
Correct spelling exhibits:
    some simple high frequency words eg I, go, to
Spelling attempts:
    exhibit some initial letters eg benks (because)
    exhibit some known letter sounds eg fienuym (from)
    are not closely linked to phonetic/visual patterns eg sieenr (should)

(continued)

BOX 4-5 **Continued**

The line in the middle of the box is the mean; the top and bottom of the boxes show the 80th and 20th percentiles, respectively; and the ends of the "whiskers" show the 90th and 10th percentiles. The left panel alone allows the usual interpretations—e.g., grade 5 achievement is above that of grade 3, with the average grade 5 student being at about the same level as the 80th percentile of grade 3 students, but considerably below the level of the 80th percentile of grade 5 students. Looking at the right panel, one can interpret these results in a criterion-referenced way in the context of spelling. For example, one can see the difference between those in the 80th percentile of the grade 3 students and their equivalent among the grade 5 students. While these excellent grade 3 students are spelling many words correctly and their writing is quite readable (e.g., they are spelling many common words correctly), the excellent grade 5 students are spelling most words correctly (e.g., they are spelling correctly a number of words with two or more syllables and words containing silent letters). One can thus obtain a richer educational interpretation of the results of the national survey, an interpretation that can be consistent with an in-classroom one.

SOURCE: Management Committee for the National School English Literacy Survey (1997, p. 84). Used with permission of the Commonwealth of Australia Department of Employment, Education, Training, and Youth Affairs.

complexities are well modeled by an extra dimension, which may not be the case. A number of tools have been developed to examine the ways in which the models do not fit the data; these tools are generally used to relate these discrepancies to features of the test content. For example, within the Rasch approach to continuous IRM, a technique has been developed for interpreting discrepancies in the prediction of individual student responses to individual items. (These types of diagnostics can also be constructed for items with most IRM software packages.) This technique, called KIDMAP (Mead, 1976), presents a graphical display of a student's actual responses, along with a graphical indication of what the expected responses would be under the estimated model. This is a kind of residual analysis, where the residual is the difference between expected and observed. The task is then to generate a substantive interpretation of the resulting patterns. Box 4-6 illustrates some results from a test of "number" items, using output from the Quest program

(Adams and Khoo, 1992). A different format for displaying these diagnostic data is shown in Box 4-7, which presents an example constructed by the GradeMap software (Wilson, Draney, and Kennedy, 2001) for the IEY curriculum.

These fit investigation techniques can be applied broadly across many contexts. When one has substantive theoretical underpinnings based on cognitive analysis, one can probe in greater detail. An example is the *rule-space* representation of Tatsuoka (1990, 1995). The first component of this representation is an analysis of correct and incorrect rules, or attributes, underlying student performance on a set of items. These rules arise from cognitive theory and an examination of the way people solve the problems presented in the items. The second is a measure of the fit of each student's pattern of right and wrong answers to a unidimensional IRM, sometimes called a "caution index" in this literature; the closer to zero is the caution index, the better is the fit of the student's response pattern to the IRM.

Each student is thus assigned an ability value and a caution index value. All student pairs of ability and caution indices are plotted as in the schematic. The ability-by-caution index plot is called a "rule-space plot"; it is a way of examining residuals for the IRM. Usually the students cluster in some way in rule space (in Figure 4-13, five clusters can be seen). Roughly speaking, one now examines the response patterns for the students in each cluster to see what combination of correct and incorrect rules accounts for most of the answer patterns in each cluster. In Figure 4-13, all the clusters are already distinguished by their ability values, except the clusters labeled A and B. The IRM assigns a subset of the cluster B proficiencies to cluster A; the two clusters are initially distinguished only by their caution indices. It is also likely that a different combination of correct and incorrect rules explains the response patterns of students in the two clusters. The rule-space plot shows how answer pattern residuals from a unidimensional IRM can be used to seek patterns in the data that are more complex than the model itself accounts for.

Regardless of whether one finds these enhancements satisfying in a formal statistical modeling sense, there are three important points to be made about the use of such strategies. First, they provide a bridge from familiar to new and from simpler to more complex formulations; thus they may be needed to aid the comprehension of those not immersed in the details of measurement modeling. Second, they may provide an easier stance from which to prepare reports for consumers and others for whom statistical testing is not the primary purpose of assessment. Third, strategies such as these may always be necessary, given that the complex models of today are probably going to be the simple models of tomorrow.

BOX 4-6 A KIDMAP

Opposite is an example of a KIDMAP. The symbol "XXX" shows the location of a student named Kim on the item map. Items the student answered correctly are represented by the items in the left-hand panel (with the locations indicating their relative difficulty). Items the student answered incorrectly are indicated in the same way in the right-hand panel. Under the standard IRM convention for representing item and student location, the probability of success is 0.50 for items located at exactly the same point as the student; the probability increases as the item drops below the student and decreases as it rises above. Thus, we would expect items located below the student (i.e., near the "XXX") to be ones the student would be more likely to get right; we would expect items located above the student to be ones the student would be more likely to get wrong; and we would not be surprised to see items located near the student to be gotten either right or wrong.

The exact delineation of "near" is somewhat arbitrary, and the Quest authors have chosen a particular value that we will not question here. What they have done is divide the map into three regions: above, near, and below the student (indicated by the dotted lines in the figure). Items on the left-hand side below the dotted line should not be surprising (i.e., they are relatively easy for Kim), nor should items above the dotted line on the right-hand side (i.e., they are relatively difficult for Kim). But the items in the top left and bottom right quadrants are ones for which Kim has given surprising responses; she has responded to the relatively difficult item 37 correctly and the relatively easy items 30 and 25 incorrectly. With more information about these items and about student Kim, we could proceed to a tentative interpretation of these results.

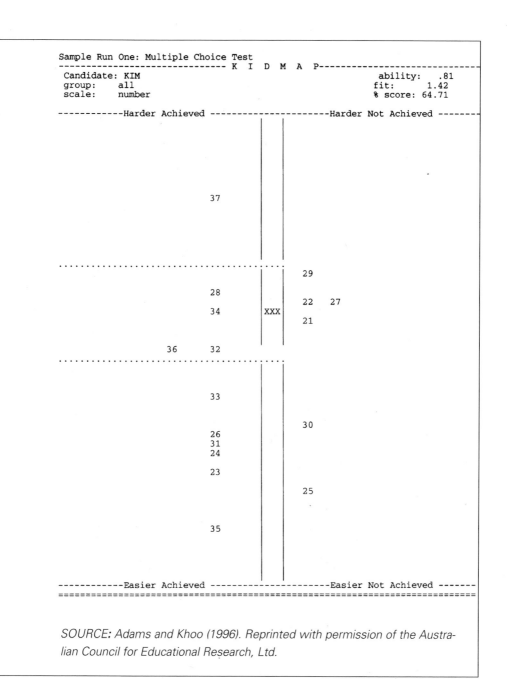

SOURCE: Adams and Khoo (1996). Reprinted with permission of the Australian Council for Educational Research, Ltd.

BOX 4-7 **Diagnostic Results: An Example of a Target Performance Map for the IEY Curriculum**

The figure below shows a target performance map for the IEY curriculum. In this figure, the expected performance on each item is shown by the gray band through the middle of the figure. The actual responses for each item are shown by the height of the darker gray shading in each of the columns (representing individual items). In much the same way as discussed earlier (see Box 4-6), this graphical display can be used to examine patterns of expected and unexpected responses for individual diagnosis.

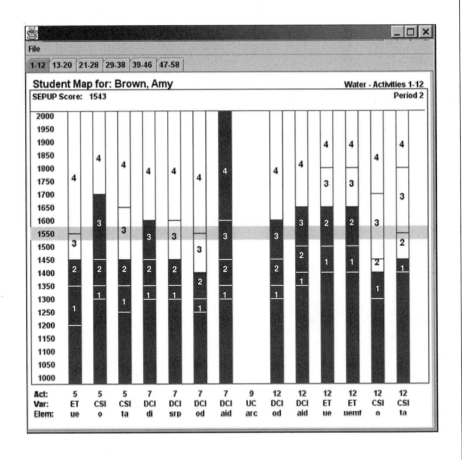

SOURCE: Wilson, Draney, and Kennedy (2001, p. 137). Used with permission of the author.

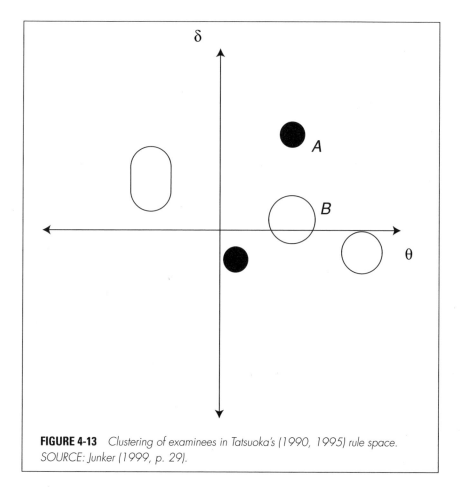

FIGURE 4-13   *Clustering of examinees in Tatsuoka's (1990, 1995) rule space.*
SOURCE: Junker (1999, p. 29).

ADDING COGNITIVE STRUCTURE TO MEASUREMENT MODELS

The preferred statistical strategy for incorporating substantive structure into measurement models is to make the measurement model more complex by adding new parameters. An example was provided in the earlier discussion of generalizability theory (see Figure 4-4), where parameters representing raters and item types were used to explain some of the parameters in the existing model (in Figure 4-5, the item difficulties). This allows formal statistical testing of effects; thus the question of whether the raters are "fair" corresponds to testing whether the effect of raters is statistically significant.

The methods described below for incorporating cognitive structural elements as parameters in standard psychometric models are but a sampling of what is at present a fairly small population of such studies. It may be hoped that further development of the current approaches and diversification of the available models will take place so that measurement models can better serve assessment.

Addition of New Parameters

A straightforward example of adding parameters to common psychometric models for substantive interpretations is the use of *differential item functioning* (DIF) methods. DIF methods have been used in examining differential response patterns for gender and ethnic groups for the last two decades and for language groups more recently. They are now being used for investigating whether different groups of examinees of approximately the same ability appear to be using differing cognitive processes to respond to test items. Such uses include examining whether differential difficulty levels are due to differential cognitive processes, language differences (Ercikan, 1998), solution strategies and instructional methods (Lane, Wang, and Magone, 1996), and skills required by the test that are not uniformly distributed across examinees (O'Neil and McPeek, 1993). Lane et al. (1996) used DIF analyses to detect differential response patterns and used analyses of differences in students' solution strategies, mathematical explanations, and mathematical errors to determine reasons for those patterns. Ercikan (1998) used DIF methods for detecting differential response patterns among language groups. The statistical detection was followed up with linguistic comparison of the test versions to determine reasons for the differential response patterns observed. DIF methods, which include Mantel-Haenzsel (Holland and Thayer, 1988), item response theory-based methods (Lord, 1980), and logistic regression (Swaminathan and Rogers, 1990), can also be used to test the validity of a measurement model. A finding of significant DIF can imply that the observation framework needs to be modified, or if the DIF is common to many items, that the underlying theory of learning is oversimplified.

Hierarchization

Returning to the Wolf et al. quotation given earlier, their initial call was for "a developmentally ordered series of accomplishments." A statistical approach to this would be to posit a measurement model consisting of a series of latent classes, each representing a specific type of tasks. Item sets would be considered to be samples from their respective latent class. Formalization of this approach would allow one to make statements about students, such as "whether the student actually possesses the 'compare fractions' skill" (Junker, 1999), by including items and an item class that represent that skill. Such a model looks like that in Figure 4-14, where "compare fractions"

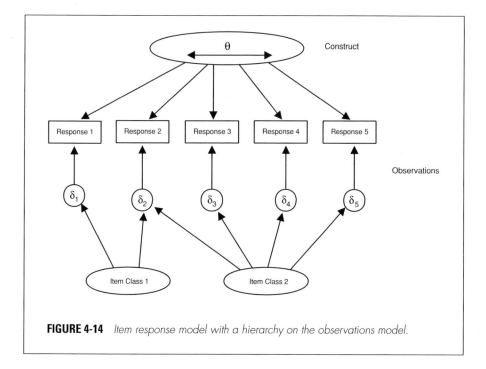

FIGURE 4-14 *Item response model with a hierarchy on the observations model.*

would be one of the item classes. Models of this sort, which one might term "hierarchical in the observations model," have been implemented by Janssen, Tuerlinckx, Meulders, and De Boeck (2000) in the context of criterion-referenced classes of achievement items. Implementing the suggestion of Wolf and colleagues would involve developmentally ordering the item classes, but that is not a major step from the model of Janssen et al.

One can also consider models that would be hierarchical on the student construct model such that the development of certain competencies would be considered to precede the development of other competencies. There are a number of ways to develop measurement models suitable for hierarchical contexts, depending on which of the several approaches outlined above—true score models, IRM, and latent class modeling—one is using. For example, *hierarchical factor analysis* has been used to postulate hierarchies of dimensions (i.e., dimensions that "cause" subdimensions). One could also postulate hierarchies of latent classes.

Figure 4-15 illustrates one variation on a class of models that is useful for thinking about the situation in which students' patterns of responses cannot be represented by a single dimension. The figure is labeled to suggest a progression of competencies into which a student population might be di-

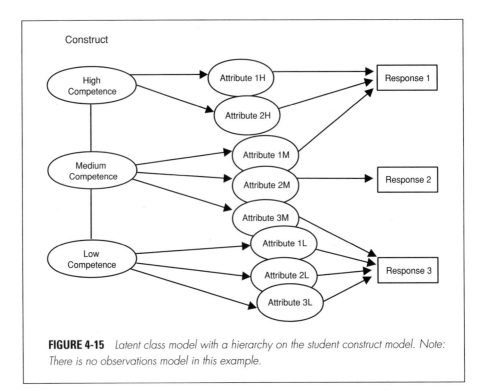

FIGURE 4-15 *Latent class model with a hierarchy on the student construct model. Note: There is no observations model in this example.*

vided or through which a single student might pass over time. In this model, a student can be in only one of three states of competence (low, medium, or high). Within a state of competence, the student has access only to the student attributes associated with that state and can apply only those attributes to each task. Thus a student in the "low competence" state would have only the tools to respond correctly to the third, easiest task; a student in the "medium competence" state would have the tools to respond correctly to all three tasks but would require a different attribute for each task; and a student in the "high competence" state could use a single attribute for all three tasks, but the first task has a twist that requires an extra attribute. Some states of competence might share attributes, but this would unnecessarily complicate the figure. The restricted latent class model of Haertel (1989) and Haertel and Wiley (1993) is similar in structure to this example. Clearly, the low/medium/high competence labels on the three knowledge states in Figure 4-15 could be replaced with labels that are merely descriptive and do not indicate ordering. Thus, the same figure could illustrate the modeling of multiple states of knowledge that simply represent different strategies for performing tasks in a particular domain.

Combining of Classes and Continua

The development of separate latent class and latent continuum approaches to psychometric modeling leads to distinct families of measurement models that can be given distinct substantive interpretations in assessment applications. Although this split in the psychometric families makes sense from a mathematical point of view, it does not fully reflect the more complex thinking of cognitive and developmental psychologists and educators. Consider, for example, the concept of Piagetian stages. Because the states are clearly intended to be ordered classes, it makes sense to model them with latent transition analysis. Yet it is easy to conceive of milestones within a given stage and to construct items of (meaningfully) varying difficulty that will identify differing levels of success *within* Piagetian stages of child development (Wilson, 1989). This sort of thinking leads one to seek ways of combining the continuum and class models we have been describing. There are a number of different possible ways to do this. One of these—the *mixture model* approach—is described by Mislevy and Verhelst (1990). In this approach, students are considered to be members of one of a set of latent classes, but each latent class may be characterized by a latent continuum or some other latent structure (for an alternative formulation, see Yamamoto and Gitomer, 1993).

For example, Wilson's (1984, 1989) Saltus model was developed to address stage-like cognitive development. Each student is characterized by two variables, one quantitative and the other qualitative. The quantitative parameter indicates the *degree* of proficiency, while the qualitative parameter indicates the *nature* of proficiency and denotes group membership. The Saltus model uses a simple IRM (Rasch, 1960, 1980) technique for characterizing development within stages and posits a certain number of developmental stages among students. A student is assumed to be in exactly one group at the time of testing, though group membership cannot be directly observed. Problem situations are also classified into a certain number of classes that match the stages. The model estimates parameters that represent the amounts by which problem classes vary in terms of difficulty for different groups. These parameter estimates can capture how certain types of problem situations become much easier relative to others as people add to or reconceptualize their content knowledge. Or they can capture how some problem situations actually become more difficult as people progress from an earlier to a more advanced group because they previously answered correctly or incorrectly for the wrong reasons. Examples of this can be found in Siegler's developmental analysis of performance on the balance scale as students' strategy rules change (see Chapter 2).

Mislevy and Wilson (1996) demonstrated how to use a mixture model approach to estimate the parameters of this model. They used an example dataset that had also been analyzed with Tatsuoka's rule-space analysis (discussed earlier). Two skills involved in mixed-number subtraction are (1) finding a common denominator and (2) converting between mixed numbers and improper fractions. In this study, three types of items in mixed-number subtraction were identified: (1) those that required neither (item class 1) (e.g., $^6/_7 - ^6/_7$); (2) those that required just finding a common denominator (item class 2) (e.g., $^5/_3 - ^3/_4$); and (3) those that required converting to improper fractions and (maybe) finding a common denominator as well (item class 3) (e.g., $3 \, ^3/_8 - 2 \, ^5/_6$). The qualitative aspect of student development is signaled by first acquiring the common-denominator skill (i.e., moving from student stage 1 to 2) and then the converting skill (i.e., moving from student stage 2 to 3). Mislevy and Wilson (1996) showed that in analyzing these data, the Saltus model does a better job of capturing the relationships among the item sets than does a Rasch model.

GENERALIZED APPROACHES TO PSYCHOMETRIC MODELING OF COGNITIVE STRUCTURES

Great effort may be required to develop and apply measurement models with features specific to particular substantive assessment contexts. The process may involve not only mastery of mathematical and statistical modeling, but also comprehension of and creative involvement in the theories of learning involved. The different assessment contexts far outnumber the existing psychometric models, and probably will continue to do so for a long time. Hence one is drawn to the possibility of establishing families of models that can be applied more broadly. Several such models have been developed and, in varying degrees, implemented. Two examples are reviewed in the next section—the unified model and M²RCML.[7] A third example, referred to as Bayes nets, is then described.

Unified Model and M²RCML

The first instance to be described was developed specifically for the sort of case in which it can be assumed that students' performance on tasks can be categorized into distinct and qualitative latent classes. DiBello, Stout, and Roussos (1995) cite four reasons why a measurement model may not adequately explain students' performance if it is based on analyses that describe tasks in terms of their component attributes (e.g., skills, bits of knowl-

---

[7]M²RCML stands for "Mixture Multidimensional Random Coefficients Multinomial Logit."

edge, beliefs). The first two reasons may be interpreted at least partially in terms of validity issues: first, students may choose a different strategy for performance in the task domain than that presumed by the task analysis; second, the task analysis may be incomplete in that it does not uncover all of the attributes required for task performance or does not incorporate all of them into the model. These are threats to construct validity to the extent that they indicate areas in which the measurement model may not map well to the underlying set of beliefs about cognition and learning in the domain.

The second two reasons may be interpreted at least partially in terms of reliability. DiBello et al. (1995) say a task has low "positivity" for a student attribute if there is either (1) a high probability that a student who possesses the attribute can fail to perform correctly when it is called for (we call this a "slip probability") or (2) a high probability that a student who lacks the attribute can still perform correctly when it is called for (we call this a "guessing probability"). Of course, this latter scenario may not be a guess at all: it may result from the student's applying an alternative strategy or a less general version of the attribute that works in the present case. Similarly, the first scenario may not be due to a "slip" but to poor question wording, transcription errors, and the like. Other deviations from the task analysis model that lead to incorrect task performance are grouped under a separate category of slips that includes such problems as transcription errors and lapses in student attention.

DiBello, Stout, and colleagues (DiBello, Stout, and Roussos, 1995; DiBello, Jiang, and Stout, 1999) have developed a multistrategy model they call the *unified model*, within which one can manipulate positivity, completeness, multiple strategies, and slips by turning on and shutting off various parts of the model. The components of the unified model can be adjusted to include a catchall strategy that is basically an IRM (for more detail, see Junker, 1999).

A second generalized scheme has been developed by Pirolli and Wilson (1998). This approach integrates the facets and multiattribute continuum models described earlier (e.g., as in Figures 4-4 and 4-6) with the Saltus model (also described above). Pirolli and Wilson developed an approach to measuring knowledge content, knowledge access, and knowledge learning. This approach has two elements. First it incorporates a theoretical view of cognition, called the Newell-Dennett framework, which the authors regard as being especially favorable to the development of a measurement approach. Second, it encompasses a class of measurement models, based on Rasch modeling, which the authors view as being particularly favorable to the development of cognitive theories. According to the model, in an observable situation, the knowledge a student has determines the actions he or she selects to achieve a desired goal. To the extent that models within the theory fit the data at hand, one considers measures of observed behavior to be manifestations of persons having specific classes of content knowledge and varying degrees of access to that knowledge. Although persons, environment, and knowledge are defined in terms of one another, successful application of this approach makes it possible to separate the parameters associated with the person from those associated with the environment.

In specifying their model, dubbed *M²RCML*, Pirolli and Wilson assume that access to knowledge within a particular knowledge state varies continuously, but perhaps multidimensionally. That is, within a particular knowledge-content state (latent class), a student may be represented by a vector of student constructs. For instance, a group of people who know a particular problem-solving strategy or a specific set of instructions may be arrayed along a continuous scale to represent their proficiency in accessing and using that knowledge. Pirolli and Wilson also assume that people can belong to different knowledge-content states, and that each state can be characterized by the probability of people being in it. Also, they suppose that the environment in which these variables operate can be represented by a vector of environment parameters (traditionally termed "item parameters"). This approach makes an important distinction between knowledge-level and symbol-level learning (Dennett, 1988; Newell, 1982): the knowledge level is seen as being modeled by the knowledge states, and the symbol level by the IRM involving the proficiency continuum and the environment parameters. Pirolli and Wilson have illustrated their approach for data related to both learning on a LISP tutor and a rule assessment analysis of reasoning involving the balance scale as described in Chapter 2.

The generalized approaches of both the unified model and M²RCML have emerged from somewhat different branches of the psychometric tradition. Together they can be regarded as addressing almost all of the calls by Wolf and colleagues (1991, pp. 63-64) as cited earlier. The last call, however, poses a somewhat more demanding challenge: ". . . we have to consider different units of analysis . . . because so much of learning occurs either in social situations or in conjunction with tools or resources, we need to consider what performance looks like in those more complex units." This call raises issues that are effectively outside the range of both general approaches discussed thus far: there are issues of the basic unit of analysis (individual or group), and of the interconnection between the different levels of analysis and the observations (whether the observations are at the individual or group level). For complications of this order (and this is certainly not the only such issue), greater flexibility is needed, and that is one of the possibilities offered by the approach described in the next section.

Bayes Nets

A more general modeling approach that has proven useful in a wide range of applications is Bayesian inference networks, also called *Bayes nets* because of their gainful use of Bayes' theorem.[8] A probability model for an inferential problem consists of variables that characterize aspects of the problem and probability distributions that characterize the user's knowledge about these aspects of the problem at any given point in time. The user builds a network of such variables, along with the interrelated probability distributions that capture their substantively important interrelationships. Conditional independence relationships introduced earlier in this chapter play a key role, both conceptually and computationally. The basic idea of conditional independence in Bayes nets is that the important interrelationships among even a large number of variables can be expressed mainly in terms of relationships within relatively small, overlapping, subgroups of these variables.

Bayes nets are systems of variables and probability distributions that allow one to draw inferences within complex networks of independent variables. Examples of their use include calculating the probabilities of disease states given symptoms and predicting characteristics of the offspring of animals in light of the characteristics of their ancestors. Spurred by applications in such diverse areas as pedigree analysis, troubleshooting, and medical diagnosis, these systems have become an active topic in statistical research (see, e.g., Almond, 1995; Andersen, Jensen, Olesen, and Jensen, 1989; Pearl, 1988).

Two kinds of variables appear in a Bayes net for educational assessment: those which concern aspects of students' knowledge and skill (construct variables in the terminology of this chapter) and those which concern aspects of the things students say, do, or make (observations). The nature and grain size of the construct variables is determined jointly by a conception of knowledge in the domain and the purpose of the assessment (see Chapter 2). The nature of the observations is determined by an understanding of how students display the targeted knowledge, that is, what students say or do in various settings that provides clues about that knowledge. The interrelationships are determined partly by substantive theory (e.g., a student who does not deeply understand the control-of-variables strategy in science may apply it in a near-transfer setting but probably not in a far-transfer setting) and partly by empirical observation (e.g., near transfer is less likely to be observed for task 1 than task 2 at any level of understanding, simply because task 2 is more difficult to read).

---

[8]Bayes' theorem concerns the relationship between two variables, described famously in a posthumously published paper by the Reverend Thomas Bayes. It concerns how one should revise his or her beliefs about one variable when one obtains information about another variable to which it is related. Let X be a variable whose probability distribution $p(x \mid z)$ depends on the variable Z. Suppose also that prior to observing X, belief about Z can be expressed in terms of a probability distribution $p(z)$. Bayes' theorem says $p(z \mid x) = p(x \mid z)p(z)/p(x)$ where $p(x)$ is the expected value of $p(x \mid z)$ over all possible values of Z.

All of the psychometric models discussed in this chapter reflect exactly this kind of reasoning, and all of them can in fact be expressed as particular implementations of Bayes nets. The models described above each evolved in their own special niches, with researchers in each gaining experience, writing computer programs, and developing a catalog of exemplars. Issues of substance and theory have accumulated in each case. As statistical methodology continues to advance (see, e.g., Gelman, Carlin, Stern, and Rubin, 1995), the common perspective and general tools of Bayesian modeling may become a dominant approach to the technical aspects of modeling in assessment. Yet researchers will continue to draw on the knowledge gained from both theoretical explorations and practical applications based on models such as those described above and will use those models as building blocks in Bayes nets for more complex assessments. The applications of Bayes nets to assessment described below have this character, reflecting their heritage in a psychometric history even as they attack problems that lie beyond the span of standard models. After presenting the rationale for Bayes nets in assessment, we provide an example and offer some speculations on the role of Bayes nets in assessment in the coming years.

Bayes nets bring together insights about the structuring of complex arguments (Wigmore, 1937) and the machinery of probability to synthesize the information contained by various nuggets of evidence. The three elements of the assessment triangle lend themselves to being expressed in this kind of framework.

Example: Mixed-Number Subtraction

The form of the data in this example is familiar—right/wrong responses to open-ended mixed-number subtraction problems—but inferences are to be drawn in terms of a more complex student model suggested by cognitive analyses. The model aims to provide short-term instructional guidance for students and teachers. It is designed to investigate which of two strategies students apply to problems and whether they can carry out the procedures necessary to solve the problems using those strategies. While competence in domains such as this can be modeled at a much finer grain size (see, e.g., VanLehn's [1990] analysis of whole-number subtraction), the model in this example does incorporate how the difficulty of an item depends on the strategy a student employs. Rather than treating this interaction as error, as would be done under CTT or IRM, the model leverages this interaction as a source of evidence about a student's strategy usage.

The example is based on studies of middle school students conducted by Tatsuoka (1987, 1990). The students she studied characteristically solved mixed-number subtraction problems using one of two strategies:

- Method A—Convert mixed numbers to improper fractions; subtract; then reduce if necessary.
- Method B—Separate mixed numbers into whole-number and fractional parts; subtract as two subproblems, borrowing one from minuend whole number if necessary; then reduce if necessary.

The responses of 530 students to 15 items were analyzed. As shown in Table 4-2, each item was characterized according to which of seven skills or subprocedures were required to solve it with Method A and which were required to solve it with Method B. The student model in the full network we build up to consists of one variable that indicates which of the two strategies a student uses and a variable for each of the subprocedures called upon by one or both strategies. If the values of these variables were known for a given pupil, one would know which strategy he or she had used on problems in this domain and which of the skills he or she had brought to bear on items when using that strategy. These unobservable constructs are connected to the observable responses through the following logic. Ideally, a student using either method would answer correctly only those items requiring the specific subprocedures the student had at his or her disposal; the student would answer incorrectly those items requiring subprocedures he or she did not know, even though the item might be solvable using the method being employed (Falmagne, 1989; Haertel and Wiley, 1993; and Tatsuoka, 1990). However, students sometimes miss items even when they do know the required subprocedures (situations called false negatives), and sometimes they answer items correctly even when they do not know the requisite subprocedures by using other, possibly faulty, strategies (false positives). The connection between observations and student-model variables is thus considered in a probabilistic sense. That is, even given the student's knowledge, skills, and strategy preference and given the demands of an item under both of the strategies, we cannot say for sure whether the student will solve the problem correctly; the best we can do is model the probability that he or she will do so.

Bayes nets rely on conditional independence relationships. In this example, conditional independence means that students' levels of skill in procedure knowledge and strategy usage explain all the relationships among the observed item responses; that is, no other constructs are needed to explain the relationships. As always, we know this is not strictly true; it is an approximation of the far more complex thinking in which students actually engage when they work through these problems. The cognitive analyses Tatsuoka and colleagues carried out to ground this application were already far more subtle than this model. Rather, the model has a more utilitarian purpose. Using the results of the cognitive analyses, the objective for the statistical model was merely to approximate students' response patterns to

TABLE 4-2 Skill Requirements for Fraction Items

| | | | Skills Used* | | | | | | | |
| | | | If Method A Used | | | | If Method B Used | | | |
Item #	Text	1	2	5	6	7	2	3	4	5
4	$3\frac{1}{2}-2\frac{3}{2}=$	x			x			x	x	x
6	$\frac{6}{7}-\frac{4}{7}=$	x								
7	$3-2\frac{1}{5}=$	x		x	x		x	x	x	x
8	$\frac{3}{4}-\frac{3}{8}=$	x								
9	$3\frac{7}{8}-2=$	x	x	x	x	x			x	
10	$4\frac{4}{12}-2\frac{7}{12}=$	x	x		x			x	x	x
11	$4\frac{1}{3}-2\frac{4}{3}=$	x	x		x			x	x	x
12	$\frac{11}{8}-\frac{1}{8}=$	x	x					x		
14	$3\frac{4}{5}-3\frac{2}{5}=$	x				x				x
15	$2-\frac{1}{3}=$	x	x	x				x	x	x
16	$4\frac{5}{7}-1\frac{4}{7}=$	x	x		x				x	
17	$7\frac{3}{5}-\frac{4}{5}=$	x	x		x				x	x
18	$4\frac{1}{10}-2\frac{8}{10}=$	x	x		x	x	x	x	x	
19	$7-1\frac{4}{3}=$	x	x	x	x	x	x	x	x	x
20	$4\frac{1}{3}-1\frac{5}{3}=$	x		x		x	x	x	x	x

*Skills:
1. Basic fraction subtraction.
2. Simplify/reduce.
3. Separate whole number from fraction.
4. Borrow one from whole number to fraction.
5. Convert whole number to fraction.
6. Convert mixed number to fraction.
7. Column borrow in subtraction.

SOURCE: Mislevy (1996, p. 399). Reprinted by permission of the National Council on Measurement in Education and by permission of the author.

see which lessons in their curriculum on mixed-number subtraction would be useful for them to work on next.

Figure 4-16 depicts the structural relationships in an inference network for Method B only. That is, it is an appropriate network if we know with certainty that a student tackles items using Method B, but we do not yet know which of the required procedures he or she can carry out. Nodes represent variables—some student-model variables, the others item responses—and arrows represent dependence relationships. The probability distribution of all variables can be represented as the product distributions for the variables that are connected in the graph. The more one knows about the domain and the more thoughtfully one structures task situations, the more parsimonious these graphs become.[9] Five nodes represent basic subprocedures a student using Method B needs to solve various kinds of items, such as basic fraction subtraction or mixed-number skills. Conjunctive nodes, such as "skills 1 and 2," represent, for example, either having or not having *both* skill 1 and skill 2. Each subtraction item is the "child" of a node representing the minimal conjunction or combination of skills needed to solve that item with Method B. The relationship between such a node and an item incorporates false positive and false negative probabilities (that is, that some students will answer the question correctly without having the requisite skills, and some students will miss the question even though they do have the needed skills).

Cognitive theory inspired the *structure* of this network; the *numerical values* of conditional probability relationships were approximated using results from Tatsuoka's (1983) "rule space" analysis of the data, based only on students classified as method B users. Ways of estimating these conditional probabilities from data or combining empirical and judgmental sources of information about them are discussed by Spiegelhalter, Dawid, Lauritzen, and Cowell (1993).

Figure 4-17 depicts base rate probabilities of students possessing a certain skill and getting a certain item correct, or the prior knowledge one would have about a student known to use method B before observing any of the student's responses to the items. Figure 4-18 shows how one's beliefs about a particular student change after seeing that student answer correctly

---

[9]A *recursive representation* of the joint distribution of a set of random variables $x_1,\ldots,x_N$ takes the form

$$p(x_1,\ldots,x_n) = p(x_n|x_{n-1},\ldots,x_1)p(x_{n-1}|x_{n-2},\ldots,x_1)\cdots p(x_2|x_1)p(x_1) = \prod_{j=1}^{n} p(x_j|x_{j-1},\ldots,x_1).$$

A recursive representation can be written for any ordering of the variables, but one that exploits conditional independence relationships is useful because variables drop out of the conditioning lists. This is equivalent to omitting edges from the graph.

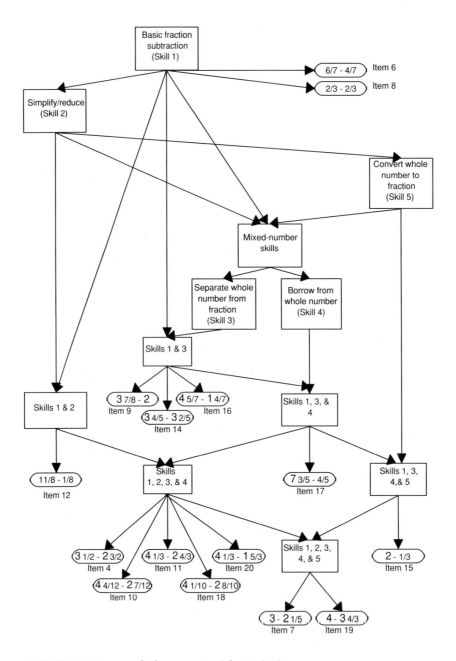

FIGURE 4-16 *Structure of inference network for Method B.*
SOURCE: Mislevy (1996, p. 400). *Reprinted by permission of the National Council on Measurement in Education and by permission of the author.*

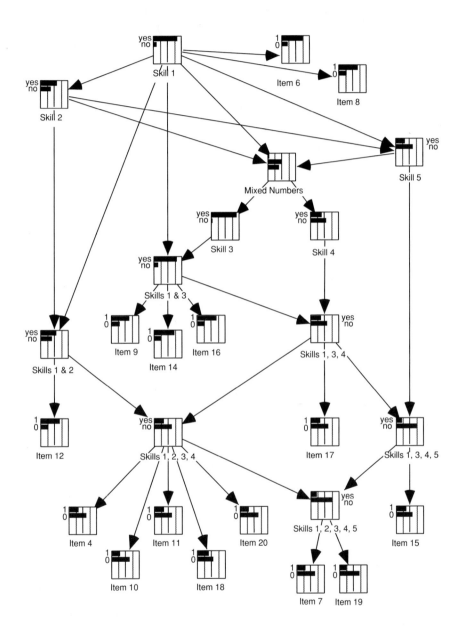

FIGURE 4-17 *Base rate probabilities for Method B. NOTE: Bars represent probabilities, summing to one for all possible values of a variable.*
SOURCE: Mislevy (1996, p. 402). Reprinted by permission of National Council on Measurement in Education and by permission of author.

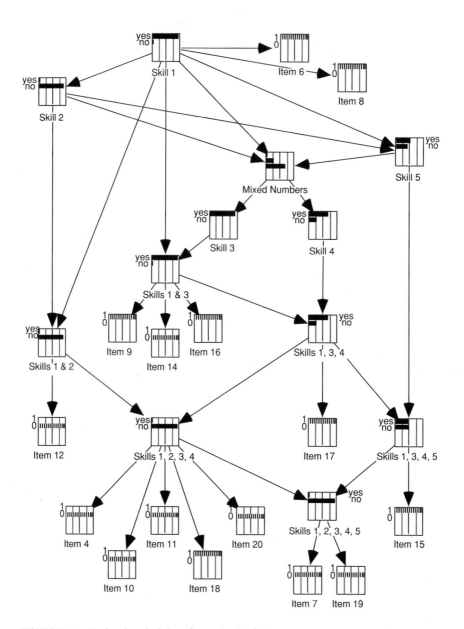

FIGURE 4-18 *Updated probabilities for Method B following item responses. NOTE: Bars represent probabilities, summing to one for all the possible values of a variable. A shaded bar extendign the full width of a node represents certainty, due to having observed the value of that variable; i.e., a student's actual responses to tasks.*
SOURCE: Mislevy (1996, p. 403). Reprinted by permission of National Council on Measurement in Education and by permission of author.

TABLE 4-3 Base Rate and Updated Probabilities of Subprocedure Profile

Skill(s)*	Prior Probability	Posterior Probability
1	.883	.999
2	.618	.056
3	.937	.995
4	.406	.702
5	.355	.561
1 & 2	.585	.056
1 & 3	.853	.994
1, 3, & 4	.392	.702
1, 2, 3, & 4	.335	.007
1, 3, 4, & 5	.223	.492
1, 2, 3, 4, & 5	.200	.003

*Skills:
1. Basic fraction subtraction.
2. Simplify/reduce.
3. Separate whole number from fraction.
4. Borrow one from whole number to fraction.
5. Convert whole number to fraction.
6. Convert mixed number to fraction.
7. Column borrow in subtraction.

SOURCE: Mislevy (1996, p. 404). Reprinted by permission of the National Council on Measurement in Education and by permission of the author.

most of the items that do not require skill 2 and answer incorrectly the items that do require skill 2. The updated probabilities for the five skills shown in Table 4-3 show substantial shifts away from the base rate toward the belief that the student commands skills 1, 3, 4, and possibly 5, but almost certainly not skill 2. This is shown graphically in the comparison between the initial base rate probabilities in Figure 4-17 and the probabilities updated in light of the student's responses in Figure 4-18.

A similar network was built for Method A, and then a network was built incorporating both it and the Method B network into a single model that is appropriate when one does not know which strategy a student is using. Each item now has three parents: minimally sufficient sets of procedures under Method A and Method B, plus a new node, "Is the student using Method A or Method B?" An item with mixed fractions and large numbers but no borrowing from the first whole number, such as $7^2/_3 - 5^1/_3$, is difficult under Method A but easy under Method B; an item with simple numbers that does require borrowing, such as $2^1/_3 - 1^2/_3$, is easy under Method A but difficult under Method B. A student who responds correctly to most of the first kind of items and incorrectly to most of the second kind is probably using Method B; a student who gets most of the first kind wrong but most of the second kind right is probably using Method A.

This example could be extended in many ways with regard to both the nature of the observations and the nature of the student model. With the present student model, one might explore additional sources of evidence about strategy use, such as monitoring response times, tracing solution steps, or simply asking the students to describe their solutions. Each such extension involves trade-offs in terms of cost and the value of the evidence, and each could be sensible in some applications but not others. An important extension of the student model would be to allow for strategy switching (Kyllonen, Lohman, and Snow, 1984). Although the students in Tatsuoka's application were not yet operating at this level, adults often decide whether to use Method A or Method B for a given item only after gauging which strategy would be easier to apply. The variables in the more complex student model needed to account for this behavior would express the tendencies of a student to employ different strategies under different conditions. Students would then be mixed cases in and of themselves, with "always use Method A" and "always use Method B" as extremes. Situations involving such mixes pose notoriously difficult statistical problems, and carrying out inference in the context of this more ambitious student model would certainly require the richer information mentioned above.

Some intelligent tutoring systems of the type described in Chapter 3 make use of Bayes nets, explicitly in the case of VanLehn's OLEA tutor (Martin and VanLehn, 1993, 1995) and implicitly in the case of John Anderson's LISP and algebra tutors (Corbett and Anderson, 1992). These applications highlight again the interplay among cognitive theory, statistical modeling, and assessment purpose. Another example of this type, the HYDRIVE intelligent tutoring system for aircraft hydraulics, is provided in Annex 4-1 at the end of this chapter.

Potential Future Role of Bayes Nets in Assessment

Two implications are clear from this brief overview of the use of Bayes nets in educational assessment. First, this approach provides a framework for tackling one of the most challenging issues now faced: how to reason about complex student competencies from complex data when the standard models from educational measurement are not sufficient. It does so in a way that incorporates the accumulated wisdom residing within existing models and practices while providing a principled basis for its extension. One can expect further developments in this area in the coming years as computational methods improve, examples on which to build accumulate, and efforts to apply different kinds of models to different kinds of assessments succeed and fail.

Second, classroom teachers are not expected to build formal Bayes nets in their classrooms from scratch. This is so even though the intuitive, often subconscious, reasoning teachers carry out every day in their informal assessments and conversations with students share key principles with formal networks. Explicitly disentangling the complex evidentiary relationships that characterize the classroom simply is not necessary. Nevertheless, a greater understanding of how one would go about doing this should it be required would undoubtedly improve everyday reasoning about assessment by policy makers, the public at large, and teachers. One can predict with confidence that the most ambitious uses of Bayes nets in assessments would not require teachers to work with the nuts and bolts of statistical distributions, evidence models, and Lauritzen-Spiegelhalter updating. Aside from research uses, one way these technical elements come into play is by being built into instructional tools. The computer in a microwave oven is an analogy, and some existing intelligent tutoring systems are an example. Neither students learning to troubleshoot the F-15 hydraulics nor their trainers know or care that a Bayes net helps parse their actions and trigger suggestions (see the HYDRIVE example presented in Annex 4-1). The difficult work is embodied in the device. More open systems than these will allow teachers or instructional designers to build tasks around recurring relationships between students' understandings and their problem solving in a domain, and to link these tasks to programs that handle the technical details of probability-based reasoning.

The most important lesson learned thus far, however, is the need for coordination across specialties in the design of complex assessments. An assessment that simultaneously pushes the frontiers of psychology, technology, statistics, and a substantive domain cannot succeed unless all of these areas are incorporated into a coherent design from the outset. If one tries to develop an ambitious student model, create a complex simulation environment, and write challenging task scenarios—all before working through the relationships among the elements of the assessment triangle needed to make sense of the data—one will surely fail. The familiar practice of writing test items and handing them off to psychometricians to model the results cannot be sustained in complex assessments.

MODELING OF STRATEGY CHANGES[10]

In the preceding account, measurement models were discussed in order of increasing complexity with regard to how aspects of learning are mod-

---

[10]This section draws heavily on the commissioned paper by Brian Junker. For the paper, go to <http://www.stat.cmu.edu/~brian/nrc/cfa/>. [March 2, 2001].

eled. Alternatively, one could organize the discussion in accordance with specific ideas from cognitive psychology. For example, one highly salient concept for cognitive psychologists is *strategy*. This section examines how the models described above might be used to investigate this issue.

It is not difficult to believe that different students bring different problem-solving strategies to an assessment setting; sufficiently different curricular backgrounds provide a prima facie argument that this must happen. Moreover, comparative studies of experts and novices (e.g., Chi, Glaser, and Farr, 1988) and theories of expertise (e.g., Glaser, 1991) suggest that the strategies one uses to solve problems change as one's expertise grows. Kyllonen et al. (1984) show that strategies used by the same person also change from task to task, and evidence from research on intelligent tutoring systems suggests it is not unusual for students to change strategy within a task as well. Thus one can distinguish at least four cases for modeling of differential strategy use, listed in increasing order of difficulty for statistical modeling and analysis:

- Case 0—no modeling of strategies.
- Case 1—strategy changes from person to person.
- Case 2—strategy changes from task to task for individuals.
- Case 3—strategy changes within a task for individuals.

Which case is selected for a given application depends, as with all assessment modeling decisions, on trade-offs between capturing what students are actually doing and serving the purpose of the assessment. Consider, for example, the science assessment study of Baxter, Elder, and Glaser (1996), which examined how middle school students' attempts to learn what electrical components were inside "mystery boxes" revealed their understanding of electrical circuits. One might decide to conduct an assessment specifically to identify which attributes of high competence a particular student has, so that the missing attributes can be addressed without regard to what low-competence attributes the student possesses; this could be an instance of Case 0. On the other hand, if the goal were to identify the competency level of the student—low, medium, or high—and remediate accordingly, a more complete person-to-person model, as in Case 1, would be appropriate. In addition, if the difficulty of the task depended strongly on the strategy used, one might be forced to apply Case 1 or one of the other cases to obtain an assessment model that fit the data well, even if the only valuable target of inference were the high-competence state.

Many models for Case 1 (that is, modeling strategy changes among students, but assuming that strategy is constant across assessment tasks) are variations on the latent class model of Figure 4-8. For example, the Haertel/

Wiley latent class model, which defines latent classes in terms of the sets of attributes class members possess, maps directly onto Figure 4-8.

The Mislevy and Verhelst (1990) model used to account for strategy effects on item difficulty in IRM also models strategy use at the level of Case 1. This approach uses information about the difficulties of the tasks under different strategies to draw inferences about what strategy is being used. Wilson's Saltus model (Wilson, 1989; Mislevy and Wilson, 1996) is quite similar, positing specific interactions on the θ scale between items of a certain type and developmental stages of examinees. The M^2RCML model of Pirolli and Wilson (1998) allows not only for mixing of strategies that drive item difficulty (as in the Mislevy and Verhelst and the Saltus models), but also for mixing over combinations of student proficiency variables. All of these Case 1 approaches are likely to succeed if the theory for positing differences among task difficulties under different strategies produces some large differences in task difficulty across strategies.

Case 2, in which individual students change strategy from task to task, is more difficult. One example of a model intended to accommodate this case is the unified model of DiBello and colleagues (DiBello et al., 1995; DiBello, et al., 1999). In fact, one can build a version of the Mislevy and Verhelst model that does much the same thing; one simply builds the latent class model within task instead of among tasks. It is not difficult to build the full model or to formulate estimating equations for it. However, it is very difficult to fit, because wrong/right or even polytomously scored responses do not contain much information about the choice of strategy.

To make progress with Case 2, one must collect more data. Helpful additions include building response latency into computerized tests; requesting information about the performance of subtasks within a task (if informative about the strategy); asking students to answer strategy-related auxiliary questions, as did Baxter, Elder, and Glaser (1996); asking students to explain the reasoning behind their answers; or even asking them directly what strategy they are using. In the best case, gathering this kind of information reduces the assessment modeling problem to the case in which each student's strategy is known with certainty.

Case 3, in which the student changes strategy within task, cannot be modeled successfully without rich within-task data. Some intelligent tutoring systems try to do this under the rubric of "model tracing" or "plan recognition." The tutors of Anderson and colleagues (e.g., Anderson, Corbett, Koedinger, and Pelletier, 1995) generally do so by keeping students close to a modal solution path, but they have also experimented with asking students directly what strategy they are pursuing in ambiguous cases. Others keep track of other environmental variables to help reduce ambiguity about the choice of strategy within performance of a particular task (e.g., Hill and Johnson, 1995). Bayesian networks are commonly used for this purpose.

The Andes tutor of mechanics problems in physics (e.g., Gertner, Conati, and VanLehn, 1998) employs a Bayesian network to do model tracing. The student attributes are production rules, the observed responses are problem-solving actions, and strategy-use variables mediate the relationships between attributes and responses. Various approaches have been proposed for controlling the potentially very large number of states as the number of possible strategies grows. Charniak and Goldman (1993), for example, build a network sequentially, adding notes for new evidence with respect to plausible plans along the way.

CONCLUSIONS

Advances in methods of educational measurement include the development of formal measurement (psychometric) models, which represent a particular form of reasoning from evidence. These models provide explicit, formal rules for integrating the many pieces of information that may be relevant to specific inferences drawn from observation of assessment tasks. *Certain kinds of assessment applications require the capabilities of formal statistical models for the interpretation element of the assessment triangle.* These tend to be applications with one or more of the following features: high stakes, distant users (i.e., assessment interpreters without day-to-day interaction with the students), complex student models, and large volumes of data.

Measurement models currently available can support many of the kinds of inferences that cognitive science suggests are important to pursue. In particular, it is now possible to characterize students in terms of multiple aspects of proficiency, rather than a single score; chart students' progress over time, instead of simply measuring performance at a particular point in time; deal with multiple paths or alternative methods of valued performance; model, monitor, and improve judgments on the basis of informed evaluations; and model performance not only at the level of students, but also at the levels of groups, classes, schools, and states.

Nonetheless, *many of the newer models and methods are not widely used because they are not easily understood or packaged in accessible ways for those without a strong technical background.* Technology offers the possibility of addressing this shortcoming. For instance, building statistical models into technology-based learning environments for use in their classrooms enables teachers to employ more complex tasks, capture and replay students' performances, share exemplars of competent performance, and in the process gain critical information about student competence.

Much hard work remains to focus psychometric model building on the critical features of models of cognition and learning and on observations that reveal meaningful cognitive processes in a particular domain. If anything, the task has become more difficult because an additional step is now required—determining in tandem the inferences that must be drawn, the observations needed, the tasks that will provide them, and the statistical models that will express the necessary patterns most efficiently. Therefore, *having a broad array of models available does not mean that the measurement model problem has been solved.* The long-standing tradition of leaving scientists, educators, task designers, and psychometricians each to their own realms represents perhaps the most serious barrier to progress.

ANNEX 4-1: AN APPLICATION OF BAYES NETS IN AN INTELLIGENT TUTORING SYSTEM

As described in Chapter 3, intelligent tutoring systems depend on some form of student modeling to guide tutor behavior. Inferences about what a student does and does not know affect the presentation and pacing of problems, the quality of feedback and instruction, and the determination of when a student has achieved tutorial objectives. The following example involves the HYDRIVE intelligent tutoring system, which, in the course of implementing principles of cognitive diagnosis, adapts concepts and tools of test theory to implement principles of probability-based reasoning (Mislevy and Gitomer, 1996).

HYDRIVE is an intelligent tutoring/assessment system designed to help trainees in aircraft mechanics develop troubleshooting skills for the F-15's hydraulics systems. These systems are involved in the operation of the flight controls, landing gear, canopy, jet fuel starter, and aerial refueling. HYDRIVE simulates many of the important cognitive and contextual features of troubleshooting on the flightline. A problem begins with a video sequence in which a pilot who is about to take off or has just landed describes some aircraft malfunction to the hydraulics technician (for example, the rudders do not move during preflight checks). HYDRIVE's interface allows the student to perform troubleshooting procedures by accessing video images of aircraft components and acting on those components; to review on-line technical support materials, including hierarchically organized schematic diagrams; and to make instructional selections at any time during troubleshooting, in addition to or in place of the instruction recommended by the system itself. HYDRIVE's system model tracks the state of the aircraft system, including changes brought about by user actions.

Annex Figure 4-1 is a simplified version of portions of the Bayes net that supports inference in HYDRIVE. Four groups of variables can be distinguished (the last three of which comprise the student model). First, the rightmost nodes are the "observable variables"—actually the results of rule-driven analyses of a student's actions in a given situation. Second, their immediate parents are knowledge and strategy requirements for two proto-

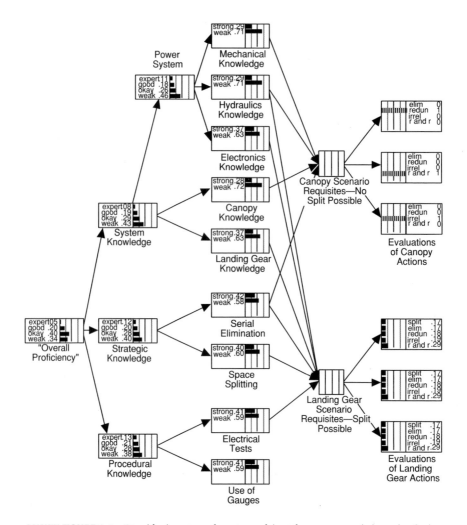

ANNEX FIGURE 4-1 *Simplified version of portions of the inference network through which the HYDRIVE student model is operationalized and updated. NOTE: Bars represent probabilities, summing to one for all the possible values of a variable. A shaded bar extending the full width of a node represents certainty, due to having observed the value of that variable; i.e., a student's actual responses to tasks.*
SOURCE: Mislevy (1996, p. 407). Used with permission of the author.

typical situations addressed in this simplified diagram; the potential values of these variables are combinations of system knowledge and troubleshooting strategies that are relevant in these situations. Third, the long column of variables in the middle concerns aspects of subsystem and strategic knowledge, corresponding to instructional options. And fourth, to their left are summary characterizations of more generally construed proficiencies. The structure of the network, the variables that capture the progression from novice to expert hydraulics troubleshooter, and the conditional probabilities implemented in the network are based on two primary sources of information: in-depth analyses of how experts and novices verbalize their problem-solving actions and observations of trainees actually working through the problems in the HYDRIVE context.

Strictly speaking, the observation variables in the HYDRIVE Bayes net are not observable behaviors, but outcomes of analyses that characterize sequences of actions as "serial elimination," "redundant action," "irrelevant action," "remove-and-replace," or "space-splitting"—all interpreted in light of the current state of the system and results of the student's previous actions. HYDRIVE employs a relatively small number of interpretation rules (about 25) to classify each troubleshooting action in these terms. The following is an example:

> IF active path which includes failure has **not** been created and the student creates an active path which does **not** include failure and edges removed from the active problem area are of one power class, THEN the student strategy is power path splitting.

Potential observable variables cannot be predetermined and uniquely defined in the manner of usual assessment items since a student could follow countless paths through the problem. Rather than attempting to model all possible system states and specific possible actions within them, HYDRIVE posits equivalence classes of system-situation states, each of which could arise many times or not at all in a given student's work. Members of these equivalence classes are treated as conditionally independent, given the status of the requisite skill and knowledge requirements. Two such classes are illustrated in Annex Figure 4-1: canopy situations, in which space-splitting[11]

---

[11]Space-splitting refers to a situation in which there is a chain of components that must all work for an event to happen (e.g., a car to start when the ignition key is turned), and a fault has occurred somewhere along that chain. The solution space includes the possibility that any components could have failed. Space-splitting means checking a point somewhere along the chain to see if things are working up to that point. If so, one can strip away the early portion of the solution space because all the components up to that point have worked; if not, one can strip away the latter part of the solution space and focus on the components up to that point.

is not possible, and landing gear situations, in which space-splitting is possible.

Annex Figure 4-1 depicts how one changes belief after observing the following actions in three separate situations from the canopy/no-split class: one redundant and one irrelevant action (both ineffectual troubleshooting moves) and one remove-and-replace action (serviceable but inefficient). Serial elimination would have been the best strategy in such cases, and is most likely to be applied when the student has strong knowledge of this strategy and all relevant subsystems. Remove-and-replace is more likely when a student possesses some subsystem knowledge but lacks familiarity with serial elimination. Weak subsystem knowledge increases chances of irrelevant and redundant actions. It is possible to get any of these classes of actions from a trainee with any combination of values of student-model variables; sometimes students with good understanding carry out redundant tests, for example, and sometimes students who lack understanding unwittingly take the same action an expert would. These possibilities must be reflected in the conditional probabilities of actions, given the values of student-model variables.

The grain size and the nature of a student model in an intelligent tutoring system should be compatible with the instructional options available (Kieras, 1988). The subsystem and strategy student-model variables in HYDRIVE summarize patterns in trouble shooting solutions at the level addressed by the intelligent tutoring system's instruction. As a result of the three aforementioned inexpert canopy actions, Annex Figure 4-1 shows belief shifted toward lower values for serial elimination and for all subsystem variables directly involved in the situation—mechanical, hydraulic, and canopy knowledge. Any or all of these variables could be a problem, since all are required for a high likelihood of expert action. Values for subsystem variables not directly involved in the situation are also lower because, to varying degrees, students familiar with one subsystem tend to be familiar with others, and, to a lesser extent, students familiar with subsystems tend to be familiar with troubleshooting strategies. These relationships are expressed by means of the more generalized system and strategy knowledge variables at the left of the figure. These variables take advantage of the indirect information about aspects of knowledge that a given problem does not address directly, and they summarize more broadly construed aspects of proficiency that are useful in evaluation and problem selection.

Part III

Assessment Design and Use: Principles, Practices, and Future Directions

INTRODUCTION

Part III sets forth the foundations for educational assessment in terms of contemporary scientific understanding of the nature of human cognition and methods of measurement. These two bodies of knowledge jointly provide a set of principles and methods for assessment design and use. As in any design activity, the scientific foundations provide direction and constrain the set of choices and possibilities, but they do not prescribe the exact nature of the design, nor do they preclude ingenuity to achieve a final product. Design is always a complex process that, while guided by theory and research, involves optimization under a series of practical constraints outside the realm of science. Thus the design is influenced in important ways by the purpose of the assessment (e.g., to assist learning, measure individual attainment, or evaluate a program), the context in which it will be used (classroom or large-scale), and practical constraints (e.g., resources and time). The following chapters explore issues of how the foundations play out in the design of real assessment situations. A variety of existing assessments are described to illustrate the points.

Chapter 5 presents features of a new approach to assessment design that capitalizes on the scientific advances described in Part II. Using the assessment triangle defined in Chapter 2 as a framework, we discuss various aspects of design—including identification of the targets for assessment, item and test design, validation, reporting, and fairness—always focusing on how a cognitive approach to design would differ from current approaches.

Chapter 6 broadens the discussion beyond assessment to explore the interactions of assessment with curriculum and instruction; how assessments could best be used to support learning, first in classroom contexts and second in large-scale contexts; and the need for systems of multiple assessments that would work together to help achieve a common set of learning goals.

Chapter 7 considers the role current and future information technologies could play in realizing the full potential of the new kinds of assessment the committee envisions. Technology is enabling the assessment of a wider array of performances and simultaneously changing the nature of learning environments and the potential targets of assessment. The opportunities as well as the challenges are considered.

Two kinds of suggestions are presented in these chapters. Some relate to how scientific developments in the foundational areas of cognition and measurement could improve assessment. Others involve changes that could be made to the educational system to accommodate effective use of these assessments. Many of the suggestions in this latter area are consistent with the scientific developments, but those developments themselves are not sufficient to determine how educational systems should function. Political and societal decisions come into play with regard to organizational changes, resource implications, and investment priorities, and the committee recognizes that these are issues on which knowledgeable people may disagree.

Five key features of a new approach to assessment design serve as the organizing themes for this chapter:

- A model of cognition and learning, or a description of how people represent knowledge and develop competence in a subject domain, is a cornerstone of the assessment development enterprise. Unfortunately, the model of learning is not made explicit in most assessment development efforts, is not empirically derived, and/or is impoverished relative to what it could be.

- To increase the chances of collecting evidence that supports the types of inferences one wants to draw, the design and selection of assessment tasks, along with the procedures for evaluating students' responses, should be guided jointly by the cognition and interpretation elements of the assessment triangle. An assessment should be more than a collection of tasks that work well individually. The utility of assessment information can be enhanced by considering how to design and/or select tasks so that the information derived from them can be combined to support the desired inferences.

- The process of construct validation during test design should rest, in part, on evidence that tasks actually tap the cognitive content and processes intended.

- Although reporting of results occurs at the end of an assessment cycle, assessments must be designed from the beginning to ensure that reporting of the desired types of information will be possible and effective. When results are reported, well-delineated descriptions of learning in the domain are key to their effectiveness for communicating about student performance.

- Fairness in testing is defined in many ways, but at its core is the idea of comparable validity: a fair assessment is one that yields comparably valid inferences from person to person and group to group. One way of thinking about fairness is to take into account individual learners' instructional histories when designing an assessment.

5

Implications of the New Foundations for Assessment Design

This chapter describes features of a new approach to assessment design that is based on a synthesis of the cognitive and measurement foundations set forth in Chapters 3 and 4. Ways in which the three elements of the assessment triangle defined in Chapter 2—cognition, observation, and inter-pretation—must work together are described and illustrated with examples. This chapter does not aim to describe the entire assessment design process. A number of existing documents, most notably *Standards for Educational and Psychological Testing* (American Educational Research Association [AERA], American Psychological Association, and National Council of Measurement in Education, 1999), present experts' consensus guidelines for test design. We have not attempted to repeat here all of the important guidance these sources provide, for instance, about standards for validity, reliability, and fairness in testing. Instead, this chapter focuses on ways in which assess-ment design and practice could be enhanced by forging stronger connec-tions between advances in the cognitive sciences and new approaches to measurement.

Three important caveats should be borne in mind when reading this chapter. First, the presentation of topics in this chapter corresponds to a general sequence of stages in the design process. Yet to be most effective, those stages must be executed recursively. That is, design decisions about late stages in the assessment process (e.g., reporting) will affect decisions about earlier stages (e.g., task design), causing assessment developers to revisit their choices and refine the design. All aspects of an assessment's design, from identifying the targets of inference to deciding how results will be reported, must be considered—all within the confines of practical con-straints—during the initial conceptualization.

Second, the design principles proposed in this chapter apply to assessments intended to serve a variety of purposes. The different ways in which the principles play out in specific contexts of use and under different sets of constraints are illustrated with a diverse set of examples. In other words, it should not be assumed that the principles proposed in this chapter pertain only to formal, large-scale assessment design. These principles also apply to informal forms of assessment in the classroom, such as when a teacher asks students oral questions or creates homework assignments. All assessments will be more fruitful when based on an understanding of cognition in the domain and on the precept of reasoning from evidence.

Finally, the features of assessment design described here represent an ideal case that is unlikely to be fully attained with any single assessment. The examples provided of actual assessments are approximations of this ideal. They illustrate how advances in the cognitive and measurement sciences have informed the development of many aspects of such an ideal design, and provide evidence that further efforts in this direction could enhance teaching and learning. In turn, these examples point to the limitations of current knowledge and technology and suggest the need for further research and development, addressed in Part IV.

THE IMPORTANCE OF A MODEL OF COGNITION AND LEARNING

Deciding what to assess is not as simple as it might appear. Existing guidelines for assessment design emphasize that the process should begin with a statement of the purpose for the assessment and a definition of the content domain to be measured (AERA et al., 1999; Millman and Greene, 1993). This report expands on current guidelines by emphasizing that the targets of inference should also be largely determined by a model of cognition and learning that describes how people represent knowledge and develop competence in the domain (the cognition element of the assessment triangle). Starting with a model of learning is one of the main features that distinguishes the committee's proposed approach to assessment design from current approaches. The model suggests the most important aspects of student achievement about which one would want to draw inferences and provides clues about the types of assessment tasks that will elicit evidence to support those inferences.

For example, if the purpose of an assessment is to provide teachers with a tool for determining the most appropriate next steps for arithmetic instruction, the assessment designer should turn to the research on children's development of number sense (see also Chapter 3). Case, Griffin, and colleagues have produced descriptions of how young children develop understanding in various mathematical areas (Case, 1996; Case, Griffin, and

Kelly, 1999; Griffin and Case, 1997). A summary of their cognitive theory for the development of whole-number sense is presented in Box 5-1. Drawing from their extensive research on how children develop mathematical understanding as well as the work of other cognitive development researchers—such as Gelman, Siegler, Fuson, and Piaget—Case, Griffin and colleagues have constructed a detailed theory of how children develop number sense. This theory describes the understandings that children typically exhibit at various stages of development, the ways they approach problems, and the processes they use to solve them. The theory also describes how children typically progress from the novice state of understanding to expertise.

Case, Griffin, and colleagues have used their model of cognition and learning to design mathematics readiness programs for economically disadvantaged young children. The model has enabled them to (1) specify what knowledge is most crucial for early success in mathematics, (2) assess where any given population stands with regard to this knowledge, and (3) provide children who do not have all this knowledge with the experience they need to construct it (Case et al., 1999). These researchers have implemented their Rightstart program in different communities in Canada and the United States and have consistently found that children in the experimental program perform significantly better on a variety of measures of number sense than those in control groups (Griffin and Case, 1997; Griffin, Case, and Sandieson, 1992; Griffin, Case, and Siegler, 1994). Later in this chapter we present an assessment they have developed to assess student understanding relative to this theory.

Features of the Model of Cognition and Learning

The model of learning that informs assessment design should have several key features. First, it should be based on empirical studies of learners in the domain. Developing a model of learning such as the example in Box 5-1 requires an intensive analysis of the targeted performances, using the types of scientific methods described in Chapter 3. The amount of work required should not be underestimated. Research on cognition and learning has produced a rich set of descriptions of domain-specific performance that can serve as the basis for assessment design, particularly for certain areas of mathematics and science (e.g., National Research Council [NRC], 2001; American Association for the Advancement of Science, 2001) (see also the discussion of domain-based models of learning and performance in Chapter 3). Yet much more research is needed. The literature contains analyses of children's thinking conducted by various types of professionals, including teachers, curriculum developers, and research psychologists, for a variety of purposes. Existing descriptions of thinking differ on a number of dimensions: some are highly detailed, whereas others are coarser-grained; some

BOX 5-1 Example of a Model of Cognition and Learning: How Children Come to Understand the Whole Number System

Below is a brief summary of the theory of Case, Griffin, and colleagues of how children gain understanding of the whole-number system, based on empirical study of learners. For a more detailed discussion see Case (1996) or Griffin and Case (1997).

1. *Initial counting and quantity schemas*. Four-year-olds generally possess a good deal of knowledge about quantity that permits them to answer questions about more and less (Starkey, 1992). Children by this age can also reliably count a set of objects and understand that the final number tag assigned to a set is the answer to the question, "How many objects are there in this group?" (Gelman, 1978). However, they appear to be incapable of integrating these competencies. Thus when asked, "Which is more—four or five?" they respond at chance level, even though they can successfully count to five and make relative quantity judgments about arrays containing five versus four objects.

2. *Mental counting line structure*. As children move from age 4 to 6, they gradually become capable of answering such questions, suggesting that these two earlier structures have merged into a "mental number line." Case and colleagues refer to the mental number line as an example of a *central conceptual structure* because of the pivotal role it assumes in children's subsequent scientific and mathematical thought. Children's knowledge representation is now such that forward and backward counting words are merged into a single set of entries that can be "read off" in either direction, whether or not a concrete set of objects is present. As children develop this unified conceptual structure, they come to realize through practice of ideas and other work that a question about addition or subtraction can be answered in the absence of any concrete set of objects, simply by counting forward or backward along the string of counting words. Also during this period,

focus on procedures, whereas others emphasize conceptual understanding; and some focus on individual aspects of learning, whereas others emphasize the social nature of learning. Differing theoretical descriptions of learning should not be viewed as competitive. Rather, aspects of existing theoretical descriptions can often be combined to create a more complete picture of student performance to better achieve the purposes of an assessment.

children begin to learn the system of notation that is used for representing numbers on paper, further serving to bind together the elements of the new cognitive structure.

3. *Double mental counting line structure.* Between the ages of 6 and 8, once children understand how mental counting works, they gradually form representations of multiple number lines, such as those for counting by 2s, 5s, 10s, and 100s. The construction of these representations gives new meaning to problems such as double-digit addition and subtraction, which can now be understood as involving component problems that require thinking in terms of different number lines. For instance, the relationship between the 10s column and the 1s in the base-10 number system becomes more apparent to them.

4. *Understanding of full system.* With further growth and practice, by about age 10 children gain a generalized understanding of the entire whole-number system and the base-10 system on which it rests. Addition or subtraction with regrouping, estimation problems using large numbers, and mental mathematics problems involving compensation all are grasped at a higher level as this understanding gradually takes shape.

Case and Griffin explain that although most children develop these competencies, there are always some who do not. This usually does not mean that they are incapable of achieving these understandings, but rather that there has not been a heavy emphasis on counting and quantity in their early environment. The researchers have designed educational interventions to help disadvantaged children develop these competencies because they are so important for later mathematical learning.

Second, the model of cognition and learning should identify performances that differentiate beginning and expert learners in the domain. The nature of subject matter expertise has been the focus of numerous studies in human cognition (see also Chapter 3). From this type of research it is known that experts have acquired extensive knowledge in their disciplines, and that this knowledge affects what they notice and how they organize, represent, and interpret information. The latter characteristics in turn affect their ability to remember, reason, and solve problems. Most useful for assessment design are descriptions of how characteristics of expertise are manifested in particular school subject domains. Studies of expert performance describe what the results of highly successful learning look like, suggesting targets for instruction and assessment.

It is not, however, the goal of education to make all school children experts in every subject area, and many would argue that "literacy" and "competency" are more appropriate goals. Ideally, then, a model of learning will also provide a developmental perspective, laying out one or more typical progressions from novice levels toward competence and then expertise, identifying milestones or landmark performances along the way. The model of learning might also describe the types of experiences that provoke change or learning. Models of learning for some content areas will depict children as starting out with little or no knowledge in the domain and through instruction gradually building a larger and larger knowledge base. An example is learning to represent large-scale space. Children's drawings provide a starting point for cartography, but they need to learn how to represent position and direction (e.g., coordinate systems) to create maps of spaces. In other domains, such as physics, students start with a good deal of naive or intuitive knowledge based on observations of the world around them. Some of this knowledge includes deeply entrenched misconceptions or concepts that must be disentangled through instruction. Given a developmental description of learning, assessments can be designed to identify current student thinking, likely antecedent understandings, and next steps to move the student toward more sophisticated understandings. Developmental models are also the starting point for designing assessment systems that can capture growth in competence.

There is no single way in which knowledge is represented by competent performers, and there is no single path to competence. But some paths are traveled more than others. When large samples of learners are studied, a few predominant patterns tend to emerge. For instance, as described in Box 5-2, the majority of students who have problems with subtraction demonstrate one or more of a finite set of common conceptual errors (Brown and Burton, 1978; Brown and VanLehn, 1980).[1] The same is true with fractions (Resnick et al., 1989; Hart, 1984) and with physics (diSessa and Minstrell, 1998). Research conducted with populations of children speaking different languages shows that many of the difficulties children experience in comprehending and solving simple mathematics word problems apply consistently across a wide range of languages and instructional settings. The re-

---

[1]While the range of bugs that students demonstrate is quite limited and predictable, this research also shows that students with incomplete subtraction skill will often show variability in the strategies they use from moment to moment and problem to problem.

BOX 5-2   Manifestations of Some Subtraction Bugs

143   The student subtracts the smaller digit in each column from the larger digit
−28   regardless of which is on top.
125

143   When the student needs to borrow, s/he adds 10 to the top digit of the
−28   current column without subtracting 1 from the next column to the left.
125

1300   When borrowing from a column whose top digit is 0, the student writes 9
−522   but does not continue borrowing from the column to the left of the 0.
878

140   Whenever the top digit in a column is 0, the student writes the bottom digit
−21   in the answer; i.e., 0 − N = N.
121

140   Whenever the top digit in a column is 0, the student writes 0 in the answer;
−21   i.e., 0 − N = 0.
120

1300   When borrowing from a column where the top digit is 0, the student
−522   borrows from the next column to the left correctly, but writes 10 instead of
788   9 in this column.

321   When borrowing into a column whose top digit is 1, the student gets 10
−89   instead of 11.
231

662   Once the student needs to borrow from a column, s/he continues to
−357   borrow from every column whether s/he needs to or not.
205

662   The student always subtracts all borrows from the leftmost digit in the top
−357   number.
115

SOURCE: Brown and Burton (1978, p. 163). Used with permission of the Cognitive Science Society and by permisson of the authors.

search reveals that children's difficulties are derived from underlying conceptual representation issues that transcend linguistic differences (Verschaffel, Greer, and DeCorte, 2000).

Differences among learners should not be ignored. Thus a third key feature of a model of learning is that it should convey a *variety* of typical ways in which children come to understand the subject matter of interest. Children are exposed to different content depending on the curriculum and family environment they encounter, and this affects what they learn (see Chapter 3). When developing models of learning, one starting point for capturing such differences is to study a group of learners that reflects the diversity of the population to be instructed and assessed in terms of such factors as age, culture, socioeconomic status, gender, and region.

Fourth, starting with a theory of how people learn the subject matter of interest, the designers of an assessment will need to select a slice or subset of the larger theory of cognition and learning as the assessment targets. That is, any given model of learning underlying an assessment will capture some, but not all, aspects of what is known about how students think and learn in the domain. That selection should depend on the purpose for the assessment. For instance, the purpose of an intelligent tutor is to determine the precise topic or skill area in which a student is struggling at the moment so that the student can be directed to further help. To develop this kind of assessment, a detailed description of how people at different levels of expertise use correct and incorrect rules during problem solving is often needed (such as that illustrated by the model of cognition underlying the Anderson tutor, described below). More typical classroom assessments, such as quizzes administered by teachers to a class several times each week or month, provide individual students with feedback about their learning and areas for improvement. They help the teacher identify the extent of mastery and appropriate next steps for instruction. To design such assessments, an extraction from the theory that is not quite so detailed, but closer to the level at which concepts are discussed in classroom discourse, is most helpful. The model of cognition and learning underlying a classroom assessment might focus on common preconceptions or incomplete understandings that students tend to have and that the teacher can identify and build on (as illustrated by the Facets example described below). If the purpose for the assessment is to provide summative information following a larger chunk of instruction, as is the case with statewide achievement tests, a coarser-grained model of learning that focuses on the development of central conceptual structures in the subject domain may suffice.

Finally, a model of learning will ideally lend itself to being aggregated in a principled way so that it can be used for different assessment purposes. For example, a fine-grained description of cognition underlying an intelligent tutoring system should be structured so the information can be combined to report less detailed summary information for students, parents, and teachers. The model should, in turn, be compatible with a coarse-grained model of learning used as a basis for an end-of-year summative assessment.

To be sure, there will always be school subjects for which models of cognition and learning have not yet been developed. Policies about what topics should be taught and emphasized in school change, and theories of how people learn particular content will evolve over time as understanding of human cognition advances. In such situations, the assessment developer may choose to start from scratch with a cognitive analysis of the domain. But when resources do not allow for that, basic principles of cognition and learning described in Chapter 3—such as the importance of how people organize knowledge, represent problems, and monitor their own learning—can inform the translation of curriculum into instruction and assessment. The principle that learning must start with what students currently understand and know about a topic and build from there will always hold.

Some existing assessments have been built on the types of models of learning described above. The following examples have been chosen to illustrate the variation in theories that underlie assessments for different purposes. First, we use the example of intelligent tutoring systems (used to illustrate a number of points in this volume). Existing intelligent tutoring systems are built on detailed cognitive theories of expert problem solving (Anderson, Boyle, Corbett, and Lewis, 1990; VanLehn and Martin, 1998). The tutors use assessment constantly to (1) provide continuous, individualized feedback to learners as they work problems; (2) offer help when appropriate or when requested by the learner; and (3) select and present appropriate next activities for learning. The second example describes a classroom assessment approach that teachers can use for diagnosing qualitatively different states of student understanding in physics. An important point of this report is that a model of learning can take different forms and encompass different research perspectives. Thus the third example illustrates a model of learning that focuses on the situative and participatory aspects of learning mathematics. The fourth example demonstrates how models of learning can be used as the basis for large-scale as well as classroom assessments.

Underlying Models of Cognition and Learning: Examples

PAT Algebra Tutor

John Anderson's ACT-R research group has developed intelligent tutoring systems for algebra and geometry that are being used successfully in a number of classrooms (Koedinger, Anderson, Hadley, and Mark, 1997). The cognitive models of learning at the core of their systems are based on the group's more general theory of human cognition, ACT-R, which has many features consistent with the cognitive architecture and structure of knowledge as described in Chapter 3. ACT-R theory aims to describe how people acquire and organize knowledge and produce successful performance in a wide range of simple and complex cognitive tasks, and it has been subjected to rigorous scientific testing (Anderson et al., 1990). The model of learning is written as a system of "if-then" production rules that are capable of generating the multitude of solution steps and missteps typical of students. As a simple example, below is a small portion of an ACT-R production system for algebra:

Rule:	IF the goal is to solve $a(bx + c) = d$
	THEN rewrite this as $bx + c = d/a$
Rule:	IF the goal is to solve $a(bx + c) = d$
	THEN rewrite this as $abx + ac = d$
Bug rule:	IF the goal is to solve $a(bx + c) = d$
	THEN rewrite this as $abx + c = d$

The cognitive model consists of many rules—some correct and some flawed—and their inclusion is based on empirical studies of student performance on a wide range of algebra problems. As the student is working, the tutor uses two techniques to monitor his or her activities: *model tracing* and *knowledge tracing*. Model tracing is used to monitor the student's progress through a problem (Anderson et al., 1990). This tracing is done in the background by matching student actions to those the cognitive model might generate; the tutor is mostly silent through this process. However, when the student asks for help, the tutor has an estimate of where he or she is and can provide hints that are tailored to that student's particular approach to the problem. Knowledge tracing is used to monitor students' learning from problem to problem (Corbett and Anderson, 1992). A Bayesian estimation procedure, of the type described in Chapter 4, identifies students' strengths and weaknesses by seeking a match against a subset of the production rules in the cognitive model that best captures what a student knows at that point in time. This information is used to individualize problem selection and pace students optimally through the curriculum.

Facet-Based Instruction and Assessment

The Facets program provides an example of how student performance can be described at a medium level of detail that emphasizes the progression or development toward competence and is highly useful for classroom assessment (Hunt and Minstrell, 1994; Minstrell, 2000). Developed through collaboration between Jim Minstrell (an experienced high school science teacher) and Earl Hunt (a cognitive psychologist), the assessment approach is based on models of learning termed *facets of student thinking*. The approach is predicated on the cognitive principle that students come to instruction with initial ideas and preconceptions that the teacher should identify and build on.

The term *facets* refers to pieces of knowledge or reasoning, processes, beliefs, or constructions of pieces of knowledge that serve as a convenient unit of thought for analysis of student behavior. In many ways they behave like general rules that students have in their knowledge base about how the world works. Facets are derived from research and from teachers' observations of student learning. For instance, students in introductory physics classes often enter instruction with the belief (or facet) that air pressure has something to do with weight, since air presses down on objects. Another widely held facet is that if two bodies of different sizes and speeds collide, larger, faster bodies exert more force than do smaller, slower bodies. Whereas neither of these facets is consistent with actual physical principles, both are roughly satisfactory explanations for understanding a variety of situations. Facets are gathered in three ways: by examining relevant research when it exists, by consulting experienced teachers, and by examining student responses to open-ended questions intended to reveal the students' initial ideas about a topic.

Facet clusters are sets of related facets, grouped around a physical situation, such as forces on interacting objects, or some conceptual idea, such as the meaning of average velocity. Within the cluster, facets are sequenced in an approximate order of development, and for recording purposes they are numerically coded. Those ending with 0 or 1 in the units digit tend to be appropriate, acceptable understandings for introductory physics; those ending in 9, 8, or 7 are more problematic facets that should be targeted with remedial instruction. An example of a facets cluster is presented in Box 5-3 (another example was presented earlier in Box 3-10).

Starting with a model of learning expressed in terms of facets, Minstrell and Hunt have carefully crafted assessment tasks and scoring procedures to provide evidence of which facets a student is likely to be using (illustrated later in this chapter).

Middle School Math Through Applications Project

Greeno and colleagues have designed curriculum and assessment practices based on situative theories of cognition and learning (see Chapter 3) (Cole, Coffey, and Goldman, 1999; Greeno, 1991). From a situative perspective, one who knows mathematics is able to participate successfully in the mathematical practices that prevail in one or more of the communities where mathematical knowledge is developed, used, or simply valued. Learning mathematics is a process of becoming more effective, responsible, and au-

BOX 5-3   **Sample Facets Cluster: Separating Medium Effects from Gravitational Effects**

A common goal of an introductory physics course is for students to understand the nature of gravity and its effects, as well as the effects of ambient, fluid mediums (e.g., air or water) on objects they contain, whether the objects are at rest or moving them. Below is a facets cluster that corresponds to this domain of understanding. It lays out the pieces of knowledge that studies of learners have shown students apply as they attempt to make sense of such phenomena. The facets of student thinking are ordered along a continuum, from correct to problematic understandings.

310   **Pushes from above and below by a surrounding fluid medium lend a slight support (net upward push due to differences in depth pressure gradient).**

310-1   The difference between the upward and downward pushes by the surrounding air results in a slight upward support or buoyancy.

310-2   Pushes from above and below an object in a liquid medium yield a buoyant upward force due to the larger pressure from below.

311   **A mathematical formulaic approach (e.g. $\rho \times g \times h_1 - \rho \times g \times h_2 =$ net buoyant pressure).**

314   **Surrounding fluids don't exert any forces or pushes on objects.**

thoritative in the ways in which an individual participates in mathematical practices. Through participation in a community, such as through interactions with other learners and people who use mathematics in their work and everyday lives, individuals develop identities as learners and knowers of mathematics (Greeno and The Middle-School Mathematics Through Applications Group, 1997).

The Middle School Mathematics Through Applications Program is a collaboration of curriculum developers, teachers, and researchers. They have developed software and print curriculum that present mathematics mainly as a resource for a variety of design activities. They have also developed curriculum-embedded assessment activities.

315	**Surrounding fluids exert equal pushes all around an object.**
315-1	Air pressure has no up or down influence (neutral).
315-2	Liquid presses equally from all sides regardless of depth.
316	**Whichever surface has the greater amount of fluid above or below the object has the greater push by the fluid on the surface.**
317	**Fluid mediums exert an upward push only.**
317-1	Air pressure is a big up influence (only direction).
317-2	Liquid presses up only.
317-3	Fluids exert bigger up forces on lighter objects.
318	**Surrounding fluid mediums exert a net downward push.**
318-1	Air pressure is a down influence (only direction).
318-2	Liquid presses (net press) down.
319	**Weight of an object is directly proportional to medium pressure on it.**
319-1	Weight is proportional to air pressure.
319-2	Weight is proportional to liquid pressure.

SOURCE: Minstrell (2000, p. 52).

For example, to assess student learning as part of a seventh-grade unit called the Antarctica Project, students work in groups to design a research station for scientists. Self- and peer-assessment strategies are used. Students are asked to continually consider and discuss four general questions while they work on classroom projects: What are we learning? What is quality work? To whom do we hold ourselves accountable? and How do we use assessment tools to learn more? Assessment activities include journal writing, group design of scoring rubrics (or criteria), and group presentations followed by peer critiques based on the rubrics. The group conversations that define the rubric, together with peer and self-evaluation of how a particular piece of work fares against that rubric, create a shared vocabulary and standards for quality work (Cole, Coffey, and Goldman, 1999).

Australia's Developmental Assessment

The Australian Council for Educational Research has developed the Developmental Assessment program, which is being used in several states in Australia. As discussed and illustrated in Chapter 4, central to the program are models of learning known as *progress maps,* intended to serve as a basis for the design of both large-scale and classroom assessments. Progress maps provide a description of skills, understandings, and knowledge in the sequence in which they typically develop—a picture of what it means to improve over time in an area of learning. Australia's Developmental Assessment is used as an example throughout this report, not because the progress maps are particularly reflective of recent advances in cognitive research, but because the Developmental Assessment approach represents a notable attempt to measure growth in competence and to convey the nature of student achievement in ways that can benefit teaching and learning.

These maps can serve as the basis for assessments for both large-scale and classroom purposes. "Progress is monitored in much the same way as a child's physical growth is monitored: from time to time an estimate is made of a student's location on a developmental continuum, and changes in location provide measures of growth over time" (Masters and Forster, 1996, p. 1). Progress maps have been developed for a variety of areas of the curriculum, and several states in Australia use them as a basis for reporting assessment results back to schools and parents (Meiers and Culican, 2000). Box 5-4 presents a sample progress map for counting and ordering (for additional examples of progress maps see Chapter 4).

The progress maps are based on a combination of expert experience and research. Developers talked with teachers and curriculum experts about what kinds of understandings they typically see in children by the end of particular grade levels. They also reviewed available research on learning in the subject domain. Once an initial map had been drafted, it was validated or tested. Teachers were interviewed and probed about whether the map was consistent with their experience and whether it covered the kinds of skills and understandings they viewed as important in the domain.

In addition, more empirical evidence was often collected by constructing tasks designed to tap specific performances on the map, having students respond, analyzing the responses, and looking at whether the statistical analyses produced patterns of performance consistent with the progressions on the maps. Areas of discrepancy were pointed out to the developers so they could refine the maps. This process is a good example of the assessment triangle at work: the process moves back and forth between the cognition, observation, and interpretation corners of the triangle so that each informs the others.

BOX 5-4   Progress Map for Counting and Ordering

Following (below and on the next two pages) is the lower portion of a counting and ordering progress map. The map shows examples of knowledge, skills, and understandings in the sequence in which they are generally expected to develop from grades one through five. This type of map is useful for tracking the progress of an individual child over time. An evaluation using tasks designed to tap specific performances on the map can provide a "snapshot" showing where a student is located on the map, and a series of such evaluations is useful for assessing a student's progress over the course of several years.

5   Uses unitary ratios of the form 1 part to X parts
        (the ratio of cordial to water was 1 to 4)
     Understands that common fractions are used to describe ratios of
     parts to whole
        (2 in 5 students ride to school. In school of 550, 220 ride bikes)
     Uses percentages to make straightforward comparisons
        (26 balls from 50 tries is 52%; 24 from 40 tries is 60%, so that
        is better)
     Uses common equivalences between decimals, fractions, and
     percentages
        (one-third off is better than 30% discount)
     Uses whole number powers and square roots in describing things
        (finds length of side of square of area 225 sq cm as a square
        root of 225)

4   Counts in decimal fraction amounts (0.3, 0.6, 0.9, 1.2, …)
     Compares and orders decimal fractions
        (orders given weight data for babies to two decimal places)
     Uses place value to explain the order of decimal fractions
        (which library book comes first—65.6 or 65.126? why?)
     Reads scales calibrated in multiples of ten
        (reads 3.97 on a tape measure marked in hundredths,
        labeled in tenths)
     Uses the symbols =, <, and > to order numbers and make
     comparisons
        $(6.75 < 6.9; 5 \times \$6 > 5 \times \$5.95)$

continued

BOX 5-4 **Continued**

Compares and orders fractions (one-quarter is less than three-eighths)

3 Counts in common fractional amounts

   (two and one-third, two and two-thirds, three, three
   and one-third)

Uses decimal notation to two places

   (uses 1.25 m for 1 m 25 cm; $3.05 for three $1 coins
   and one 5 cent coin; 1.75 kg for 1750 kg)

Regroups money to fewest possible notes and coins

   (11 × $5 + 17 × $2 + 8 × $1 regrouped as 1 × $50 +
   2 × $20 + $5 + $2)

Uses materials and diagrams to represent fractional amounts

   (folds tape into five equal parts, shades 3 parts to show 3/5)

Expresses generalizations about fractional numbers symbolically

   (1 quarter = 2 eighths and 1/4 = 2/8)

2 Counts forward and backward from any whole number, including
   skip counting in 2s, 3s, and 10s

Uses place value to distinguish and order whole numbers

   (writes four ten dollar notes and three one dollar coins as $43)

Estimates the size of a collection (up to about 20)

THE DESIGN OF OBSERVATIONAL SITUATIONS

Once the purpose for an assessment, the underlying model of cognition in the domain, and the desired types of inferences to be drawn from the results have been specified, observational situations must be designed for collecting evidence to support the targets of inference. This design phase includes the development of tasks and procedures for evaluating students' responses, the construction of sets of tasks, and the assembly of an assessment instrument. These processes involve both reflection and empirical observation, and require several iterations of the steps described below.

In addition to starting with a model of learning for the subject domain, assessment design should be led by the interpretation element of the assessment triangle, which guides how information from the assessment tasks will be filtered and combined to produce results (that is, how observations will be transformed into measurements). A central message of this report is that

Uses fractional language (one-half, third, quarter, fifth, tenth)
appropriately in describing and comparing things
Shows and compares unit fractions (finds a third of a cup of sugar)
Describes and records simple fractional equivalents
 (The left over half pizza was as much as two quarters put together)

1   Counts collections of objects to answer the question 'How many are
there?'
Makes or draws collections of a given size
 (responds correctly to Give me 6 bears)
Makes sensible estimates of the size of small collections up to 10
 (for 7 buttons, 2 or 15 would not be a sensible estimate, but
 5 would be)
Skip counts in 2s or 3s using a number line, hundred chart, or mental
counting (2, 4, 6, ...)
Uses numbers to decide which is bigger, smaller, same size
 (If he has 7 mice at home and I have 5, then he has more)
Uses the terms first, second, third (I finished my lunch second)

SOURCE: Adapted from Masters and Forster (1996, p. 2). Used with permission of
the authors.

the interpretation model must be consistent with the underlying model of learning. While there are a variety of ways of achieving this consistency (see Chapter 4), it frequently is not achieved in current practice.

Task Design Guided by Cognitive and Measurement Principles

Many people consider the designing of assessment tasks to be an art. But to produce high-quality information for educational decision making, a more scientific and principled approach is needed. Only through such an approach is it possible to design tasks that precisely tap the intended aspects of learning and provide evidence that can lead to valid, fair, and useful inferences.

Messick (1994) distinguishes between a *task-centered* and a *construct-centered* approach to assessment design, the latter being the approach espoused here. With a task-centered approach, the focus is on having students perform meaningful and important tasks, and the target of inference is, implicitly, the tendency to do well on those tasks. Such an approach makes sense under certain circumstances, such as an arts contest or figure-skating competition, when evaluation of the product or performance per se is the focus. But educational decision makers are rarely concerned with one particular performance. They tend to be more interested in the underlying competencies that enable performance on a task, as well as on a range of related activities. In such cases, a construct-centered approach is needed. Such an approach starts with identifying the knowledge, skills, or other attributes that should be assessed (expressed through the model of learning), which then guide the selection or construction of relevant tasks and scoring procedures. Messick notes that the movement toward performance assessment in the last decade has often been task-centered, with an emphasis on creating assessment tasks that are "authentic" and representative of important activities students should be able to perform, but without specification of the underlying constructs that are the targets of inference. Simply because a task is "authentic" does not mean it is a valid observation of a particular construct (Baker, 1997).

A related point is that design should focus on the cognitive demands of tasks (the mental processes required for successful performance), rather than primarily on surface features, such as how tasks are presented to students or the format in which students are asked to respond. For instance, it is commonly believed that multiple-choice items are limited to assessing low-level processes such as recall of facts, whereas performance tasks elicit more complex cognitive processes. However, the relationship between item format and cognitive demands is not so straightforward. Although multiple-choice items are often used to measure low-level skills, a variety of item formats, including carefully constructed multiple-choice questions, can in fact tap complex cognitive processes (as illustrated later in Box 5-7). Similarly, performance tasks, usually intended to assess higher-level cognitive processes, may inadvertently tap low-level ones (Baxter and Glaser, 1998; Hamilton, Nussbaum, and Snow, 1997; Linn, Baker, and Dunbar, 1991).

Linking tasks to the model of cognition and learning forces attention to a central principle of task design—that tasks should emphasize those features relevant to the construct being measured and minimize extraneous features (AERA et al., 1999; Messick, 1993). This means that ideally, a task will not measure aspects of cognition that are irrelevant to the targeted performance. For instance, when assessing students' mathematical reasoning, one should avoid presenting problems in contexts that might be unfamiliar to a particular population of students. Similarly, mathematics tasks should not make heavy demands for reading or writing unless one is explicitly aiming to assess students' abilities to read or communicate about mathematics. Thus surface features of tasks do need to be considered to the extent that they affect or change the cognitive demands of the tasks in unintended ways.

Ideally, task difficulty should be explained in terms of the underlying knowledge and cognitive processes required, rather than simply in terms of statistical item difficulty indices, such as the proportion of respondents answering the item correctly. Beyond knowing that 80 percent of students answered a particular item incorrectly, it would be educationally useful to know *why* so many did so, that is, to identify the sources of the difficulty so they could be remedied (assuming, of course, that they represented important construct-relevant variance). Cognitive theory and analysis can be helpful here.

For instance, one cognitive principle emphasized in Chapter 3 is that tasks in which children are asked to apply their knowledge in novel situations tend to be more difficult than those in which children apply what they have learned in the context in which they learned it. Similarly, research shows that a mathematics word problem that describes the combining of quantities and seeks the resultant total (e.g., John has 3 marbles and Mary has 5, How many do they have altogether?) is easier to comprehend than one that describes the same actors but expresses a comparison of their respective quantities (e.g., John has 3 marbles. He has 2 less than Mary. How many does she have?). Although the solution to both problems is to add the quantities, the success rate on the first problem is much higher than on the second (Riley and Greeno, 1988). Part of the difficulty for children is the conflict between the relational expression *less than,* which implies subtraction, and the operation required, which involves addition. No such conflict arises for the first problem, in which the expression clearly implies addition. Cognitive research also shows that in comprehending a portion of narrative or expository text, inferring why an event occurred is more difficult if the causes are widely dispersed in the text and relatively remote from the description of the resultant event (Lorch and van den Broek, 1997).

The point is not that such sources of difficulty should necessarily be avoided. Rather, these kinds of cognitive complexities should be introduced into the assessment tasks in principled ways only in those cases in which one wants to draw inferences about whether students can handle them. For instance, there are many reasons why educators might want to assess students' abilities to apply integrated sets of skills (e.g., literacy and mathematics capabilities) to complex problems. That is entirely consistent with the approach being set forth here as long as assessment design begins with a model of learning that describes the complex of skills, understandings, and communicative practices about which one is interested in drawing inferences, and tasks are specifically designed to provide evidence to support those inferences.

The most commonly used statistical measures of task difficulty ignore the fact that two tasks with similar surface features can be equally difficult, but for different reasons. For example, two language tasks that require combined reading and writing skills may exhibit the same overall level of difficulty according to the statistical item parameters, even though one task places greater demands on compositional skills and the other on reading comprehension.

There has been some exploration of the cognitive demands of achievement tasks in semantically rich domains, including Marshall's (1995) work on assessing students' schemas for story problems and White and Frederiksen's (1998) exploration of levels of understanding of electrical circuits. As described in Chapter 4, several existing measurement models are able to incorporate and analyze aspects of item difficulty. Yet while some of these models have been available for several years, their use in mainstream assessment has been infrequent (e.g., Wilson and Wang, 1995).

It would also be educationally useful to analyze the difficulty of an assessment task in terms of *which* students get it wrong, and *why* it is so problematic for those students. Part of the answer might lie in differences in the communicative practices students bring to the assessment. Some researchers have used the differential item functioning methods described in Chapter 4 to help study such issues.

No existing assessment examples embody all of the principles set forth above. However, some assessments have begun to approximate certain of these features. The following is an example of an assessment composed of tasks that were designed to correspond directly to a model of learning.

Example: Number Knowledge Test

The Number Knowledge Test (Griffin and Case, 1997), presented in Box 5-5, was originally designed by Case and Griffin as a research tool to test out their theory about the development of children's central conceptual structures for whole numbers (see Box 5-1). Over the past decade, the test has increasingly been used in the United States and Canada as an educational diagnostic tool to determine most appropriate next steps for arithmetic instruction.

Referring back to the model of learning presented in Box 5-1, items at the 4-year-old level, which are presented to students with physical objects, provide evidence of whether children have acquired the initial counting schema. Items at the 6-year-old level, presented without physical objects, assess whether children have acquired the "mental counting line" structure. Items at the 8-year-old level assess whether children have acquired the "double mental counting line" structure. Finally, items at the 10-year-old level indicate whether children can handle double- and triple-digit numbers in a more fully integrated fashion.

The teacher administers the test orally and individually to children. The few items included at each age level yield a wealth of information about children's developing understanding. Testing stops when a child does not pass a sufficient number of items to go on to the next level. This is an example of a set of questions for which the interpretation of responses is relatively simple. The strength of the assessment derives from the underlying model of cognition and learning.

The researchers have found that although many teachers express some hesitation about having to administer and score an individual oral test, they usually end up feeling that it was not as difficult as they had feared and that the results are highly worthwhile. Teachers report that the experience reveals differences in children's thinking that they had not previously noticed, prompts them to listen more actively to each child in their class, and gives them a sense of what developmental instruction entails (Griffin and Case, 1997).

Evaluation of Student Responses

The observation corner of the assessment triangle includes tasks for eliciting student performance in combination with scoring criteria and procedures, or other methods for evaluating student responses to the tasks. For convenience, we often refer to this process simply as "scoring," while recognizing that in many cases student responses might be evaluated using other means, such as informal evaluation by the teacher during class discussion.

Tasks and the procedures to be used for drawing the relevant evidence from students' responses to those tasks must be considered together. That is, the ways in which student responses will be scored should be conceptualized during the design of a task. A task may stimulate creative thinking or problem solving, but such rich information will be lost unless the means used to interpret the responses capture the evidence needed to draw inferences about those processes. Like tasks, scoring methods must be carefully constructed to be sensitive to critical differences in levels and types of student understanding identified by the model of learning. At times one may be interested in the quantity of facts a student has learned, for instance, when one is measuring mastery of the alphabet or multiplication table. However, a cognitive approach generally implies that when evaluating students' responses, the focus should be on the quality or nature of their understanding, rather than simply the quantity of information produced. In many cases, quality can be modeled quantitatively; that is, even in highly qualitative contexts, ideas of order and orderliness will be present (see also Chapter 4).

BOX 5-5 **Number Knowledge Test**

Below are the 4-, 6-, 8-, and 10-year-old sections of the Number Knowledge Test.

Preliminary

Let's see if you can count from 1 to 10. Go ahead.

Level 0 (4-year-old level): Go to Level 1 if 3 or more correct

1. (Show 5 unordered chips.) Would you count these for me?
2. I'm going to show you some counting chips (show mixed array of 3 red and 4 blue chips). Count just the blue chips and tell me how many there are.
3. Here are some circles and triangles (show mixed array of 7 circles and 8 triangles). Count just the triangles and tell me how many there are.
4. Pretend I'm going to give you 2 pieces of candy and then I'm going to give you 1 more (do so). How many will you have altogether?

Level 1 (6-year-old level): Go to Level 2 if 5 or more correct

1. If you had 4 chocolates and someone gave you 3 more, how many chocolates would you have altogether?
2. What number comes right after 7?
3. What number comes two numbers after 7?
4a. Which is bigger: 5 or 4?
4b. Which is bigger: 7 or 9?
5a. (This time, I'm going to ask you about smaller numbers.) Which is smaller: 8 or 6?
5b. Which is smaller: 5 or 7?
6a. (Show visual array.) Which number is closer to 5: 6 or 2?
6b. (Show visual array.) Which number is closer to 7: 4 or 9?
7. How much is 2+4? (OK to use fingers for counting)
8. How much is 8 take away 6? (OK to use fingers for counting)
9a. (Show visual array—8, 5, 2, 6—ask child to point to and name each numeral.) When you are counting, which of these numbers do you say first?
9b. When you are counting, which of these numbers do you say last?

Level 2 (8-year-old level): Go to Level 3 if 5 or more correct

1. What number comes 5 numbers after 49?
2. What number comes 4 numbers before 60?
3a. Which is bigger: 69 or 71?
3b. Which is bigger: 32 or 28?
4a. (This time I'm going to ask you about smaller numbers.) Which is smaller: 27 or 32?
4b. Which is smaller: 51 or 39?
5a. (Show visual array.) Which number is closer to 21: 25 or 18?
5b. (Show visual array.) Which number is closer to 28: 31 or 24?
6. How many numbers are there in between 2 and 6? (Accept either 3 or 4)
7. How many numbers are there in between 7 and 9? (Accept either 1 or 2)
8. (Show card "12, 54") How much is 12+54? (No credit if number increased by one with fingers.)
9. (Show card "47, 21") How much is 47 take away 21? (No credit if number decreased by one with fingers.)

Level 3 (10-year-old level): Go to Level 4 if 4 or more correct

1. What number comes 10 numbers after 99?
2. What number comes 9 numbers after 999?
3a. Which difference is bigger: the difference between 9 and 6 or the difference between 8 and 3?
3b. Which difference is bigger: the difference between 6 and 2 or the difference between 8 and 5?
4a. Which difference is smaller: the difference between 99 and 92 or the difference between 25 and 11?
4b. Which difference is smaller: the difference between 48 and 36 or the difference between 84 and 73?
5. (Show card, "13, 39") How much is 13+39?
6. (Show card, "36, 18") How much is 36-18?
7. How much is 301 take away 7?

SOURCE: Griffin and Case (1997, pp. 12-13). Used with permission of the authors.

Silver, Alacaci, and Stylianou (2000) have demonstrated some limitations of scoring methods used by the National Assessment of Educational Progress (NAEP) for capturing the complexities of learning. They reanalyzed a sample of written responses to an NAEP item that asked students to compare two geometric figures and found important differences in the quality of the reasoning demonstrated: some students showed surface-level reasoning (paying attention to the appearance of the figures), others showed analytic reasoning (paying attention to geometric features), and still others demonstrated more sophisticated reasoning (looking at class membership). Despite these qualitative differences, however, the NAEP report simply indicated that 11 percent of students gave satisfactory or better responses—defined as providing at least two reasons why the shapes were alike or different—while revealing little about the nature of the students' understanding. Whereas the current simple NAEP scoring strategy makes it relatively easy to control variation among raters who are scoring students' responses, much other information that could have educational value is lost. Needed are enhanced scoring procedures for large-scale assessments that capture more of the complexity of student thinking while still maintaining reliability. When the scoring strategy is based on a strong theory of learning, the interpretation model can exploit the extra information the theory provides to produce a more complex and rich interpretation, such as those presented in Chapter 4.

Task Sets and Assembly of an Assessment Instrument

An assessment should be more than a collection of items that work well individually. The utility of assessment information can be enhanced by carefully selecting tasks and combining the information from those tasks to provide evidence about the nature of student understanding. Sets of tasks should be constructed and selected to discriminate among different levels and kinds of understanding that are identified in the model of learning. To illustrate this point simply, it takes more than one item or a collection of unrelated items to diagnose a procedural error in subtraction. If a student answers three of five separate subtraction questions incorrectly, one can infer only that the student is using some faulty process(es), but a carefully crafted collection of items can be designed to pinpoint the limited concepts or flawed rules the student is using.

In Box 5-6, a typical collection of items designed to work independently to assess a student's general understanding of subtraction is contrasted with a set of tasks designed to work together to diagnose the common types of subtraction errors presented earlier in Box 5-2. As this example shows, significantly more useful information is gained in the latter case that can be used to provide the student with feedback and determine next steps for instruction. (A similar example of how sets of items can be used to diagnose

BOX 5-6 Using Sets of Items to Diagnose Subtraction Bugs

The traditional testing approach is to present students with a sample of independent or disconnected items that tap the same general set of skills in order to obtain a reliable estimate of students' abilities to solve such problems. Thus to assess a student's understanding of multidigit subtraction, items such as the following might be used:

$$
\begin{array}{ccccc}
834 & 999 & 254 & 783 & 402 \\
-92 & -486 & -19 & -86 & -100 \\
\hline
842 & 513 & 165 & 703 & 302
\end{array}
$$

In this case, the student answered three of the five problems incorrectly (the first, third, and fourth items from the left). Typically, the number of correct answers would be summed, and the student would receive a score of 40 percent correct; from this evidence it might be inferred that the student has a poor understanding of subtraction.

In contrast, consider the information gained from the following set of five items (Siegler, 1998, p. 294) that are linked to the theory of subtraction errors (Brown and Burton, 1978) presented in Box 5-2.

$$
\begin{array}{ccccc}
307 & 856 & 606 & 308 & 835 \\
-182 & -699 & -568 & -287 & -217 \\
\hline
285 & 157 & 168 & 181 & 618
\end{array}
$$

Here the pattern of errors (the first, third, and fourth problems from the left) and the particular answers given suggest the existence of two bugs. First, whenever a problem required subtraction from zero, the student simply flipped the two numbers in the column with the zero. For example, in the problem 307 – 182, the student treated 0 – 8 as 8 – 0 and wrote 8 as the answer. The second bug involved not decrementing the number to the left of the zero (e.g, not reducing the 3 to 2 in 307 – 182). This lack of decrementing is not surprising because, as indicated by the first bug, the student did not borrow anything from this column. Thus, this particular pattern of correct and incorrect responses can be explained by positing a basically correct subtraction procedure with two particular bugs.

Note that in both the traditional and cognitive research-based examples shown here, the student answered three problems incorrectly and two correctly. However, the interpretations afforded by the two approaches are qualitatively quite different.

student understandings is provided by the balance-scale problems presented in Boxes 2-1, 2-2, and 2-3 in Chapter 2.)

When using such an approach, however, measurement issues arise that must be addressed by the interpretation element of the assessment triangle. Making sense of students' responses to patterns of items requires an interpretation model that can handle the added complexity. Statistical and informal interpretation models not only serve to make sense of the data after the assessment has been administered, but also play a crucial role in selecting the optimal set of items to include so that one can differentiate among profiles of understanding on the basis of pilot test data. Interpretation models tell the assessment designer how much and what types of tasks and evidence are needed to support the desired inferences and at what point additional assessment tasks will provide unnecessarily redundant information.

The interpretation model also serves as the "glue" that holds together the information gleaned from the items and transforms it into interpretable results. Traditional classical and item response models (as discussed in Chapter 4) would not allow for the diagnostic interpretation afforded by the second set of problems in Box 5-6. But some of the more complex models discussed in Chapter 4 could be used to exploit the model of learning for subtraction to produce a richer interpretation. The validity of these richer interpretations depends on the correctness of the model of learning for the situation at hand, and hence will be somewhat less robust than an interpretation based on the simpler measurement methods. On the other hand, the richer interpretations afforded by the more complex measurement methods and underlying cognitive theory offer hope for making assessments much more educationally useful.

We now return to the Facets program to illustrate how the cognitive and interpretation elements guide the design of observations (tasks, scoring, and sets of tasks) that make it possible to collect instructionally useful information about a student's understanding.

Example: Facets-Based Assessment

The Facets instructional program begins with various facet clusters (model of learning) of the type shown earlier in Box 5-3. Teachers can use the facet clusters as the basis for crafting questions to initiate class discussion of a topic or to develop a preinstruction quiz. Minstrell (2000) describes one such quiz that he has used to start a physics unit on separating effects of gravity from effects of the ambient medium. In the quiz, students are asked a question carefully designed to provide evidence of facets of student thinking on this topic.

> First, suppose we weigh some object on a large spring scale, not unlike the ones we have at the local market. The object apparently weighs 10

pounds, according to the scale. Now we put the same apparatus, scale, object and all, under a very large glass dome, seal the system around the edges, and pump out all the air. That is, we use a vacuum pump to allow all the air to escape out from under the glass dome. What will the scale reading be now? Answer as precisely as you can at this point in time. [pause] And in the space provided, briefly explain how you decided. (p. 50)

Students write their answers and rationales. From their words a facet diagnosis can be made relatively easily using the facets continuum as a scoring guide for locating student understanding. Students who give an answer of zero pounds for the scale reading in a vacuum usually are thinking that air only presses down, and "without air there would be no weight, like in space" (Facet 319). Other students suggest a number "a little less than 10" because "air is very light, so it doesn't press down very hard, but does press down some, thus, taking the air away will only decrease the scale reading slightly" (Facet 318). Other students suggest there will be no change at all: "Air has absolutely no effect on scale reading." The explanation could convey a belief that media do not exert any force or pressure on objects in them (Facet 314), or that fluid pressures on the top and bottom of an object are equal (Facet 315). A few students suggest that while there are pressures from above and below, there is a net upward pressure by the fluid: "There is a slight buoyant force" (Facet 310, an acceptable workable idea at this point).

The numbering scheme for the facets enables the teacher to do more than simply mark the answers "right" or "wrong." When data are coded, the teacher or researcher can scan the class results to identify dominant targets for the focus of instruction, and movement along the continuum from high- to low-numbered facets indicates growth.

Multiple-choice questions have also been designed to identify facets of student thinking by having each of the answer choices map back to a particular facet. That is, each "wrong" answer represents a particular naive or unformed conception, while the "right" answer indicates the goal of instruction. In fact, the computerized DIAGNOSER, designed to facilitate facet-based instruction, relies entirely on multiple-choice questions of the sort shown in Box 5-7.

The Facets program also provides an example of how sets of items can be used to diagnose characteristics of student understanding. The set of questions in Box 5-7 was developed to determine whether students' knowledge is organized *theoretically* in a coordinated, internally consistent manner, or students have a more fragmentary *knowledge-in-pieces* understanding. Minstrell (Minstrell, 1992; Minstrell, Stimpson, and Hunt, 1992) gave these questions to 60 students at the end of a high school introductory physics course and developed an informal interpretation model. He determined beforehand that students answering in the pattern of line 1 could be characterized as taking a *Newtonian* perspective; this ended up being true of

BOX 5-7   Use of Multiple-Choice Questions to Test for Theoretical vs. Knowledge-in-Pieces Perspective

Problem: In the following situation, two identical steel marbles M1 and M2 are to be launched horizontally off their respective tracks. They each leave the ends of their respective tracks at the same time, but M2 will leave its track travelling twice as fast as M1. The track for M1 can be set at any height in relation to M2.

(a) If we want the two marbles to collide, how will we need to arrange the horizontal launch tracks?

A. The track for M1 should be much higher than the track for M2.
B. The tracks for M1 and M2 should be at the same elevation.
C. The track for M1 should be much lower than the track for M2.

Now, suppose we have set the track for M1 at an appropriate height so that the marbles will collide in the space between and below the two tracks.

(b) The picture below is just before the two marbles collide. Diagram (arrows with appropriate relative lengths) and label the forces on each marble.

[A for horizontal component in the forward direction]
[B for no horizontal component in the forward direction]

(c) When they collide, which marble will exert the greater force on the other?

A. M2 will exert the greater force on M1.
B. M1 will exert the greater force on M2.
C. M2 and M1 will exert equal forces on each other.

Briefly justify your answer.

(d) After the marbles collide, they fall the rest of the way to the floor. Which would reach the floor the soonest?

A. They will reach the floor at the same time.
B. M1 will reach the floor before M2.
C. M2 will reach the floor before M1.

Briefly justify your answer.

Combinations of answers are more consistent with a knowledge-in-pieces perspective than with a theoretical perspective.

Answer Combination	Problem Parts				Frequency Count (Students)
	(a)	(b)	(c)	(d)	
1. Newtonian	B*	B*	C*	A*	7
2.	B*	B*	A$	A*	8
3.	C	B*	C*	A*	3
4.	B*	A$	C*	A*	4
5.	A$	B*	C*	C$	1
6.	A$	A$	C*	A*	2
7.	C	A$	C*	A*	1
8.	C	B*	A$	A*	3
9.	A$	B*	A$	A*	4
10.	B*	A$	A$	A*	10
11.	0	A$	C*	A*	2
12.	C	A$	C*	C$	1
13.	C	B*	A$	B$	1
14.	C	A4	A$	A*	3
15.	A$	A$	A$	A*	8
16.	0	A$	A$	A*	1
17. Novice	A$	A$	A$	C$	1

NOTE: 0 indicates no answer, * indicates answer consistent with a Newtonian perspective, and $ indicates answer consistent with a novice perspective.

SOURCE: Adapted from Minstrell (1992). Used with permission of the author.

7 of the 60 students. Students taking an *Aristotelian* or novice perspective would show the pattern of line 17 (1 student). The rest of the combinations reflect a *knowledge-in-pieces* understanding. Note that across the four questions, 81 ($3 \times 3 \times 3 \times 3$) response combinations would have been possible, but students tended to produce certain patterns of responses. For example, line 10 shows that 10 students apparently understood the independence of horizontal and vertical motions (problem parts a and d) without understanding the forces on projectiles (part b) or forces during collisions (part c). (The list of answer combinations in Box 5-7 is not meant to imply a linear progression from novice to Newtonian). Such profiles of student understanding are more instructionally useful than simply knowing that a student answered some combination of half of the test questions correctly.

On a single physics assessment, one could imagine having many such sets of items corresponding to different facet clusters. Interpretation issues could potentially be addressed with the sorts of measurement models presented in Chapter 4. For instance, how many bundles of items are needed for reliable diagnosis? And could the utility of the information produced be enhanced by developing interpretation models that could generate profiles of student performance across numerous topics (facet clusters)? Doing so would require not only cognitive descriptions of developing competence within a topic, but also a model of how various topics are related and which topics are more difficult or build on earlier ones. A statistical interpretation model could articulate these aspects of learning and also help determine how many and which items should be included on the test to optimize the reliability of the inferences drawn.

TASK VALIDATION

Once a preliminary set of tasks and corresponding scoring rubrics have been developed, evidence of their validity must be collected. Traditionally, validity concerns associated with achievement tests have tended to center around test content, that is, the degree to which the test samples the subject matter domain about which inferences are to be drawn. Evidence is typically collected through expert appraisal of the alignment between the content of the assessment tasks and the subject matter framework (e.g., curriculum standards). Sometimes an empirical approach to validation is used, whereby items are included in a test on the basis of data. Test items might be selected primarily according to their empirical relationship with an external criterion, their relationship with one another, or their power to differentiate among groups of individuals. Under such circumstances, it is likely that the selection of some items will be based on chance occurrences in the data (AERA et al., 1999).

There is increasing recognition within the assessment community that traditional forms of validation emphasizing consistency with other measures, as well as the search for indirect indicators that can show this consistency statistically, should be supplemented with evidence of the cognitive or substantive aspect of validity (e.g., Linn et al., 1991; Messick, 1993). That is, the trustworthiness of the interpretation of test scores should rest in part on empirical evidence that the assessment tasks actually tap the intended cognitive processes.

Situative and sociocultural research on learning (see Chapter 3) suggests that validation should be taken a step further. This body of research emphasizes that cognitive processes are embedded in social practices. From this perspective, the performance of students on tests is understood as an activity in the situation presented by the test and success depends on ability to participate in the practices of test taking (Greeno, Pearson, and Schoenfeld, 1996). It follows that validation should include the collection of evidence that test takers have the communicative practices required for their responses to be actual indicators of such abilities as understanding and reasoning. The assumption that students have the necessary communicative skills has been demonstrated to be false in many cases. For instance, Cole, Gay, and Glick (1968) conducted research in Liberia in which they assessed various cognitive capabilities, such as conservation and classification. From a standard assessment perspective, the Liberian test takers appeared to lack the skills being tested. But when assessments were designed that made sense in their practices, a much more positive picture of their competencies emerged.

Approaches to Task Validation

As described by Messick (1993) and summarized by Magone, Cai, Silver and Wang (1994), a variety of techniques can be used to examine the processes examinees use during task performance to evaluate whether prospective items are functioning as intended. One such method is *protocol analysis*, in which students are asked to think aloud as they solve problems or to describe retrospectively how they solved the problems (see Ericsson and Simon, 1984). Another method is *analysis of reasons*, in which students are asked to provide rationales for their responses to the tasks. A third method is *analysis of errors*, in which one draws inferences about processes from incorrect procedures, concepts, or representations of the problems. All of these methods were described earlier in Chapter 3 as part of the scientific reasoning process used by researchers to develop and test theories of the knowledge and processes underlying performance on cognitive tasks.

Baxter and Glaser (1998) used some of these techniques to examine how well test developers' intentions are realized in performance assessments that purport to measure complex cognitive processes. They developed a simple framework, a *content-process space* that depicts tasks' demands for content knowledge as lying on a continuum from rich to lean. At one extreme are knowledge-rich tasks that require in-depth understanding of subject matter topics; at the other extreme are tasks that depend not on prior knowledge or experience but on information given in the assessment situation. Similarly, tasks' demands for process skills are arrayed on a continuum from constrained to open. Assessment tasks can involve many possible combinations of content knowledge and process skills. Analyzing a diverse range of science assessments from state and district testing programs, Baxter and Glaser found matches and mismatches between the intentions of test developers and what the tasks actually measured, and varying degrees of correspondence between observed cognitive activity and performance scores. Box 5-8 provides an example of a concept mapping task that was found to overestimate quality of understanding.

In another study, Hamilton et al. (1997) investigated the usefulness of small-scale interview studies as a means of exploring the validity of both multiple-choice and performance-based science achievement tests. Interviews illuminated unanticipated cognitive processes used by test takers. One finding was the importance of distinguishing between the demands of open-ended tasks and the opportunities such tasks provide students. Some open-ended tasks enabled students to reason scientifically but did not explicitly require them to do so. If a task did not explicitly require scientific reasoning, students often chose to construct answers using everyday concepts and language. More-structured multiple-choice items, in contrast, did not offer students this choice and forced them to attend to the scientific principles. Clarifying the directions and stems of the open-ended tasks helped resolve these ambiguities.

Though the research studies described above analyzed tasks after they had already been administered as part of a large-scale assessment, the researchers concluded that cognitive task analysis should not be an afterthought, done only to make sense of the data after the test has been developed and administered to large numbers of students. Rather, such analyses should be an integral part of the test development process to ensure that instructions are clear and that tasks and associated scoring rubrics are functioning as intended. Some developers of large-scale assessments are beginning to heed this advice. For example, as part of the development of the Voluntary National Test, the contractor, American Institutes for Research, used cognitive laboratories to gauge whether students were responding to the items in ways the developers intended. The laboratories were intended to improve the quality of the items in two ways: by providing specific information about items, and by making it possible to generalize the findings to evaluate the quality of other items not tried out in the laboratories (NRC, 1999a).

It should be noted that exploring validity in the ways suggested here could also enhance the quality of informal assessments used in the classroom, such as classroom questioning, and the kinds of assignments teachers give students in class and as homework. The formulation of tasks for class work calls for similar reflection on the cognitive basis and functions of the assignments. The next example describes the design of the QUASAR assessment, which included efforts to collect evidence of the cognitive validity of the assessment tasks. This example also illustrates several of the other features of design proposed in this chapter, such as the central role of a model of learning and the highly recursive nature of the design process, which continually refers back to the model of learning.

Example: QUASAR Cognitive Assessment Instrument

QUASAR is an instructional program developed by Silver and colleagues to improve mathematics instruction for middle school students in economically disadvantaged communities (Silver, Smith, and Nelson, 1995; Silver and Stein, 1996). To evaluate the impact of this program, which emphasizes the abilities to solve problems, reason, and communicate mathematically, assessments were needed that would tap the complex cognitive processes targeted by instruction. In response to this need, the QUASAR Cognitive Assessment Instrument was developed (Lane, 1993; Silver and Lane, 1993).

Assessment design began with the development of a model of learning. Using the *Curriculum and Evaluation Standards for School Mathematics* (National Council of Teachers of Mathematics, 1989), augmented with findings from cognitive research, the assessment developers specified a number of cognitive processes important to competent performance in the domain: understanding and representing problems; discerning mathematical relations; organizing information; using and discovering strategies, heuristics, and procedures; formulating conjectures; evaluating the reasonableness of answers; generalizing results; justifying an answer or procedures; and communicating. These processes were defined more specifically in each of the content categories covered by the assessment: number and operations; estimation; patterns; algebra, geometry, and measurement; and data analysis, probability, and statistics. Specifications of the targeted content and processes served as the basis for developing preliminary tasks and scoring rubrics that would provide evidence of those processes.

Preliminary tasks were judged by a team of internal reviewers familiar with the QUASAR goals and the curricular and instructional approaches being used across different school sites. After internal review involving much group discussion, tasks were revised and pilot tested with samples of students. In addition to collecting students' written responses to the tasks, some students were interviewed individually. A student was asked to "think aloud"

BOX 5-8   **Cognitive Complexity of Science Tasks**

Baxter and Glaser (1998) studied matches and mismatches between the intentions of test developers and the nature of cognitive activity elicited in an assessment situation. The Connecticut Common Core of Learning Assessment Project developed a number of content-rich, process-constrained tasks around major topics in science. Baxter and Glaser analyzed a task that asked high school students to write an explanation in response to the following: "For what would you want your blood checked if you were having a transfusion?" (Lomask, Baron, Greig, and Harrison, 1992). Concept maps were developed for scoring student explanations. The expert's (teacher's) concept map below served as a template against which students' performances were evaluated.

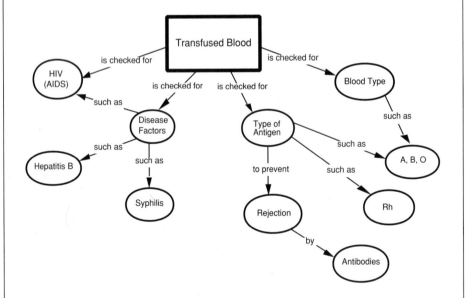

On the surface, concept maps appear to be an excellent way to showcase the differential quality of student responses for teachers and students because they explicitly attend to the organization and structure of knowledge. However, Baxter and Glaser found that an overestimate of students' understanding stems from two features of the concept map: (1) the knowledge assumed, with half of the core concepts (e.g., HIV, disease, blood type) being learned in contexts outside science class, and (2) the relations among the concepts, 90 percent of which are at the level of examples or procedural links (such as, is checked for) rather than processes or underlying causal mechanisms. Unless proficient performance displayed by the concept map requires inferences or reasoning about subject matter relations or causal mechanisms reflective of principled knowledge, the concept map serves primarily as a checklist of words and misrepresents (overestimates in this case) students' understanding.

SOURCE: Lomask, Baron, Greig, and Harrison (1992, p. 27). Used with permission of the authors.

as he or she completed the task, and also to elaborate retrospectively on certain aspects of the solution. Interviews were recorded, transcribed, and analyzed to determine whether the student had interpreted each task as intended and the task had elicited the intended processes.

The judgments of the internal reviewers, along with the pilot data, were used to answer a series of questions related to the quality of the tasks: Does the task assess the skill/content it was designed to assess? Does the task assess the high-level cognitive processes it was designed to assess? Does the task elicit different representations and strategies? What are they, and how often do they occur in the pilot data? If the task asks for an explanation, are the students providing high-level conceptual explanations? If the task requires students to show their work, are they complete in providing the steps involved in their solutions?

On the basis of the answers to these questions, a task was either discarded, revised and pilot tested again, or judged satisfactory and forwarded to the next stage of external review. External review was conducted by teams of outside expert mathematics educators, mathematicians, and psychometricians. This review served as a check on whether important mathematical content and processes were being assessed, and whether the tasks were free from bias and technically sound.

BOX 5-9　**Revising Tasks**

The Pattern Task was designed to assess reasoning skills for identifying the underlying regularities of a figural pattern, using these regularities to extend the pattern, and communicating these regularities effectively. The following is the original version of this task:

For homework, Allan's teacher asked him to look at the pattern below and draw the figure that should come next.

Allan doesn't know how to find the next figure.

Write a description for Allan telling him which figure comes next.

The pilot data showed that in response to this initial version, many students simply drew a fifth figure rather than providing a description of the pattern regularities, making it difficult to obtain a sense of their solution strategies. The task was therefore revised so it asked students to describe *how* they knew which figure comes next. This change increased

The development process for the QUASAR Cognitive Assessment Instrument required continual interplay among the validation procedures of logical analysis, internal review, pilot testing, and external review. Sometimes a task would undergo several iterations of a subset of these procedures before it was considered ready for the next stage of development. An example is given in Box 5-9.

REPORTING OF ASSESSMENT RESULTS

Although reporting of results occurs at the end of an assessment cycle, assessments must be designed from the outset to ensure that reporting of the desired types of information will be possible. As emphasized at the beginning of this chapter, the purpose for the assessment and the kinds of inferences one wants to draw from the results should drive the design, including the cognitive complexity of the students' responses. On the basis of further pilot testing and expert review, the task was revised to its present form.

For homework Miguel's teacher asked him to look at the pattern below and draw the figure that should come next.

Miguel does not know how to find the next figure.

A. Draw the next figure for Miguel.

B. Write a description for Miguel telling him how you knew which figure comes next.

SOURCE: Magone, Cai, Silver, and Wang (1994, p. 324). Reprinted with permission from Elsevier Science.

the selection of an appropriate model of learning, the observations, and the interpretation model.

The familiar distinction between norm-referenced and criterion-referenced testing is salient in understanding the central role of a model of learning in the reporting of assessment results. Traditionally, achievement tests have been designed to provide results that compare students' performance with that of other students. The results are usually *norm-referenced* since they compare student performance with that of a norm group (that is, a representative sample of students who took the same test). Such information is useful, just as height and weight data are informative when placed in the context of such data on other individuals. Comparative test information can help parents, teachers, and others determine whether students are progressing at the same rate as their peers or whether they are above or below the average. Norm-referenced data are limited, however, because they do not show what a student actually can or cannot do. A score indicating that a student is in the 40th percentile in mathematics does not reveal what mathematics knowledge the student does or does not have. The student may have answered most items correctly if the norm group was high-performing, or may have answered many questions incorrectly if the norm group performed less well. Nor does the norm-referenced score indicate what a student needs to do to improve. In the 1960s, Glaser (1963) drew attention to the desirability of shifting to *criterion-referenced* testing so that a student's performance would be reported in absolute terms, that is, in terms of what the student can or cannot do.

> . . . the specific behaviors implied at each level of proficiency can be identified and used to describe the specific tasks a student must be capable of performing before he achieves one of these knowledge levels. . . . Measures which assess student achievement in terms of a criterion standard thus provide information as to the degree of competence attained by a particular student which is independent of reference to the performance of others. (pp. 519-520)

The notion of criterion-referenced testing has gained popularity in the last few decades, particularly with the advent of standards-based reforms in the 1990s. As a result of these reforms, many states are implementing tests designed to measure student performance against standards in core content areas. A number of states are combining these measures with more traditional norm-referenced reports to show how students' performance compares with that of students from other states as well (Council of Chief State School Officers, 2000).

Because criterion-referenced interpretations depend so directly on a clear explication of what students can or cannot do, well-delineated descriptions of learning in the domain are key to their effectiveness in communicating about student performance. Test results should be reported in relation to a model of learning. The ways people learn the subject matter and different states of competence should be displayed and made as recognizable as possible to educators, students, and the public to foster discussion and shared understanding of what constitutes academic achievement. Some examples of enhanced reporting afforded by models of learning (e.g., progress maps) are presented in Chapter 4.

FAIRNESS

Fairness in testing is defined in many ways (see AERA et al., 1999; NRC, 1999b), but at its core is the idea of *comparable validity*: a fair test is one that yields comparably valid inferences from person to person and group to group. An assessment task is considered biased if construct-irrelevant characteristics of the task result in different meanings for different subgroups.

For example, it is now common wisdom that a task used to observe mathematical reasoning should include words and expressions in general use and not those associated with particular cultures or regions; the latter might result in a lack of comparable score meanings across groups of examinees.

Currently, bias tends to be identified through expert review of items. Such a finding is merely judgmental, however, and in and of itself may not warrant removal of items from an assessment. Also used are statistical differential item functioning (DIF) analyses, which identify items that produce differing results for members of particular groups after the groups have been matched in ability with regard to the attribute being measured (Holland and Thayer, 1988). However, DIF is a statistical finding and again may not warrant removal of items from an assessment. Some researchers have therefore begun to supplement existing bias-detection methods with cognitive analyses designed to uncover the reasons why items are functioning differently across groups in terms of how students think about and approach the problems (e.g., Lane, Wang, and Magone, 1996; Zwick and Ercikan, 1989).

A particular set of fairness issues involves the testing of students with disabilities. A substantial number of children who participate in assessments do so with accommodations intended to permit them to participate meaningfully. For instance, a student with a severe reading and writing disability might be able to take a chemistry test with the assistance of a computer-based reader and dictation system. Unfortunately, little evidence currently exists about the effects of various accommodations on the inferences one might wish to draw about the performance of individuals with disabilities (NRC, 1997), though some researchers have taken initial steps in studying these issues (Abedi, Hofstetter, and Baker, 2001). Therefore, cognitive analyses are also needed to gain insight into how accommodations affect task demands, as well as the validity of inferences drawn from test scores obtained under such circumstances.

In some situations, rather than aiming to design items that are culture- or background-free, a better option may be to take into account learner history in the interpretation of responses to the assessment. The distinction between *conditional* and *unconditional* inferences deserves attention because it may provide a key to resolving some of the thorniest issues in assessment today, including equity and student choice of tasks.

Conditional Versus Unconditional Inferences

To some extent in any assessment, given students of similar ability, what is relatively difficult for some students may be relatively easy for others, depending on the degree to which the tasks relate to the knowledge structures students have, each in their own way, constructed (Mislevy, 1996). From the traditional perspective, this is "noise," or measurement error, and if excessive leads to low reliability (see Chapter 4). For inferences concerning overall proficiency in this sense, tasks that do not rank individuals in the same order are less informative than ones that do.

Such interactions between tasks and prior knowledge are fully expected from modern perspectives on learning, however, since it is now known that knowledge typically develops first in context, then is extended and decontextualized so it can be applied more broadly to other contexts. An in-depth project that dovetails with students' prior knowledge provides solid information, but becomes a waste of time for students for whom this connection is lacking. The same task can therefore reveal either vital evidence or little at all, depending on the target of inference and the relationship of the information involved to what is known from other sources.

Current approaches to assessment, particularly large-scale testing, rely on *unconditional* interpretation of student responses. This means that evaluation or interpretation of student responses does not depend on any other information the evaluator might have about the background of the examinee. This approach works reasonably well when there is little unique interaction between students and tasks (less likely for assessments connected with instruction than for those external to the classroom) or when enough tasks can be administered to average over the interactions (thus the SAT has 200 items). The disadvantage of unconditional scoring is that it precludes saying different things about a student's performance in light of other information that might be known about the student's instructional history.

An alternative way to interpret evidence from students' responses to tasks is referred to as *conditional* interpretation. Here the observer or scorer has additional background information about the student that affects the interpretation. This can be accomplished in one of three ways, each of which is illustrated using the example of all assessment of students' understanding of control of variables in scientific experimentation (Chen and Klahr, 1999).

Example: Assessment of Control-of-Variables Strategy

In their study, Chen and Klahr (1999) exposed children to three levels of training in how to design simple unconfounded experiments. One group received explicit training and repeated probe questions. Another group received only probe questions and no direct training. Finally, the third group served as a control: they received equal exposure to the materials, but no instruction at all. Three different kinds of materials were used for subgroups of children in each training condition. Some children were initially exposed to ramps and balls, other to springs and weights, and still other to sinking objects.

Children in each training condition were subsequently assessed on how well they could transfer their knowledge about the control-of-variables procedures. The three assessments were designed to be increasingly "distant" from the materials used during the training.

(a) "Very near transfer": This assessment was in the same domain as was the initial exposure (e.g., children trained on ramps were asked to design additional experiments using ramps).

(b) "Near transfer": In this assessment, children initially exposed to one domain (e.g., springs) were asked to design experiments in a different domain (e.g., ramps).

(c) "Far transfer": Here, children were presented with a task that was amenable to the same control-of-variables strategy but had different surface features (e.g., paper-and-pencil assessments of good and bad experimental designs in domains outside physics).

Two points are central to the present discussion:

• The targets of assessment were three factors: tendency to subsequently use the control-of-variables strategy in the instructional context, in near-transfer contexts, and in far-transfer contexts. All the tasks were carefully designed to make it possible to determine whether a child used the strategy.

• Whether a task was an example task, a near-transfer task, or a far-transfer task was not a property of the task, but of the match between the task and the student. Tasks were even counterbalanced within groups with regard to which was the teaching example and which was the near-transfer task.

The results of the study showed clear differences among groups across the different kinds of tasks: negligible differences on the repeat of the task on which a child had been instructed; a larger difference on the near-transfer task, favoring children who had been taught the strategy; and a difference again favoring these children on far-transfer tasks, which turned out to be difficult for almost all the children. What is important here is that no such pattern could have emerged if the researchers had simply administered the post test task to all students without knowing either the training that constituted the first half of the experiment or the match between each child's post test task and the training he or she had received. The evidence is not in the task performance data, but in the evaluation of those data in light of other information the researchers possessed about the students.

Methods of Conditional Inference

The first method of conditional inference is that the observer influences the observational setting (the assessment task presented to the student) or the conditions that precede the observation in ways that ensure a certain task-examinee matchup. This method is demonstrated by the design of the control-of-variables study just described.

A second way to condition the extraction of information from student performances is to obtain relevant background information about students from which to infer key aspects of the matchups. In the Klahr et al. (in press) example, this approach would be appropriate if the researchers could only give randomly selected post-test tasks to students, but could try to use curriculum guides and teacher interviews to determine how each student's post-test happened to correspond with his or her past instruction (if at all).

A third method is to let students choose among assessment tasks in light of what they know about themselves—their interests, their strengths, and their backgrounds. In the control-of-variables study, students might be shown several tasks and asked to solve one they encountered in instruction, one a great deal like it, and one quite dissimilar (making sure the student identified which was which). A complication here is that some students will likely be better at making such decisions than others.

The forms of conditional inference described above offer promise for tackling persisting issues of equity and fairness in large-scale assessment. Future assessments could be designed that take into account students' opportunity to learn what is being tested. Similarly, such approaches could help address issues of curriculum fairness, that is, help protect against external assessments that favor one curriculum over another. Issues of opportunity to learn and the need for alignment among assessment, curriculum, and instruction are taken up further in Chapter 6.

CONCLUSIONS

The design of high-quality classroom and large-scale assessments is a complex process that involves numerous components best characterized as iterative and interdependent, rather than linear and sequential. A design decision made at a later stage can affect one occurring earlier in the process. As a result, assessment developers must often revisit their choices and refine their designs.

One of the main features that distinguishes the committee's proposed approach to assessment design from current approaches is the central role of a model of cognition and learning, as emphasized above. This model may be fine-grained and very elaborate or more coarsely grained, depending on the purpose of the assessment, but it should always be based on empirical studies of learners in a domain. Ideally, the model of learning will also provide a developmental perspective, showing typical ways in which learners progress toward competence.

Another essential feature of good assessment design is an interpretation model that fits the model of learning. Just as sophisticated interpretation techniques used with assessment tasks based on impoverished models of learning will produce limited information about student competence, assessments based on a contemporary and detailed understanding of how students learn will not yield all the information they otherwise might if the statistical tools available to interpret the data, or the data themselves, are not sufficient for the task. *Observations, which include assessment tasks along with the criteria for evaluating students' responses, must be carefully designed to elicit the knowledge and cognitive processes that the model of learning suggests are most important for competence in the domain.* The interpretation model must incorporate this evidence in the results in a manner consistent with the model of learning.

Validation that tasks tap relevant knowledge and cognitive processes, often lacking in assessment development, is another essential aspect of the development effort. Starting with hypotheses about the cognitive demands of a task, a variety of research techniques, such as interviews, having students think aloud as they work problems, and analysis of errors, can be used to analyze the mental processes of examinees during task performance. Conducting such analyses early in the assessment development process can help ensure that assessments do, in fact, measure what they are intended to measure.

Well-delineated descriptions of learning in the domain are key to being able to communicate effectively about the nature of student performance. *Although reporting of results occurs at the end of an assessment cycle, assessments must be designed from the outset to ensure that reporting of the desired types of information will be possible.* The ways in which people learn the subject matter, as well as different types or levels of competence, should be displayed and made as recognizable as possible to educators, students, and the public.

Fairness is a key issue in educational assessment. *One way of addressing fairness in assessment is to take into account examinees' histories of instruction—or opportunities to learn the material being tested—when designing assessments and interpreting students' responses.* Ways of drawing such conditional inferences have been tried mainly on a small scale, but hold promise for tackling persistent issues of equity in testing.

Some examples of assessments that approximate the above features already exist. They are illustrative of the new approach to assessment the committee advocates, and they suggest principles for the design of new assessments that can better serve the goals of learning.

Four themes guide the discussion in this chapter of how advances in the cognitive sciences and new approaches to measurement have created opportunities, not yet fully realized, for assessments to be used in ways that better serve the goals of learning.

- One type of assessment does not fit all. The purpose and context of an assessment set priorities and constraints on the design. The power of classroom assessment resides in its close connections to instruction and teachers' knowledge of their students' instructional histories. Large-scale, standardized assessments can communicate across time and place, but by so constraining the content and timeliness of the message that they often have limited utility in the classroom. These kinds of trade-offs are an inescapable aspect of assessment design.

- It is in the context of classroom assessment that the most significant benefit can be gained from advances in cognitive theory. Learning is enhanced by assessment that provides feedback to students about particular qualities of their work and what they can do to improve their understanding. To provide this kind of information, teachers must have a foundation of knowledge about how students learn the subject matter.

- Large-scale assessments are further removed from instruction, but can still benefit learning if well designed and properly used. They can signal worthy goals and display to the public what competency in a domain looks like, along with typical learning pathways. They can also play an important role in communicating and fostering public dialogue about educational goals. However, fully capitalizing on a merger of cognitive and measurement principles will require relaxing some of the constraints that drive current large-scale assessment practices.

- Multiple measures are needed to serve the assessment needs of an educational system. Currently, however, conflicts between classroom and large-scale assessments in terms of both goals and feedback cause confusion for educators, students, and parents. We describe a vision of coordinated systems of assessment in which multiple assessments work together, along with curriculum and instruction, to support a shared set of learning goals. In this vision, a greater portion of the investment in assessment is shifted toward the classroom, where it can be used most directly to assist learning.

6

Assessment in Practice

Although assessments are currently used for many purposes in the educational system, a premise of this report is that their effectiveness and utility must ultimately be judged by the extent to which they promote student learning. The aim of assessment should be "*to educate and improve* student performance, not merely to *audit* it" (Wiggins, 1998, p.7). To this end, people should gain important and useful information from every assessment situation. In education, as in other professions, good decision making depends on access to relevant, accurate, and timely information. Furthermore, the information gained should be put to good use by informing decisions about curriculum and instruction and ultimately improving student learning (Falk, 2000; National Council of Teachers of Mathematics, 1995).

Assessments do not function in isolation; an assessment's effectiveness in improving learning depends on its relationships to curriculum and instruction. Ideally, instruction is faithful and effective in relation to curriculum, and assessment reflects curriculum in such a way that it reinforces the best practices in instruction. In actuality, however, the relationships among assessment, curriculum, and instruction are not always ideal. Often assessment taps only a subset of curriculum and without regard to instruction, and can narrow and distort instruction in unintended ways (Klein, Hamilton, McCaffrey, and Stecher, 2000; Koretz and Barron, 1998; Linn, 2000; National Research Council [NRC], 1999b). In this chapter we expand on the idea, introduced in Chapter 2, that synergy can best be achieved if the three parts of the system are bound by or grow out of a shared knowledge base about cognition and learning in the domain.

PURPOSES AND CONTEXTS OF USE

Educational assessment occurs in two major contexts. The first is the classroom. Here assessment is used by teachers and students mainly to assist learning, but also to gauge students' summative achievement over the longer term. Second is large-scale assessment, used by policy makers and educational leaders to evaluate programs and/or obtain information about whether individual students have met learning goals.

The sharp contrast that typically exists between classroom and large-scale assessment practices arises because assessment designers have not been able to fulfill the purposes of different assessment users with the same data and analyses. To guide instruction and monitor its effects, teachers need information that is intimately connected with the work their students are doing, and they interpret this evidence in light of everything else they know about their students and the conditions of instruction. Part of the power of classroom assessment resides in these connections. Yet precisely because they are individualized and highly contextualized, neither the rationale nor the results of typical classroom assessments are easily communicated beyond the classroom. Large-scale, standardized tests do communicate efficiently across time and place, but by so constraining the content and timeliness of the message that they often have little utility in the classroom. This contrast illustrates the more general point that one size of assessment does not fit all. The purpose of an assessment determines priorities, and the context of use imposes constraints on the design, thereby affecting the kinds of information a particular assessment can provide about student achievement.

Inevitability of Trade-Offs in Design

To say that an assessment is a good assessment or that a task is a good task is like saying that a medical test is a good test; each can provide useful information only under certain circumstances. An MRI of a knee, for example, has unquestioned value for diagnosing cartilage damage, but is not helpful for diagnosing the overall quality of a person's health. It is natural for people to understand medical tests in this way, but not educational tests. The same argument applies nonetheless, but in ways that are less familiar and perhaps more subtle.

In their classic text *Psychological Tests and Personnel Decisions*, Cronbach and Gleser (1965) devote an entire chapter to the trade-off between *fidelity* and *bandwidth* when testing for employment selection. A high-fidelity, narrow-bandwidth test provides accurate information about a small number of focused questions, whereas a low-fidelity, broad-bandwidth test provides noisier information for a larger number of less-focused questions. For a

fixed level of resources—the same amount of money, testing time, or tasks—
the designer can choose where an assessment will fall along this spectrum.
Following are two examples related to the fidelity-bandwidth (or depth versus breadth) trade-offs that inevitably arise in the design of educational assessments. They illustrate the point that the more purposes one attempts to
serve with a single assessment, the less well that assessment can serve any
given purpose.

Trade-Offs in Assessment Design: Examples

Accountability Versus Instructional Guidance for Individual Students

The first example expands on the contrast between classroom and large-
scale assessments described above. A starting point is the desire for statewide accountability tests to be more helpful to teachers or the question of
why assessment designers cannot incorporate in the tests items that are
closely tied to the instructional activities in which students are engaged (i.e.,
assessment tasks such as those effective teachers use in their classrooms). To
understand why this has not been done, one must look at the distinct purposes served by standardized achievement tests and classroom quizzes: who
the users are, what they already know, and what they want to learn.

In this example, the chief state school officer wants to know whether
students have been studying the topics identified in the state standards.
(Actually, by assessing these topics, the officer wants to increase the likelihood that students will be studying them.) But there are many curriculum
standards, and she or he certainly cannot ascertain whether each has been
studied by every student. A broad sample from each student is better for his
or her purposes—not enough information to determine the depth or the
nature of any student's knowledge across the statewide curriculum, but enough
to see trends across schools and districts about broad patterns of performance. This information can be used to plan funding and policy decisions
for the coming year.

The classroom teacher wants to know how well an individual student, or class of
students, is learning the things they have been studying and what they ought to be
working on next. What is important is the match among what the teacher already
knows about the things students have been working on, what the teacher
needs to learn about their current understanding, and how that knowledge
will help shape what the students should do now to learn further.

For the chief state school officer, the ultimate question is whether larger
aggregates of students (such as schools, districts, or states) have had "the
opportunity to learn." The state assessment is constructed to gather information to support essentially the same inference about all students, so the

information can most easily be combined to meet the chief officer's purpose. For the teacher, the starting point is knowing what each student as an individual has had the opportunity to learn. The classroom quiz is designed to reveal patterns of individual knowledge (compared with the state grade-level standards) within the small content domain in which students have been working so the teacher can make tailored decisions about next steps for individual students or the class. For the teacher, combining information across classes that are studying and testing different content is not important or possible. Ironically, the questions that are of most use to the state officer are of the least use to the teacher.

National Assessment of Educational Progress (NAEP): Estimates for Groups Versus Individual Students

The current public debate over whether to provide student-level reports from NAEP highlights a trade-off that goes to the very heart of the assessment and has shaped its sometimes frustratingly complex design from its inception (see Forsyth, Hambleton, Linn, Mislevy, and Yen, 1996 for a history of NAEP design trade-offs). NAEP was designed to survey the knowledge of students across the nation with respect to a broad range of content and skills, and to report the relationships between that knowledge and a large number of educational and demographic background variables. The design selected by the founders of NAEP (including Ralph Tyler and John Tukey) to achieve this purpose was multiple-matrix sampling. Not all students in the country are sampled. A strategically selected sample can support the targeted inferences about groups of students with virtually the same precision as the very familiar approach of testing every student, but for a fraction of the cost. Moreover, not all students are administered all items. NAEP can use hundreds of tasks of many kinds to gather information about competencies in student populations without requiring any student to spend more than a class period performing those tasks; it does so by assembling the items into many overlapping short forms and giving each sampled student a single form.

Schools can obtain useful feedback on the quality of their curriculum, but NAEP's benefits are traded off against several limitations. Measurement at the level of individual students is poor, and individuals can not be ranked, compared, or diagnosed. Further analyses of the data are problematic. But a design that served any of these purposes well (for instance, by testing every student, by testing each student intensively, or by administering every student parallel sets of items to achieve better comparability) would degrade the estimates and increase the costs of the inferences NAEP was created to address.

Reflections on the Multiple Purposes for Assessment

As noted, the more purposes a single assessment aims to serve, the more each purpose will be compromised. Serving multiple purposes is not necessarily wrong, of course, and in truth few assessments can be said to serve a single purpose only. But it is incumbent on assessment designers and users to recognize the compromises and trade-offs such use entails. We return to notions of constraints and trade-offs later in this chapter.

Multiple assessments are thus needed to provide the various types of information required at different levels of the educational system. This does not mean, however, that the assessments need to be disconnected or working at cross-purposes. If multiple assessments grow out of a shared knowledge base about cognition and learning in the domain, they can provide valuable multiple perspectives on student achievement while supporting a core set of learning goals. Stakeholders should not be unduly concerned if differing assessments yield different information about student achievement; in fact, in many circumstances this is exactly what should be expected. However, if multiple assessments are to support learning effectively and provide clear and meaningful results for various audiences, it is important that the purposes served by each assessment and the aspects of achievement sampled by any given assessment be made explicit to users.

Later in the chapter we address how multiple assessments, including those used across both classroom and large-scale contexts, could work together to form more complete assessment systems. First, however, we discuss classroom and large-scale assessments in turn and how each can best be used to serve the goals of learning.

CLASSROOM ASSESSMENT

The first thing that comes to mind for many people when they think of "classroom assessment" is a midterm or end-of-course exam, used by the teacher for summative grading purposes. But such practices represent only a fraction of the kinds of assessment that occur on an ongoing basis in an effective classroom. The focus in this section is on assessments used by teachers to support instruction and learning, also referred to as *formative* assessment. Such assessment offers considerable potential for improving student learning when informed by research and theory on how students develop subject matter competence.

As instruction is occurring, teachers need information to evaluate whether their teaching strategies are working. They also need information about the current understanding of individual students and groups of students so they can identify the most appropriate next steps for instruction. Moreover, students need feedback to monitor their own success in learning and to know how to improve. Teachers make observations of student understanding and performance in a variety of ways: from classroom dialogue, questioning, seatwork and homework assignments, formal tests, less formal quizzes, projects, portfolios, and so on.

Black and Wiliam (1998) provide an extensive review of more than 250 books and articles presenting research evidence on the effects of classroom assessment. They conclude that ongoing assessment by teachers, combined with appropriate feedback to students, can have powerful and positive effects on achievement. They also report, however, that the characteristics of high-quality formative assessment are not well understood by teachers and

BOX 6-1 **Transforming Classroom Assessment Practices**

A project at King's College London (Black and Wiliam, 2000) illustrates some of the issues encountered when an effort is made to incorporate principles of cognition and reasoning from evidence into classroom practice. The project involved working closely with 24 science and mathematics teachers to develop their formative assessment practices in everyday classroom work. During the course of the project, several aspects of the teaching and learning process were radically changed.

One such aspect was the teachers' practices in asking questions in the classroom. In particular, the focus was on the notion of wait time (the length of the silence a teacher would allow after asking a question before speaking again if nobody responded), with emphasis on how short this time usually is. The teachers altered their practice to give students extended time to think about any question posed, often asking them to discuss their ideas in pairs before calling for responses. The practice of students putting up their hands to volunteer answers was forbidden; anyone could be asked to respond. The teachers did not label answers as right or wrong, but instead asked a student to explain his or her reasons for the answer offered. Others were then asked to say whether they agreed and why. Thus questions opened up discussion that helped expose and explore students' assumptions and reasoning. At the same time, wrong answers became useful input, and the students realized that the teacher was interested in knowing what they thought, not in evaluating whether they were right or wrong. As a consequence, teachers asked fewer questions, spending more time on each.

that formative assessment is weak in practice. High-quality classroom assessment is a complex process, as illustrated by research described in Box 6-1 that encapsulates many of the points made in the following discussion. In brief, the development of good formative assessment requires radical changes in the ways students are encouraged to express their ideas and in the ways teachers give feedback to students so they can develop the ability to manage and guide their own learning. Where such innovations have been instituted, teachers have become acutely aware of the need to think more clearly about their own assumptions regarding how students learn.

In addition, teachers realized that their lesson planning had to include careful thought about the selection of informative questions. They discovered that they had to consider very carefully the aspects of student thinking that any given question might serve to explore. This discovery led them to work further on developing criteria for the quality of their questions. Thus the teachers confronted the importance of the cognitive foundations for designing assessment situations that can evoke important aspects of student thinking and learning. (See Bonniol [1991] and Perrenoud [1998]) for further discussion of the importance of high-quality teacher questions for illuminating student thinking.)

In response to research evidence that simply giving grades on written work can be counterproductive for learning (Butler, 1988), teachers began instead to concentrate on providing comments without grades—feedback designed to guide students' further learning. Students also took part in self-assessment and peer-assessment activities, which required that they understand the goals for learning and the criteria for quality that applied to their work. These kinds of activities called for patient training and support from teachers, but fostered students' abilities to focus on targets for learning and to identify learning goals for which they lacked confidence and needed help (metacognitive skills described in Chapter 3). In these ways, assessment situations became opportunities for learning, rather than activities divorced from learning.

There is a rich literature on how classroom assessment can be designed and used to improve instruction and learning (e.g., Falk, 2000; Niyogi, 1995; Shepard, 2000; Stiggins, 1997; Wiggins, 1998). This literature presents powerful ideas and practical advice to assist teachers across the K-16 spectrum in improving their classroom assessment practices. We do not attempt to summarize all of the insights and implications for practice presented in this literature. Rather, our emphasis is on what could be gained by thinking about classroom assessment in light of the principles of cognition and reasoning from evidence emphasized throughout this report.

Formative Assessment, Curriculum, and Instruction

At the 2000 annual meeting of the American Educational Research Association, Shepard (2000) began her presidential address by quoting Graue's (1993, p. 291) observation, that "assessment and instruction are often conceived as *curiously separate* in both time and purpose." Shepard asked:

> How might the culture of classrooms be shifted so that students no longer feign competence or work to perform well on the test as an end separate from real learning? Could we create a learning culture where students and teachers would have a shared expectation that finding out what makes sense and what doesn't is a joint and worthwhile project, essential to taking the next steps in learning? ...How should what we do in classrooms be changed so that students and teachers look to assessment as a source of insight and help instead of its being the occasion for meting out reward and punishments. To accomplish this kind of transformation, we have to make assessment more useful, more helpful in learning, and at the same time change the social meaning of evaluation. (pp. 12-15)

Shepard proceeded to discuss ways in which classroom assessment practices need to change: the content and character of assessments need to be significantly improved to reflect contemporary understanding of learning; the gathering and use of assessment information and insights must become a part of the ongoing learning process; and assessment must become a central concern in methods courses in teacher preparation programs. Shepard's messages were reflective of a growing belief among many educational assessment experts that if assessment, curriculum, and instruction were more integrally connected, student learning would improve (e.g., Gipps, 1999; Pellegrino, Baxter, and Glaser, 1999; Snow and Mandinach, 1991; Stiggins, 1997).

Sadler (1989) provides a conceptual framework that places classroom assessment in the context of curriculum and instruction. According to this framework, three elements are required for formative assessment to promote learning:

- A clear view of the learning goals.
- Information about the present state of the learner.
- Action to close the gap.

These three elements relate directly to assessment, curriculum, and instruction. The *learning goals* are derived from the curriculum. The *present state of the learner* is derived from assessment, so that the gap between it and the learning goals can be appraised. *Action* is then taken through instruction to close the gap. An important point is that assessment information by itself simply reveals student competence at a point in time; the process is considered formative assessment only when teachers use the information to make decisions about how to adapt instruction to meet students' needs.

Furthermore, there are ongoing, dynamic relationships among formative assessment, curriculum, and instruction. That is, there are important bidirectional interactions among the three elements, such that each informs the other. For instance, formulating assessment procedures for classroom use can spur a teacher to think more specifically about learning goals, thus leading to modification of curriculum and instruction. These modifications can, in turn, lead to refined assessment procedures, and so on.

The mere existence of classroom assessment along the lines discussed here will not ensure effective learning. The clarity and appropriateness of the curriculum goals, the validity of the assessments in relationship to these goals, the interpretation of the assessment evidence, and the relevance and quality of the instruction that ensues are all critical determinants of the outcome. Starting with a model of cognition and learning in the domain can enhance each of these determinants.

Importance of a Model of Cognition and Learning

For most teachers, the ultimate goals for learning are established by the curriculum, which is usually mandated externally (e.g., by state curriculum standards). However, teachers and others responsible for designing curriculum, instruction, and assessment must fashion intermediate goals that can serve as an effective route to achieving the ultimate goals, and to do so they must have an understanding of how people represent knowledge and develop competence in the domain.

National and state standards documents set forth learning goals, but often not at a level of detail that is useful for operationalizing those goals in instruction and assessment (American Federation of Teachers, 1999; Finn, Petrilli, and Vanourek, 1998). By dividing goal descriptions into sets appropriate for different age and grade ranges, current curriculum standards provide broad guidance about the nature of the progression to be expected in various subject domains. Whereas this kind of epistemological and conceptual analysis of the subject domain is an essential basis for guiding assessment, deeper cognitive analysis of how people learn the subject matter is also needed. Formative assessment should be based on cognitive theories about how people learn particular subject matter to ensure that instruction centers on what is most important for the next stage of learning, given a learner's current state of understanding. As described in Chapter 3, cognitive research has produced a rich set of descriptions of how people develop problem-solving and reasoning competencies in various content areas, particularly for the domains of mathematics and science. These models of learning provide a fertile ground for designing formative assessments.

It follows that teachers need training to develop their understanding of cognition and learning in the domains they teach. Preservice and professional development are needed to uncover teachers' existing understandings of how students learn (Strauss, 1998), and to help them formulate models of learning so they can identify students' naive or initial sense-making strategies and build on those strategies to move students toward more sophisticated understandings. The aim is to increase teachers' diagnostic expertise so they can make informed decisions about next steps for student learning. This has been a primary goal of cognitively based approaches to instruction and assessment that have been shown to have a positive impact on student learning, including the Cognitively Guided Instruction program (Carpenter, Fennema, and Franke, 1996) and others (Cobb et al., 1991; Griffin and Case, 1997), some of which are described below. As these examples point out, however, such approaches rest on a bedrock of informed professional practice.

Cognitively Based Approaches to Classroom Assessment: Examples

Cognitively Guided Instruction and Assessment

Carpenter, Fennema, and colleagues have demonstrated that teachers who are informed regarding children's thinking about arithmetic will be in a better position to craft more effective mathematics instruction (Carpenter et al., 1996; Carpenter, Fennema, Peterson, and Carey, 1988). Their approach, called Cognitively Guided Instruction (CGI), borrows much from cognitive science, yet recasts that work at a higher level of abstraction, a midlevel model designed explicitly to be easily understood and used by teachers. As noted earlier, such a model permits teachers to "read and react" to ongoing events in real time as they unfold during the course of instruction. In a sense, the researchers suggest that teachers use this midlevel model to support a process of continuous formative assessment so that instruction can be modified frequently as needed.

The cornerstone of CGI is a coarse-grained model of student thinking that borrows from work done in cognitive science to characterize the semantic structure of word problems, along with typical strategies children use for their solution. For instance, teachers are informed that problems apparently involving different operations, such as 3 + 7 = 10 and 10 − 7 = 3, are regarded by children as similar because both involve the action of combining sets. The model that summarizes children's thinking about arithmetic word problems involving addition or subtraction is summarized by a three-dimensional matrix, in which the rows define major classes of semantic relations, such as combining, separating, or comparing sets; the columns refer to the unknown set (e.g., 7 + 3 = ? vs. 7 + ? = 10); and the depth is a compilation of typical strategies children employ to solve problems such as these. Cognitive-developmental studies (Baroody, 1984; Carpenter and Moser, 1984; Siegler and Jenkins, 1989) suggest that children's trajectories in this space are highly consistent. For example, direct modeling strategies are acquired before counting strategies; similarly, counting on from the first addend (e.g., 2 + 4 = ?, 2, 3(1), 4(2), 5(3), 6(4)) is acquired before counting on from the larger addend (e.g., 4, 5(1), 6(2)).

Because development of these strategies tends to be robust, teachers can quickly locate student thinking within the problem space defined by CGI. Moreover, the model helps teachers locate likely antecedent understandings and helps them anticipate appropriate next steps. Given a student's solution to a problem, a classroom teacher can modify instruction in a number of ways: (1) by posing a developmentally more difficult or easier problem; (2) by altering the size of the numbers in the set; or (3) by comparing and contrasting students' solution strategies, so that students can come to appreciate the utility and elegance of a strategy they might not yet be able to generate on their own. For example, a student directly modeling a joining of sets with counters (e.g., 2 + 3 solved by combining 2 chips with 3 chips and then counting all the chips) might profit by observing how a classmate uses a counting strategy (such as 2, 3(1), etc.) to solve the same problem. In a program such as CGI, formative assessment is woven seamlessly into the fabric of instruction (Carpenter et al., 1996).

Intelligent Tutors

As described in previous chapters, intelligent tutoring systems are powerful examples of the use of cognitively based classroom assessment tools blended with instruction. Studies indicate that when students work alone with these computer-based tutors, the relationship between formative assessment and the model of student thinking derived from research is comparatively direct. Students make mistakes, and the system offers effective

BOX 6-2 Effects of an Intelligent Tutoring System on Mathematics Learning

A large-scale experiment evaluated the benefits of intelligent tutoring in an urban high school (Koedinger, Anderson, Hadley, and Mark, 1997). Researchers compared achievement levels of ninth-grade students who received the PUMP curriculum, which is supported by an intelligent tutor, the PUMP Algebra Tutor (PAT) (experimental group), with those of students who received more traditional algebra instruction (control group).* The results, presented below, demonstrate strong learning benefits from using the curriculum that included the intelligent tutoring program.

The researchers did not collect baseline data to ensure similar starting achievement levels across experimental and control groups. However, they report that the groups were similar in terms of demographics. In addition, they looked at students' mathematics grades in the previous school year to check for differences in students' prior knowledge that would put the experimental group at an advantage. In fact, the average prior grades for the experimental group were lower than those for the control group.

———————————

*The researchers note that their research strategy is first to establish the success of the whole package and then to examine the effects of the curriculum and intelligent tutoring components independently; this work is still to be finished.

remediation. As a result, students on average learn more with the system than with other, traditional instruction (see Box 6-2).

On the other hand, some research suggests that the relationship between formative assessment and cognitive theory can be more complex. In a study of Anderson's geometry tutor with high school students and their teachers, Schofield and colleagues found that teachers provided more articulate and better-tuned feedback than did the intelligent tutor (Schofield, Eurich-Fulcer, and Britt, 1994). Nevertheless, students preferred tutor-based to traditional instruction, not for the reasons one might expect, but because the tutor helped teachers tune their assistance to problems signaled by a student's interaction with the tutor. Thus, student interactions with the tutor

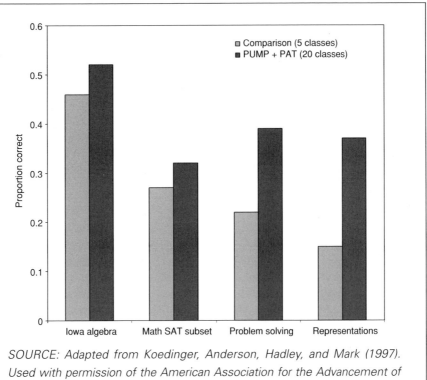

SOURCE: Adapted from Koedinger, Anderson, Hadley, and Mark (1997). Used with permission of the American Association for the Advancement of Science.

(and sometimes their problems with it) served to elicit and inform more knowledgeable teacher assistance, an outcome that students apparently appreciated. Moreover, the assistance provided by teachers to students was less public. Hence, formative assessment and subsequent modification of instruction—both highly valued by these high school students—were mediated by a triadic relationship among teacher, student, and intelligent tutor. Interestingly, these interactions were not the ones originally intended by the designers of the tutor. Not surprisingly, rather than involving direct correspondence between model-based assessments and student learning, these relationships are more complex in actual practice. And the Schofield et al. study suggests that some portion of the effect may be due to stimulating positive teacher practices.

Reflections on the Teacher's Role

Intelligent tutors and instructional programs such as Facets (described in Chapter 5) and CGI share an emphasis on providing clearer benchmarks of student thinking so that teachers can understand precursors and successors to the performances they are observing in real time. Thus these programs provide a "space" of student development in which teachers can work, a space that emphasizes ongoing formative assessment as an integral part of teaching practice. Yet these approaches remain under specified in important senses. Having good formative benchmarks in mind directs attention to important components and landmarks of thinking, yet teachers' flexible and sensitive repertoires of assistance are still essential to achieving these goals. In general, these programs leave to teachers the task of generating and testing these repertoires. Thus, as noted earlier, the effectiveness of formative assessment rests on a bedrock of informed professional practice. Models of learning flesh out components and systems of reasoning, but they derive their purpose and character from the practices within which they are embedded. Similarly, descriptions of typical practices make little sense in the absence of careful consideration of the forms of knowledge representation and reasoning they entail (Cobb, 1998).

Complex cognitively based measurement models can be embedded in intelligent tutoring systems and diagnostic assessment programs and put to good use without the teacher's having to participate in their construction. Many of the examples of assessments described in this report, such as Facets, intelligent tutoring systems, and BEAR (see Chapter 4), use statistical models and analysis techniques to handle some of the operational challenges. Providing teachers with carefully designed tools for classroom assessment can increase the utility of the information obtained. A goal for the future is to develop tools that make high-quality assessment more feasible for teachers. The topic of technology's impact on the implementation of classroom assessment is one to which we return in Chapter 7.

The Quality of Feedback

As described in Chapter 3, learning is a process of continuously modifying knowledge and skills. Sometimes new inputs call for additions and extensions to existing knowledge structures; at other times they call for radical reconstruction. In all cases, feedback is essential to guide, test, challenge, or redirect the learner's thinking.

Simply giving students frequent feedback in the classroom may or may not be helpful. For example, highly atomized drill-and-practice software can provide frequent feedback, but in so doing can foster rote learning and context dependency in students. A further concern is whether such software is being used appropriately given a student's level of skill development. For instance, a drill-and-practice program may be appropriate for developing fluency and automatizing a skill, but is usually not as appropriate during the early phase of skill acquisition (Goldman, Mertz, and Pellegrino, 1989). It is also noteworthy that in an environment where the teacher dominates all transactions, the frequent evocation and use of feedback can make that dominance all the more oppressive (Broadfoot, 1986).

There is ample evidence, however, that formative assessment can enhance learning when designed to provide students with feedback about particular qualities of their work and guidance on what they can do to improve. This conclusion is supported by several reviews of the research literature, including those by Natriello (1987), Crooks (1988), Fuchs and Fuchs (1986), Hattie (1987, 1990), and Black and Wiliam (1998). Many studies that have examined gains between pre- and post-tests, comparing programs in which formative assessment was the focus of the innovation and matched control groups were used, have shown effect sizes in the range of 0.4 to 0.7[1] (Black and Wiliam, 1998).

When different types of feedback have been compared in experimental studies, certain types have proven to be more beneficial to learning than others. Many studies in this area have shown that learning is enhanced by feedback that focuses on the mastery of learning goals (e.g., Butler, 1988; Hattie, 1987, 1990; Kluger and DeNisi, 1996). This research suggests that other types of feedback, such as when a teacher focuses on giving grades, on granting or withholding special rewards, or on fostering self-esteem (trying to make the student feel better, irrespective of the quality of his or her work), may be ineffective or even harmful.

The culture of focusing on grades and rewards and of seeing classroom learning as a competition appears to be deeply entrenched and difficult to change. This situation is more apparent in the United States than in some other countries (Hattie, Biggs, and Purdie, 1996). The competitive culture of many classrooms and schools can be an obstacle to learning, especially when linked to beliefs in the fixed nature of ability (Vispoel and Austin, 1995; Wolf, Bixby, Glen, and Gardner, 1991). Such beliefs on the part of educators can lead both to the labeling—overtly or covertly—of students as "bright" or "dull" and to the confirmation and enhancement of such labels through tracking practices.

International comparative studies—notably case studies and video studies conducted for the Third International Mathematics and Science Study

---

[1]To give a sense of the magnitude of such effect sizes, an effect size of 0.4 would mean that the average student who received the treatment would achieve at the same level as a student in the top 35 percent of those who did not receive the treatment. An effect size of 0.7, if realized in the Third International Mathematics and Science Study, would raise the United States from the middle of the 41 countries participating to one of the top 5.

that compare mathematics classrooms in Germany, Japan, and the United States—highlight the effects of these cultural beliefs. The studies underscore the difference between the culture of belief in Japan that the whole class can and should succeed through collaborative effort and the culture of belief endemic to many western countries, particularly the United States, that emphasizes the value of competition and differentiation (Cnen and Stevenson, 1995; Holloway, 1988).

The issues involved in students' views of themselves as learners may be understood at a more profound level by regarding the classroom as a community of practice in which the relationships formed and roles adopted between teacher and students and among students help to form and interact with each member's sense of personal identity (Cobb et al., 1991; Greeno and The Middle-School Mathematics Through Applications Group, 1997). Feedback can either promote or undermine the student's sense of identity as a potentially effective learner. For example, a student might generate a conjecture that was later falsified. One possible form of feedback would emphasize that the conjecture was wrong. A teacher might, instead, emphasize the disciplinary value of formulating conjectures and the fruitful mathematics that often follows from generating evidence about a claim, even (and sometimes especially) a false one.

A voluminous research literature addresses characteristics of learners that relate to issues of feedback. Important topics of study have included students' attributions for success and failure (e.g., Weiner, 1986), intrinsic versus extrinsic motivation (e.g., Deci and Ryan, 1985), and self-efficacy (e.g., Bandura and Schunk, 1981). We have not attempted to synthesize this large body of literature (for reviews see Graham and Weiner, 1996; Stipek, 1996). The important point to be made here is that teachers should be aware that different types of feedback have motivational implications that affect how students respond. Black and Wiliam (1998) sum up the evidence on feedback as follows:

> . . . the way in which formative information is conveyed to a student, and the context of classroom culture and beliefs about ability and effort within which feedback is interpreted by the individual recipient, can affect these personal features for good or ill. The hopeful message is that innovations which have paid careful attention to these features have produced significant gains when compared with the existing norms of classroom practice. (p. 25)

The Role of the Learner

Students have a crucial role to play in making classroom assessment effective. It is their responsibility to use the assessment information to guide their progress toward learning goals. Consider the following assessment example, which illustrates the benefits of having students engage actively in peer and self-assessment.

Researchers White and Frederiksen (2000) worked with teachers to develop the ThinkerTools Inquiry Project, a computer-enhanced middle school science curriculum that enables students to learn about the processes of scientific inquiry and modeling as they construct a theory of force and motion.[2] The class functions as a research community, and students propose competing theories. They then test their theories by working in groups to design and carry out experiments using both computer models and real-world materials. Finally, students come together to compare their findings and to try to reach consensus about the physical laws and causal models that best account for their results. This process is repeated as the students tackle new research questions that foster the evolution of their theories of force and motion.

The ThinkerTools program focuses on facilitating the development of metacognitive skills as students learn the inquiry processes needed to create and revise their theories. The approach incorporates a reflective process in which students evaluate their own and each other's research using a set of criteria that characterize good inquiry, such as reasoning carefully and collaborating well. Studies in urban classrooms revealed that when this reflective process is included, the approach is highly effective in enabling all students to improve their performance on various inquiry and physics measures and helps reduce the performance gap between low- and high-achieving students (see Box 6-3).

As demonstrated by the ThinkerTools example, peer and self-assessment are useful techniques for having learners share and grasp the criteria of quality work—a crucial step if formative assessment is to be effective. Just as teachers should adopt models of cognition and learning to guide instruction, they should also convey a model of learning (perhaps a simplified version) to their students so the students can monitor their own learning. This can be done through techniques such as the development of scoring rubrics or criteria for evaluating student work. As emphasized in Chapter 3, metacognitive awareness and control of one's learning are crucial aspects of developing competence.

Students should be taught to ask questions about their own work and revise their learning as a result of reflection—in effect, to conduct their own formative assessment. When students who are motivated to improve have opportunities to assess their own and others' learning, they become more capable of managing their own educational progress, and there is a transfer of power from teacher to learner. On the other hand, when formative feed-

---

[2]Website: <garnet.berkeley.edu:7019/mchap.html>. [September 5, 2000].

BOX 6-3   **Impact of Reflective Inquiry on Learning**

White and Frederiksen (2000) carried out a controlled study comparing ThinkerTools classes in which students engaged in the reflective-assessment process with matched control classes in which they did not. Each teacher's classes were evenly divided between the two treatments. In the reflective-assessment classes, the students continually engaged in monitoring and evaluating their own and each other's research. In the control classes, the students were not given an explicit framework for reflecting on their research; instead, they engaged in alternative activities in which they commented on what they did and did not like about the curriculum. In all other respects, the classes participated in the same ThinkerTools inquiry-based science curriculum. There were no significant differences in students' initial average standardized test scores (the Comprehensive Test of Basic Skills [CTBS] was used as a measure of prior achievement) between the classes assigned (randomly) to the different treatments.

One of the outcome measures was a written inquiry assessment that was given both before and after the ThinkerTools Inquiry Curriculum was administered. Presented below are the gain scores on this assessment for both low- and high-achieving students and for students in the reflective-assessment and control classes. Note first that students in the reflective-assessment classes gained more on this inquiry

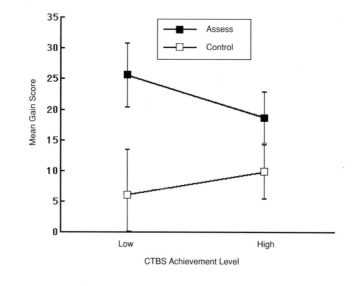

assessment. Note also that this was particularly true for the low-achieving students. This is evidence that the metacognitive reflective-assessment process is beneficial, particularly for academically disadvantaged students.

This finding was further explored by examining the gain scores for each component of the inquiry test. As shown in the figure below, one can see that the effect of reflective assessment is greatest for the more difficult aspects of the test: making up results, analyzing those results, and relating them back to the original hypotheses. In fact, the largest difference in the gain scores is that for a measure termed "coherence," which reflects the extent to which the experiments the students designed addressed their hypotheses, their made-up results related to their experiments, their conclusions followed from their results, and their conclusions were related back to their original hypotheses. The researchers note that this kind of overall coherence is a particularly important indication of sophistication in inquiry.

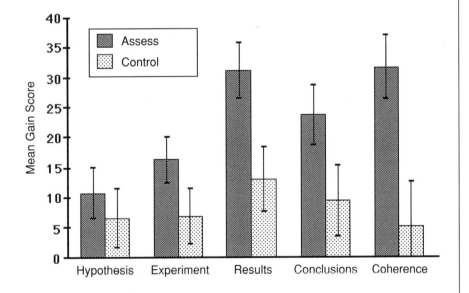

SOURCE: White and Frederiksen (2000, p. 347). Used with permission of the American Association for the Advancement of Science.

back is "owned" entirely by the teacher, the power of the learner in the classroom is diminished, and the development of active and independent learning is inhibited (Deci and Ryan, 1994; Fernandes and Fontana, 1996; Grolnick and Ryan, 1987).

Fairness

Because the assessor, in this context typically the classroom teacher, has interactive contact with the learner, many of the construct-irrelevant barriers associated with external standardized assessments (e.g., language barriers, unfamiliar contexts) can potentially be detected and overcome in the context of classroom assessment. However, issues of fairness can still arise in classroom assessment. Sensitive attention by the teacher is paramount to avoid potential sources of bias. In particular, differences between the cultural backgrounds of the teacher and the students can lead to severe difficulties. For example, the kinds of questions a middle-class teacher asks may be quite unlike, in form and function, questions students from a different socioeconomic or cultural group would experience at home, placing those students at a disadvantage (Heath, 1981, 1983).

Apart from the danger of a teacher's personal bias, possibly unconscious, against any particular individual or group, there is also the danger of a teacher's subscribing to the belief that learning ability or intelligence is fixed. Teachers holding such a belief may make self-confirming assumptions that certain children will never be able to learn, and may misinterpret or ignore assessment evidence to the contrary. However, as emphasized in the above discussion, there is great potential for formative assessment to assist and improve learning, and some studies, such as the ThinkerTools study described in Box 6-3, have shown that students initially classified as less able show the largest learning gains. There is some indication from other studies that the finding of greater gains for less able students may be generalizable, and this is certainly an area to be further explored.[3] For now, these initial findings suggest that effective formative assessment practices may help overcome disadvantages endured at earlier stages in education.

Another possible source of bias may arise when students do not understand or accept learning goals. In such a case, responses that should provide the basis for formative assessment may not be meaningful or forthcoming.

---

[3]The literature reviews on mastery learning by Block and Burns (1976), Guskey and Gates (1986), and Kulik, Kulik, and Bangert-Drowns (1990) confirm evidence of extra learning gains for the less able, gains that have been associated with the feedback enhancement in such regimes. However, Livingston and Gentile (1996) have cast doubt on this attribution. Fuchs and Fuchs (1986) report that studies with children with learning handicaps showed mean gain effect sizes of 0.73, compared with a mean of 0.63 for nonhandicapped children.

This potential consequence argues for helping learners understand and share learning goals.

LARGE-SCALE ASSESSMENT

We have described ways in which classroom assessment can be used to improve instruction and learning. We now turn to a discussion of assessments that are used in large-scale contexts, primarily for policy purposes. They include state, national, and international assessments. At the policy level, large-scale assessments are often used to evaluate programs and/or to set expectations for individual student learning (e.g., for establishing the minimum requirements individual students must meet to move on to the next grade or graduate from high school). At the district level, such assessments may be used for those same purposes, as well as for matching students to appropriate instructional programs. At the classroom level, large-scale assessments tend to be less relevant but still provide information a teacher can use to evaluate his or her own instruction and to identify or confirm areas of instructional need for individual students. Though further removed from day-to-day instruction than classroom assessments, large-scale assessments have the potential to support instruction and learning if well designed and appropriately used. For parents, large-scale assessments can provide information about their own child's achievement and some information about the effectiveness of the instruction their child is receiving.

Implications of Advances in Cognition and Measurement

Substantially more valid and useful information could be gained from large-scale assessments if the principles set forth in Chapter 5 were applied during the design process. However, fully capitalizing on the new foundations described in this report will require more substantial changes in the way large-scale assessment is approached, as well as relaxation of some of the constraints that currently drive large-scale assessment practices.

As described in Chapter 5, large-scale summative assessments should focus on the most critical and central aspects of learning in a domain as identified by curriculum standards and informed by cognitive research and theory. Large-scale assessments typically will reflect aspects of the model of learning at a less detailed level than classroom assessments, which can go into more depth because they focus on a smaller slice of curriculum and instruction. For instance, one might need to know for summative purposes whether a student has mastered the more complex aspects of multicolumn subtraction, including borrowing from and across zero, rather than exactly which subtraction bugs lead to mistakes. At the same time, while policy makers and parents may not need all the diagnostic detail that would be useful to a teacher and student during the course of instruction, large-scale summative assessments should be based on a model of learning that is compatible with and derived from the same set of knowledge and beliefs about learning as classroom assessment.

Research on cognition and learning suggests a broad range of competencies that should be assessed when measuring student achievement, many of which are essentially untapped by current assessments. Examples are knowledge organization, problem representation, strategy use, metacognition, and kinds of participation in activity (e.g., formulating questions, constructing and evaluating arguments, contributing to group problem solving). Furthermore, large-scale assessments should provide information about the nature of student understanding, rather than simply ranking students according to general proficiency estimates.

A major problem is that only limited improvements in large-scale assessments are possible under current constraints and typical standardized testing scenarios. Returning to issues of constraints and trade-offs discussed earlier in this chapter, large-scale assessments are designed to serve certain purposes under constraints that often include providing reliable and comparable scores for individuals as well as groups; sampling a broad set of curriculum standards within a limited testing time per student; and offering cost-efficiency in terms of development, scoring, and administration. To meet these kinds of demands, designers typically create assessments that are given at a specified time, with all students taking the same (or parallel) tests under strictly standardized conditions (often referred to as "on-demand" assessment). Tasks are generally of the kind that can be presented in paper-and-pencil format, that students can respond to quickly, and that can be scored reliably and efficiently. In general, competencies that lend themselves to being assessed in these ways are tapped, while aspects of learning that cannot be observed under such constrained conditions are not addressed. To design new kinds of situations for capturing the complexity of cognition and learning will require examining the assumptions and values that currently drive assessment design choices and breaking out of the current paradigm to explore alternative approaches to large-scale assessment.

Alternative Approaches

To derive real benefits from the merger of cognitive and measurement theory in large-scale assessment requires finding ways to cover a broad range of competencies and to capture rich information about the nature of student understanding. This is true even if the information produced is at a coarse-grained as opposed to a highly detailed level. To address these challenges it is useful to think about the constraints and trade-offs associated with issues of sampling—sampling of the content domain and of the student population.

The tasks on any particular assessment are supposed to be a representative sample of the knowledge and skills encompassed by the larger content domain. If the domain to be sampled is very broad, which is usually the case with large-scale assessments designed to cover a large period of instruction, representing the domain may require a large number and variety of assessment tasks. Most large-scale test developers opt for having many tasks that can be responded to quickly and that sample broadly. This approach limits the sorts of competencies that can be assessed, and such measures tend to cover only superficially the kinds of knowledge and skills students are supposed to be learning. Thus there is a need for testing situations that enable the collection of more extensive evidence of student performance.

If the primary purpose of the assessment is program evaluation, the constraint of having to produce reliable individual student scores can be relaxed, and population sampling can be useful. Instead of having all students take the same test (also referred to as "census testing"), a population sampling approach can be used whereby different students take different portions of a much larger assessment, and the results are combined to obtain an aggregate picture of student achievement.

If individual student scores are needed, broader sampling of the domain can be achieved by extracting evidence of student performance from classroom work produced during the course of instruction (often referred to as "curriculum-embedded" assessment). Student work or scores on classroom assessments can be used to supplement the information collected from an on-demand assessment to obtain a more comprehensive sampling of student performance. Although rarely used today for large-scale assessment purposes, curriculum-embedded tasks can serve policy and other external purposes of assessment if the tasks are centrally determined to some degree, with some flexibility built in for schools, teachers, and students to decide which tasks to use and when to have students respond to them.

Curriculum-embedded assessment approaches afford additional benefits. In on-demand testing situations, students are administered tasks that are targeted to their grade levels but not otherwise connected to their personal educational experiences. It is this relatively low degree of contextualization that renders these data good for some inferences, but not as good for others (Mislevy, 2000). If the purpose of assessment is to draw inferences about whether students can solve problems using knowledge and experiences they have learned in class, an on-demand testing situation in which every student receives a test with no consideration of his or her personal instruction history can be unfair. In this case, to provide valuable evidence of learning, the assessment must tap what the student has had the opportunity to learn (NRC, 1999b). In contrast to on-demand assessment, embedded assessment approaches use techniques that link assessment tasks to concepts and materials of instruction. Curriculum-embedded assessment offers an alternative to on-demand testing for cases in which there is a need for correspondence among the curriculum, assessment, and actual instruction (see the related discussion of conditional versus unconditional inferences at the end of Chapter 5).

The following examples illustrate some cases in which these kinds of alternative approaches are being used successfully to evaluate individuals and programs in large-scale contexts. Except for DIAGNOSER, these examples are not strictly cognitively based and do not necessarily illustrate the features of design presented in Chapter 5. Instead they were selected to illustrate some alternative ways of approaching large-scale assessment and the trade-offs entailed. The first two examples show how population sampling has been used for program evaluation at the national and state levels to enable coverage of a broader range of learning goals than would be possible if each student were to take the same form of a test. The third and fourth examples involve approaches to measuring individual attainment that draw evidence of student performance from the course of instruction.

Alternative Approaches to Large-Scale Assessment: Examples

National Assessment of Educational Progress

As described earlier in this chapter, NAEP is a national survey intended to provide policy makers and the public with information about the academic achievement of students across the nation. It serves as one source of information for policy makers, school administrators, and the public for evaluating the quality of their curriculum and instructional programs. NAEP is a unique case of program evaluation in that it is not tied to any specific curriculum. It is based on a set of assessment frameworks that describe the knowledge and skills to be assessed in each subject area. The performances assessed are intended to represent the leading edge of what all students should be learning. Thus the frameworks are broader than any particular curriculum (NRC, 1999a). The challenge for NAEP is to assess the breadth of learning goals that are valued across the nation. The program approaches this challenge through the complex matrix sampling design described earlier.

NAEP's design is beginning to be influenced by the call for more cognitively informed assessments of educational programs. Recent evaluations of NAEP (National Academy of Education, 1997; NRC, 1999a) emphasize that the current survey does not adequately capitalize on advances in our understanding of how people learn particular subject matter. These study committees have strongly recommended that NAEP incorporate a broader conceptualization of school achievement to include aspects of learning that are not well specified in the existing NAEP frameworks or well measured by the current survey methods. The National Academy of Education panel recommended that particular attention be given to such aspects of student cognition as problem representation, the use of strategies and self-regulatory skills, and the formulation of explanations and interpretations, contending that consideration of these aspects of student achievement is necessary for NAEP to provide a complete and accurate assessment of achievement in a subject area. The subsequent review of NAEP by the NRC reiterated those recommendations and added that large-scale survey instruments alone cannot reflect the scope of these more comprehensive goals for schooling. The NRC proposed that, in addition to the current assessment blocks, which are limited to 50-minute sessions and paper-and-pencil responses, NAEP should include carefully designed, targeted assessments administered to smaller samples of students that could provide in-depth descriptive information about more complex activities that occur over longer periods of time. For instance, smaller data collections could involve observations of students solving problems in groups or performing extended science projects, as well as analysis of writing portfolios compiled by students over a year of instruction.

Thus NAEP illustrates how relaxing the constraint of having to provide individual student scores opens up possibilities for population sampling and coverage of a much broader domain of cognitive performances. The next example is another illustration of what can be gained by such a sampling approach.

Maryland State Performance Assessment Program

The Maryland State Performance Assessment Program (MSPAP) is designed to evaluate how well schools are teaching the basic and complex skills outlined in state standards called Maryland Learner Outcomes. Maryland is one of the few states in the country that has decided to optimize the use of assessment for program evaluation, forgoing individual student scores.[4] A population sampling design is used, as opposed to the census testing design used by most states.

MSPAP consists of criterion-referenced performance tests in reading, mathematics, writing, language usage, science, and social studies for students in grades 3, 5, and 8. The assessment is designed to measure a broad range of competencies. Tasks require students to respond to questions or directions that lead to a solution for a problem, a recommendation or decision, or an explanation or rationale for their responses. Some tasks assess one content

---

[4]Website: <www.mdk12.org>. [June 29, 2000].

area; others assess multiple content areas. The tasks may encompass group or individual activities; hands-on, observation, or reading activities; and activities that require extended written responses, limited written responses, lists, charts, graphs, diagrams, webs, and/or drawings. A few MSPAP items are released each year to educators and the public to provide a picture of what the assessment looks like and how it is scored.[5]

To cover this broad range of learning outcomes, Maryland uses a sampling approach whereby each student takes only one-third of the entire assessment. This means an individual student's results do not give a complete picture of how that child is performing (although parents can obtain a copy of their child's results from the local school system). What is gained is a program evaluation instrument that covers a much more comprehensive range of learning goals than that addressed by a traditional standardized test.

AP Studio Art

The above two examples do not provide individual student scores. The AP Studio Art portfolio assessment is an example of an assessment that is designed to certify individual student attainment over a broad range of competencies and to be closely linked to the actual instruction students have experienced (College Board, 1994). Student work products are extracted during the course of instruction, collected, and then evaluated for summative evaluation of student attainment.

AP Studio Art is just one of many Advanced Placement (AP) programs designed to give highly motivated high school students the opportunity to take college-level courses in areas such as biology, history, calculus, and English while still in high school. AP programs provide course descriptions and teaching materials, but do not require that specific textbooks, teaching techniques, or curricula be followed. Each program culminates in an exam intended to certify whether individual students have mastered material equivalent to that of an introductory college course. AP Studio Art is unique in that at the end of the year, instead of taking a written summative exam, students present a portfolio of materials selected from the work they have produced during the AP course for evaluation by a group of artists and teachers. Preparation of the portfolio requires forethought; work submitted for the various sections must meet the publicly shared criteria set forth by the AP program.

The materials presented for evaluation may have been produced in art classes or on the student's own time and may cover a period of time longer than a single school year. Instructional goals and the criteria by which students' performance will be evaluated are made clear and explicit. Portfolio

---

[5]Website: <www.mdk12.org/mspp/mspap/look/prt_mspap.html>. [June 29, 2000].

requirements are carefully spelled out in a poster distributed to students and teachers; scoring rubrics are also widely distributed. Formative assessment is a critical part of the program as well. Students engage in evaluation of their own work and that of their peers, then use that feedback to inform next steps in building their portfolios. Thus while the AP Studio Art program is not directly based on cognitive research, it does reflect general cognitive principles, such as setting clear learning goals and providing students with opportunities for formative feedback, including evaluation of their own work.

Portfolios are scored quickly but fairly by trained raters. It is possible to assign reliable holistic scores to portfolios in a short amount of time. Numerous readings go into the scoring of each portfolio, enhancing the fairness of the assessment process (Mislevy, 1996). In this way, technically sound judgments are made, based on information collected through the learning process, that fulfill certification purposes. Thus by using a curriculum-embedded approach, the AP Studio Art program is able to collect rich and varied samples of student work that are tied to students' instructional experiences over the course of the year, but can also be evaluated in a standardized way for the purposes of summative assessment.

It should be noted that some states attempting to implement large-scale portfolio assessment programs have encountered difficulties (Koretz and Barron, 1998). Therefore, while this is a good example of an alternative approach to on-demand testing, it should be recognized that there are many implementation challenges to be addressed.

Facets DIAGNOSER

We return to Minstrell and Hunt's facets-based DIAGNOSER (Minstrell, 2000), described in some detail in Chapter 5, to illustrate another way of thinking about assessment of individuals' summative achievement. The DIAGNOSER, developed for use at the classroom level to assist learning, does not fit the mold of traditional large-scale assessment. Various modules (each of which takes 15 to 20 minutes) cover small amounts of material fairly intensively. However, the DIAGNOSER could be used to certify individual attainment by noting the most advanced module a student had completed at a successful level of understanding in the course of instruction. For instance, the resulting assessment record would distinguish between students who had completed only Newtonian mechanics and those who had completed modules on the more advanced topics of waves or direct-circuit electricity. Because the assessment is part of instruction, there would be less concern about instructional time lost to testing.

Minstrell (2000) also speculates about how a facets approach could be applied to the development of external assessments designed to inform decisions at the program and policy levels. Expectations for learning, currently conveyed by state and national curriculum standards, would be enhanced by facets-type research on learning. Current standards based on *what we want our students to know and be able to do* could be improved by incorporating findings from research on *what students know and are able to do along the way to competence.* By using a matrix sampling design, facet clusters could be covered extensively, providing summary information for decision makers about specific areas of difficulty for learners—information that would be useful for curriculum revision.

Use of Large-Scale Assessment to Signal Worthy Goals

Large-scale assessments can serve the purposes of learning by signaling worthwhile goals for educators and students to pursue. The challenge is to use the assessment program to signal goals at a level that is clear enough to provide some direction, but not so prescriptive that it results in a narrowing of instruction. Educators and researchers have debated the potential benefits of "teaching to a test." Proponents of performance-based assessment have suggested that assessment can have a positive impact on learning if authentic tasks are used that replicate important performances in the discipline. The idea is that high-quality tasks can clarify and set standards of academic excellence, in which case teaching to the test becomes a good thing (Wiggins, 1989). Others (Miller and Seraphine, 1993) have argued that teaching to a test will always result in narrowing of the curriculum, given that any test can only sample the much broader domain of learning goals.

These views can perhaps be reconciled if the assessment is based on a well-developed model of learning that is shared with educators and learners. To make appropriate instructional decisions, teachers should teach to the model of learning—as conveyed, for example, by progress maps and rubrics for judging the quality of student work—rather than focusing on the particular items on a test. Test users must understand that any particular set of assessment tasks represents only a sample of the domain and that tasks will change from year to year. Given this understanding, assessment items and sample student responses can provide valuable exemplars to help teachers and students understand the underlying learning goals. Whereas teaching directly to the items on a test is not desirable, teaching to the set of beliefs about learning that underlie an assessment—which should be the same set of beliefs that underlies the curriculum—can provide positive direction for instruction.

High-quality summative assessment tasks are ones for which students can prepare only through active learning, as opposed to rote drill and practice or memorization of solutions. The United Kingdom's Secondary School Certification Exam in physics (described in more detail later in this chapter) produces a wide variety of evidence that can be used to evaluate students' summative achievement. The exam includes some transfer tasks that have been observed to be highly motivating for students (Morland, 1994). For instance, there is a task that assesses whether students can read articles dealing with applications of physics that lie outside the confines of the syllabus. Students know they will be presented with an article they have not seen before on a topic not specified in the syllabus, but that it will be at a level they should be able to understand on the basis of the core work of the syllabus. This task assesses students' competency in applying their understanding in a new context in the process of learning new material. The only way for students to prepare for this activity is to read a large variety of articles and work systematically to understand them.

Another goal of the U.K. physics curriculum is to develop students' capacity to carry out experimental investigations on novel problems. Students are presented with a scientific problem that is not included in the routine curriculum materials and must design an experiment, select and appropriately use equipment and procedures to implement the design, collect and analyze data, and interpret the data. Again, the only way students can prepare for this task is by engaging in a variety of such investigations and learning how to take responsibility for their design, implementation, and interpretation. In the United Kingdom, these portions of the physics exam are administered by the student's own teacher, with national, standardized procedures in place for ensuring and checking fairness and rigor. When this examination was first introduced in the early 1970s, it was uncommon in classrooms to have students read on topics outside the syllabus and design and conduct their own investigations. The physics exam has supported the message, also conveyed by the curriculum, that these activities are essential, and as a result students taking the exam have had the opportunity to engage in such activities in the course of their study (Tebbutt, 1981).

Feedback and Expectations for Learning

In Chapters 4 and 5, we illustrated some of the kinds of information that could be obtained by reporting large-scale assessment results in relation to developmental progress maps or other types of learning models. Assessment results should describe student performance in terms of different states and levels of competence in the domain. Typical learning pathways should be displayed and made as recognizable as possible to educators, students, and the public.

Large-scale assessments of individual achievement could be improved by focusing on the potential for providing feedback that not only measures but also enhances future learning. Assessments can be designed to say both that *this person is unqualified to move on* and that *this person's difficulty lies in these particular areas, and that is what has to be improved, the other components being at the desired level.*

Likewise, assessments designed to evaluate programs should provide the kinds of information decision makers can use to improve those programs. People tend to think of school administrators and policy makers as removed from concerns about the details of instruction. Thus large-scale assessment information aimed at those users tends to be general and comparative, rather than descriptive of the nature of learning that is taking place in their schools. Practices in some school districts, however, are challenging these assumptions (Resnick and Harwell, 1998).

Telling an administrator that mathematics is a problem is too vague. Knowing how a school is performing in mathematics relative to past years, how it is performing relative to other schools, and what proportions of students fall in various broadly defined achievement categories also provides little guidance for program improvement. Saying that *students do not understand probability* is more useful, particularly to a curriculum planner. And knowing that *students tend to confuse conditional and compound probability* can be even more useful for the modification of curriculum and instruction. Of course, the sort of feedback needed to improve instruction depends on the program administrator's level of control.

Not only do large-scale assessments provide means for reporting on student achievement, but they also convey powerful messages about the kinds of learning valued by society. Large-scale assessments should be used by policy makers and educators to operationalize and communicate among themselves, and to the public, the kinds of thinking and learning society wishes to encourage in students. In this way, assessments can foster valuable dialogue about learning and its assessment within and beyond the education system. Models of learning should be shared and communicated in accessible ways to show what competency in a domain looks like. For example, Developmental Assessment based on progress maps is being used in the Commonwealth of Victoria to assess literacy. An evaluation of the program revealed that users were "overwhelmingly positive about the value and potential of Developmental Assessment as a means for developing shared understandings and a common language for literacy development" (Meiers and Culican, 2000, p. 44).

Example: The New Standards Project

The New Standards Project, as originally conceived (New Standards™, 1997a, 1997b, 1997c), illustrates ways to approach many of the issues of large-scale assessment discussed above. The program was designed to provide clear goals for learning and assessments that are closely tied to those goals. A combination of on-demand and embedded assessment was to be used to tap a broad range of learning outcomes, and priority was given to communicating the performance standards to various user communities. Development of the program was a collaboration between the Learning Research and Development Center of the University of Pittsburgh and the National Center on Education and the Economy, in partnership with states and urban school districts. Together they developed challenging standards for student performance at grades 4, 8, and 10, along with large-scale assessments designed to measure attainment of those standards.[6]

The New Standards Project includes three interrelated components: performance standards, a portfolio assessment system,[7] and an on-demand exam. The performance standards describe what students should know and the ways they should demonstrate the knowledge and skills they have acquired. The performance standards include samples of student work that illustrate high-quality performances, accompanied by commentary that shows how the work sample reflects the performance standards. They go beyond most content standards by describing how good is good enough, thus providing clear targets to pursue.

The Reference Exam is a summative assessment of the national standards in the areas of English Language Arts and Mathematics at grades 4, 8, and 10. The developers state explicitly that the Reference Exam is intended to address those aspects of the performance standards that can be assessed in a limited time frame under standardized conditions. The portfolio assessment system was designed to complement the Reference Exam by providing evidence of achievement of those performance standards that depend on extended work and the accumulation of evidence over time.

The developers recognized the importance of making the standards clear and presenting them in differing formats for different audiences. One version of the standards is targeted to teachers. It includes relatively detailed language about the subject matter of the standards and terms educators use to describe differences in the quality of work produced by students. The standards are also included in the portfolio material provided for student use. In these materials, the standards are set forth in the form of guidelines to help students select work for inclusion in their portfolios. In addition, there were plans to produce a less technical version for parents and the community in general.

---

[6]Aspects of the program have since changed, and the Reference Exam is now administered by Harcourt Educational Measurement.

[7]The portfolio component was field tested but has not been administered on a large scale.

ASSESSMENT SYSTEMS

In the preceding discussion we have addressed issues of practice related to classroom and large-scale assessment separately. We now return to the matter of how such assessments can work together conceptually and operationally.

As argued throughout this chapter, one form of assessment does not serve all purposes. Given that reality, it is inevitable that multiple assessments (or assessments consisting of multiple components) are required to serve the varying educational assessment needs of different audiences. A multitude of different assessments are already being conducted in schools. It is not surprising that users are often frustrated when such assessments have conflicting achievement goals and results. Sometimes such discrepancies can be meaningful and useful, such as when assessments are explicitly aimed at measuring different school outcomes. More often, however, conflicting assessment goals and feedback cause much confusion for educators, students, and parents. In this section we describe a vision for *coordinated systems* of multiple assessments that work together, along with curriculum and instruction, to promote learning. Before describing specific properties of such systems, we consider issues of balance and allocation of resources across classroom and large-scale assessment.

Balance Between Classroom and Large-Scale Assessment

The current educational assessment environment in the United States clearly reflects the considerable value and credibility accorded external, large-scale assessments of individuals and programs relative to classroom assessments designed to assist learning. The resources invested in producing and using large-scale testing in terms of money, instructional time, research, and development far outweigh the investment in the design and use of effective classroom assessments. It is the committee's position that to better serve the goals of learning, the research, development, and training investment must be shifted toward the classroom, where teaching and learning occurs.

Not only does large-scale assessment dominate over classroom assessment, but there is also ample evidence of accountability measures negatively impacting classroom instruction and assessment. For instance, as discussed earlier, teachers feel pressure to teach to the test, which results in a narrowing of instruction. They also model their own classroom tests after less-than-ideal standardized tests (Gifford and O'Connor, 1992; Linn, 2000; Shepard, 2000). These kinds of problems suggest that beyond striking a better balance between classroom and large-scale assessment, what is needed are coordinated assessment systems that collectively support a common set of learning goals, rather than working at cross-purposes.

Ideally in a balanced assessment environment, a single assessment does not function in isolation, but rather within a nested assessment system involving states, local school districts, schools, and classrooms. Assessment systems should be designed to optimize the credibility and utility of the resulting information for both educational decision making and general monitoring. To this end, an assessment system should exhibit three properties: comprehensiveness, coherence, and continuity. These three characteristics describe an assessment system that is aligned along three dimensions: vertically, across levels of the education system; horizontally, across assessment, curriculum, and instruction; and temporally, across the course of a student's studies. These notions of alignment are consistent with those set forth by the National Institute for Science Education (Webb, 1997) and the National Council of Teachers of Mathematics (1995).

Features of a Balanced Assessment System

Comprehensiveness

By *comprehensiveness*, we mean that a range of measurement approaches should be used to provide a variety of evidence to support educational decision making. Educational decisions often require more information than a single measure can provide. As emphasized in the NRC report *High Stakes: Testing for Tracking, Promotion, and Graduation,* multiple measures take on particular importance when important, life-altering decisions (such as high school graduation) are being made about individuals. No single test score can be considered a definitive measure of a student's competence. Multiple measures enhance the validity and fairness of the inferences drawn by giving students various ways and opportunities to demonstrate their competence. The measures could also address the quality of instruction, providing evidence that improvements in tested achievement represent real gains in learning (NRC, 1999c).

One form of comprehensive assessment system is illustrated in Table 6-1, which shows the components of a U.K. examination for certification of top secondary school students who have studied physics as one of three chosen subjects for 2 years between ages 16 and 18. The results of such examinations are the main criterion for entrance to university courses. Components A, B, C, and D are all taken within a few days, but E and F involve activities that extend over several weeks preceding the formal examination.

This system combines external testing on paper (components A, B, and C) with external performance tasks done using equipment (D) and teachers' assessment of work done during the course of instruction (E and F). While

TABLE 6-1 Six Components of an A-Level Physics Examination

Component	Title	No. of Questions or Tasks	Time	Weight in Marks	Description
A	Coded Answer	40	75 min.	20%	Multiple choice questions, all to be attempted.
B	Short Answer	7 or 8	90 min.	20%	Short with structured subcomponents, fixed space for answer, all to be attempted.
C	Comprehension	3	150 min.	24%	a) Answer questions on a new passage. b) Analyze and draw conclusions from a set of presented data. c) Explain phenomena described in short paragraphs: select 3 from 5.
D	Practical Problems	8	90 min.	16%	Short problems with equipment set up in a laboratory, all to be attempted.
E	Investigation	1	About 2 weeks	10%	In normal school laboratory time, investigate a problem of the student's own choice.
F	Project Essay	1	About 2 weeks	10%	In normal school time, research and write about a topic chosen by the student.

SOURCE: *Adapted from Morland (1994).*

this particular physics examination is now subject to change,[8] combining the results of external tests with classroom assessments of particular aspects of achievement for which a short formal test is not appropriate is an established feature of achievement testing systems in the United Kingdom and

---

[8]Because the whole structure of the 16-18 examinations is being changed, this examination and the curriculum on which it is based, which have been in place for 30 years, will no longer be in use after 2001. They will be replaced by a new curriculum and examination, based on the same principles.

several other countries. This feature is also part of the examination system for the International Baccalaureate degree program. In such systems, work is needed to develop procedures for ensuring the comparability of standards across all teachers and schools.

Overall, the purpose is to reflect the variety of the aims of a course, including the range of knowledge and simple understanding explored in A, the practical skills explored in D, and the broader capacities for individual investigation explored in E and F. Validity and comprehensiveness are enhanced, albeit through an expensive and complex assessment process.

There are other possible ways to design comprehensive assessment systems. Portfolios are intended to record "authentic" assessments over a period of time and a range of classroom contexts. A system may assess and give certification in stages, so that the final outcome is an accumulation of results achieved and credited separately over, say, 1 or 2 years of a learning course; results of this type may be built up by combining on-demand externally controlled assessments with work samples drawn from coursework. Such a system may include assessments administered at fixed times or at times of the candidate's choice using banks of tasks from which tests can be selected to match the candidate's particular opportunities to learn. Thus designers must always look to the possibility of using the broader approaches discussed here, combining types of tasks and the timing of assessments and of certifications in the optimum way.

Further, in a comprehensive assessment system, the information derived should be technically sound and timely for given decisions. One must be able to trust the accuracy of the information and be assured that the inferences drawn from the results can be substantiated by evidence of various types. The technical quality of assessment is a concern primarily for external, large-scale testing; but if classroom assessment information is to feed into the larger assessment system, the reliability, validity, and fairness of these assessments must be addressed as well. Researchers are just beginning to explore issues of technical quality in the realm of classroom assessment (e.g., Wilson and Sloane, 2000).

Coherence

For the system to support learning, it must also have a quality the committee refers to as *coherence*. One dimension of coherence is that the conceptual base or models of student learning underlying the various external and classroom assessments within a system should be compatible. While a large-scale assessment might be based on a model of learning that is coarser than that underlying the assessments used in classrooms, the conceptual base for the large-scale assessment should be a broader version of one that makes sense at the finer-grained level (Mislevy, 1996). In this way, the external assessment results will be consistent with the more detailed understanding of learning underlying classroom instruction and assessment. As one moves up and down the levels of the system, from the classroom through the school, district, and state, assessments along this vertical dimension should align. As long as the underlying models of learning are consistent, the assessments will complement each other rather than present conflicting goals for learning.

To keep learning at the center of the educational enterprise, assessment information must be strongly linked to curriculum and instruction. Thus another aspect of coherence, emphasized earlier, is that alignment is needed among curriculum, instruction, and assessment so that all three parts of the education system are working toward a common set of learning goals. Ideally, assessment will not simply be aligned with instruction, but integrated seamlessly into instruction so that teachers and students are receiving frequent but unobtrusive feedback about their progress. If assessment, curriculum, and instruction are aligned with common models of learning, it follows that they will be aligned with each other. This can be thought of as alignment along the horizontal dimension of the system.

To achieve both the vertical and horizontal dimensions of coherence or alignment, models of learning are needed that are shared by educators at different levels of the system, from teachers to policy makers. This need might be met through a process that involves gathering together the necessary expertise, not unlike the approach used to develop state and national curriculum standards that define the content to be learned. But current definitions of content must be significantly enhanced based on research from the cognitive sciences. Needed are user-friendly descriptions of how students learn the content, identifying important targets for instruction and assessment (see, e.g., American Association for the Advancement of Science, 2001). Research centers could be charged with convening the appropriate experts to produce a synthesis of the best available scientific understanding of how students learn in particular domains of the curriculum. These models of learning would then guide assessment design at all levels, as well as curriculum and instruction, effecting alignment in the system. Some might argue that what we have described are the goals of current curriculum standards. But while the existing standards emphasize *what* students should learn, they do not describe *how* students learn in ways that are maximally useful for guiding instruction and assessment.

Continuity

In addition to comprehensiveness and coherence, an ideal assessment system would be designed to be *continuous*. That is, assessments should measure student progress over time, akin more to a videotape record than to the snapshots provided by the current system of on-demand tests. To provide such pictures of progress, multiple sets of observations over time must be linked conceptually so that change can be observed and interpreted. Models of student progression in learning should underlie the assessment system, and tests should be designed to provide information that maps back to the progression. With such a system, we would move from "one-shot" testing situations and cross-sectional approaches for defining student performance toward an approach that focused on the processes of learning and an individual's progress through that process (Wilson and Sloane, 2000). Thus, continuity calls for alignment along the third dimension of time.

Approximations of a Balanced System

No existing assessment systems meet all three criteria of comprehensiveness, coherence, and continuity, but many of the examples described in this report represent steps toward these goals. For instance, the Developmental Assessment program shows how progress maps can be used to achieve coherence between formative and summative assessments, as well as among curriculum, instruction, and assessment. Progress maps also enable the measurement of growth (continuity). The Australian Council for Educational Research has produced an excellent set of resource materials for teachers to support their use of a wide range of assessment strategies—from written tests to portfolios to projects at the classroom level—that can all be designed to link back to the progress maps (comprehensiveness) (see, e.g., Forster and Masters, 1996a, 1996b; Masters and Forster, 1996). The BEAR assessment shares many similar features; however, the underlying models of learning are not as strongly tied to cognitive research as they could be. On the other hand, intelligent tutoring systems have a strong cognitive research base and offer opportunities for integrating formative and summative assessments, as well as measuring growth, yet their use for large-scale assessment purposes has not yet been explored. Thus, examples in this report offer a rich set of opportunities for further development toward the goal of designing assessment systems that are maximally useful for both informing and improving learning.

CONCLUSIONS

Guiding the committee's work were the premises that (1) something important should be learned from every assessment situation, and (2) the information gained should ultimately help improve learning. The power of classroom assessment resides in its close connections to instruction and teachers' knowledge of their students' instructional histories. Large-scale, standardized assessments can communicate across time and place, but by so constraining the content and timeliness of the message that they often have limited utility in the classroom. Thus *the contrast between classroom and large-scale assessments arises from the different purposes they serve and contexts in which they are used.* Certain trade-offs are an inescapable aspect of assessment design.

Students will learn more if instruction and assessment are integrally related. *In the classroom, providing students with information about particular qualities of their work and about what they can do to improve is crucial for maximizing learning.* It is in the context of classroom assessment that theories of cognition and learning can be particularly helpful by providing a picture of intermediary states of student understanding on the pathway from novice to competent performer in a subject domain.

Findings from cognitive research cannot always be translated directly or easily into classroom practice. Most effective are programs that interpret the findings from cognitive research in ways that are useful for teachers. Teachers need theoretical training, as well as practical training and assessment tools, to be able to implement formative assessment effectively in their classrooms.

Large-scale assessments are further removed from instruction, but can still benefit learning if well designed and properly used. Substantially more valid and useful inferences could be drawn from such assessments if the principles set forth in this report were applied during the design process.

Large-scale assessments not only serve as a means for reporting on student achievement, but also reflect aspects of academic competence societies consider worthy of recognition and reward. *Thus large-scale assessments can provide worthwhile targets for educators and students to pursue.* Whereas teaching directly to the items on a test is not desirable, teaching to the theory of cognition and learning that underlies an assessment can provide positive direction for instruction.

To derive real benefits from the merger of cognitive and measurement theory in large-scale assessment, it will be necessary to devise ways of covering a broad range of competencies and capturing rich information about the nature of student understanding. *Indeed, to fully capitalize on the new foundations described in this report will require substantial changes in the way large-scale assessment is approached and relaxation of some of the constraints that currently drive large-scale assessment practices.* Alternatives to on-demand, census testing are available. If individual student scores are needed, broader sampling of the domain can be achieved by extracting evidence of student performance from classroom work produced during the course of instruction. If the primary purpose of the assessment is program evaluation, the constraint of having to produce reliable individual student scores can be relaxed, and population sampling can be useful.

For classroom or large-scale assessment to be effective, students must understand and share the goals for learning. Students learn more when they understand (and even participate in developing) the criteria by which their work will be evaluated, and when they engage in peer and self-assessment during which they apply those criteria. These practices develop students' metacognitive abilities, which, as emphasized above, are necessary for effective learning.

The current educational assessment environment in the United States assigns much greater value and credibility to external, large-scale assessments of individuals and programs than to classroom assessment designed to assist learning. The investment of money, instructional time, research, and development for large-scale testing far outweighs that for effective classroom assessment. *More of the research, development, and training investment must be shifted toward the classroom, where teaching and learning occur.*

A vision for the future is that assessments at all levels—from classroom to state—will work together in a system that is comprehensive, coherent, and continuous. In such a system, assessments would provide a variety of evidence to support educational decision making. Assessment at all levels would be linked back to the same underlying model of student learning and would provide indications of student growth over time.

Three themes underlie this chapter's exploration of how information technologies can advance the design of assessments, based on a merging of the cognitive and measurement advances reviewed in Part II.

- Technology is providing new tools that can help make components of assessment design and implementation more efficient, timely, and sophisticated. We focus on advances that are helping designers forge stronger connections among the three elements of the assessment triangle set forth in Chapter 2. For instance, technology offers opportunities to strengthen the cognition-observation linkage by enabling the design of situations that assess a broader range of cognitive processes than was previously possible, including knowledge-organization and problem-solving processes that are difficult to assess using traditional, paper-and-pencil assessment methods.

- Technology offers opportunities to strengthen the cognitive coherence among assessment, curriculum, and instruction. Some programs have been developed to infuse ongoing formative assessment into portions of the current mathematics and science curriculum. Other projects illustrate how technology fundamentally changes what is taught and how it is taught. Exciting new technology-based learning environments now being designed provide complete integration of curriculum, instruction, and assessment aimed at the development of new and complex skills and knowledge.

- The chapter concludes with a possible future scenario in which cognitive research, advances in measurement, and technology combine to spur a radical shift in the kinds of assessments used to assist learning, measure student attainment, evaluate programs, and promote accountability.

7

Information Technologies: Opportunities for Advancing Educational Assessment

Technology has long been a major force in assessment. The science of measurement took shape at the same time that technologies for standardization were transforming industry. In the decades since, test designers and measurement experts have often been among the early advocates and users of new technologies. The most common kinds of assessments in use today are, in many ways, the products of technologies that were once cutting-edge, such as automated scoring and item-bank management.

Today, sophisticated information technologies, including an expanding array of computing and telecommunications devices, are making it possible to assess what students are learning at very fine levels of detail, from distant locations, with vivid simulations of real-world situations, and in ways that are barely distinguishable from learning activities. However, the most provocative applications of new technologies to assessment are not necessarily those with the greatest sophistication, speed, or glitz. The greater potential lies in the role technology could play in realizing the central ideas of this report: that assessments should be based on modern knowledge of cognition and its measurement, should be integrated with curriculum and instruction, and should inform as well as improve student achievement. Currently, the promise of these new kinds of assessments remains largely unfulfilled, but technology could substantially change this situation.

Within the next decade, extremely powerful information technologies will become ubiquitous in educational settings. They are almost certain to provoke fundamental changes in learning environments at all levels. Indeed, some of these changes are already occurring, enabling people to conjecture about their consequences for children, teachers, policy makers, and the public. Other applications of technology are beyond people's speculative capacity. A decade ago, for example, few could have predicted the sweeping effects of the Internet on education and other segments of society. The range of computational devices and their applications is expanding at a geometric rate, fundamentally changing how people think about communication, connectivity, and the role of technology in society (National Research Council [NRC], 1999b).

The committee believes new information technologies can advance the design of assessments based on a merger of the cognitive and measurement sciences. Evidence in support of this position comes from several existing projects that have created technology-enhanced learning environments incorporating assessment. These prototype cases also suggest some future directions and implications for the coupling of cognition, measurement, and technology.

Two important points of clarification are needed about our discussion of the connections between technology and assessment. First, various technologies have been applied to bring greater efficiency, timeliness, and sophistication to multiple aspects of assessment design and implementation. Examples include technologies that generate items; immediately adapt items on the basis of the examinee's performance; analyze, score, and report assessment data; allow learners to be assessed at different times and in distant locations; enliven assessment tasks with multimedia; and add interactivity to assessment tasks. In many cases, these technology tools have been used to implement conventional theories and methods of assessment, albeit more effectively and efficiently. Although these applications can be quite valuable for various user groups, they are not central to this committee's work and are therefore not discussed here. Instead, we focus on those instances in which a technology-based innovation or design enhances (1) the connections among the three elements of the assessment triangle and/or (2) the integration of assessment with curriculum and instruction.

The second point is that many of the applications of technology to learning and assessment described in this chapter are in the early stages of development. Thus, evidence is often limited regarding certain technical features (e.g., reliability and validity) and the actual impact on learning. The committee believes technological advances such as those described here have enormous potential for advancing the science, design, and use of educational assessment, but further study will clearly be needed to determine the effectiveness of particular programs and approaches.

NEW TOOLS FOR ASSESSMENT DESIGN AND IMPLEMENTATION

Computer and telecommunications technologies provide powerful new tools for meeting many of the challenges inherent in designing and implementing assessments that go beyond conventional practices and tap a broader repertoire of cognitive skills and knowledge. Indeed, many of the design principles and practices described in the preceding chapters would be difficult to implement without technology. For purposes of discussing these matters, a useful frame of reference is the assessment triangle introduced in Chapter 2.

The role of any given technology advance or tool can often be differentiated by its primary locus of effect within the assessment triangle. For the link between *cognition* and *observation*, technology makes it possible to design tasks with more principled connections to cognitive theories of task demands and solution processes. Technology also makes it possible to design and present tasks that tap complex forms of knowledge and reasoning. These aspects of cognition would be difficult if not impossible to engage and assess through traditional methods. With regard to the link between *observation* and *interpretation*, technology makes it possible to score and interpret multiple aspects of student performance on a wide range of tasks carefully chosen for their cognitive features, and to compare the resulting performance data against profiles that have interpretive value. In the sections that follow we explore these various connections by considering specific cases in which progress has been made.

Enhancing the Cognition-Observation Linkage

Theory-Based Item Generation

As noted in Chapter 5, a key design step is the generation of items and tasks that are consistent with a model of student knowledge and skill. Currently, this is usually a less-than-scientific process because many testing programs require large numbers of items for multiple test forms. Whether the items are similar in their cognitive demands is often uncertain. Computer programs that can automatically generate assessment items offer some intriguing possibilities for circumventing this problem and improving the linkage between cognitive theory and observation. The programs are based on a set of item specifications derived from models of the knowledge structures and processes associated with specific characteristics of an item form. For example, the Mathematics Test Creation Assistant has been programmed

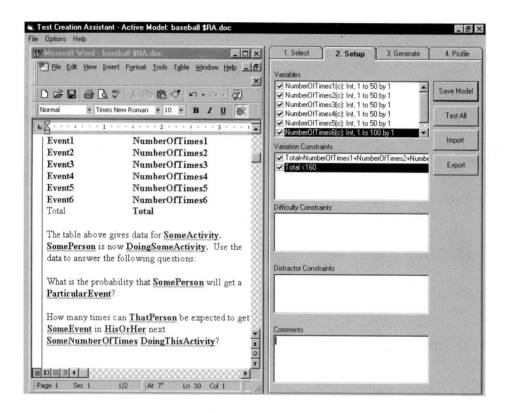

FIGURE 7-1 *Item template from the Test Creation Assistant.*
SOURCE: Bennett (1999, p. 7) and Educational Testing Service (1998). Used with permission of the Educational Testing Service.

with specifications for different classes of mathematics problem types for which theory and data exist on the processes involved and the sources of solution difficulty (see Figure 7-1 for an example). The computer program automatically generates multiple variations of draft assessment items that are similar to each other in terms of problem types, but sometimes different in terms of the semantic context that frames the problem. Test designers then review, revise, and select from the draft items. Such methodologies hold promise for promoting test design that is more systematic and cognitively principled (Bennett, 1999).

There are, however, challenges associated with ensuring thoughtful generation and use of items employing such automated methods. Sometimes simply changing the semantic context of an item (e.g., from a business scenario to a baseball scenario) can fundamentally change the knowledge that is activated and the nature of the performance assessed. A shift in the problem context can create knowledge and comprehension difficulties not intended as a source of solution variance. The need for sensitivity to semantic context is but one illustration of the importance of recursively executing the design stages described in Chapter 5, especially the process of validating the intended inferences for an item form across the multiple instances generated.

Concept Organization

As noted in Chapter 3, one of the most important differences between experts and novices lies in how their knowledge is organized. Various attempts have been made to design assessment situations for observing learners' knowledge representations and organization (see e.g., Mintzes, Wandersee, and Novak, 2000). An example can be found in software that enables students, working alone or in groups, to create concept maps on the computer. Concept maps are a form of graphical representation in which students arrange and label nodes and links to show relationships among multiple concepts in a domain; they are intended to elicit students' understanding of a domain's conceptual structure (Edmondson, 2000; Mintzes et al., 2000; O'Neil and Klein, 1997; Shavelson and Ruiz-Primo, 2000).

Software developed by O'Neil and Klein provides immediate scoring of students' concept maps based on the characteristics found in concept maps developed by experts and provides feedback to the students. The researchers are also developing an approach that uses networked computers to capture how effectively students work in a team to produce such maps by analyzing such characteristics as the students' adaptability, communication skills, timely organization of activities, leadership, and decision-making skills. The researchers have informally reported finding correlations of around $r = 0.7$ between performance on individually produced concept maps and an essay task (NRC, 1999a).

This concept map research offers just one example of how technology can enhance the assessment of collaborative skills by facilitating the execution of group projects and recording individual involvement in group activities. The ThinkerTools Inquiry Project (White and Frederiksen, 2000) described in Chapter 6 and later in this chapter provides another such example.

Complex Problem Solving

Many aspects of cognition and expertise have always been difficult to assess given the constraints of traditional testing methods and formats. For example, it is difficult to assess problem-solving strategies with paper-and-pencil formats. Although conventional test formats can do many things well, they can present only limited types of tasks and materials and provide little or no opportunity for test takers to manipulate information or record the sequence of moves used in deriving an answer. This limitation in turn restricts the range of performances that can be observed, as well as the types of cognitive processes and knowledge structures about which inferences can be drawn.

Technology is making it possible to assess a much wider range of important cognitive competencies than was previously possible. Computer-enhanced assessments can aid in the assessment of problem-solving skills by presenting complex, realistic, open-ended problems and simultaneously collecting evidence about how people go about solving them. Technology also permits users to analyze the sequences of actions learners take as they work through problems and to match these actions against models of knowledge and performance associated with different levels of expertise.

One example of this use of technology is for the assessment of spatial and design competencies central to the discipline of architecture. To assess these kinds of skills, as well as problem-solving approaches, Katz and colleagues (Katz, Martinez, Sheehan, and Tatsuoka, 1993) developed computerized assessment tasks that require architecture candidates to use a set of tools for arranging or manipulating parts of a diagram. For instance, examinees might be required to lay out the plan for a city block. On the bottom of the screen are icons representing various elements (e.g., library, parking lot, and playground). Explicit constraints are stated in the task. Examinees are also expected to apply implicit constraints, or prior knowledge, that architects are expected to have (e.g., a playground should not be adjacent to a parking lot). The computer program collects data as examinees construct their solutions and also records the time spent on each step, thus providing valuable evidence of the examinee's solution process, not just the product.

To develop these architecture tasks, the researchers conducted studies of how expert and novice architects approached various design tasks and compared their solution strategies. From this research, they found that experts and novices produced similar solutions, but their processes differed in important ways. Compared with novices, experts tended to have a consistent focus on a few key constraints and engaged in more planning and evaluation with respect to those constraints. The task and performance analyses led the researchers to design the tasks and data collection to provide evidence of those types of differences in solution processes (Katz et al., 1993).

Several technology-enhanced assessments rely on sophisticated modeling and simulation environments to capture complex problem-solving and reasoning skills. An example is the Dental Interactive Simulation Corporation (DISC) assessment for licensing dental hygienists (Mislevy, Steinberg, Breyer, Almond, and Johnson, 1999). A key issue with assessments based on simulations is whether they capture the critical skills required for successful performance in a domain. The DISC developers addressed this issue by basing the simulations on extensive research into the ways hygienists at various levels of expertise approach problems.

The DISC computerized assessment is being developed for a consortium of dental organizations for the purpose of simulating the work performed by dental hygienists as a means of providing direct evidence about how candidates for licensure would interact with patients. The foundation for the assessment was a detailed analysis of the knowledge hygienists apply when they assess patients, plan treatments, and monitor progress; the analysis was derived from interviews with and observations of several expert and competent hygienists and novice students of dental hygiene. Thus, the initial phase of the effort involved building the student model by using some of the methods for cognitive analysis described in Chapter 3.

The interactive, computer-based simulation presents the examinee with a case study of a virtual patient with a problem such as bruxism (chronic teeth grinding). The simulation provides evidence about such key points as whether the examinee detects the condition, explores connections with the patient's history and lifestyle, and discusses implications. Some information, such as the patient's medical history questionnaire, is provided up front. Other information, such as radiographs, is made available only if the examinee requests it. Additional information stored in the system is used to perform dynamic computations of the patient's status, depending on the actions taken by the examinee.

This mode of assessment has several advantages. It can tap skills that could not be measured by traditional licensing exams. The scenarios are open-ended to capture how the examinee would act in a typical professional situation. And the protocols are designed to discern behaviors at various levels of competency, based on actual practices of hygienists.

MashpeeQuest is an example of an assessment designed to tap complex problem solving in the K-12 education context. As described by Mislevy, Steinberg, Almond, Haertel, and Penuel (2000), researchers at SRI International have developed an on-line performance task to use as an evaluation tool for Classroom Connect's AmericaQuest instructional program. One of the goals of AmericaQuest is to help students learn to develop persuasive arguments supported by evidence they acquire from the course's website or their own research. The MashpeeQuest assessment task gives students an opportunity to put these skills to use in a web-based environment that structures their work (see Box 7-1). In this example, technology plays at least two roles in enabling the assessment of complex problem solving. The first is conceptual: the information analysis skills to be assessed and the behaviors that serve as evidence are embedded within a web-based environment. The second role is more operational: since actions take place in a technological environment, some of the observations of student performance can be made

BOX 7-1   **MashpeeQuest**

The AmericaQuest instructional program develops reasoning skills that are central to the practices of professional historians and archaeologists. The MashpeeQuest performance task is designed to tap the following subset of the skills that the AmericaQuest program is intended to foster:

Information Analysis Skills
• Ability to analyze and synthesize information from a variety of sources.
• Ability to evaluate/critique both content and sources.

Problem-Solving Skills
• Ability to synthesize disparate ideas through reasoning in a problem-solving context.
• Ability to offer reasoned arguments rather than brief guesses.
• Ability to formulate creative, well-founded theories for unsolved questions in science and history.

During instruction, students participate via the Internet in an expedition with archaeologists and historians who are uncovering clues about the fate of a Native American tribe, the Anasazi, who are believed to have abandoned their magnificent cliff dwellings in large numbers between 1200 and 1300. To collect observations of students' acquisition of the targeted skills, the MashpeeQuest assessment task engages students in deciding a court case involving recognition of another tribe, the Mashpee Wampanoags, who some believe disappeared just as the Anasazi did. A band of people claiming Wampanoag ancestry has been trying for some years to gain recognition from the federal government as a tribe that still exists. Students are asked to investigate the evidence, select websites that provide evidence to support their claim, and justify their choices based on the evidence. They are also asked to identify one place to go to find evidence that does not support their claim, and to address how their theory of what happened to the Mashpee is still justified.

SOURCE: Adapted from Mislevy et al. (2000).

automatically (e.g., number of sources used and time per source). Other observations, such as those requiring information analysis, are made by human raters.

Enhancing the Observation-Interpretation Linkage

Text Analysis and Scoring

Extended written responses are often an excellent means of determining how well someone has understood certain concepts and can express their interrelationships. In large-scale assessment contexts, the process of reading and scoring such written products can be problematic because it is so time- and labor-intensive, even after raters have been given extensive training on standardized scoring methods. Technology tools have been developed to aid in this process by automatically scoring a variety of extended written products, such as essays. Some of the most widely used tools of this type are based on a cognitive theory of semantics called latent semantic analysis (LSA) (Landauer, Foltz, and Laham, 1998). LSA involves constructing a multidimensional semantic space that expresses the meaning of words on the basis of their co-occurences in large amounts of text. Employing mathematical techniques, LSA can be used to "locate" units of text within this space and assign values in reference to other texts. For example, LSA can be used to estimate the semantic similarity between an essay on how the heart functions and reference pieces on cardiac structure and functioning that might be drawn from a high school text and a medical reference text.

LSA can be applied to the scoring of essays for assessment purposes in several ways. It can be used to compare a student's essay with a set of pregraded essays at varying quality levels or with one or more model essays written by experts. Evaluation studies suggest that scores obtained from LSA systems are as reliable as those produced by pairs of human raters (Landauer, 1998). One of the benefits of such an automated approach to evaluating text is that it can provide not just a single overall score, but multiple scores on matches against different reference texts or based on subsets of the total text. These multiple scores can be useful for diagnostic purposes, as discussed subsequently.

Questions exist about public acceptance of the machine scoring of essays for high-stakes testing. There are also potential concerns about the impact of these approaches on the writing skills teachers emphasize, as well as the potential to reduce the opportunities for teacher professional development (Bennett, 1999).

Analysis of Complex Solution Strategies

We have already mentioned the possibility of using technology to assess solution moves in the context of problem-solving simulations. One of the most sophisticated examples of such analyses is offered by the IMMEX (Interactive Multimedia Exercises) program (Vendlinski and Stevens, 2000), which uses complex neural network technology to make sense of (interpret) the actions students take during the course of problem solving. IMMEX was originally developed for use in teaching and assessing the diagnostic skills of medical students. It now consists of a variety of software tools for authoring complex, multimove problem-solving tasks and for collecting performance data on those tasks, with accompanying analysis methods. The moves an individual makes in solving a problem in the IMMEX system are tracked, and the path through the solution space can be presented graphically, as well as compared against patterns previously exhibited by both skilled and less-skilled problem solvers. The IMMEX tools have been used for the design and analysis of complex problem solving in a variety of contexts, ranging from medical school to science at the college and K-12 level.

In one IMMEX problem set called True Roots, learners play the part of forensic scientists trying to identify the real parents of a baby who may have been switched with another in a maternity ward. Students can access data from various experts, such as police and hospital staff, and can conduct laboratory tests such as blood typing and DNA analysis. Students can also analyze maps of their own problem-solving patterns, in which various nodes and links represent different paths of reasoning (Lawton, 1998).

A core technology used for data analysis in the IMMEX system is artificial neural networks. These networks are used to abstract identifiable patterns of moves on a given problem from the data for many individuals who have attempted solutions, including individuals separately rated as excellent, average, or poor problem solvers. In this way, profiles can be abstracted that support the assignment of scores reflecting the accuracy and quality of the solution process. In one example of such an application, the neural network analysis of solution patterns was capable of identifying different levels of performance as defined by scores on the National Board of Medical Examiners computer-based clinical scenario exam (Casillas, Clyman, Fan, and Stevens, 2000). Similar work has been done using artificial neural network analysis tools to examine solution strategy patterns for chemistry problems (Vendlinski and Stevens, 2000).

Enhancing the Overall Design Process

The above discussion illustrates specific ways in which technology can assist in assessment design by supporting particular sets of linkages within the assessment triangle. The Educational Testing Service has developed a more general software system, Portal, to foster cognitively based assessment design. The DISC assessment for licensing dental hygienists, described earlier, is being designed using the Portal approach.

Portal includes three interrelated components: a conceptual framework, an object model, and supporting tools. The *conceptual framework* is Mislevy and colleagues' evidentiary reasoning framework (Mislevy et al., 2000), which the committee adapted and simplified to create the assessment triangle referred to throughout this report. This conceptual framework (like the assessment triangle) is at a level of generality that supports a broad range of assessment types. The *object model* is a set of specifications or blueprints for creating assessment design "objects." A key idea behind Portal is that different kinds of objects are not defined for different kinds of tests; rather, the same general kinds of objects are tailored and assembled in different ways to meet different purposes. The object model for a particular assessment describes the nature of the objects and their interconnections to ensure that the design reflects attention to all the assessment elements—cognition, observation, and interpretation—and coordinates their interactions to produce a coherent assessment. Finally, the *supporting tools* are software tools for creating, manipulating, and coordinating a structured database that contains the elements of an assessment design.

The Portal system is a serious attempt to impose organization on the process of assessment design in a manner consistent with the thinking described elsewhere in this report on the general process of assessment design and the specific roles played by cognitive and measurement theory. Specifications and blueprints are becoming increasingly important in assessment design because, as companies and agencies develop technology-based assessments, having common yet flexible standards and language is essential for building inter-operable assessment components and processes.

STRENGTHENING THE COGNITIVE COHERENCE AMONG CURRCULUM, INSTRUCTION, AND ASSESSMENT

Technology is changing the nature of the economy and the workplace, as well as other aspects of society. To perform competently in an information society, people must be able to communicate, think, and reason effectively; solve complex problems; work with multidimensional data and sophisticated representations; navigate through a sea of information that may or may not be accurate; collaborate in diverse teams; and demonstrate self-motivation and other skills (Dede, 2000; NRC, 1999c; Secretary's Commission on Achieving Necessary Skills [SCANS], 1991). To be prepared for this future, students must acquire different kinds of content knowledge and thinking skills than were emphasized in the past, and at higher levels of attainment. Numerous reports and standards documents reinforce this point of view with regard to expectations about the learning and understanding of various aspects of science, mathematics, and technology (National Council of Teachers of Mathematics, 2000; NRC, 1996, 1999b; SCANS, 1991).

Consistent with these trends and pressures, many schools are moving toward instructional methods that encourage students to learn mathematics and science content in greater depth, and to learn advanced thinking skills through longer-term projects that emphasize a scientific process of inquiry, involve the use of complex materials, and cut across multiple disciplines. Many of these reforms incorporate findings from cognitive research, and many assign technology a central role in this transformation.

In numerous areas of the curriculum, information technologies are changing what is taught, when and how it is taught, and what students are expected to be able to do to demonstrate their knowledge and skill. These changes in turn are stimulating people to rethink what is assessed, how that information is obtained, and how it is fed back into the educational process in a productive and timely way. This situation creates opportunities to center curriculum, instruction, and assessment around cognitive principles. With technology, assessment can become richer, more timely, and more seamlessly interwoven with curriculum and instruction.

In this section we consider two ways in which this integration is under way. In the first set of scenarios, the focus is on using technology tools and systems to assist in the integration of cognitively based assessment into classroom practice in ways consistent with the discussion in Chapter 6. In the second set of scenarios, the focus is on technology-enhanced learning environments that provide for a more thorough integration of curriculum, instruction, and assessment guided by models of cognition and learning.

Facilitating Formative Assessment

As discussed in earlier chapters, the most useful kinds of assessment for enhancing student learning often support a process of individualized instruction, allow for student interaction, collect rich diagnostic data, and provide timely feedback. The demands and complexity of these types of assessment can be quite substantial, but technology makes them feasible. In diagnostic assessments of individual learning, for example, significant amounts of information must be collected, interpreted, and reported. No individual, whether a classroom teacher or other user of assessment data, could realistically be expected to handle the information flow, analysis demands, and decision-making burdens involved without technological support. Thus, technology removes some of the constraints that previously made high-quality formative assessment difficult or impractical for a classroom teacher.

Several examples illustrate how technology can help infuse ongoing formative assessment into the learning process. Notable among them are intelligent tutors, described previously in this report (see Chapters 3 and 6). Computer technology facilitates fine-grained analysis of the learner's cognitive processes and knowledge states in terms of the theoretical models of domain learning embedded within a tutoring system. Without technology, it would not be possible to provide individualized and interactive instruction, extract key features of the learner's responses, immediately analyze student errors, and offer relevant feedback for remediating those errors—let alone do so in a way that would be barely identifiable as assessment to the learner.

Another example is the DIAGNOSER computerized assessment tool used in the Facets-based instructional program (described in Chapters 5 and 6). DIAGNOSER allows students to test their own understanding as they work through various modules on key math and science concepts (Minstrell, Stimpson, and Hunt, 1992). On the basis of students' responses to the carefully constructed questions, the program can pinpoint areas of possible misunderstanding, give feedback on reasoning strategies, and prescribe relevant instruction. The program also keeps track of student responses, which teachers can use for monitoring overall class performance. As illustrated in Chapter 5, the assessment questions are in a multiple-choice format, in which each possible answer corresponds to a facet of reasoning. Although the assessment format is rather conventional, this basic model could be extended to other, more complex applications. Minstrell (2000; see also Hunt and Minstrell, 1994) has reported data on how use of a Facets instructional approach that includes the DIAGNOSER software system has significantly enhanced levels of student learning in high school physics.

ThinkerTools (also described in Chapter 6) is a computer-enhanced middle school science curriculum that promotes metacognitive skills by encouraging students to evaluate their own and each others' work using a set of well-considered criteria (White and Frederiksen, 2000). Students propose and test competing theories, carry out experiments using the computer and real-world materials, compare their findings, and try to reach consensus about the best model. The software enables students to simulate experiments, such as turning gravity on and off, that would be impossible to perform in the real world, and to accurately measure distances, times, and velocities that would similarly be difficult to measure in live experiments. Feedback about the correctness of student conjectures is provided as part of the system. According to a project evaluation, students who learned to use the self-assessment criteria produced higher-quality projects than those who did not, and the benefits were particularly obvious for lower-achieving students.

The IMMEX program was discussed in the preceding section as an example of a powerful set of technology tools for assessing student problem solving in areas of science. Teachers participate in professional development experiences with the IMMEX system and learn to use the various tools to develop problem sets that then become part of their overall curriculum-instruction-assessment environment. Students work on problems in the IMMEX system, and feedback can be generated at multiple levels of detail for both teacher and student. For the teacher, data are available on how individual students and whole classes are doing on particular problems, as well as over time on multiple problems. At a deeper level of analysis, teachers and students can obtain visual maps of their search through the problem space for the solution to a given problem. These maps are rich in information, and teachers and students can use them in multiple ways to review and discuss the problem-solving process. By comparing earlier maps with later ones, teachers and students can also judge refinements in problem-solving processes and strategies (see Vendelinski and Stevens, 2000, for examples of this process).

Technology-based assessment tools are not limited to mathematics and science. Summary Street, experimental software for language arts, helps middle school students improve their reading comprehension and writing skills by asking them to write summaries of materials they have read. Using a text analysis program based on LSA, the computer compares the summary with the original text and analyzes it for certain information and features. The program also gives students feedback on how to improve their summaries before showing them to their teachers (Kintsch, Steinhart, Stahl, LSA Research Group, Matthews, and Lamb, 2000). Research with this system has shown substantial improvements in students' summary generation skills, which generalize to other classes and are independent of having further access to the Summary Street software program (Kintsch et al., 2000).

The preceding examples are not an exhaustive list of instances in which technology has been used to create formative assessment tools that incorporate various aspects of cognitive and measurement theory. An especially important additional example is the integration of concept mapping tools, discussed earlier, into instructional activities (see Mintzes et al., 1998). In the next section, we consider other examples of the use of technology-assisted formative assessment tools in the instructional process. In many of these cases, the tools are an integral part of a more comprehensive, technology-enhanced learning environment.

Technology-Enhanced Learning Environments

Some of the most powerful technology-enhanced innovations that link curriculum, instruction, and assessment focus on aspects of the mathematics and science curriculum that have heretofore been difficult to teach. Many of these designs were developed jointly by researchers and educators using findings from cognitive science and classroom practice. Students and teachers in these environments use technology to conduct research, solve problems, analyze data, interact with others, track progress, present their results, and accomplish other goals. Typically, these environments emphasize learning through the processes of inquiry and collaborative, problem-based learning, and their learning goals are generally consistent with those discussed in the National Council of Teachers of Mathematics (2000) mathematics standards and the NRC (1996) science standards. In many ways, they also go beyond current standards by emphasizing new learning outcomes students need to master to perform competently in an information society.

In these environments, it is not uncommon for learners to form live and on-line communities of practice, evaluating their own and each others' reasoning, hypotheses, and work products. These programs also tend to have multiple learning goals; in addition to teaching students important concepts in biology, physics, or earth science, for example, they may seek to teach students to think, work, and communicate as scientists do. These environments, examples of which are described below, illustrate the importance of carefully designed assessment to an effective learning environment (NRC, 1999d) and show how technology makes possible the integration of assessment with instruction in powerful ways.

Use of Technology to Enhance Learning Environments: Examples

SMART Model   An example of embedding assessment strategies within extended-inquiry activities can be found in work pursued by the Cognition and Technology Group at Vanderbilt University (CTGV) on the development of a conceptual model for integrating curriculum, instruction, and assessment in science and mathematics (Barron et al., 1995; CTGV, 1994, 1997). The resultant SMART (Scientific and Mathematical Arenas for Refining Thinking) Model incorporates frequent opportunities for formative assessment by both students and teachers, and reflects an emphasis on self-assessment to help students develop the ability to monitor their own understanding and find resources to deepen it when necessary (Vye et al., 1998). The SMART Model involves the explicit design of multiple cycles of problem solving, self-assessment, and revision in an overall problem-based to project-based learning environment.

Activity in the problem-based learning portion of SMART typically begins with a video problem scenario, for example, from the *Adventures of Jasper Woodbury* mathematics problem-solving series (CTGV, 1997) or the *Scientists in Action* series. An example of the latter is the Stones River Mystery (Sherwood, Petrosino, Lin, and CTGV, 1998), which tells the story of a group of high school students who, in collaboration with a biologist and a hydrologist, are monitoring the water in Stones River. The video shows the team visiting the river and conducting various water quality tests. Students in the classroom are asked to assess the water quality at a second site on the river. They are challenged to select tools they can use to sample macroinvertebrates and test dissolved oxygen, to conduct these tests, and to interpret the data relative to previous data from the same site. Ultimately, they find that the river is polluted as a result of illegal dumping of restaurant grease. Students must then decide how to clean up the pollution.

The problem-based learning activity includes three sequential modules: macroinvertebrate sampling, dissolved oxygen testing, and pollution cleanup. The modules are preliminary to the project-based activity, in which students conduct actual water quality testing at a local river. In executing the latter, they are provided with a set of criteria by which an external agency will evaluate written reports and accompanying videotaped presentations.

The ability of students and teachers to progress through the various cycles of work and revision within each module and devise an effective solution to the larger problem depends on a variety of resource materials carefully designed to assist in the learning and assessment process (see Box 7-2). Students who use these resources and tools learn significantly more than students who go through the same instructional sequence for the same amount of time, but without the benefit of the tools and the embedded formative assessment activities. Furthermore, their performance in a related project-based learning activity is significantly enhanced (Barron et al., 1995).

Genscope™ This is an innovative computer-based program designed to help students learn key concepts of genetics and develop scientific reasoning skills (see Hickey, Kindfield, and Horwitz, 1999; Horwitz, 1998). The program includes curriculum, instructional components, and assessments. The centerpiece is an open-ended software tool that permits students to manipulate models of genetic information at multiple levels, including cells, family trees, and whole populations. Using GenScope™, students can create and vary the biological traits of an imaginary species of dragons—for example, by altering a gene that codes for the dragon's color and exploring how this alteration affects generations of offspring and the survivability of a population.

The developers of GenScope™ have pursued various approaches to the assessment of student learning outcomes. To compare the performance of ninth graders who used this program and those in more traditional classrooms, the researchers administered a paper-and-pencil test. They concluded that many GenScope™ students were not developing higher-order reasoning skills as intended. They also found that some classrooms that used these curriculum materials did not complete the computerized activities because of various logistical problems; nevertheless, the students in these classrooms

BOX 7-2 Web-Based Resources for SMART Science

Solution of the Stones River Mystery requires students to work through three successive activity modules focused on macroinvertebrate sampling, dissolved oxygen testing, and pollution cleanup. Each module follows the same cycle of activities: initial selection of a method for testing or cleanup, feedback on the initial choice, revision of the choice, and a culminating task. Within each activity module, selection, feedback, and revision make use of the SMART web site, which organizes the overall process and supports three high-level functions.

First, it provides individualized feedback to students and serves as a formative evaluation tool. As with DIAGNOSER, the feedback suggests aspects of students' work that are in need of revision and classroom resources students can use to help them make these revisions. The feedback does not tell students the "right answer." Instead, it sets a course for independent inquiry by the student. The Web feedback is generated from data entered by individual students.

The second function of SMART web site is to collect, organize, and display the data collected from multiple distributed classrooms, a function performed by SMART Lab. Data displays are automatically updated as students submit new data. The data in SMART Lab consist of students' answers to problems and explanations for their answers. Data from each class can be displayed separately from those of the distributed classroom. This feature enables the teacher and her or his class to discuss different solution strategies, and in the process address important concepts and misconceptions. These discussions provide a rich source of information for the teacher on how students are thinking about a problem and are designed to stimulate further student reflection.

The third function of SMART web site is performed by Kids Online. Students are presented with the explanations of student-actors. The explanations are text-based with audio narration, and they are errorful by design. Students are asked to critically evaluate the explanations and provide feedback to the student-actors. The errors seed thinking and discussion on concepts that are frequently misconceived by students. At the same time, students learn important critical evaluation skills.

showed the same reasoning gains as their schoolmates who used the software. To address the first concern, the researchers developed a set of formative assessments, including both worksheets and computer activities, that encouraged students to practice specific reasoning skills. To address the second concern, the developers refined the program and carefully designed a follow-up evaluation with more rigorous controls and comparison groups; this evaluation showed that GenScope™ was notably more effective than traditional methods in improving students' reasoning abilities in genetics.

Recently, the researchers have begun testing a new assessment software tool, BioLogica, which embeds formative assessment into the computerized GenScope™ activities. This system poses sequences of challenges to students as they work, monitors their actions, intervenes with hints or feedback, asks questions intended to elicit student understanding, provides tools the students can use to meet the challenge, and directs them to summon the teacher for discussion. The BioLogica scripts are based on numerous hours of observation and questioning of children as they worked. The system can also create personal portfolios of a student's notes and images and record the ongoing interactions of multiple students in a massive log that can be used for formative or summative assessment.

Knowledge Integration Environment   The Knowledge Integration Environment (KIE) is another technology-based instructional environment that engages middle and high school students in scientific inquiry using the Internet. KIE consists of a set of complementary software components that provide browsing, note-taking, discussion, argument-building, and guidance capabilities. The instructional goal is to foster knowledge integration by encouraging students to make connections between scientific concepts and relate these concepts to personally relevant situations and problems. As part of the design process, developers conducted research with students in real classroom environments to gain a better understanding of the cognitive benefits of different kinds of prompts, ways in which perspective taking can be scaffolded,[1] and the effects of evidence presentation on student interpretation (Bell, 1997). The KIE curriculum consists of units, called "projects," that typically last three to ten class periods. Projects include debates, critiques, and design projects. Box 7-3 describes an example of a KIE project.

KIE is related to another program, the Computer as Learning Partner (CLP), which is based on many of the same principles. The developers of CLP have used a variety of measures to evaluate its impact on learning (Linn and Hsi, 2000). Students engaged in a CLP unit on heat and temperature, for

---

[1]Scaffolding consists of explicit and sequentially organized support and guidance about possible strategies.

example, showed substantial gains in understanding and outperformed comparable twelfth-grade students in traditional classrooms. Researchers are also working on designing assessments that can similarly be used to evaluate the impact of KIE on learning. Early results from this research suggest benefits comparable to those of CLP (Linn and Hsi, 2000).

Additional Examples   The list of technology-enhanced learning environments, as well as other applications of technology tools in educational settings, continues to grow (see CILT.org and LETUS.org). Two other environments with a significant research and development history bear mentioning for their consideration of issues associated with the integration of curriculum, instruction, and assessment. The first is the CoVis (Learning Through Collaborative Visualization) project. The goal of the CoVis project is to support the formation and work of learning communities by providing media-rich communication and scientific visualization tools in a highly interactive, networked, collaborative context. For instance, students collaborate with distant peers to study meteorological phenomena using computational tools. A variety of technological tools make it possible for participants to record, carry out, and discuss their project work with peers in other locations (Edelson, 1997).

The second such environment is MOOSE Crossing, an innovative technology-based program that uses an on-line learning environment to improve the reading, writing, and programming skills of children aged 8 to 14. The program enables children to build virtual objects, creatures, and places and to program their creations to move, change, and interact in the virtual environment (Bruckman, 1998). The broader goal of the project is to create a self-directed and self-supporting on-line community of learners who provide technical and social support, collaborate on activities, and share examples of completed work. Initially the project encompassed no formal assessment, consistent with its philosophy of encouraging self-motivated learning, but over time the developers realized the need to evaluate what students were learning. Assessments of programming skills indicated that most participants were not attempting to write programming scripts of any complexity, so the project designers introduced a merit badge system to serve as a motivator, scaffold, and assessment tool. To win a badge, students must work with a mentor to complete a portfolio, which is reviewed by anonymous reviewers.

Assessment Issues and Challenges for Technology-Enhanced Learning Environments

As the preceding examples illustrate, many technology-enhanced learning environments have integrated formative and summative assessments into

BOX 7-3   Knowledge Integration Environment: How Far Does Light Go?

KIE is organized around projects that involve students in using the Internet. The How Far Does Light Go? project (Bell, 1997) asks students to contrast two theoretical positions about the propagation of light using text and multimedia evidence derived from both scientific and everyday sources. The first theoretical position in the debate is the scientifically normative view that "light goes forever until it is absorbed," while the second is the more phenomenological perception that "light dies out as you move farther from a light source."

Students begin the project by stating their personal position on how far light goes. They review a set of evidence and determine where each piece fits into the debate. After creating some evidence of their own, the students then synthesize the evidence by selecting the pieces that in their opinion factor most prominently into the debate and composing written explanations to that effect. The result is a scientific argument supporting one of the two theoretical positions. Student teams present their arguments in a classroom discussion and respond to questions from the other students and the teacher. As the project concludes, students are asked to reflect upon issues that arose during the activity and once again state their position in the debate.

Sensemaker is one software component of KIE. It provides a spatial and categorical representation for a collection of web-based evidence. The sample screen below shows a SenseMaker argument constructed jointly by a student pair for use in a classroom debate as part of the How Far Does Light Go? project.

their ongoing instructional activities. This was not always the case from the outset of these programs. Sometimes the designers planned their curriculum, instructional programs, and activities without giving high priority to assessment. But as researchers and teachers implemented these innovations, they realized that the environments would have to incorporate better assessment strategies.

Several factors led to this realization. First, after analyzing students' interactions, researchers and teachers often discovered that many learners re-

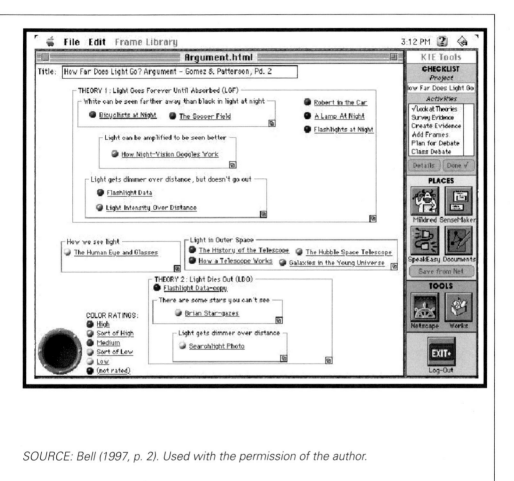

SOURCE: Bell (1997, p. 2). Used with the permission of the author.

quired more scaffolding to motivate them to tackle challenging tasks and help them acquire a deep level of understanding. Thus, components were added to programs such as GenScope™, Moose Crossing, and SMART to give students more advice, encouragement, and practice.

Second, researchers found that teachers and students needed formative assessment to help them monitor what was being learned and develop their metacognitive skills (CTGV, 1997; White and Frederiksen, 1998). Consequently, many of these environments included methods of recording and analyzing students' inquiry processes and ways of encouraging them to reflect on and revise their thinking. An interesting example is the cognitively based scheme for computerized diagnosis of study skills (e.g., self-explanation) recently produced and tested by Conati and VanLehn (1999). The development of metacognitive skills is also an explicit part of the designs used in SMART.

Third, researchers and educators realized that to document the learning effects of these innovations for parents, policy makers, funding agencies, and other outside audiences, it would be necessary to have assessments that captured the complex knowledge and skills that inquiry-based learning environments are designed to foster. Not surprisingly, traditional assessments of mathematics and science typically reveal little about the benefits of these kinds of learning environments. Indeed, one can understand why there is often no evidence of benefit when typical standardized tests are used to evaluate the learning effects of many technology-based instructional programs. The use of such tests constitutes an instance of a poor fit between the observation and cognitive elements of the assessment triangle. The tasks used for typical standardized tests provide observations that align with a student model focused on specific types of declarative and procedural knowledge that may or may not have been acquired with the assistance of the technology-based programs. Thus, it should come as no surprise that there is often a perceived mismatch between the learning goals of many educational technology programs and the data obtained from standardized tests. Despite their inappropriateness, however, many persist in using such data as the primary basis for judging the effectiveness and value of investments in educational technology.

Unfortunately, this situation poses a significant assessment and evaluation challenge for the designers and implementers of technology-enhanced learning environments. For example, if such environments are to be implemented on a wider scale, evidence must be produced that students are learning things of value, and this evidence must be convincing and accepted as valid by outside audiences. In many technology-enhanced learning environments, the data provided are from assessments that are highly contextualized: assessment observations are made while students are engaged in learning activities, and the model used to interpret these observations is linked specifically to that project. Other concerns relate to the technical quality of the assessment information. Is it derived from a representative sample of learners? Are the results generalizable to the broad learning goals in that domain? Are the data objective and technically defensible? Such concerns often make it difficult to use assessment data closely tied to the learning environment to convince educators and the public of the value of these new kinds of learning environments. Without such data it is difficult to expand the audience for these programs so that they are used on a larger scale. This dilemma represents yet another example of the point, made earlier in this report, that assessment that serves the purpose of supporting student learning may not serve the purpose of program evaluation equally well.

While this dilemma is complex and often poorly understood, it can begin to be addressed by starting with a clear definition of both the goals for learning in such environments and the targets of inference. By following the design principles set forth in this report, it is possible to design fair assessments of student attainment that are not totally embedded in the learning environment or confounded with technology use. Assessing the knowledge students acquire in specific technology-enhanced learning environments requires tasks and observations designed to provide evidence consistent with an appropriate student model. The latter identifies the specific knowledge and skills students are expected to learn and the precise form of that knowledge, including what aspects are tied to specific technology tools. An interesting example of this principled approach to assessment design is the Mashpee Quest task (described earlier in Box 7-1) (Mislevy et al., 2000).

LINKAGE OF ASSESSMENTS FOR CLASSROOM LEARNING AND ACCOUNTABILITY PURPOSES

A Vision of the Possible

While it is always risky to predict the future, it appears clear that advances in technology will continue to impact the world of education in powerful and provocative ways. Many technology-driven advances in the design of learning environments, which include the integration of assessment with instruction, will continue to emerge and will reshape the terrain of what is both possible and desirable in education. Advances in curriculum, instruction, assessment, and technology are likely to continue to move educational practice toward a more individualized and mastery-oriented approach to learning. This evolution will occur across the K-16 spectrum. To manage learning and instruction effectively, people will want and need to know considerably more about what has been mastered, at what level, and by whom.

One of the limiting factors in effectively integrating assessment into educational systems to address the range of questions that need to be answered about student achievement is the lack of models of student learning for many aspects of the curriculum. This situation will change over time, and it will become possible to incorporate much of the necessary theoretical and empirical knowledge into technology-based systems for instruction and assessment.

It is both intriguing and useful to consider the possibilities that might arise if assessment were integrated into instruction in multiple curricular areas, and the resultant information about student accomplishment and understanding were collected with the aid of technology. In such a world, programs of on-demand external assessment might not be necessary. It might be possible to extract the information needed for summative and program evaluation purposes from data about student performance continuously available both in and out of the school context.

Extensive technology-based systems that link curriculum, instruction, and assessment at the classroom level might enable a shift from today's assessment systems that use different kinds of assessments for different purposes to a balanced design in which the features of comprehensiveness, coherence, and continuity would be assured (see Chapter 6). One can imagine a future in which the audit function of external assessments would be significantly reduced or even unnecessary because the information needed to assess students at the levels of description appropriate for various external assessment purposes could be derived from the data streams generated by students in and out of their classrooms. Technology could offer ways of creating over time a complex stream of data about how students think and reason while engaged in important learning activities. Information for assessment purposes could be extracted from this stream and used to serve both classroom and external assessment needs, including providing individual feedback to students for reflection about their metacognitive habits. To realize this vision, research on the data representations and analysis methods best suited for different audiences and different assessment objectives would clearly be needed.

A metaphor for this shift exists in the world of retail outlets, ranging from small businesses to supermarkets to department stores. No longer do these businesses have to close down once or twice a year to take inventory of their stock. Rather, with the advent of automated checkout and barcodes for all items, these businesses have access to a continuous stream of information that can be used to monitor inventory and the flow of items. Not only can business continue without interruption, but the information obtained is far richer, enabling stores to monitor trends and aggregate the data into various kinds of summaries. Similarly, with new assessment technologies, schools no longer have to interrupt the normal instructional process at various times during the year to administer external tests to students.

While the committee is divided as to the practicality and advisability of pursuing the scenario just described, we offer it as food for thought about future states that might be imagined or invented. Regardless of how far one wishes to carry such a vision, it is clear that technological advances will allow for the attainment of many of the goals for assessment envisioned in this report. When powerful technology-based systems are implemented in multiple classrooms, rich sources of information about student learning will be continuously available across wide segments of the curriculum and for individual learners over extended periods of time. The major issue is not whether this type of data collection and information analysis is feasible in the future. Rather, the issue is how the world of education will anticipate and embrace this possibility, and how it will explore the resulting options for effectively using assessment information to meet the multiple purposes served by current assessments and, most important, to aid in student learning.

It is sometimes noted that the best way to predict the future is to invent it. Multiple futures for educational assessment could be invented on the basis of synergies that exist among information technologies and contemporary knowledge of cognition and measurement. In considering these futures, however, one must also explore a number of associated issues and challenges.

Issues and Challenges

Visions of assessment integrated with instruction and of the availability of complex forms of data coexist with other visions of education's future as a process of "distributed learning": educational activities orchestrated by means of information technology across classrooms, workplaces, homes, and community settings and based on a mix of presentational and constructivist pedagogies (guided inquiry, collaborative learning, mentoring) (Dede, 2000). Recent advances in groupware and experiential simulation enable guided, collaborative inquiry-based learning even though students are in different locations and often are not on line at the same time. With the aid of telementors, students can create, share, and master knowledge about authentic real-world problems. Through a mix of emerging instructional media, learners and educators can engage in synchronous or asynchronous interaction: face-to-face or in disembodied fashion or as an "avatar" expressing an alternate form of individual identity. Instruction can be distributed across space, time, and multiple interactive media. These uses of technology for distributed learning add a further layer of complexity to issues raised by the potential for using technology to achieve the integrated forms of assessment envisioned in this report.

Policy Issues

Although powerful, distributed learning strategies render assessment and evaluation for comparative and longitudinal purposes potentially more problematic. A major question is whether assessment strategies connected to such environments would be accepted by policy makers and others who make key decisions about current investments in large-scale assessment programs. Many people will be unfamiliar with these approaches and concerned about their fairness, as well as their fit with existing standards in some states. Questions also arise about how to compare the performance of students in technology-enhanced environments with that of students in more traditional classrooms, as well as students who are home-schooled or educated in settings without these technologies.

Pragmatic Issues

Issues of utility, practicality, and cost would have to be addressed to realize the vision of integrated assessments set forth above. First is the question of how different users would make sense of the masses of data that might be available and which kinds of information should be extracted for various purposes. Technical issues of data quality and validity would also become paramount. With regard to costs, designing integrated assessments would be labor-intensive and expensive, but technological tools that would aid in the design and implementation process could eventually reduce the costs and effort involved. The costs would also need to be spread over time and amortized by generating information that could be used for multiple purposes: diagnosis and instructional feedback, classroom summative assessment, and accountability.

Equity Issues

Many of the innovations described in this chapter have the potential to improve educational equity. Initial evaluations of technology-enhanced learning projects have suggested that they may have the power to increase learning among students in low-income areas and those with disabilities (Koedinger, Anderson, Hadley, and Mark, 1997; White and Frederiksen, 1998). Technology-enhanced instruction and assessment may also be effective with students who have various learning styles—for example, students who learn better with visual supports than with text or who learn better through movement and hands-on activities. These approaches can also encourage communication and performances by students who are silent and passive in classroom settings, are not native English speakers, or are insecure about their capabilities. Technology is already being used to assess students with physical disabilities and other learners whose special needs preclude representative performance using traditional media for measurement (Dede, 2000).

Evidence indicates that hands-on methods may be better than textbook-oriented instruction for promoting science mastery among students with learning disabilities. At-risk students may make proportionately greater gains than other students with technology-enhanced programs. The GenScope™ program, for example, was conducted in three ninth-grade biology classrooms of students who were not college bound; about half of the students in all three classrooms had been identified as having learning or behavioral disabilities. An auspicious finding of the program evaluation was that the gains in reasoning skills in the two classrooms using GenScope™ were much greater than those in the classroom following a more traditional approach (Hickey et al., 1999).

An example of the potential of technology-enhanced learning can be found in the Union City, New Jersey, school district, which has reshaped its curriculum, instruction, and assessment around technology. Evaluations have demonstrated positive and impressive gains in student learning in this diverse, underfinanced district (Chang et al., 1998).

Privacy Issues

Yet another set of critical issues relates to privacy. On the one hand, an integrated approach to assessment would eliminate the need for large banks of items to maintain test security, because the individual trail of actions taken while working on a problem would form the items. On the other hand, such an approach raises different kinds of security issues. When assessments record students' actions as they work, a tension exists between the need to protect students' privacy and the need to obtain information for demonstrating program effectiveness. Questions arise of what consequences these new forms of embedded assessment would have for learning and experimentation if students (and teachers) knew that all or many of their actions—successes and failures—were being recorded. Other questions relate to how much information would be sampled and whether that information would remain private.

Learners and parents have a right to know how their performance will be judged and how the data being collected will be used. Existing projects that record student interactions for external evaluations have obtained informed consent from parents to extract certain kinds of information. Scaling up these kinds of assessments to collect and extract information from complex data streams could be viewed as considerably more invasive and could escalate concerns about student privacy.

CONCLUSIONS

Information technologies are helping to remove some of the constraints that have limited assessment practice in the past. Assessment tasks no longer need be confined to paper-and-pencil formats, and the entire burden of classroom assessment no longer need fall on the teacher. At the same time, *technology will not in and of itself improve educational assessment.* Improved methods of assessment require a design process that connects the three elements of the assessment triangle to ensure that the theory of cognition, the observations, and the interpretation process work together to support the intended inferences. Fortunately, there exist multiple examples of technology tools and applications that enhance the linkages among cognition, observation, and interpretation.

Some of the most intriguing applications of technology extend the nature of the problems that can be presented and the knowledge and cognitive processes that can be assessed. By enriching task environments through the use of multimedia, interactivity, and control over the stimulus display, it is possible to assess a much wider array of cognitive competencies than has heretofore been feasible. New capabilities enabled by technology include directly assessing problem-solving skills, making visible sequences of actions taken by learners in solving problems, and modeling and simulating complex reasoning tasks. Technology also makes possible data collection on concept organization and other aspects of students' knowledge structures, as well as representations of their participation in discussions and group projects. *A significant contribution of technology has been to the design of systems for implementing sophisticated classroom-based formative assessment practices.* Technology-based systems have been developed to support individualized instruction by extracting key features of learners' responses, analyzing patterns of correct and incorrect reasoning, and providing rapid and informative feedback to both student and teacher.

A major change in education has resulted from the influence of technology on what is taught and how. Schools are placing more emphasis on teaching critical content in greater depth. Examples include the teaching of advanced thinking and reasoning skills within a discipline through the use of technology-mediated projects involving long-term inquiry. Such projects often integrate content and learning across disciplines, as well as integrate assessment with curriculum and instruction in powerful ways.

A possibility for the future arises from the projected growth across curricular areas of technology-based assessment embedded in instructional settings. Increased availability of such systems could make it possible to pursue balanced designs representing a more coordinated and coherent assessment system. Information from such assessments could possibly be used for multiple purposes, including the audit function associated with many existing external assessments.

Finally, *technology holds great promise for enhancing educational assessment at multiple levels of practice, but its use for this purpose also raises issues of utility, practicality, cost, equity, and privacy.* These issues will need to be addressed as technology applications in education and assessment continue to expand, evolve, and converge.

Part IV

Conclusion

8

Implications and Recommendations for Research, Policy, and Practice

The Committee on the Foundations of Assessment produced this report, with the support of the National Science Foundation (NSF), to review and synthesize advances in the cognitive and measurement sciences and to explore the implications of those advances for improving educational assessment. Interest in the intersection of these two fields is not new. Prompted by calls for assessments that can better inform and support learning, a number of education researchers have put forth the potential benefits of merging modern knowledge in the areas of cognition and learning and methods of educational measurement (Baker, 1997; Cronbach and Gleser, 1965; Glaser, 1981; Glaser and Silver, 1994; Messick, 1984; Mislevy, 1994; National Academy of Education, 1996; Nichols, 1994; Pellegrino, Baxter, and Glaser, 1999; Snow and Lohman, 1993; Wilson and Adams, 1996).

Several decades of research in the cognitive sciences has advanced the knowledge base about how children develop understanding, how people reason and build structures of knowledge, which thinking processes are associated with competent performance, and how knowledge is shaped by social context (National Research Council [NRC], 1999b). These findings, presented in Chapter 3, suggest directions for revamping assessment to provide better information about students' levels of understanding, their thinking strategies, and the nature of their misunderstandings.

During this same period, there have been significant developments in measurement (psychometric) methods and theory. As presented in Chapter 4, a wide array of statistical measurement methods are currently available to support the kinds of inferences that cognitive research suggests are important to pursue when assessing student achievement.

Meanwhile, computer and telecommunications technologies are making it possible to assess what students are learning at very fine levels of detail, with vivid simulations of real-world situations, and in ways that are tightly integrated with instruction. Chapter 7 provides examples of how technology is making it feasible, for instance, for students to receive ongoing individualized feedback as they work with a computerized tutoring system—feedback more detailed than what a teacher could have provided a class of 30 students in the past.

This report describes a variety of promising assessment innovations that represent first steps in capitalizing on these opportunities. However, most of these examples have been limited to small-scale applications that have yet to affect mainstream assessment practice. In this final chapter, we discuss priorities for research, practice, and policy to enable the emergence of a "new science of assessment." First, however, we summarize some of the main points from the preceding chapters by describing a vision for a future generation of educational assessments based on the merger of modern cognitive theory and methods of measurement.

A VISION FOR THE FUTURE OF ASSESSMENT

In the future envisioned by the committee, educational assessments will be viewed as a facilitator of high levels of student achievement. They will help students learn and succeed in school by making as clear as possible to them, their teachers, and other education stakeholders the nature of their accomplishments and the progress of their learning.

Teachers will assess students' understanding frequently in the classroom to provide them with feedback and determine next steps for instruction. Their classroom practices will be grounded in principles of how students think and learn in content domains and of assessment as a process of reasoning from evidence. Teachers will use this knowledge to design assessments that provide students with feedback about particular qualities of their work and what they can do to improve.

Students will provide evidence of their understanding and thinking in a variety of ways—by responding to teachers' questions, writing or producing projects, working with computerized tutoring systems, or attempting to explain concepts to other students. Teachers, in turn, will use this information to modify instruction for the class and for individuals on the basis of their understanding and thinking patterns.

Teachers will have a clear picture of the learning goals in subject domains, as well as typical learning pathways for reaching those goals. Ultimate and intermediate learning goals will be shared regularly with students as a part of instruction. Students will be engaged in activities such as peer and self-assessment to help them internalize the criteria for high-quality work and develop metacognitive skills.

Teachers will also use summative assessments for ongoing reflection and feedback about overall progress and for reporting of this information to others. External summative assessments, such as state tests, will reinforce the same ultimate goals and beliefs about learning that are operating in the classroom. Large-scale assessments will set valuable learning goals for students to pursue. Such assessments will broadly sample the desired outcomes for learning by using a variety of methods, such as on-demand assessment combined with a sampling of work produced during the course of instruction.

Policy makers, educators, and the public will come to expect more than the general comparisons and rankings that characterize current test results. Performance on large-scale assessments will be explicitly and publicly displayed so that students, parents, and teachers can see the concepts and processes entailed at different levels of competence. Assessments will be able to show, for instance, how a competent performer proceeds on a mathematics problem and forms an answer, in comparison with a student who is less proficient. Large-scale assessments will help show the different kinds of interpretations, procedural strategies, explanations, and products that differentiate among various levels or degrees of competence.

Within an education system, teachers, administrators, and policy makers will be working from a shared knowledge base about how students learn subject matter and what aspects of competence are important to assess. Resource materials that synthesize modern scientific understanding of how people learn in areas of the curriculum will serve as the basis for the design of classroom and large-scale assessments, as well as curriculum and instruction, so that all the system's components work toward a coherent set of learning goals.

In many ways, this vision for assessment represents a significant departure from the types of assessments typically available today and from the ways in which such assessments are most commonly used. Current knowledge could serve as the basis for a number of improvements to the assessment design process (as described in Chapters 3, 4, and 5 of this report) to produce assessment information that would be more useful, valid, and fair. Full realization of the committee's broader vision for educational assessment, however, will require more knowledge about how to design and use such assessments, as well as about the underlying fundamental properties of learning and measurement. Furthermore, the committee recognizes that the maximum potential of new forms of assessment cannot be realized unless educational practices and policies adapt in significant ways. Some of the constraints that currently limit assessment practice will need to be relaxed if the full benefits of a merger between the cognitive and measurement sciences are to be realized. The new kinds of assessment described in this report do not necessarily conform to the current mode of on-demand, paper-and-pencil tests that students take individually at their desks under strictly standardized conditions. Furthermore, realizing the potential benefits of new forms of assessment will depend on making compatible changes in curriculum and instruction.

BRIDGING RESEARCH AND PRACTICE

Like other groups before us (NRC, 1999c; National Academy of Education, 1999), the committee recognizes that the bridge between research and practice takes time to build and that research and practice must proceed interactively. It is unlikely that the insights gained from current or new knowledge about cognition, learning, and measurement will be sufficient by themselves to bring about transformations in assessment such as those described in this report. As the NRC's Committee on Learning Research and Educational Practice pointed out, research and practice need to be connected more directly through the building of a cumulative knowledge base that serves both sets of interests. In the context of this study, that knowledge base would focus on the development and use of theory-based assessment. Furthermore, it is essential to recognize that research impacts practice indirectly through the influence of the existing knowledge base on four important mediating arenas: educational tools and materials; teacher education and professional development; education policies; and public opinion and media coverage (NRC, 1999c). By affecting each of these arenas, an expanding knowledge base on the principles and practices of effective assessment can help change educational practice. And the study of changes in practice, in turn, can help in further developing the knowledge base. These organizing ideas regarding the connections between research and practice are illustrated in Figure 8-1.

In this chapter we outline a proposed research and development agenda for expanding the knowledge base on the integration of cognition and measurement and consider the implications of such a knowledge base for each of the four mediating arenas that directly influence educational practice. In doing so we propose two general guidelines for how future work should proceed.

First, the committee advocates increased and sustained multidisciplinary collaboration around theoretical and practical matters of assessment. We apply this precept not only to the collaboration between researchers in the cognitive and measurement sciences, but also to the collaboration of these groups with teachers, curriculum specialists, and assessment developers. The committee believes the potential for an improved science and design of educational assessment lies in a mutually catalytic merger of the two foundational disciplines, especially as such knowledge is brought to bear on conceptual and pragmatic problems of assessment development and use.

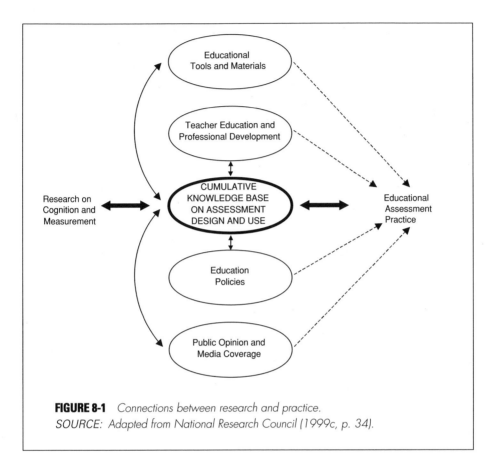

FIGURE 8-1 *Connections between research and practice.*
SOURCE: Adapted from National Research Council (1999c, p. 34).

Second, the committee urges individuals in multiple communities, from research through practice and policy, to consider the conceptual scheme and language used in this report as a guide for stimulating further thinking and discussion about the many issues associated with the productive use of assessments in education. The assessment triangle set forth in Chapter 2 and summarized in Box 8-1 provides a conceptual framework for principled thinking about the assumptions and foundations underlying an assessment. In the next section of this chapter we consider some of the implications of our conceptual scheme for research that can contribute to the advancement of both theory and practice.

Before discussing specific implications for research and practice and presenting our recommendations in each of these areas, we would be remiss if we did not note our concern about continuing with the present system of educational assessment, including the pattern of increasing investment in large-scale assessment designs and practices that have serious limi-

BOX 8-1 Summary of the Assessment Triangle

The process of reasoning from evidence can be portrayed as a triangle referred to throughout this report as the *assessment triangle*. As shown below, the corners of the triangle represent three key elements that underlie any assessment: (1) a model of student *cognition* and learning in the domain, (2) a set of beliefs about the kinds of *observations* that will provide evidence of students' competencies, and (3) an *interpretation* process for making sense of the evidence.

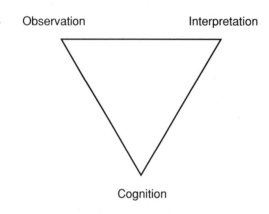

Observation   Interpretation

Cognition

These three elements form the foundations on which every assessment rests. The three elements are represented as corners of a triangle because each is connected to and dependent on the others. To have an effective assessment, all three should be explicitly coordinated as part of the design. A major tenet of this report is that most assessments in current use are based on outmoded conceptions of cognition and learning and on impoverished observation and interpretation methods, as compared with what could be the case given modern scientific knowledge of cognition and measurement.

tations and in some cases do more harm than good. This concern underlines the importance of seizing the opportunity that now exists to reshape the assessment landscape while simultaneously reinforcing many of the social and political reasons for investing in high-quality educational assessment materials, designs, and practices. That opportunity should not be lost just because every theoretical and operational detail has yet to be established for the design and implementation of assessments based on a merger of the cognitive and measurement sciences. There is much that can be done in the near term to improve assessment design and use on the basis of existing knowledge, while an investment is being made in the research and development needed to build assessments appropriate for the educational systems of the 21st century.

IMPLICATIONS AND RECOMMENDATIONS FOR RESEARCH

The research needed to approach the new science of assessment envisioned by the committee needs to focus on those issues that lie at the intersection of cognitive and measurement science. In this section we present the committee's recommendations for research organized into three broad categories: (1) synthesis of existing knowledge, (2) research to expand the current knowledge base, and (3) some initial steps for building the knowledge base.

For all the research recommendations presented below, we advocate a general approach to research and development that differs from conventional practices. In the traditional view of research, development, and implementation, scientists begin with basic research that involves gathering fundamental knowledge and developing theories about an area of inquiry. Other scientists and practitioners use this basic research, together with their experience, to design prototypes that apply the knowledge in practical settings. Still others then design ways to implement the prototypes on a larger scale.

The committee believes that, in the case of the assessments we envision, research should focus on design and implementation. The committee takes this position for two reasons. The first is strategic. As described throughout this report, some promising prototype assessments based on modern cognitive theory and measurement principles have already been developed. While the prototypes have been used effectively in selected classrooms and educational settings, there is generally limited experience with their application outside of relatively controlled settings or in large-scale contexts. In part this is because the new forms of assessment are often complex and have not been tailored for widespread practical use. In addition, there are issues involved in large-scale assessment that designers of classroom-based tools have yet to confront. The committee takes the position that practical implementation should be studied to raise questions about fundamental science.

In his book *Pasteur's Quadrant*, Stokes (1997) argues that the traditional dichotomy between "basic" and "applied" research is not always applicable. In many instances, research aimed at solving practical problems can test the validity and generality of fundamental principles and knowledge. Pasteur's work is an archetype of this approach. By focusing on a very real practical problem—developing ways to combat harmful bacteria—Pasteur pursued "use-inspired strategic research" that not only helped solve the immediate problem, but also contributed greatly to enhancing fundamental knowledge about biology and biochemistry. Similarly, Hargreaves (1999) argues that research results cannot be applied directly to classroom practice, but must be transformed by practitioners; that is, teachers need to participate in creating new knowledge.

In a report to the National Education Research Policies and Priorities Board of the Office of Educational Research and Improvement, a panel of the National Academy of Education argues that federal agencies should fund research in Pasteur's Quadrant as well as basic research (National Academy of Education, 1999). The panel states that "problem-solving research and development" (the equivalent of what Stokes describes as use-inspired strategic research) is characterized by four features:

- Commitment to the improvement of complex systems.
- Co-development by researchers and practitioners, with recognition of differences in expertise and authority.
- Long-term engagement that involves continual refinement.
- Commitment to theory and explanation.

The panel notes that this last feature would enable prototypes generated in one site or context of use to "travel" to other settings (the panel contrasts its view with the traditional notion of "dissemination"). To permit wider adoption, the research would have to generate principles to ensure that others would not simply replicate the surface features of an innovation. Also required would be consideration of tools that could help others apply the innovation faithfully, as well as people familiar with the design who could help others implement it. The committee is sympathetic to this argument and believes research that addresses ways to design assessments for use in either classrooms or large-scale settings can simultaneously enhance understanding of the design principles inherent in such assessments and improve basic knowledge about cognition and measurement.

We advocate that the research recommended below be funded by federal agencies and private foundations that currently support research on teaching and learning, as well as private-sector entities involved in commercial assessment design and development. Among the salient federal agencies are the Department of Education, the NSF, and the National Institute of Child Health and Human Development. The research agenda is expansive in both scope and likely duration. It would be sensible for the funding of such work to be coordinated across agencies and, in many instances, pursued cooperatively with foundations and the private sector.

Synthesis of Existing Knowledge

Recommendation 1: Accumulated knowledge and ongoing advances from the merger of the cognitive and measurement sciences should be synthesized and made available in usable forms to multiple educational constituencies. These constituencies include educational researchers, test developers, curriculum specialists, teachers, and policy makers.

As discussed throughout this report, a great deal of the foundational research needed to move the science of assessment forward has already been conducted; however, it is not widely available or usable in synthetic form. This report is an initial attempt at such a synthesis, but the committee recognized from the start of its work that a comprehensive critique, synthesis, and extrapolation of all that is known was beyond the scope of a study such as this and remains a target for the future. Furthermore, there is an ongoing need to accumulate, synthesize, and disseminate existing knowledge—that is, to construct the cumulative knowledge base on assessment design and use that lies at the center of Figure 8-1.

Expanding the Knowledge Base

Recommendation 2: Funding should be provided for a major program of research, guided by a synthesis of cognitive and measurement principles, focused on the design of assessments that yield more valid and fair inferences about student achievement. This research should be conducted collaboratively by multidisciplinary teams comprising both researchers and practitioners.
• A priority should be the development of cognitive models of learning that can serve as the basis for assessment design for all areas of the school curriculum. Research on how students learn subject matter should be conducted in actual educational settings and with groups of learners representative of the diversity of the student population to be assessed.

- **Research on new statistical measurement models and their applicability should be tied to modern theories of cognition and learning. Work should be undertaken to better understand the fit between various types of cognitive theories and measurement models to determine which combinations work best together.**
- **Research on assessment design should include exploration of systematic and fair methods for taking into account aspects of examinees' instructional background when interpreting their responses to assessment tasks. This research should encompass careful examination of the possible consequences of such adaptations in high-stakes assessment contexts.**

One priority for research is the development of cognitive models of learning for areas of the school curriculum. As noted in Chapter 3, researchers have developed sophisticated models of student cognition in various areas of the curriculum, such as algebra and physics. However, an understanding of how people learn remains limited for many other areas. Moreover, even in subject domains for which characteristics of expertise have been identified, a detailed understanding of patterns of growth that would enable one to identify landmarks on the way to competence is often lacking. Such landmarks are essential for effective assessment design and implementation.

The development of models of learning should not be done exclusively by scientists in laboratory settings. As argued earlier, it would be more fruitful if such investigations were conducted, at least in part, in actual educational contexts by collaborative teams of researchers and practitioners. Such collaborations would help enhance both the quality and utility of the knowledge produced by the research.

To develop assessments that are fair—that are comparably valid across different groups of students—it is crucial that patterns of learning for different populations of students are studied. Much of the development of cognitive theories has been conducted with a restricted group of students (i.e., mostly middle-class whites). In many cases it is not clear whether current theories of learning apply equally well with diverse populations of students, including those who have been poorly served in the educational system, underrepresented minority students, English-language learners, and students with disabilities. There are typical learning pathways, but not a single pathway to competence. Furthermore, students will not necessarily respond in similar ways to assessment probes designed to diagnose knowledge and understanding. These kinds of natural variations among individuals need to be better understood through empirical study and incorporated into the cognitive models of learning that serve as a basis for assessment design.

Sophisticated models of learning by themselves do not produce high-quality assessment information. Also needed are methods and tools both for eliciting appropriate and relevant data from students and for interpreting the data collected about student performance. As described in Chapter 4, the measurement methods now available enable a much broader range of inferences to be drawn about student competence than many people realize. But research is needed to investigate the relative utility of existing and future statistical models for capturing critical aspects of learning specified in cognitive theories.

Most of the new measurement models have been applied only on a limited scale. Thus, there is a need to explore the utility and feasibility of the new models for a wider range of assessment applications and contexts. Within such a line of inquiry, a number of issues will need to be understood in more depth, including the level of detail at which models of student learning must be specified for implementing various types of classroom or large-scale assessments. Furthermore, there is a vital need for research on ways to make a broader range of measurement models usable by practitioners, rather than exclusively by measurement specialists. Many of the currently available measurement methods require complex statistical modeling that only people with highly specialized technical skills can use to advantage. If these tools are to be applied more widely, understandable interfaces will need to be built that rise above statistical complexity to enable widespread use, just as users of accounting and management programs need not understand all the calculations that go into each element of the software.

Another priority for assessment design is the exploration of new ways to address persisting issues of fairness and equity in testing. People often view fairness in testing in terms of ensuring that students are placed in test situations that are as similar or standardized as possible. But another way of approaching fairness is to take into account examinees' histories of instruction or opportunities to learn the material being tested when interpreting their responses to assessment tasks. Ways of drawing such conditional inferences have been tried mainly on a small scale but hold promise for tackling persisting issues of equity in assessment.

Recommendation 3: Research should be conducted to explore how new forms of assessment can be made practical for use in classroom and large-scale contexts and how various new forms of assessment affect student learning, teacher practice, and educational decision making.

- **Research should explore ways in which teachers can be assisted in integrating new forms of assessment into their in-**

structional practices. It is particularly important that such work be done in close collaboration with practicing teachers who have varying backgrounds and levels of teaching experience.

• Also to be studied are ways in which school structures (e.g., length of time of classes, class size, and opportunity for teachers to work together) impact the feasibility of implementing new types of assessments and their effectiveness.

The committee firmly believes that the kinds of examples described in this report—all of which are currently being used in classrooms or large-scale contexts—represent positive steps toward the development of assessments that can not only inform but also improve learning. However, for these kinds of innovations to gain more widespread adoption, work is needed to make them practical for use in classroom and large-scale contexts, and evidence of their impact on student learning is needed.

Furthermore, the power offered by assessments to enhance learning in large numbers of classrooms depends on changes in the relationship between teacher and student, the types of lessons teachers use, the pace and structure of instruction, and many other factors. To take advantage of the new tools, many teachers will have to change their conception of their role in the classroom. They will have to shift toward placing much greater emphasis on exploring students' understanding with the new tools and then undertaking a well-informed application of what has been revealed by use of the tools. This means teachers must be prepared to use feedback from classroom and external assessments to guide their students' learning more effectively by modifying the classroom and its activities. In the process, teachers must guide their students to be more engaged actively in monitoring and managing their own learning—to assume the role of student as self-directed learner.

The power of new assessments depends on substantial changes not only in classroom practice, but also in the broader educational context in which assessments are conducted. For assessment to serve the goals of learning, there must be alignment among curriculum, instruction, and assessment. Furthermore, the existing structure and organization of schools may not easily accommodate the type of instruction users of the new assessments will need to employ. For instance, if teachers are going to gather more assessment information during the course of instruction, they will need time to assimilate that information. If these kinds of systemic and structural issues are not addressed, new forms of assessment will not live up to their full potential. This is a common fate for educational innovations. Many new techniques and procedures have failed to affect teaching and learning on a large scale because the innovators did not address all the factors that affect

teaching and learning (Elmore, 1996). Despite the promise of new procedures, most teachers tend to teach the way they have always taught, except
in the "hothouse" settings where the innovations were designed.

Thus, if assessments based on the foundations of cognitive and measurement science are to be implemented on a broad scale, changes in school
structures and practices will likely be needed. However, the precise nature
of such changes is uncertain. As new assessments are implemented, researchers will need to examine the effects of such factors as class size and
the length of the school day on the power of assessments to inform teachers
and administrators about student learning. Also needed is a greater understanding of what structural changes are required for teachers to modify their
practice in ways that will enable them to incorporate such assessments effectively.

Some Initial Steps for Building the Knowledge Base

**Recommendation 4: Funding should be provided for in-depth
analyses of the critical elements (cognition, observation, and
interpretation) underlying the design of existing assessments
that have attempted to integrate cognitive and measurement
principles (including the multiple examples presented in this
report). This work should also focus on better understanding
the impact of such exemplars on student learning, teacher
practice, and educational decision making.**

The committee believes an ideal starting point for much of the research
agenda is further study of the types of assessment examples provided in the
preceding chapters, which represent initial attempts at synthesizing advances
in the cognitive and measurement sciences. While these examples were
presented to illustrate features of the committee's proposed approach to
assessment, the scope of this study did not permit in-depth analyses of all
the design and operational features of each example or their impact on
student learning, teacher practice, and educational decision making. Further
analysis of these and other examples would help illuminate the principles
and practices of assessment design and use described in this report. Several
important and related directions of work need to be pursued.

First, to fully understand any assessment, one must carefully deconstruct
and analyze it in terms of its underlying foundational assumptions. The assessment triangle provides a useful framework for analyzing the foundational elements of an assessment. Questions need to be asked and answered
regarding the precise nature of the assumptions made about cognition, observation, and interpretation, including the degree to which they are in synchrony. Such an analysis should also consider ways in which current knowl-

edge from the cognitive and measurement sciences could be used to enhance the assessment in significant ways.

Second, once an assessment is well understood, its effectiveness as a
tool for measurement and for support of learning must be explored and
documented. The committee strongly believes that the examples in this report represent promising directions for further development, and where available, has presented empirical support for their effectiveness. However, there
is a strong need for additional empirical studies aimed at exploring which
tools are most effective and why, how they can best be used, and what costs
and benefits they entail relative to current forms of assessment.

Third, while it is important to carefully analyze each of the examples as
a separate instance of innovative design, they also need to be analyzed as a
collective set of instances within a complex "design space." The latter can be
thought of as a multivariate environment expressing the important features
that make specific instances simultaneously similar and different. This design space is only partially conceived and understood at the present time.
Thus, analyses should be pursued that cut across effective exemplars with
the goal of identifying and clarifying the underlying principles of the new
science of assessment design. In this way, the principles described in this
report can be refined and elaborated while additional principles and operational constructs are uncovered. If a new science of assessment grounded in
concepts from cognitive and measurement science is to develop and mature, every attempt must be made to uncover the unique elements that emerge
from the synthesis of the foundational sciences. This work can be stimulated
by further in-depth analysis of promising design artifacts and the design
space in which they exist.

> **Recommendation 5: Federal agencies and private-sector orga-
> nizations concerned about issues of assessment should sup-
> port the establishment of multidisciplinary discourse commu-
> nities to facilitate cross-fertilization of ideas among researchers
> and assessment developers working at the intersection of cog-
> nitive theory and educational measurement.**

Many of the innovative assessment practices described in this report
were derived from projects funded by the NSF or the James S. McDonnell
Foundation. These organizations have provided valuable opportunities for
cross-fertilization of ideas, but more sharing of knowledge is needed. Many
of the examples exist in relative isolation and are known only within limited
circles of scientific research and/or educational practice. The committee believes there are enough good examples of assessments based on a merger of
the cognitive and measurement sciences so that designers can start building
from existing work. However, a discourse among multidisciplinary commu-

nities will need to be established to promote and sustain such efforts. As mentioned earlier, this report provides a language and conceptual base for discussing the ideas embedded in existing innovative assessment practices and for the broader sharing and critique of those ideas.

IMPLICATIONS AND RECOMMENDATIONS FOR POLICY AND PRACTICE

Research often does not directly affect educational practice, but it can effect educational change by influencing the four mediating arenas of the education system that do influence practice, shown previously in Figure 8-1. For the earlier committee that identified these arenas, the question was how to bridge research on student learning and instructional practice in classrooms. The focus of the present committee is on a related part of the larger question: how to link research on the integration of cognition and measurement with actual assessment practice in schools and classrooms. By influencing and working through the four mediating arenas, the growing knowledge base on cognition and measurement can ultimately have an effect on assessment and instructional practice in classrooms and schools.

It is important to note that the path of influence does not flow only in one direction. Just as we believe that research on the integration of cognition and measurement should focus on use-inspired strategic research, we believe that practical matters involving educational tools and materials, teacher education and professional development, education policies, and public opinion and media coverage will influence the formulation of research questions that can further contribute to the development of a cumulative knowledge base. Research focused on these arenas will enhance understanding of practical matters related to how students learn and how learning can best be measured in a variety of school subjects.

Educational Tools and Materials

Recommendation 6: Developers of assessment instruments for classroom or large-scale use should pay explicit attention to all three elements of the assessment triangle (cognition, observation, and interpretation) and their coordination.

• All three elements should be based on modern knowledge of how students learn and how such learning is best measured.

• Considerable time and effort should be devoted to a theory-driven design and validation process before assessments are put into operational use.

When designing new tools for classroom or large-scale use, assessment developers are urged to use the assessment triangle as a guiding framework, as set forth and illustrated in Chapters 5, 6, and 7. As discussed under Recommendation 1 above, a prerequisite for the development of new forms of assessment is that current knowledge derived from research be conveyed to assessment and curriculum developers in ways they can access and use.

A key feature of the approach to assessment development proposed in this report is that the effort should be guided by an explicit, contemporary cognitive model of learning that describes how people represent knowledge and develop competence in the subject domain, along with an interpretation model that is compatible with the cognitive model. Assessment tasks and procedures for evaluating responses should be designed to provide evidence of the characteristics of student understanding identified in the cognitive model of learning. The interpretation model must incorporate this evidence in the assessment results in a way that is consistent with the model of learning. Assessment designers should explore ways of using sets of tasks that work in combination to diagnose student understanding while at the same time maintaining high standards of reliability. The interpretation model must, in turn, reflect consideration of the complexity of such sets of tasks.

An important aspect of assessment validation often overlooked by assessment developers is the collection of evidence that tasks actually tap the intended cognitive content and processes. Starting with hypotheses about the cognitive demands of a task, a variety of research techniques, such as interviews, having students think aloud as they solve problems, and analysis of errors, can be used to explore the mental processes in which examinees actually engage during task performance. Conducting such analyses early in the assessment development process ensures that the assessments do, in fact, measure what they are intended to measure.

Recommendation 7: Developers of educational curricula and classroom assessments should create tools that will enable teachers to implement high-quality instructional and assessment practices, consistent with modern understanding of how students learn and how such learning can be measured.

• Assessments and supporting instructional materials should interpret the findings from cognitive research in ways that are useful for teachers.

• Developers are urged to take advantage of opportunities afforded by technology to assess what students are learning at fine levels of detail, with appropriate frequency, and in ways that are tightly integrated with instruction.

The committee believes a synthesis of cognitive and measurement principles has particularly significant potential for the design of high-quality tools for classroom assessment that can inform and improve learning. However, teachers should not be expected to devise on their own all the assessment tasks for students or ways of interpreting responses to those tasks. Some innovative classroom assessments that have emerged from this synthesis and are having a positive impact on learning have been described in preceding chapters. A key to the effectiveness of these tools is that they must be packaged in ways that are practical for use by teachers. As described in Chapter 7, computer and telecommunications technologies offer a rich array of opportunities for providing teachers with sophisticated assessment tools that will allow them to present more complex cognitive tasks, capture and reply to students' performances, share exemplars of competent performance, engage students in peer and self-reflection, and in the process gain critical information about student competence.

Recommendation 8: Large-scale assessments should sample the broad range of competencies and forms of student understanding that research shows are important aspects of student learning.
- **A variety of matrix sampling, curriculum-embedded, and other assessment approaches should be used to cover the breadth of cognitive competencies that are the goals of learning in a domain of the curriculum.**
- **Large-scale assessment tools and supporting instructional materials should be developed so that clear learning goals and landmark performances along the way to competence are shared with teachers, students, and other education stakeholders. The knowledge and skills to be assessed and the criteria for judging the desired outcomes should be clearly specified and available to all potential examinees and other concerned individuals.**
- **Assessment developers should pursue new ways of reporting assessment results that convey important differences in performance at various levels of competence in ways that are clear to different users, including educators, parents, and students.**

Though further removed from day-to-day instruction than classroom assessments, large-scale assessments also have the potential to support instruction and learning if well designed and appropriately used. Deriving real benefits from the merger of cognitive and measurement theory in large-scale assessment requires finding ways to cover a broad range of competencies and capture rich information about the nature of student understanding. Alternatives to the typical on-demand testing scenario—in which every student takes the same test at a specified time under strictly standardized conditions—should be considered to enable the collection of more diverse evidence of student achievement.

Large-scale assessments have an important role to play in providing dependable information for educational decision making by policy makers, school administrators, teachers, and parents. Large-scale assessments can also convey powerful messages about the kinds of learning valued by society and provide worthy goals to pursue. If such assessments are to serve these purposes, however, it is essential that externally set goals for learning be clearly communicated to teachers, students, and other education stakeholders.

Considerable resources should be devoted to producing materials for teachers and students that clearly present both the learning goals and landmark performances along the way to competence. Those performances can then be illustrated with samples of the work of learners at different levels of competence, accompanied by explanations of the aspects of cognitive competence exemplified by the work. These kinds of materials can foster valuable dialogue among teachers, students, and the public about what achievement in a domain of the curriculum looks like. The criteria by which student work will be judged on an assessment should also be made as explicit as possible. Curriculum materials should encourage the use of activities such as peer and self-assessment to help students internalize the criteria for high-quality work and foster metacognitive skills. All of these points are equally true for classroom assessments.

The use of assessments based on cognitive and measurement science will also necessitate different forms of reporting on student progress, both to parents and to administrators. The information gleaned from such assessments is far more nuanced than that obtainable from the assessments commonly used today, and teachers may want to provide more detail in reports to parents about the nature of their children's understanding. In formulating reports based on new assessments, test developers, teachers, and school administrators should ensure that the reports include the information parents want and can appropriately use to support their children's learning. Reports on student performance could also provide an important tool to assist administrators in their supervisory roles. Administrators could use such information to see how teachers are gauging their students' learning and how they are responding to the students' demonstration of understanding. Such information could help administrators determine where to focus resources for professional development. In general, for the information to be useful and meaningful, it will have to include a profile consisting of multiple elements and not just a single aggregate score.

Teacher Education and Professional Development

Recommendation 9: Instruction in how students learn and how learning can be assessed should be a major component of teacher preservice and professional development programs.

• This training should be linked to actual experience in classrooms in assessing and interpreting the development of student competence.

• To ensure that this occurs, state and national standards for teacher licensure and program accreditation should include specific requirements focused on the proper integration of learning and assessment in teachers' educational experience.

Research on the integration of cognition and measurement also has major implications for teacher education. Teachers need training to understand how children learn subject matter and how assessment tools and practices can be used to obtain useful information about student competence. Both the initial preparation of teachers and their ongoing professional development can incorporate insights and examples from research on the integration of cognitive and measurement science and equip teachers with knowledge and skills they can use to employ high-quality assessments. At the same time, such learning opportunities can enable teachers to transform their practice in ways that will allow them to profit from those assessments.

If such assessments are to be used effectively, teacher education needs to equip beginning teachers with a deep understanding of many of the approaches students might take toward understanding a particular subject area, as well as ways to guide students at different levels toward understanding (Carpenter, Fennema, and Franke, 1996; Griffin and Case 1997). Teachers also need a much better understanding of the kinds of classroom environments that incorporate such knowledge (NRC, 1999b). Typically, teacher education programs provide very little preparation in assessment (Plake and Impara, 1997). Yet teaching in ways that integrate assessment with curriculum and instruction requires a strong understanding of methods of assessment and the uses of assessment data. This does not mean that all teachers need formal training in psychometrics. However, teachers need to understand how to use tools that can yield valid inferences about student understanding and thinking, as well as methods of interpreting data derived from assessments.

In addition, school administrators need to provide teachers with ample opportunities to continue their learning about assessment throughout their professional practice. Professional development is increasingly seen as a vital element in improving of practice, for veteran as well as new teachers

(Cohen and Hill, 1998; Elmore and Burney, 1998). This continued learning should include the development of cognitive models of learning. Teachers' professional development can be made more effective if it is tied closely to the work of teaching (e.g., National Academy of Education, 1999). The "lesson study" in which Japanese teachers engage offers one way to forge this link (Stigler and Hiebert, 1999). In that approach, teachers develop lessons on their own, based on a common curriculum. They try these lessons out in their classrooms and share their findings with fellow teachers. They then modify the lessons and try them again, collecting data as they implement the lessons and again working collaboratively with other teachers to polish them. The resulting lessons are often published and become widely used by teachers throughout the country.

Education Policies

Recommendation 10: Policy makers are urged to recognize the limitations of current assessments, and to support the development of new systems of multiple assessments that would improve their ability to make decisions about education programs and the allocation of resources.

• **Important decisions about individuals should not be based on a single test score. Policy makers should instead invest in the development of assessment systems that use multiple measures of student performance, particularly when high stakes are attached to the results.**

• **Assessments at the classroom and large-scale levels should grow out of a shared knowledge base about the nature of learning. Policy makers should support efforts to achieve such coherence.**

• **Policy makers should promote the development of assessment systems that measure growth or progress of students and the education system over time and that support multilevel analyses of the influences responsible for such change.**

Recommendation 11: The balance of mandates and resources should be shifted from an emphasis on external forms of assessment to an increased emphasis on classroom formative assessment designed to assist learning.

Another arena through which research can influence practice is education policy. This is a particularly powerful arena in the case of assessment. Policy makers currently are putting great stock in large-scale assessments and using them for a variety of purposes. There is a good deal of evidence that assessments used for policy purposes have had effects on educational practice, not all of them positive (e.g., Herman, 1992; NRC, 1999a; Koretz and Barron, 1998).

Research on the integration of cognition and measurement can affect practice through policy in several ways. Most directly, the research can enhance the assessments used for policy decisions. Furthermore, the decisions of policy makers could be better informed than is the case today by assessments that provide a broader picture of student learning. Since test developers respond to the marketplace, a demand from policy makers for new assessments would likely spur their development.

A range of assessment approaches should be used to provide a variety of evidence to support educational decision making. There is a need for comprehensive systems of assessment consisting of multiple measures, including those that rely on the professional judgments of teachers and that together meet high standards of validity and reliability. Single measures, while useful, are unlikely to tap all the dimensions of competence identified by learning goals. Multiple measures are essential in any system in which high-stakes decisions are made about individuals on the basis of assessment results (NRC, 1999a).

Currently, assessments at the classroom and large-scale levels often convey conflicting goals for learning. As argued in Chapter 6, coherence is needed in the assessment system. A coherent assessment system supports learning for all students. If a state assessment were not designed from the same conceptual base as classroom assessments, the mismatch could undermine the potential for improved learning offered by a system of assessment based on the cognitive and measurement sciences.

To be sure, coherence in an educational system is easier to wish for than to achieve—particularly in an education system with widely dispersed authority such as that of the United States. In many ways, standards-based reform is a step toward achieving some of this coherence. But current content standards are not as useful as they could be. Cognitive research can contribute to the development of next-generation standards that are more effective for guiding curriculum, instruction, and assessment—standards that define not only the content to be learned, but also the ways in which subject matter understanding is acquired and develops. Classroom and large-scale assessments within a coherent system should grow from a shared knowledge base about how students think and learn in a domain of the curriculum. This kind of coherence could help all assessments support common learning goals.

Assessments should be aimed at improving learning by providing information needed by those at all levels of the education system on the aspects of schooling for which they are responsible. If properly conducted, assessments can also serve accountability purposes by providing valuable information to teachers and administrators about the progress or growth of the education system over time. The committee refers to this feature as continuity. And if the assessments are instructionally sensitive—that is, if they show the effects of high-quality teaching—they can provide important information about the effectiveness of teaching practices as well (NRC, 1999d).

Developing and implementing a system of multiple assessments would likely be more costly than continuing with the array of tests now being used by states and school districts. Currently, states spend about $330 million for testing (Achieve, 2000). While this sum appears considerable, it represents less than one-tenth of 1 percent of the total amount spent on precollege education (National Center for Education Statistics, 2001). If used properly, the total spending for assessment should not be considered money for tests alone. Funds spent for teachers to score assessments, included in the cost of assessment, also serve an important professional development function. Moreover, spending on assessments that inform instruction represents an investment in teaching and learning, not just in system monitoring. Therefore, policy makers need to invest considerably more in assessment than is currently the case, presuming that the investment is in assessment systems of the type advocated in this report.

Public Opinion and Media Coverage

Recommendation 12: Programs for providing information to the public on the role of assessment in improving learning and on contemporary approaches to assessment should be developed in cooperation with the media. Efforts should be made to foster public understanding of basic principles of appropriate test interpretation and use.

A fourth arena in which research on the integration of cognitive and measurement science can affect practice is through public opinion and the media. Current interest among the public and the news media in testing and test results suggests that public opinion and media coverage can be a powerful arena for change. Information communicated to the public through the media can influence practice in at least two ways. First, the media influence the constituencies responsible for assessment development and practice, including teachers, school administrators, policy makers, and test developers. Perhaps of greater significance is recognition that the more the public is made aware of how assessment practice could be transformed to better serve the goals of learning, the greater will be the support that educators and policy makers have for the kinds of changes proposed in this volume.

Researchers should therefore undertake efforts to communicate with the media what student development toward competence looks like and how it can best be measured; the media can, in turn, communicate those messages to the public. An attempt should also be made through the media and other avenues for communication with the public to foster understanding of basic principles of appropriate test interpretation and use. Assessment consumers, including the public, should understand that no test is a perfect measure, that more valid decisions are based on multiple indicators, and that the items on a particular assessment are only a sample from the larger domain of knowledge and skill identified as the targets of learning. As part of the design and delivery of such programs, research needs to be conducted on the public's understanding of critical issues in assessment and the most effective ways to communicate outcomes from educational assessment.

CONCLUDING COMMENTS

As noted at the beginning of this report, educational assessment is an integral part of the quest for improved education. Through assessment, education stakeholders seek to determine how well students are learning and whether students and institutions are progressing toward the goals that have been set for educational systems. The problem is that the vital purposes of informing and improving education through assessment are being served only partially by present assessment practices.

The principles and practices of educational assessment have changed over the last century, but not sufficiently to keep pace with the substantial developments that have accrued in the understanding of learning and its measurement. It is time to harness the scientific knowledge of cognition and measurement to guide the principles and practices of educational assessment. There is already a substantial knowledge base about what better assessment means, what it looks like, and principled ways that can be used to build and use it. That knowledge base needs to be put into widespread practice, as well as continually expanded.

Educators, the public, and particularly parents should not settle for impoverished assessment information. They should be well informed about criteria for meaningful and helpful assessment. To do justice to the students in our schools and to support their learning, we need to recognize that the process of appraising them fairly and effectively requires multiple measures constructed to high standards. Useful and meaningful evidence includes profiling of multiple elements of proficiency, with less emphasis on overall aggregate scores. A central theme of this report is that it is essential to assess diverse aspects of knowledge and competence, including how students understand and explain concepts, reason with what they know, solve problems, are aware of their states of knowing, and can self-regulate their learning and performance.

Achieving these goals requires a strong connection between educational assessments and modern theories of cognition and learning. Without this connection, assessment results provide incomplete, and perhaps misleading, information about what has been learned and appropriate next steps for improvement. Creating better assessments should not be viewed as a luxury, but as a necessity.

Perhaps the greatest challenges to the new science and design of educational assessment relate to disciplinary boundaries and established practices. For instance, there is currently an implicit assumption that one can create good tasks or good assessments and then leave it up to technical people to figure out how to analyze and report the results. Instead, the assessment design process must be a truly multidisciplinary and collaborative activity, with educators, cognitive scientists, subject matter specialists, and psychometricians informing one another during the design process. Other obstacles to pursuing new approaches to assessment stem from existing social structures in which familiar assessment practices are now deeply embedded and thus difficult to change. Professional development and public education are needed to convey how assessment should be designed and how it can be used most effectively in the service of learning.

The investment required to improve educational assessment and further develop the knowledge base to support that effort is substantial. However, this investment in our children and their educational futures is a reasonable one given the public's legitimate expectation that assessment should both inform and enhance student achievement.

References

CHAPTER 1

Achieve. (2000). *Testing: Setting the record straight*. Washington, DC: Author.

American Federation of Teachers. (1999). *Making standards matter 1999*. Washington, DC: Author.

Appelbaum, E., Bailey, T., Berg, P., and Kalleberg, A.L. (2000). *Manufacturing advantage: Why high-performance work systems pay off*. Ithaca, NY: Cornell University Press.

Baker, E.L. (1997). Model-based performance assessment. *Theory into Practice, 36*(4), 247-254.

Barley, S.R., and Orr, J.E. (1997). *Between craft and science: Technical work in U.S. settings*. Ithaca, NY: Cornell University.

Baxter, G.P., and Glaser, R. (1998). Investigating the cognitive complexity of science assessments. *Educational Measurement: Research and Practice, 17*(3), 37-45.

Black, P., and Wiliam, D. (1998). Assessment and classroom learning. *Assessment in Education, 5*(1), 7-73.

Bresnahan, T.F., Brynjolfsson, E., and Hitt, L.M. (1999). Technology, organization, and the demand for skilled labor. In M.M. Blair and T.A. Kochan (Eds.), *The new relationship: Human capital in the American corporation* (pp. 145-193). Washington, DC: Brookings Institution Press.

Bureau of Labor Statistics. (2000). *Occupational outlook handbook, 2000-01 edition*. Washington, DC: U.S. Department of Labor.

Cizek, G.J. (2000). Pockets of resistance in the education revolution. *Educational Measurement: Issues and Practice, 19*(1), 16-23; 33.

Cole, N.S., and Moss, P.A. (1993). Bias in test use. In R.L. Linn (Ed.), *Educational measurement* (*Third Edition*) (pp. 201-220). Phoenix, AZ: American Council on Education and The Oryx Press.

Council of Chief State School Officers. (1999). *Data from the annual survey. State student assessment programs. Volume 2*. Washington, DC: Author.

Dwyer, C.A. (1998). Assessment and classroom learning: Theory and practice. *Assessment in Education, 5*(1), 131-137.

Edelson, D.C., Gordon, D.N., and Pea, R.D. (1999). Designing scientific investigation environments for learners: Lessons from experiences with scientific visualization. *Journal of the Learning Sciences, 8*(3/4), 391-450.

Education Week. (1999). *Quality counts '99: Rewarding results, punishing failure.* Bethesda, MD: Author.

Finn, C.E., Jr., Petrilli, M.J., and Vanourek, G. (1998). The state of state standards. *Fordham Report* (*Volume 2*). Washington, DC: The Thomas B. Fordham Foundation.

Glaser, R., Linn, R., and Bohrnstedt, G. (1997). *Assessment in transition: Monitoring the nation's educational progress.* New York: National Academy of Education.

Glaser, R., and Silver, E. (1994). Assessment, testing, and instruction: Retrospect and prospect. In L. Darling-Hammond (Ed.), *Review of research in education* (*Volume 20*). (pp. 393-419). Washington, DC: American Educational Research Association.

Klein, S.P., Hamilton, L.S., McCaffrey, D.F., and Stecher, B.M. (2000). *What do test scores in Texas tell us?* Santa Monica, CA: RAND.

Koretz, D.M., and Barron, S.I. (1998). *The validity of gains in scores on the Kentucky Instructional Results Information System (KIRIS).* Santa Monica, CA: RAND.

Lemann, N. (1999). *The big test: The secret history of the American meritocracy.* New York: Farrar, Straus, and Giroux.

Lindquist, E.F. (1951). Preliminary considerations in objective test construction. In E.F. Lindquist (Ed.), *Educational measurement* (pp. 119-184). Washington, DC: American Council on Education.

Linn, R. (2000). Assessments and accountability. *Educational Researcher, 29*(2), 4-16.

Linn, R.L., Baker, E.L., and Dunbar, S.B. (1991). Complex, performance-based assessment: Expectations and validation criteria. *Educational Researcher, 20*(8), 15-21.

Mehrens, W.A. (1998). Consequences of assessment: What is the evidence? *Educational Policy Analysis Archives, 6*(13). <http://epaa.asu.edu/epaa/v6n13.html>. [March 28, 2000].

Messick, S. (1984). The psychology of educational measurement. *Journal of Educational Measurement, 21*(3), 215-237.

Mislevy, R.J. (1993). Foundations of a new test theory. In N. Frederiksen, R.J. Mislevy, and I.I. Bejar (Eds.), *Test theory for a new generation of tests.* Hillsdale, NJ: Erlbaum.

Mislevy, R.J. (1994). *Test theory reconceived.* (CSE Technical Report 376). Los Angeles: National Center for Research on Evaluation, Standards, and Student Testing, University of California, Los Angeles.

National Academy of Education. (1996). *Implications for NAEP of research on learning and cognition.* Stanford, CA: Author.

National Center for Education Statistics. (1996). *Technical issues in large-scale performance assessment.* Washington, DC: U.S. Department of Education.

National Council of Teachers of Mathematics. (2000). *Principles and standards for school mathematics.* Reston, VA: Author.

National Research Council. (1996). *National science education standards.* National Committee on Science Education Standards and Assessment. Coordinating Council for Education. Washington, DC: National Academy Press.

National Research Council. (1999a). *The changing nature of work: Implications for occupational analysis.* Committee on Techniques for the Enhancement of Human Performance: Occupational Analysis. Commission on Behavioral and Social Sciences and Education. Washington, DC: National Academy Press.

National Research Council. (1999b). *Grading the nation's report card: Evaluating NAEP and transforming the assessment of educational progress.* Committee on the Evaluation of National and State Assessments of Educational Progress. J.W. Pellegrino, L.R. Jones, and K.J. Mitchell, (Eds.). Commission on Behavioral and Social Sciences and Education. Washington, DC: National Academy Press.

National Research Council. (1999c). *High stakes: Testing for tracking, promotion, and graduation.* Committee on Appropriate Test Use. J.P. Heubert and R.M. Hauser, (Eds.). Commission on Behavioral and Social Sciences and Education. Washington, DC: National Academy Press.

National Research Council. (2001). *Building a workforce for the information economy.* Committee on Workforce Needs in Information Technology. Board on Testing and Assessment; Board on Science, Technology, and Economic Policy; and Office of Scientific and Engineering Personnel. Washington, DC: National Academy Press.

New Standards™. (1997). *Performance standards: English language arts, mathematics, science, applied learning (Volume 1, Elementary school).* Washington, DC: National Center for Education Statistics and the University of Pittsburgh.

Nichols, P.D. (1994). A framework for developing cognitively diagnostic assessments. *Review of Educational Research, 64*(4), 575-603.

Pellegrino, J.W., Baxter, G.P., and Glaser, R. (1999). Addressing the "two disciplines" problem: Linking theories of cognition and learning with assessment and instructional practice. In A. Iran-Nejad and P.D. Pearson (Eds.), *Review of research in education (Volume 24)* (pp. 307-353). Washington, DC: American Educational Research Association.

Popham, W.J. (2000). *Modern educational measurement: Practical guidelines for educational leaders.* Needham, MA: Allyn and Bacon.

Resnick, L.B., and Resnick, D.P. (1992). Assessing the thinking curriculum: New tools for educational reform. In B.R. Gifford and M.C. O'Connor (Eds.), *Changing assessments: Alternative views of aptitude, achievement, and instruction.* Boston: Kluwer.

Rothman, R., Slattery, J.B., Vranek, J.L., and Resnick, L.B. (in press). *The alignment of standards and assessments.* Los Angeles: National Center for Research on Evaluation, Standards, and Student Testing. Graduate School of Education, University of California.

Secretary's Commission on Achieving Necessary Skills (SCANS). (1991). *What work requires of schools: A SCANS report for America 2000.* Washington, DC: U.S. Department of Labor.

Snow, R.E., and, D.F. (1989). Implications of cognitive psychology for educational measurement. In R.L. Linn (Ed.), *Educational measurement (3rd Edition).* (pp. 263-330). New York: Macmillan.

Steele, C.M. (1995). Stereotype threat and the intellectual test performance of African Americans. *Journal of Personality and Social Psychology, 69*(5), 797-811.

Steele, C.M. (1997). How stereotypes shape intellectual identity and performance. *American Psychological Association, 55*(6), 613-629.

U.S. Congress, Office of Technology Assessment. (1992). *Testing in American schools: Asking the right questions.* Washington, DC: U.S. Government Printing Office.

Wilson, M., and Adams, R.J. (1996). Evaluating progress with alternative assessments: A model for chapter 1. In M.B. Kane (Ed.), *Implementing performance assessment: Promise, problems, and challenges.* Hillsdale, NJ: Lawrence Erlbaum Associates.

CHAPTER 2

American Educational Research Association, American Psychological Association, and National Council on Measurement in Education. (1999). *Standards for educational and psychological testing.* Washington, DC: American Educational Research Association.

Black, P., and Wiliam, D. (1998). Assessment and classroom learning. *Assessment in Education, 5*(1), 7-73.

Council of Chief State School Officers. (1999). *Data from the annual survey. State student assessment programs. Volume 2.* Washington, DC: Author.

Falk, B. (2000). *The heart of the matter: Using standards and assessment to learn.* Portsmouth, NH: Heinemann.

Goldman, S.R., Pellegrino, J.W., and Mertz, D.L. (1988). Extended practices of basic addition facts: Strategy changes in learning disabled students. *Cognition and Instruction, 5,* 223-265.

Haertel, E.H. (1999). Performance assessment and education reform. *Phi Delta Kappan, 80*(9), 662-666.

Linn, R. (2000). Assessments and accountability. *Educational Researcher, 29*(2), 4-16.

Mislevy, R.J. (1994). Evidence and inference in educational assessment. *Psychometrika, 59*(4), 439-483.

Mislevy, R.J. (1996). Test theory reconceived. *Journal of Educational Measurement, 33*(4), 379-416.

National Council of Teachers of Mathematics. (1995). *Assessment standards for school mathematics.* Reston, VA: Author.

National Council of Teachers of Mathematics. (2000). *Principles and standards for school mathematics.* Reston, VA: Author.

National Research Council. (1996). *National science education standards.* National Committee on Science Education Standards and Assessment. Coordinating Council for Education. Washington, DC: National Academy Press.

National Research Council. (1999a). *High stakes: Testing for tracking, promotion, and graduation.* Committee on Appropriate Test Use. J.P. Heubert and R.M. Hauser, (Eds.). Commission on Behavioral and Social Sciences and Education. Washington, DC: National Academy Press.

National Research Council. (1999b). *How people learn: Bridging research and practice.* Committee on Learning Research and Educational Practice. M.S. Donovan, J.D. Bransford, and J.W. Pellegrino, (Eds.). Commission on Behavioral and Social Sciences and Education. Washington, DC: National Academy Press.

National Research Council. (2001). *Classroom assessment and the national science education standards.* Committee on Classroom Assessment and the *National Science Education Standards.* J.M. Atkin, P. Black, and J. Coffey, (Eds.). Division of Behavioral and Social Sciences and Education. Washington, DC: National Academy Press.

Niyogi, N.S. (1995). *The intersection of instruction and assessment: The classroom.* Princeton, NJ: ETS Policy Information Center.

Pellegrino, J.W., Baxter, G.P., and Glaser, R. (1999). Addressing the "two disciplines" problem: Linking theories of cognition and learning with assessment and instructional practice. In A. Iran-Nejad and P.D. Pearson (Eds.), *Review of Research in Education* (*Volume 24*). (pp. 307-353). Washington, DC: American Educational Research Association.

Schauble, L. (1990). Belief revision in children: The role of prior knowledge and strategies for generating evidence. *Journal of Experimental Child Psychology, 49,* 31-67.

Schum, D.A. (1987). *Evidence and inference for the intelligence analyst* (*Volume II*). Lanham, MD: University Press of America.

Scriven, M. (1991). *Evaluation thesaurus* (*4th Edition*). Newbury Park, CA: Sage.

Shepard, L.A. (2000). The role of assessment in a learning culture. Presidential Address presented at the annual meeting of the American Educational Research Association, New Orleans, April 26.

Siegler, R.S. (1976). Three aspects of cognitive development. *Cognitive Psychology, 8,* 481-520.

Siegler, R.S. (1998). *Children's thinking* (*3rd Edition*). Upper Saddle River, NJ: Prentice Hall.

Siegler, R.S., and Crowley, K. (1991). The microgenetic method: A direct means for studying cognitive development. *American Psychologist, 46*(6), 606-620.

Stiggins, R.J. (1997). *Student-centered classroom assessment.* Old Tappan, NJ: Prentice Hall.

Webb, N.L. (1992). Assessment of students' knowledge of mathematics: Steps toward a theory. In D.A. Grouws (Ed.), *Handbook of research on mathematics teaching and learning.* New York: Macmillan.

Webb, N.L. (1997). *Criteria for alignment of expectations and assessments in mathematics and science education.* National Institute for Science Education and Council of Chief State School Officers Research Monograph No. 6. Washington, DC: Council of Chief State School Officers.

Wiggins, G. (1998). *Educative assessment. Designing assessments to inform and improve student performance.* San Francisco: Jossey-Bass.

CHAPTER 3

Alibali, M.W., and Goldin-Meadow, S. (1993). Gesture-speech mismatch and mechanisms of learning: What the hands reveal about a child's state of mind. *Cognitive Psychology, 25*(4), 468-523.

Anderson, J.R. (1982). Acquisition of cognitive skill. *Psychological Review, 89*(4), 369-406.

Anderson, J.R. (1990). *Cognitive psychology and its implications (3rd Edition)*. New York: W.H. Freeman.

Anderson, J.R., and Boyle, C.F. (1985). Intelligent tutoring systems. *Science, 228*(4698), 456-462.

Anderson, J.R., Boyle, C.F., Corbett, A., and Lewis, M.W. (1990). Cognitive modeling and intelligent tutoring. *Artificial Intelligence, 42*, 7-49.

Anderson, J.R. and Gluck, K. (2001). What role do cognitive architectures play in intelligent tutoring systems? In S.M. Carver and D. Klahr (Eds.), *Cognition & instruction: 25 years of progress*. Mahwah, NJ: Lawrence Erlbaum Associates.

Anderson, J.R., Greeno, J.G., Reder, L.M., and Simon, H.A. (2000). Perspectives on learning, thinking, and activity. *Educational Researcher, 29*(4), 11-13.

Anderson, J.R., Kushmerick, N., and Lebiere, C. (1993). Navigation and conflict resolution. In J.R. Anderson (Ed.), *Rules of the mind* (pp. 93-120). Mahwah, NJ: Lawrence Erlbaum Associates.

Baddeley, A. (1986). *Working memory*. Oxford: Clarendon Press/Oxford University Press.

Baker, E.L. (1997). Model-based performance assessment. *Theory into Practice, 36*(4), 247-254.

Ball, D.L., and Bass, H. (in press). Making believe: The collective construction of public mathematical knowledge in the elementary classroom. In D. Phillips (Ed.), *Yearbook of the National Society for the Study of Education, Constructivism in Education*. Chicago: University of Chicago Press.

Bartlett, F.C. (1932). *Remembering: a study in experimental and social psychology*. New York: Macmillan.

Bassok, M., and Holyoak, K.J. (1989). Interdomain transfer between isomorphic topics in algebra and physics. *Journal of Experimental Psychology: Memory, Learning, and Cognition, 15*(1), 153-166.

Binet, A., and Simon, T. (1980). *The development of intelligence in children*. (Reprint. Originally published: Baltimore: Williams and Wilkins, 1916). Nashville, TN: Williams.

Bjork, R.A., and Richardson-Klavhen, A. (1989). On the puzzling relationship between environment context and human memory. In C. Izawa (Ed.), *Current issues in cognitive processes: The Tulane Flowerree Symposium on Cognition*. Hillsdale, NJ: Erlbaum.

Briars, D.J., and Larkin, J. (1984). An integrated model of skill in solving elementary word problems. *Cognition-and-Instruction, 1*(3), 245-296.

Bruer, J.T. (1997). Education and the brain: A bridge too far. *Educational Researcher, 26*(8), 4-16.

Bruer, J.T. (1999). In search of . . . brain-based education. *Phi Delta Kappan, 80*(9), 648-657.

Buonomano, D.V., and Merzenich, M.M. (1998). Cortical plasticity: From synapses and maps. *Annual Review of Neuroscience, 21*, 149-186.

Carpenter, T., Ansell, E., Franke, M.L., and Fennema, E. (1993). Models of problem-solving: A study of kindergarten children's problem-solving processes. *Journal for Research in Mathematics Education, 24*(5), 428-444.

Carpenter, T.P., Fennema, E., and Franke, M.L. (1996). Cognitively guided instruction: A knowledge base for reform in primary mathematics instruction. *The Elementary School Journal, 97*(1), 3-20.

Carpenter, P.A., Just, M.A., and Shell, P. (1990). What one intelligence test measures: A theoretical account of the processing in the Raven Progressive Matrices Test. *Psychological Review, 97*(3), 404-431.

Carpenter, T.P., and Moser, J.M. (1982). The development of addition and subtraction problem-solving skills. In T.P. Carpenter, J.M. Moser, and T. Romberg (Eds.), *Addition and subtraction: A cognitive perspective.* Hillsdale, NJ: Erlbaum.

Carraher, T.N. (1986). From drawings to buildings: Mathematical scales at work. *International Journal of Behavioral Development, 9*, 527-544.

Carroll, J.B. (1993). *Human cognitive abilities.* Cambridge: Cambridge University Press.

Carstens, C.B., Huskins, E., and Hounshell, G.W. (1995). Listening to Mozart may not enhance performance on the revised Minnesota Paper Form Board Test. *Psychological Reports, 77*, 111-114.

Case, R. (1992). The mind's staircase: Exploring the conceptual underpinnings of children's thought and knowledge. Hillsdale, NJ: Lawrence Erlbaum Associates.

Case, R., and Okamoto, Y. (Eds.) (1996). The role of central conceptual structures in the development of children's thought. *Monographs of the Society for Research in Child Development, 61*(1-2), Serial 246.

Chase, W.G., and Simon, H.A. (1973). Perception in chess. *Cognitive Psychology, 1*, 33-81.

Chen, Z., and Klahr, D. (1999). All other things being equal: Children's acquisition of the control of variables strategy. *Child Development, 70*(5), 1098-1120.

Cheng, P.W., and Holyoak, K.J. (1985). Pragmatic reasoning schemas. *Cognitive Psychology, 17*(4), 391-416.

Chi, M.T.H., Bassok, M., Lewis, M.W., Reiman, P., and Glaser, R. (1989). Self explanation: How students study and use examples in learning to solve problems. *Cognitive Science, 13*, 145-182.

Chi, M.T.H., Feltovich, P.J., and Glaser, R. (1981). Categorization and representation of physics problems by experts and novices. *Cognitive Science, 5*, 121-152.

Chi, M.T.H., Glaser, R., and Rees, E. (1982). Expertise in problem-solving. In R.J. Sternberg (Ed.), *Advances in the psychology of human intelligence (Volume 1).* Hillsdale, NJ: Erlbaum.

Chi, M.T.H., and Koeske, R.D. (1983). Network representation of a child's dinosaur knowledge. *Developmental Psychology, 19*, 29-39.

Chi, M.T.H., and VanLehn, K. (1991). The content of physics self-explanations. *Journal of the Learning Sciences, 1*(1), 69-106.

Clement, J.J. (1982). Students' preconceptions in introductory mechanics. *American Journal of Physics, 50*, 66-71.

Cobb, P. (1998). Learning from distributed theories of intelligence. *Mind, Culture, and Activity, 5*(3), 187-204.

Cobb, P., and McClain, K. (in press). Participating in classroom mathematical practices. *Journal of the Learning Sciences.*

Cognition and Technology Group at Vanderbilt. (1997). *The Jasper Project: Lessons in curriculum, instruction, assessment, and professional development.* Mahwah, NJ: Erlbaum.

Dillon, R.F. (1985). Predicting academic achievement with models based on eye movement data. *Journal of Psychoeducational Assessment, 3*, 157-165.

Driver, R., Squires, A., Rushworth, P., and Wood-Robinson, V. (1994*). Making sense of secondary science: Research into children's ideas.* New York: Routledge.

Dunbar, K. (1999). How scientists build models in vivo sciene as a window on the scientific mind. In L. Magnani and N.J. Neressian (Eds.), *Model-based reasoning in scientific discovery* (pp. 85-99). New York: Kluwer Academic/Plenum Pubilshers.

Dweck, C., and Legget, E. (1988). A social-cognitive approach to motivation and personality. *Psychological Review, 95*, 256-273.

Ericsson, K.A., and Simon, H.A. (1984). *Protocol analysis: Verbal reports as data.* Cambridge, MA: MIT Press.

Fay, A., and Klahr, D. (1996). Knowing about guessing and guessing about knowing: Preschoolers' understanding of indeterminacy. *Child Development, 67*, 689-716.

Fitch, R.H., Miller, S., and Tallal, P. (1997). Neurobiology of speech. *Annual Review of Neuroscience, 20*, 331-353.

Gabel, D. (Ed.) (1994). *Handbook of research on science teaching and learning.* New York: MacMillan.

Geary, D. (1995). Reflections of evolution and culture in children's cognition: Implications for mathematical development and instruction. *American Psychologist, 50*(1), 24-37.

Gelman, R., and Gallistel, C.R. (1978). *The child's understanding of number.* Cambridge, MA: Harvard University Press.

Glaser, R. (1992). Expert knowledge and processes of thinking. In D.F. Halpern (Ed.), *Enhancing thinking skills in the sciences and mathematics* (pp. 63-75). Hillsdale, NJ: Lawrence Erlbaum Associates.

Glaser, R., and Baxter, G.P. (1999). *Assessing active knowledge.* Paper presented at the 1999 CRESST Conference, Benchmarks for Accountability: Are We There Yet?, September 16-17, UCLA, Los Angeles, CA.

Goodwin, C. (2000). Practices of color classification. *Mind, Culture, and Activity, 7*(1&2), 19-36.

Greeno, J.G., Collins, A.M., and Resnick, L.B. (1996a). Cognition and learning. In D.C. Berliner and R.C. Calfee (Eds.), *Handbook of educational psychology* (pp. 15-46). New York: Macmillan.

Greeno, J.G., Pearson, P.D., and Schoenfeld, A.H. (1996b). *Implications for NAEP of research on learning and cognition. Report of a study commissioned by the National Academy of Education.* Panel on the NAEP Trial State Assessment, Conducted by the Institute for Research on Learning. Stanford, CA: National Academy of Education.

Greenough, W.T. (1976). Enduring brain effects of differential experience and training. In M.R. Rosenzweig and E.L. Bennet (Eds.), *Neural mechanisms of learning and memory* (pp. 255-278). Cambridge, MA: MIT Press.

Griffin, S.A., Case, R., and Siegler, R.S. (1994). Rightstart: Providing the central conceptual prerequisites for first formal learning of arithmetic to students at risk for school failure. In K. McGilly (Ed.), *Classroom lessons: Integrating cognitive theory and classroom practice* (pp. 1-50). Cambridge, MA: MIT Press/Bradford Books.

Harvard-Smithsonian Center for Astrophysics, Science Education Department. (1987). *A private universe* (Video). Cambridge, MA: Science Media Group.

Hatano, G. (1990). The nature of everyday science: A brief introduction. *British Journal of Developmental Psychology, 8,* 245-250.

Hayes, J.R., and Flower, L. (1986). Writing research and the writer. *American Psychologist, 41,* 1106-1113.

Heath, S.B. (1981). Questioning at home and school: A comprehensive study. In G. Spindler (Ed.), *Doing ethnography: Educational anthropology in action.* New York: Holt, Rinehart, and Winston.

Heath, S.B. (1983). *Ways with words: Language, life, and work in communities and classrooms.* Cambridge, England: Cambridge University Press.

Hellige, J. (1993). *Hemispheric asymmetry: What's right and what's left?* Cambridge, MA: Harvard University Press.

Holzman, T.G., Pelligrino, J.W., and Glaser, R. (1983). Cognitive variables in series completion. *Journal of Educational Psychology, 75* (4), 603-618.

Horn, J.L., and Noll, J. (1994). A system for understanding cognitive capabilities: A theory and the evidence on which it is based. In D. Detterman (Ed.), *Theories of intelligence* (*Volume 4*) (pp. 151-204). Norwood, NJ: Ablex.

Hull, C.L. (1943). *Principles of behavior: An introduction to behavior theory.* New York: Appleton-Century.

Hull, G., Jury, M., Ziv, O., and Schultz, K. (1994). *Changing work, changing literacy? A study of skill requirements and development in a traditional and restructured workplace* (*Interim Report Two*). University of California, Berkeley: National Center for the Study of Writing and Literacy.

Hunt, E. (1995). *Will we be smart enough? A cognitive analysis of the coming workforce.* New York: Russell Sage.

Hunt, E., and Minstrell, J. (1996). Effective instruction in science and mathematics: Psychological principles and social constraints. *Issues in Education: Contributions from Educational Psychology, 2*(2), 123-162.

Hunt, E., Streissguth, A.P., Kerr, B., and Olson, H.C. (1995). Mothers' alcohol consumption during pregnancy: Effects on spatial-visual reasoning in 14-year-old children. *Psychological Science, 6*(6), 339-342.

Just, M.A., and Carpenter, P.A. (1992). A capacity theory of comprehension. Individual differences in working memory. *Psychological Review, 90,* 122-149.

Just, M.A., Carpenter, P.A., and Keller, T.A. (1996). The capacity theory of comprehension: New frontiers of evidence and arguments. *Psychological-Review, 103*(4), 773-780.

Kaiser, M.K., Proffitt, D.R., and McCloskey, M. (1985). The development of beliefs about falling objects. *Perception & Psychophysics, 38*(6), 533-539.

Karmiloff-Smith, A. (1979). Problem-solving construction and representations of closed railway circuits. *Archives of Psychology, 47,* 37-59.

Kenealy, P., and Monsef, A. (1994). Music and IQ tests. *The Psychologist, 7,* 346.

Kintsch, W., and Greeno, J.G. (1985). Understanding and solving word arithmetic problems. *Psychological Review, 92*(1), 109-129.

Klahr, D., and Carver, S.M. (1988). Cognitive objectives in a LOGO debugging curriculum: Instruction, learning, and transfer. *Cognitive Psychology, 20*(3), 362-404.

Klahr, D., and MacWhinney, B. (1998). Information processing. In W. Damon, D. Kuhn, and R.S. Siegler (Eds.), *Cognition, perception, and language* (*5th Edition, Volume 2*). New York: Wiley.

Klahr, D., and Robinson, M. (1981). Formal assessment of problem-solving and planning processes in preschool children. *Cognitive Psychology, 13*, 113-148.

Klahr, D. and Siegler, R.S. (1978). The representations of children's knowledge. In H. Reese and L.P. Lipsitt (Eds.), *Advances in child development, 12*. New York: Academic Press.

Klahr, D., and Simon, H.A. (1999). Studies of scientific discovery: Complementary approaches and convergent findings. *Psychological Bulletin, 125*(5), 524-543.

Koedinger, K.R., and Anderson, J. (1999). *Pump Algebra Project: AI and high school math*. Available: <http://act.psy.cmu.edu/ACT/awpt/awpt-home.html>. [July 7, 2000].

Kyllonen, P.C., and Christal, R.E. (1990). Reasoning ability is (little more than) working memory capacity?! *Intelligence, 14*, 389-433.

Lampert, M. (1986). Knowing, doing, and teaching multiplication. *Cognition and Instruction, 3*, 305-342.

Larkin, J.H., McDermott, J., Simon, D.P., and Simon, H.A. (1980). Expert and novice performance in solving physics problems. *Science, 208*, 1335-1342.

Lave, J. (1988). *Cognition in practice*. Cambridge, England: Cambridge University Press.

Lehrer, R., Jacobson, C., Thoyre, G., Kemeny, V., Strom, D., Horvath, J., Gance, S., and Koehler, M. (1998). Developing understanding of geometry and space in the primary grades. In R. Lehrer and D. Chazan (Eds.), *Designing learning environments for developing understanding of geometry and space* (pp. 169-200). Mahwah, NJ: Lawrence Erlbaum Associates.

Lehrer, R., and Schauble, L. (2000). Inventing data structures for representational purposes: Elementary grade students' classification models. *Mathematical Thinking and Learning 2*(1-2), 51-74.

Lehrer, R., Schauble, L., Carpenter, S., and Penner, D.E. (2000). The inter-related development of inscriptions and conceptual understanding. In P. Cobb, E. Yackel, and K. McClain (Eds.), *Symbolizing and communicating in mathematics classrooms: Perspectives on discourse, tools, and instructional design* (pp. 325-360). Mahwah, NJ: Lawrence Erlbaum Associates.

Lopez, A., Atran, S., Coley, J.D., and Medin, D.L. (1997). The tree of life: Universal and cultural features of folkbiological taxonomies and inductions. *Cognitive Psychology, 32*(3), 251-295.

Macleod, C.M., Hunt, E., and Matthews, N.N. (1978). Individual differences in the verification of sentence-picture relationships. *Journal of Verbal Learning and Verbal Behavior, 17*, 493-507.

Marshall, S.P. (1995). *Schemas in problem-solving*. New York, NY: Cambridge University Press.

Massey, C.M., and Gelman, R. (1988). Preschoolers decide whether pictured unfamiliar objects can move themselves. *Developmental Psychology, 24*, 307-317.

Medin, D.L., Lynch, E.B., and Coley, J.D. (1997). Categorization and reasoning among tree experts: Do all roads lead to Rome? *Cognitive Psychology, 32*, 49-96.

Merzenich, M.M., Jenkins, W.M., Johnston, P., Schreiner, C., Miller, S.L., and Tallal, P. (1996). Temporal processing deficits of language-learning impaired children ameliorated by training. *Science, 271*, 77-81.

Miller, G.A. (1956). The magical number seven, plus or minus two: Some limits on our capacity for processing information. *Psychological Review, 63*, 81-97.

Minstrell, J. (2000). Student thinking and related assessment: Creating a facet-based learning environment. In Committee on the Evaluation of National and State Assessments of Educational Progress. N.S. Raju, J.W. Pellegrino, M.W. Bertenthal, K.J. Mitchell, and L.R. Jones (Eds.), *Grading the nation's report card: Research from the evaluation of NAEP* (pp. 44-73). Commission on Behavioral and Social Sciences and Education. Washington, DC: National Academy Press.

Miyake, A., Just, M.A., and Carpenter, P.A. (1994). Working memory constraints on the resolution of lexical ambiguity: Maintaining multiple interpretations in neutral contexts. *Journal of Memory and Language, 33*(2), 175-202.

Mody, M., Studdert-Kennedy, M., and Brady, S. (1997). Speech perception deficits in poor readers: Auditory processing or phonological coding? *Journal of Experimental Child Psychology, 64*, 199-231.

Mulholland, T.M., Pellegrino, J.W., and Glaser, R. (1980). Components of geometric analogy solution. *Cognitive Psychology, 12*, 252-284.

Nantais, K.M., and Schellenberg, E.G. (1999). The Mozart effect: An artifact of preference. *Psychological Science, 10*, 370-373.

National Research Council. (1999). *How people learn: Brain, mind, experience, and school.* Committee on Developments in the Science of Learning. J.D. Bransford, A.L. Brown, and R.R. Cocking, (Eds.). Commission on Behavioral and Social Sciences and Education. Washington, DC: National Academy Press.

Nelson, T.O. (1996). Consciousness and metacognition. *American Psychologist, 51*(2), 102-116.

Newcombe, N.S., and Huttenlocker, J. (2000). *Making space.* Cambridge, MA: MIT Press.

Newell, A. (1990). *Unified theories of cognition.* Cambridge, MA: Harvard University Press.

Newell, A., and Simon, H.A. (1972). *Human problem-solving.* Englewood Cliffs, NJ: Prentice Hall.

Newman, J., Rosenbach, J.H., Burns, K.L., Latimer, B.C., Matocha, H.R., and Vogt, E.E. (1995). An experimental test of "the Mozart effect": Does listening to his music improve spatial ability? *Perceptual and Motor Skills, 81*, 1379-1387.

Ochs, E., Jacoby, S., and Gonzalez, P. (1994). Interpretive journeys: How physicists talk and travel through graphic space. *Configurations, 2*, 151-172.

Ochs, E., and Schieffelin, B.B. (1984). Language acquisition and socialization: Three developmental stories and their implications. In R. Schweder and R. Levine (Eds.), *Culture and its acquisition* (pp. 276-320). Chicago: University of Chicago Press.

Okada, T., and Simon, H.A. (1997). Collaborative discovery in a scientific domain. *Cognitive Science, 21*(2), 109-146.

Olson, D.R. (1996). *The world on paper: The conceptual and cognitive implications of writing and reading.* Cambridge, MA: Cambridge University Press.

Palincsar, A.S., and Magnusson, S.J. (2001). The interplay of first-hand and second-hand investigations to model and support the development of scientific knowledge and reasoning. In S.M. Carver and D. Klahr (Eds.), *Cognition & instruction: 25 years of progress.* Mahwah, NJ: Lawrence Erlbaum Associates.

Piaget, J. (1952). *The origins of intelligence in children*, M. Cook, (Trans.) New York: International Universities Press.

Piaget, J. (1978). *Success and understanding*. Cambridge, MA: Harvard University Press.

Rauscher, F.H., Shaw, G.L., and Ky, K.N. (1993). Music and spatial task performance. *Nature, 365*, 611.

Rauscher, F.H., Shaw, G.L., and Ky, K.N. (1995). Listening to Mozart enhances spatial-temporal reasoning: Towards a neurophysiological basis. *Neuroscience Letters, 185*, 44-47.

Resnick, L.B. (1989). Developing mathematical knowledge. *American Psychologist, 44*(2), 162-169.

Riley, M.S., Greeno, J.G., and Heller, J.I. (1983). Development of children's problem-solving ability in arithmetic. In J.P. Ginsburg (Ed.), *The development of mathematical thinking* (pp.153-196). New York: Academic Press.

Rogoff, B. (1990). *Apprenticeship in thinking: Cognitive development in social context*. New York: Oxford University Press.

Rosenbloom, P., and Newell, A. (1987). Learning by chunking: A production system model of practice. In D. Klahr and P. Langley (Eds.), *Production system models of learning and development* (pp. 221-286). Cambridge, MA: MIT Press.

Roth, W. M., and McGinn, M.K. (1998). Inscriptions: Toward a theory of representing as social practice. *Review of Educational Research 68*(1), 35-59.

Shaywitz, B.A., Pugh, K.R., Jenner, A.R., Fulbright, R.K., Fletcher, J.M., Gore, J.C., and Shaywitz, S.E. (2000). The neurobiology of reading and reading disability (dyslexia). In M.L. Kamil and P.B. Mosenthal (Eds.), *Handbook of reading research* (*Volume III*). (pp. 229-249). Mahwah, NJ: Lawrence Erlbaum Associates.

Siegler, R.S. (1976). Three aspects of cognitive development. *Cognitive Psychology, 8*, 481-520.

Siegler, R.S. (1998). *Children's thinking* (*Third Edition*). Upper Saddle River, NJ: Prentice Hall.

Siegler, R.S. (in press). Microgenetic studies of self-explanation. To appear in N. Granott and J. Parziale (Eds.), *Microdevelopment: Transition processes in development and learning*. New York: Cambridge University Press.

Siegler, R.S., and Crowley, K. (1991). The microgenetic method: A direct means for studying cognitive development. *American Psychologist, 46*(6), 606-620.

Simon, H.A. (1974). How big is a chunk? *Science, 183*(4124), 482-488.

Singley, M.K., and Anderson, J.R. (1988). A keystroke analysis of learning and transfer in text editing. *Human Computer Interaction, 3*(3), 223-274.

Skinner, B.F. (1938). *The behavior of organisms: An experimental analysis*. New York: Appleton-Century-Crofts.

Sperry, R.W. (1984). Consciousness, personal identity and the divided brain. *Neuropsychologia, 22*(6), 661-673.

Springer, S.P., and Deutsch, G. (1993). *Left brain, right brain* (*Fourth Edition*). New York: W. H. Freeman.

Starkey, P. (1992). The early development of numerical reasoning. *Cognition, 43*, 93-126.

Steele, K.M., Ball, T.N., and Runk, R. (1997). Listening to Mozart does not enhance backwards digit span performance. *Perceptual Motor Skills, 84*, 1179-1184.

Steele, K.M., Bass, K.E., and Crook, M.D. (1999). The mystery of the Mozart effect: Failure to replicate it. *Psychological Science, 10*, 366-369.

Steffe, L.P. (1970). Differential performance of first-grade children when solving arithmetic addition problems. *Journal for Research in Mathematics Education 1*(3), 144-161.

Strom, D., Kemeny, V., Lehrer, R., and Forman, E. (In press). Visualizing the emergent structure of children's mathematics argument. *Cognitive Science.*

Tallal, P., Miller, S.L., Bedi, G., Byma, G., Wang, X., Nagarajan, S.S., Schreiner, C., Jenkins, W.M., and Merzenich, M.M. (1996). Language comprehension in language-learning impaired children improved with acoustically modified speech. *Science, 271*, 81-84.

Teasley, S.D. (1995). The role of talk in children's peer collaborations. *Developmental Psychology, 31*(2), 207-220.

Thompson, R.F. (2000). *The brain: A neuroscience primer* (*Third Edition*). New York: Worth.

Thorndike, E.L. (1931). *Human learning.* New York: Century.

Treisman, P.U. (1990). Teaching mathematics to a changing population: The Professional Development Program at the University of California, Berkeley. Part I. A study of the mathematics performance of black students at the University of California, Berkeley. In N. Fisher, H. Keynes, and P. Wagreich (Eds.), *Mathematicians and education reform* (pp. 33-46). Washington, DC: American Mathematical Society.

VanLehn, K., and Martin, J. (1998). Evaluation of an assessment system based on Bayesian student modeling. *International Journal of Artificial Intelligence in Education, 8*, 179-221.

Vosniadou, S., and Brewer, W.F. (1992). Mental models of the Earth: A study of conceptual change in childhood. *Cognitive Psychology, 24*(4), 535-585.

Ward, M. (1971). *Them children.* New York: Holt, Rinehart, and Winston.

Wason, P.C., and Johnson-Laird, P. (1972). *Psychology of reasoning: Structure and content.* Cambridge, MA: Harvard University Press.

Wertsch, J.V. (1998). *Mind as action.* New York: Oxford University Press.

White, B.Y., and Frederiksen, J.R. (1998). Inquiry, modeling, and metacognition: Making science accessible to all students. *Cognition and Instruction, 16*(1), 3-118.

Wiggins, G. (1989). Teaching to the (authentic) test. *Educational Leadership, 46*(7), 41-47.

Wynn, K. (1990). Children's understanding of counting. *Cognition, 36*, 155-193.

Wynn, K. (1992). Addition and subtraction by human infants. *Nature, 358*, 749-750.

CHAPTER 4

Adams, R.J., and Khoo, S-T. (1992). *Quest: The interactive test analysis system.* Hawthorn, Australia: Australian Council on Education Research Press.

Adams, R., Wilson, M., and Wang, W. (1997). The multidimensional random coefficient multinomial logit model. *Applied Psychological Measurement, 21*(1), 1-23.

Almond, R.G. (1995). *Graphical belief modeling.* London: Chapman and Hall.

Andersen, S.K., Jensen, F.V., Olesen, K.G., and Jensen, F. (1989). *HUGIN: A shell for building Bayesian belief universes for expert systems* [computer program]. Aalborg, Denmark: HUGIN Expert.

Anderson, J.R., Corbett, A.T., Koedinger, K.R., and Pelletier, R. (1995). Cognitive tutors: Lessons learned. *The Journal of the Learning Sciences, 4,* 167-207.

Baxter, G.P., Elder, A.D., and Glaser, R. (1996). Knowledge-based cognition and performance assessment in the science classroom. *Educational Psychologist, 31*(2), 133-140.

Bock, R.D. (1979). Univariate and multivariate analysis of variance of time-structured data. In J.R. Nesselroade and P.B. Baltes (Eds.). *Longitudinal research in the study of behavior and development* (pp. 199-231). New York: Academic Press.

Brennan, R.L. (1983). *The elements of generalizability theory.* Iowa City, IA: American College Testing Program.

Bryk, A.S., and Raudenbush, S. (1992*). Hierarchical linear models: Applications and data analysis methods.* Newbury Park, England: Sage Publications.

Burstein, L. (1980). The analysis of multilevel data in educational research and evaluation. *Review of Research in Education, 8,* 158-233.

Charniak, E., and Goldman, R. (1993). A Bayesian model of plan recognition. *Artificial Intelligence, 64,* 53-79.

Chi, M.T.H., Glaser, R., and Farr, M.J. (1988). *The nature of expertise.* Hillsdale, NJ: Lawrence Erlbaum Associates.

Collins, L.M., and Wugalter, S.E. (1992). Latent class models for stage-sequential dynamic latent variables. *Multivariate Behavioral Research, 27*(1), 131-157.

Connolly, A., Nachtman, W., and Pritchett, M. (1972). *Keymath diagnostic arithmetic test.* Circle Pines, MN: American Guidance Service.

Corbett, A.T., and Anderson, J.R. (1992). The LISP intelligent tutoring system: Research in skill and acquisition. In J. Larkin, R. Chabay, and C. Scheftic (Eds.), *Computer assisted instruction and intelligent tutoring systems: Establishing communication and collaboration.* Hillsdale, NJ: Lawrence Erlbaum Associates.

Cronbach, L.J., Gleser, G.C., Nanda, H., and Rajaratnam, N. (1972). *The dependability of behavioral measurements: Theory of generalizability for scores and profiles.* New York: Wiley.

Dennett, D.C. (1988). *The intentional stance.* Cambridge, MA: Bradford Books, MIT Press.

DiBello, L., Jiang, H. and Stout, W.F., (1999). A multidimensional IRT model for practical cognitive diagnosis. To appear, *Applied psychological methods.*

DiBello, L.V., Stout, W.F. and Roussos, L.A. (1995). Unified cognitive/psychometric diagnostic assessement likelihood-based classification techniques. In P.D. Nichols, S.F. Chipman, and R.L. Brennan, (Eds.), *Cognitively diagnostic assessment,* (chapter 15). Hillsdale, NJ: Lawrence Erlbaum Associates.

Embretson, S.E. (1996). Multicomponent response models. In W.J. van der Linden and R.K. Hambleton (Eds.), *Handbook of modern item response theory.* New York: Springer.

Ercikan, K. (1998). Translation effects in international assessments. *International Journal of Educational Research, 29,* 543-553.

Falmagne, J-C. (1989). A latent trait model via a stochastic learning theory for a knowledge space. *Psychometrika, 54,* 283-303.

Fischer, G.H. (1995). Linear logistic models for change. In G.H. Fisher and I.W. Molenaar (Eds.), *Rasch models: Foundations, recent developments, and applications*. New York: Springer-Verlag.

Gelman, A., Carlin, J., Stern, H., and Rubin, D.B. (1995). *Bayesian data analysis*. London: Chapman and Hall.

Gertner, A.S., Conati, C., and VanLehn, K. (1998). Procedural help in Andes: Generating hints using a Bayesian network student model. In *Proceedings of the Fifteenth National Conference on Artificial Intelligence AAAI- 98* (pp. 106-111). Cambridge MA: MIT Press.

Glaser, R. (1963). Instructional technology and the measurement of learning outcomes: Some questions. *American Psychologist, 18*, 519-521.

Glaser, R. (1991). The maturing of the relationship between the science of learning and cognition and educational practice. *Learning and Instruction, 1*(2), 129-144.

Goldstein, H., Rasbash, J., Plewis, I., and Draper, D. (1998). *A user's guide to MLwiN*. London: Institute of Education.

Haertel, E.H. (1989). Using restricted latent class models to map the skill structure of achievement items. *Journal of Educational Measurement, 26*, 301-321.

Haertel, E.H. (1990). Continuous and discrete latent structure models for item response data. *Psychometrika, 55*, 477-494.

Haertel, E.H., and Wiley, D.E. (1993). Representations of ability structures: Implications for testing. In N. Frederiksen, R.J. Mislevy, and I.I. Bejar (Eds.), *Test theory for a new generation of tests*. Hillsdale, NJ: Lawrence Earlbaum Associates.

Hagenaars, J.A., and Luijkx, R. (1990). *LCAG user's manual. Working Papers Series #17*. Tilburg University (TH Netherlands), Department of Sociology.

Hill, R.W. and Johnson, W.L. (1995). Situated plan attribution. *Journal of Artificial Intelligence in Education, 6*, 35-66.

Holland, P.W., and Thayer, D. (1988). Differential item performance and the Mantel-Haenzsel procedure. In H. Wainer and H.I. Braun (Eds.), *Test validity* (pp. 129-145). Hillsdale, NJ: Lawrence Erlbaum Associates.

Hunt, E., and Minstrell, J. (1994). A cognitive approach to the teaching of physics. In K. McGilly (Ed.), *Classroom lessons: Integrating cognitive theory and classroom practice* (pp. 51-74). Cambridge, MA: MIT Press.

Janssen, R., Tuerlinckx, F., Meulders, M., and De Boeck, P. (2000). An hierarchical IRT model for mastery classification. *Journal of Educational and Behavioral Statistics, 25*(3), 285-306.

Jöreskog, K.G., and Sörbom, D. (1979). *Advances in factor analysis and structural equation models*. Cambridge, MA: Abt Books.

Junker, B. (1999). *Some statistical models and computational methods that may be useful for cognitively-relevant assessment*. Paper prepared for the National Research Council Committee on the Foundations of Assessment. <http://www.stat.cmu.edu/~brian/nrc/cfa/>. [April 2, 2001].

Kahneman, D., Slovic, P., and Tversky, A. (1982). *Judgment under uncertainty: Heuristics and biases*. Cambridge: Cambridge University Press.

Kieras, D.E. (1988). What mental model should be taught: Choosing instructional content for complex engineered systems. In M.J. Psotka, L.D. Massey, and S.A. Mutter (Eds.), *Intelligent tutoring systems: Lessons learned* (pp. 85-111). Hillsdale, NJ: Lawrence Erlbaum.

Kreft, I., and De Leeuw, J. (1998). *Introducing multilevel modeling.* Thousand Oaks, CA: Sage.

Kyllonen, P.C., Lohman, D.F., and Snow, R.E. (1984). Effects of aptitudes, strategy training, and test facets on spatial task performance. *Journal of Educational Psychology, 76,* 130-145.

Lane, L, Wang, N., and Magone, M. (1996). Gender-related differential item functioning on a Middle-School Mathematics Performance Assessment. *Educational Measurement: Issues and Practice, 15*(4), 21-28.

Lawley, D.N. (1943). On problems connected with item selection and test construction. *Proceedings of the Royal Society of Edinburgh, 62-A* (Part I), 74-82.

Lazarsfeld, P.F. (1950). The logical and mathematical foundation of latent structure analysis. In S.A. Stouffer, L. Guttman, E. A. Suchman, P.R. Lazarsfeld, S.A. Star, and J.A. Clausen, *Measurement and prediction* (pp. 362-412). Princeton, NJ: Princeton University Press.

Lord, F.M. (1980). *Applications of item response theory to practical testing problems.* Hillsdale, NJ: Erlbaum.

Lord, R.M., and Novick, M.R. (1968). *Statistical theories of mental test scores.* Reading, MA: Addison-Wesley.

Management Committee for the National School English Literacy Survey (Commonwealth of Australia). (1997). *Mapping literacy achievement: Results of the 1996 National School English Literacy Survey.* Canberra, Australia: Commonwealth of Australia Department of Employment, Education, Training, and Youth Affairs.

Martin, J.D., and VanLehn, K. (1993). OLAE: Progress toward a multi-activity, Bayesian student modeler. In S.P. Brna, S. Ohlsson, and H. Pain (Eds.), *Artificial intelligence in education: Proceedings of AI-ED 93* (pp. 410-417). Charlottesville, VA: Association for the Advancement of Computing in Education.

Martin, J.D., and VanLehn, K. (1995). A Bayesian approach to cognitive assessment. In P. Nichols, S. Chipman, and R. Brennan (Eds.), *Cognitively diagnostic assessment* (pp. 141-165). Hillsdale, NJ: Erlbaum.

Masters, G.N., Adams, R.A., and Wilson, M. (1990). Charting of student progress. In T. Husen and T.N. Postlethwaite (Eds.), *International encyclopedia of education: Research and studies. Supplementary volume 2* (pp. 628-634). Oxford: Pergamon Press.

Masters, G.N., and Forster, M. (1996). *Developmental assessment: Assessment resource kit.* Hawthorn, Australia: Australian Council on Education Research Press.

Mead, R. (1976). *Assessment of fit of data to the Rasch model through analysis of residuals.* Unpublished doctoral dissertation, University of Chicago.

Minstrell, J. (2000). Student thinking and related assessment: Creating a facet-based learning environment. In Committee on the Evaluation of National and State Assessments of Educational Progress. N.S. Raju, J.W. Pellegrino, M.W. Bertenthal, K.J. Mitchell, and L.R. Jones (Eds.), *Grading the nation's report card: Research from the evaluation of NAEP* (pp. 44-73). Commission on Behavioral and Social Sciences and Education. Washington, DC: National Academy Press.

Mislevy, R.J. (1996). Test theory reconceived. *Journal of Educational Measurement, 33*(4), 379-416.

Mislevy, R.J., and Gitomer, D.H. (1996). The role of probability-based inference in an intelligent tutoring system. *User Modeling and User-Adapted Interaction, 5,* 253-282.

Mislevy, R.J., and Verhelst, H. (1990). Modeling item responses when different subjects employ different solution strategies. *Psychometrika, 55,* 195-215.

Mislevy, R.J., and Wilson, M.R. (1996). Marginal maximum likelihood estimation for a psychometric model of discontinuous development. *Psychometrika, 61,* 41-71.

Muthen, B.O., and Khoo, S-T. (1998). Longitudinal studies of achievement growth using latent variable modeling. *Learning and Individual Differences* (J.B. Cooney, Ed.).

Newell, A. (1982). The knowledge level. *Artificial Intelligence, 18*(1), 87-127.

O'Neil, K.A., and McPeek, W.M., (1993). In P.W. Holland, and H. Wainer (Eds.*), Differential item functioning* (pp. 255-276). Hillsdale, NJ: Erlbaum.

Pearl, J. (1988). *Probabilistic reasoning in intelligent systems: Networks of plausible inference.* San Mateo, CA: Kaufmann.

Pirolli, P., and Wilson, M. (1998). A theory of the measurement of knowledge content, access, and learning. *Psychological Review, 105*(1), 588-92.

Rasch, G. (1960). *Probabilistic models for some intelligence and attainment tests.* Copenhagen: Denmarks Paedagogiske Institut.

Rasch, G. (1980). *Probabilistic models for some intelligence and attainment tests, Expanded edition.* Chicago: University of Chicago.

Raudenbush, S.W., Bryk, A.S., and Congdon, R.T. (1999). *Hierarchical linear modeling 5* [computer program]. Lincolnwood, IL: Scientific Software International.

Reckase, M.D. (1972). Development and application of a multivariate logistic latent trait model. Unpublished doctoral dissertation, Syracuse University, Syracuse, NY.

Roberts, L., Sloane, K., and Wilson, M. (1996). *Assessment moderation: Supporting teacher change while improving professional practice* BEAR Report Series, SA-96-2. University of California, Berkeley.

Roberts, L., Wilson, M., and Draney, K. (1997, June*) The SEPUP assessment system: An overview* BEAR Report Series, SA-97-1. University of California, Berkeley.

Rock, D.A., and Pollack-Ohls, J. (1987). *Measuring gains: A new look at an old problem.* Princeton, NJ: Educational Testing Service.

Science Education for Public Understanding Program (SEPUP). (1995). *Issues, evidence, & you.* Ronkonkoma, NY: Lab-Aids.

Spearman, C. (1904). The proof and measurement of association between two things. *American Journal of Psychology, 15,* 72-101.

Spiegelhalter, D.J., Dawid, A.P., Lauritzen, S.L., and Cowell, R.G. (1993). Bayesian analysis in expert systems. *Statistical Science, 8,* 219-283.

Swaminathan, H., and Rogers, H.J. (1990). Dectecting differential item functioning using logistic regression procedures. *Journal of Educational Measurement, 27,* 361-370.

Sympson, J.B. (1978). A model for testing with multidimensional items. In D.J. Weiss (Ed.), *Proceedings of the 1977 Computerized Adaptive Testing Conference* (pp. 82-98). Minneapolis: University of Minnesota, Department of Psychology, Psychometric Methods Program.

Tatsuoka, K.K. (1983). Rule space: An approach for dealing with misconceptions based on item response theory. *Journal of Educational Measurement, 20*, 345-354.

Tatsuoka, K.K. (1987). Validation of cognitive sensitivity for item response curves. *Journal of Educational Measurement, 24*, 233-245.

Tatsuoka, K.K. (1990). Toward an integration of item response theory and cognitive error diagnosis. In N. Frederiksen, R. Glaser, A. Lesgold, and M.G. Shafto, (Eds.), *Diagnostic monitoring of skill and knowledge acquisition* (pp. 453-488). Hillsdale, NJ: Erlbaum.

Tatsuoka, K.K. (1995). Architecture of knowledge structures and cognitive diagnosis: A statistical pattern recognition and classification approach. In P.D. Nichols, S.F. Chipman, and R.L. Brennan (Eds.), *Cognitively diagnostic assessment* (chapter 14). Hillsdale, NJ: Lawrence Erlbaum Associates.

van de Pol, F., Langeheine, R., and de Jong, W. (1989). *PANMARK user manual.* Voorburg: Netherlands Central Bureau of Statistics.

VanLehn, K. (1990). *Mind bugs: The origins of procedural misconceptions.* Cambridge, MA: MIT Press.

West Australian Ministry of Education. (1991). *First steps spelling developmental continuum.* Perth, Australia: Author.

Wigmore, J.H. (1937). *The science of judicial proof (3rd Edition).* Boston: Little, Brown.

Willet, J., and Sayer, A. (1994). Using covariance structure analysis to detect correlates and predictors of individual change over time. *Psychological Bulletin, 116*(2), 363-380.

Wilson, M. (1984). A Psychometric model of hierarchical development. Unpublished doctoral dissertation, University of Chicago.

Wilson, M. (1989). Saltus: A psychometric model of discontinuity in cognitive development. *Psychological Bulletin, 105*(2), 276-289.

Wilson, M., and Draney, K. (1997, July). *Developing maps for student progress in the SEPUP Assessment System* BEAR Report Series, SA-97-2. University of California, Berkeley.

Wilson, M., Draney, K., and Kennedy, C. (2001). *GradeMap* [computer program]. Berkeley, CA: BEAR Center, University of California.

Wilson, M., and Sloane, K. (2000). From principles to practice: An embedded assessment system. *Applied Measurement in Education, 13*(2), 181-208.

Wolf, D., Bixby, J., Glenn, J., and Gardner, H. (1991). To use their minds well: Investigating new forms of student assessment. In G. Grant (Ed.), *Review of educational research, Volume 17* (pp. 31-74). Washington, DC: American Educational Research Association.

Wright, B.D., and Masters, G.N. (1982). *Rating scale analysis.* Chicago: MESA Press.

Wright, S. (1934). The method of path coefficients. *Annals of Mathematical Statistics, 5*, 161-215.

Wu, M., Adams, R.J., and Wilson, M. (1998). ACER *ConQuest* [computer program]. Hawthorn, Australia: Australian Council on Educational Research.

Yamamoto, K., and Gitomer, D.H. (1993). Application of a HYBRID model to a test of cognitive skill representation. In Fredriksen, N. and Mislevy, R.J. (Eds.) (1993). *Test theory for a new generation of tests* (chapter 11). Hillsdale, NJ: Lawrence Erlbaum Associates.

CHAPTER 5

Abedi, J., Hofstetter, and Baker, E. (2001). *NAEP math performance and test accommodations: Interactions with student language background* (CSE Technical Report 536). Los Angeles: National Center for Research on Evaluation, Standards, and Student Testing, University of California, Los Angeles.

American Association for the Advancement of Science. (2001). *Atlas of science literacy.* Washington, DC: Author.

American Educational Research Association, American Psychological Association, and National Council of Measurement in Education. (1999). *Standards for educational and psychological testing.* Washington, DC: American Educational Research Association.

Anderson, J.R., Boyle, C.F., Corbett, A., and Lewis, M.W. (1990). Cognitive modelling and intelligent tutoring. *Artificial Intelligence, 42,* 7-49.

Baker, E.L. (1997). Model-based performance assessment. *Theory into Practice, 36*(4), 247-254.

Baxter, G.P., and Glaser, R. (1998). Investigating the cognitive complexity of science assessments. *Educational Measurement: Research and Practice, 17*(3), 37-45.

Brown, J.S., and Burton, R.R. (1978). Diagnostic models for procedural bugs in basic mathematical skills. *Cognitive Science, 2,* 155-192.

Brown, J.S., and VanLehn, K. (1980). Repair theory: A generative theory of bugs in procedural skills. *Cognitive Science, 4*(4), 379-426.

Case, R. (1996). Reconceptualizing the nature of children's conceptual structures and their development in middle childhood. In R. Case and Y. Okamoto (Eds.), *The role of central conceptual structures in the development of children's thought. Monographs of The Society for Research in Child Development, Serial 246 61*(1-2), 1-26.

Case, R., Griffin, S., and Kelly, W. (1999). Socioeconomic gradients in mathematical ability and their responsiveness to intervention during early childhood. In D.P. Keating and C. Hertzman (Eds.), *Developmental health and the wealth of nations: Social, biological, and educational dynamics* (pp. 125-149). New York: Guilford Press.

Chen, Z., and Klahr, D. (1999). All other things being equal: Children's acquisition of the control of variables strategy. *Child Development, 70*(5), 1098-1120.

Cole, K., Coffey, J., and Goldman, S. (1999). Using assessments to improve equity in mathematics. *Educational Leadership, 56*(6), 56-58.

Cole, M., Gay, J., and Glick, J. (1968). Some experimental studies of Kpelle quantitative behavior. *Psychonomic Monograph Supplements, 2*(10), 173-190.

Corbett, A.T., and Anderson, J.R. (1992). The LISP intelligent tutoring system: Research in skill acquisition. In J. Larkin, R. Chabay, and C. Scheftic (Eds.), *Computer assisted instruction and intelligent tutoring systems: Establishing communication and collaboration.* Hillsdale, NJ: Lawrence Erlbaum Associates.

Council of Chief State School Officers. (2000). *Key state educational policies on k-12 education: 2000.* Washington, DC: Author.

diSessa, A., and Minstrell, J. (1998). Cultivating conceptual change with benchmark lessons. In J.G. Greeno and S. Goldman (Eds.), *Thinking practices in learning and teaching science and mathematics.* Mahwah, NJ: Lawrence Erlbaum Associates.

Ericsson, K.A., and Simon, H.A. (1984). *Protocol analysis: Verbal reports as data.* Cambridge, MA: MIT Press.

Gelman, R. (1978). Counting in the preschooler: What does and does not develop. In R.S. Siegler (Ed.), *Children's thinking: What develops?* Hillsdale, NJ: Lawrence Erlbaum Associates.

Glaser, R. (1963). Instructional technology and the measurement of learning outcomes: Some questions. *American Psychologist, 18,* 519-521.

Greeno, J.G. (1991). Mathematical cognition: Accomplishments and challenges in research. In R.R. Hoffman and D.S. Palermo (Eds.), *Cognition and the symbolic processes: Applied and ecological perspecitves* (pp. 255-279). Hillsdale, NJ: Lawrence Erlbaum Associates.

Greeno, J.G., Pearson, P.D., and Schoenfeld, A.H. (1996). *Implications for NAEP of research on learning and cognition. Report of a study commissioned by the National Academy of Education.* Panel on the NAEP Trial State Assessment, Conducted by the Institute for Research on Learning. Stanford, CA: National Academy of Education.

Greeno, J.G., and The Middle-School Mathematics Through Applications Group. (1997). Participation as fundamental in learning mathematics. In J.A. Dossey, J.O. Swafford, M. Parmantie, and A.E. Dossey (Eds.), *Volume 1: Plenary paper, discussion groups, research papers, short oral reports, poster presentations.* Columbus, OH: The ERIC Clearinghouse for Science, Mathematics, and Environmental Education.

Griffin, S., and Case, R. (1997). Re-thinking the primary school math curriculum: An approach based on cognitive science. *Issues in Education, 3*(1), 1-49.

Griffin, S.A., Case, R., and Sandieson, R. (1992). Synchrony and asynchrony in the acquisition of children's everyday mathematical knowledge. In R. Case (Ed.), *The mind's staircase: Exploring the conceptual underpinnings of children's thought and knowledge* (pp. 75-98). Hillsdale, NJ: Lawrence Erlbaum Associates.

Griffin, S.A., Case, R., and Siegler, R.S. (1994). Rightstart: Providing the central conceptual prerequisites for first formal learning of arithmetic to students at risk for school failure. In K. McGilly (Ed.), *Classroom lessons: Integrating cognitive theory and classroom practice* (pp. 1-50). Cambridge, MA: MIT Press/Bradford Books.

Hamilton, L.S., Nussbaum, E.M., and Snow, R.E. (1997). Interview procedures for validating science assessments. *Applied Measurement in Education, 10*(2), 181-200.

Hart, K.M. (1984). *Ratio: Children's strategies and errors: A report of the strategies and errors in secondary mathematics project.* Windsor, England: Nfer-Nelson.

Holland, P.W., and Thayer, D.T. (1988). Differential item performance and the Mantel-Haenszel procedure. In H. Wainer and H.I. Braun (Eds.), *Test validity* (pp. 129-145). Hillsdale, NJ: Lawrence Erlbaum Associates.

Hunt, E., and Minstrell, J. (1994). A cognitive approach to the teaching of physics. In K. McGilly (Ed.), *Classroom lessons: Integrating cognitive theory and classroom practice* (pp. 51-74). Cambridge, MA: MIT Press.

Klahr, D., Chen, Z., and Toth, E.E. (in press). From cognition to instruction to cognition: A case study in elementary school science instruction. In K. Crowley, C.D. Schunn, and T. Okada (Eds.), *Designing for science: Implications from professional, instructional, and everyday science*. Mahwah, NJ: Lawrence Erlbaum Associates.

Koedinger, K.R., Anderson, J.R., Hadley, W.H., and Mark, M.A. (1997). Intelligent tutoring goes to school in the big city. *International Journal of Artificial Intelligence in Education, 8*, 30-43.

Lane, S. (1993). The conceptual framework for the development of a mathematics performance assessment instrument. *Educational Measurement: Issues and Practice, 12*(2), 16-23.

Lane, S., Wang, N., and Magone, M. (1996). Gender-related differential item functioning on a middle-school mathematics performance assessment. *Educational Measurement: Issues and Practice, 15*(4), 21-27; 31.

Linn, R.L., Baker, E.L., and Dunbar, S.B. (1991). Complex, performance-based assessment: Expectations and validation criteria. *Educational Researcher, 20*(8), 15-21.

Lomask, M., Baron, J., Greig, J., and Harrison, C. (1992). *ConnMap: Connecticut's use of concept mapping to assess the structure of students' knowledge of science*. A symposium presented at the Annual Meeting of the National Association of Research in Science Teaching, March, Cambridge.

Lorch, R.F., Jr., and van den Broek, P. (1997). Understanding reading comprehension: Current and future contributions of cognitive science. *Contemporary Educational Psychology, 22*(2), 213-246.

Magone, M.E., Cai, J., Silver, E.A., and Wang, N. (1994). Validating the cognitive complexity and content quality of a mathematics performance assessment. *International Journal of Educational Research, 21*(3), 317-340.

Marshall, S.P. (1995). *Schemas in problem solving*. New York, NY: Cambridge University Press.

Masters, G., and Forster, M. (1996). *Developmental assessment. Assessment resource kit*. Cemberwell, Victoria, Australia: Commonwealth of Australia.

Meiers, M., and Culican, S.J. (2000). Developmental assessment: A profile of DART and its use in current literacy research. *Learning Matters, 5*(3), 41-45.

Messick, S. (1993). Validity. In R.L. Linn (Ed.), *Educational measurement (3rd Edition)* (pp. 13-103). Phoenix, AZ: Oryx Press.

Messick, S. (1994). The interplay of evidence and consequences in the validation of performance assessments. *Education Researcher, 23*(2), 13-23.

Millman, J., and Greene, J. (1993). The specification and development of tests of achievement and ability. In R.L. Linn (Ed.), *Educational measurement (3rd Edition)* (pp. 335-366). Phoenix, AZ: Oryx Press.

Minstrell, J. (1992). Constructing understanding from knowledge in pieces: A practical view from the classroom. Paper presented at the annual meeting of the American Educational Research Association, San Francisco, April 20-24, 1992.

Minstrell, J. (2000). Student thinking and related assessment: Creating a facet-based learning environment. In Committee on the Evaluation of National and State Assessments of Educational Progress. N.S. Raju, J.W. Pellegrino, M.W. Bertenthal, K.J. Mitchell, and L.R. Jones (Eds.). Commission on Behavioral and Social Sciences and Education, *Grading the nation's report card: Research from the evaluation of NAEP* (pp. 44-73). Washington, DC: National Academy Press.

Minstrell, J., Stimpson, V., and Hunt, E. (1992). Instructional design and tools to assist teachers in addressing students' understanding and reasoning. Paper presented at the annual meeting of the American Educational Research Association, San Francisco, April, 1992.

Mislevy, R.J. (1996). Test theory reconceived. *Journal of Educational Measurement, 33*(4), 379-416.

National Council of Teachers of Mathematics. (1989). *Curriculum and evaluation standards for school mathematics.* Reston, VA: Author.

National Research Council. (1997). *Educating one and all: Students with disabilities and standards-based reform.* Committee on Goals 2000 and the Inclusion of Students with Disabilities. L.M. McDonnel, M.J. McLaughlin, and P. Morison, (Eds.) Commission on Behavioral and Social Sciences and Education. Washington, DC: National Academy Press.

National Research Council. (1999a). *Evaluation of the voluntary national tests, year 2: Final report.* Committee on the Evaluation of the Voluntary National Tests, Year 2. "/images/interface/clear.gif"L.L. Wise, R.J. Noeth, and J.A. Koenig, (Eds.). Commission on Behavioral and Social Sciences and Education. Washington, DC: National Academy Press.

National Research Council. (1999b). *High stakes: Testing for tracking, promotion, and graduation.* Committee on Appropriate Test Use. J.P. Heubert and R.M. Hauser, (Eds.). Commission on Behavioral and Social Sciences and Education. Washington, DC: National Academy Press.

National Research Council. (2001). *Adding it up: Helping children learn mathematics.* Mathematics Learning Study Committee. J. Kilpatrick, J. Swafford, and B. Findell, (Eds.) Division of Behavioral and Social Sciences and Education. Washington, DC: National Academy Press.

Resnick, L.B., Nesher, P., Leonard, F., Magone, M., Omanson, S., and Peled, I. (1989). Conceptual bases of arithmetic errors: The case of decimal fractions. *Journal for Research in Mathematics Education, 20*(1), 8-27.

Riley, M.S., and Greeno, J.G. (1988). Developmental analysis of understanding language about quantities and of solving problems. *Cognition and Instruction, 5,* 49-101.

Siegler, R.S. (1998). *Children's thinking (3rd Edition).* Upper Saddle River, NJ: Prentice Hall.

Silver, E.A., Alacaci, C., and Stylianou, D.A. (2000). Students' performance on extended constructed-response tasks. In E.A. Silver and P.A. Kenney (Eds.), *Results from the seventh mathematics assessment of the National Assessment of Educational Progress* (pp. 301-341). Reston, VA: National Council of Teachers of Mathematics.

Silver, E.A., and Lane, S. (1993). Assessment in the context of mathematics instruction reform: The design of assessment in the QUASAR project. In M. Niss (Ed.), *Cases of assessment in mathematics education* (pp. 59-69). London: Kluwer.

Silver, E.A., Smith, M.S., and Nelson, B.S. (1995). The QUASAR project: Equity concerns meet mathematics instructional reform in the middle school. In W.G. Secada, E. Fennema, and L.B. Adajian (Eds.), *New directions in equity in mathematics education* (pp. 9-56). New York: Cambridge University Press.

Silver, E.A., and Stein, M.K. (1996). The QUASAR project: The "revolution of the possible" in mathematics instructional reform in urban middle schools. *Urban Education, 30*(4), 476-521.

Starkey, P. (1992). The early development of numerical reasoning. *Cognition, 43*, 93-126.

VanLehn, K., and Martin, J. (1998). Evaluation of an assessment system based on Bayesian student modeling. *International Journal of Artificial Intelligence in Education, 8*, 179-221.

Verschaffel, L., Greer, B., and De Corte, E. (2000). *Making sense of word problems.* Lisse, Netherlands: Swets and Zeitlinger.

White, B.Y., and Frederiksen, J.R. (1998). Inquiry, modeling, and metacognition: Making science accessible to all students. *Cognition and Instruction, 16*(1), 3-118.

Wilson, M., and Wang, W-C. (1995). Complex composites: Issues that arise in combining different modes of assessment. *Applied Psychological Measurement, 19*(1), 51-71.

Zwick, R., and Ercikan, K. (1989). Analysis of differential item functioning in the NAEP history assessment. *Journal of Educational Measurement, 26*(1), 55-66.

CHAPTER 6

American Association for the Advancement of Science. (2001). *Atlas of science literacy.* Washington, DC: Author.

American Federation of Teachers. (1999). *Making standards matter 1999.* Washington, DC: Author.

Bandura, A., and Schunk, D. (1981). Cultivating competence, self-efficacy, and intrinsic interest through proximal self-motivation. *Journal of Personality and Social Psychology, 41*, 586-598.

Baroody, A.J. (1984). Children's difficulties in subtraction: Some causes and questions. *Journal for Research in Mathematics Education, 15*(3), 203-213.

Black, P., and Wiliam, D. (1998). Assessment and classroom learning. *Assessment in Education, 5*(1), 7-73.

Black, P., and Wiliam, D. (2000). *The king's medway Oxford formative assessment project.* Paper presented at the Conference of the British Educational Research Association, Cardiff, United Kingdom, September 2000.

Block, J.H., and Burns, R.B. (1976). Mastery in learning. In L.S. Shulman (Ed.), *Review of research in education.* Itasca, IL: Pocock.

Bonniol, J.J. (1991). The mechanisms regulating the learning process of pupils: Contributions to a theory of formative assessment. In P. Weston (Ed.), *Assessment of pupils' achievement: Motivation and schools success* (pp. 119-137). Amsterdam: Swets and Zeitlinger.

Broadfoot, P.M. (1986). Alternatives to public examinations. In D. L. Nuttall (Ed.), *Assessing educational achievement* (pp. 54-77). London: Flamer.

Butler, R. (1988). Enhancing and undermining intrinsic motivation: The effects of task-involving and ego-involving feedback evaluation on interest and performance. *British Journal of Educational Psychology, 58*, 1-14.

Carpenter, T.P., Fennema, E., and Franke, M.L. (1996). Cognitively guided instruction: A knowledge base for reform in primary mathematics instruction. *The Elementary School Journal, 97*(1), 3-20.

Carpenter, T.P., Fennema, E., Peterson, P.L., and Carey, D.A. (1988). Teachers' pedagogical content knowledge of students' problem-solving in elementary arithmetic. *Journal of Research in Mathematics Education, 19*, 385-401.

Carpenter, T.P., and Moser, J.M. (1984). The acquisition of addition and subtraction concepts in grades one through three. *Journal for Research in Mathematics Education, 15*(3), 179-202.

Cnen, C., and Stevenson, H.W. (1995). Culture and academic achievement: Ethnic and cross-national differences. *Advances in Motivation and Achievement, 9*, 119-151.

Cobb, P. (1998). Learning from distributed theories of intelligence. *Mind, Culture, and Activity, 5*(3), 187-204.

Cobb, P., Wood, T., Yackel, E., Nicholls, J., Wheatley, G., Trigatti, B., and Perlwitz, M. (1991). Assessment of a problem-centered second-grade mathematics project. *Journal for Research in Mathematics Education, 22*(1), 3-29.

College Board. (1994). *Evaluating the advanced placement portfolio in studio art.* New York: College Entrance Examination Board and Educational Testing Service.

Cronbach, L.J., and Gleser, G.C. (1965). *Psychological tests and personnel decisions* (*Second Edition*). Urbana, IL: University of Illinois Press.

Crooks, T.J. (1988). The impact of classrom evaluation practices on students. *Review of Educational Research, 58*(4), 438-481.

Deci, E., and Ryan, R. (1985). *Intrinsic motivation and self-determination in human behavior.* New York: Plenum Press.

Deci, E.L., and Ryan, R.M. (1994). Promoting self-determined education. *Scandinavian Journal of Educational Research, 38*, 3-14.

Falk, B. (2000). *The heart of the matter: Using standards and assessment to learn.* Portsmouth, NH: Heinemann.

Fernandes, M., and Fontana, D. (1996). Changes in control beliefs in Portugese primary school pupils as a consequence of the employment of self-assessment strategies. *British Journal of Educational Psychology, 66*, 301-313.

Finn, C.E., Jr., Petrilli, M.J., and Vanourek, G. (1998). The state of state standards. *Fordham Report* (*Volume 2*). Washington, DC: The Thomas B. Fordham Foundation.

Forster, M., and Masters, G. (1996a). *Paper and pen. Assessment resource kit.* Victoria, Australia: Commonwealth of Australia.

Forster, M., and Masters, G. (1996b). *Portfolios. Assessment resource kit.* Victoria, Australia: Commonwealth of Australia.

Forsyth, R., Hambleton, R., Linn, R., Mislevy, R., and Yen, W. (1996). *Design/feasibility team: Report to the National Assessment Governing Board*. Washington, DC: National Assessment Governing Board.

Fuchs, L.S., and Fuchs, D. (1986). Effects of systemic formative evaluation: A meta-analysis. *Exceptional Children, 53*(3), 199-208.

Gifford, B.R., and O'Connor, M.C. (1992). *Changing assessments: Alternative views of aptitude, achievement, and instruction*. Boston: Kluwer Academic.

Gipps, C. (1999). Socio-cultural aspects of assessment. In A. Iran-Nejad and P.D. Pearson (Eds.), *Review of research in education (Volume 24)*. (pp. 355-392). Washington, DC: American Educational Research Association.

Goldman, S.R., Mertz, D.L., and Pellegrino, J.W. (1989). Individual differences in extended practice functions and solution strategies for basic addition facts. *Journal of Educational Psychology, 81*, 481-496.

Graham, S., and Weiner, B. (1996). Theories and principles of motivation. In D.C. Berliner and R.C. Calfee (Eds.), *Handbook of educational psychology* (pp. 63-84). New York: Simon and Schuster Macmillan.

Graue, M.E. (1993). Integrating theory and practice through instructional assessment. *Educational Assessment, 1*, 293-309.

Greeno, J.G., and The Middle-School Mathematics through Applications Group. (1997). Participation as fundamental in learning mathematics. In J.A. Dossey, J.O. Swafford, M. Parmantie, and A.E. Dossey (Eds.), *Volume 1: Plenary paper, discussion groups, research papers, short oral reports, poster presentations*. Columbus, OH: The ERIC Clearinghouse for Science, Mathematics, and Environmental Education.

Griffin, S., and Case, R. (1997). Re-thinking the primary school math curriculum: An approach based on cognitive science. *Issues in Education, 3*, 1-65.

Grolnick, W.S., and Ryan, R.M. (1987). Autonomy in children's learning: An experimental and individual difference investigation. *Journal of Personality and Social Psychology, 52*, 890-898.

Guskey, G.R., and Gates, S.L. (1986). Synthesis of research on the effects of mastery learning in elementary and secondary classrooms. *Educational Leadership, 33*(8), 73-80.

Hattie, J. (1987). Identifying the salient facets of a model of student learning: A synthesis of meta-analyses. *International Journal of Educational Research, 11*, 187-212.

Hattie, J. (1990). Measuring the effects of schools. *Australian Journal of Education, 36*, 5-13.

Hattie, J., Biggs, J., and Purdie, N. (1996). Effects of learning skills interventions on student learning: A meta-analysis. *Review of Educational Research, 66*, 99-136.

Heath, S.B. (1981). Questioning at home and school: A comprehensive study. In G. Spindler (Ed.), *Doing ethnography: Educational anthropology in action*. New York: Holt, Rinehart, and Winston.

Heath, S.B. (1983). *Ways with words: Language, life, and work in communities and classrooms*. Cambridge, England: Cambridge University Press.

Holloway, S.D. (1988). Concepts of ability and effort in Japan and the United States. *Review of Educational Research, 58*, 327-345.

Klein, S.P., Hamilton, L.S., McCaffrey, D.F., and Stecher, B.M. (2000). *What do test scores in Texas tell us?* Santa Monica, CA: RAND.

Kluger, A.N., and DeNisi, A. (1996). The effects of feedback interventions on performance: A historical review, a meta-analysis, and a preliminary feedback intervention theory. *Psychological Bulletin, 119*, 254-284.

Koedinger, K.R., Anderson, J.R., Hadley, W.H., and Mark, M.A. (1997). Intelligent tutoring goes to school in the big city. *International Journal of Artificial Intelligence in Education, 8*, 30-43.

Koretz, D.M., and Barron, S.I. (1998). *The validity of gains in scores on the Kentucky Instructional Results Information System (KIRIS)*. Santa Monica, CA: RAND.

Kulik, C.L.C., Kulik, J.A., and Bangert-Drowns, R.L. (1990). Effectiveness of mastery-learning programs: A meta-analysis. *Review of Educational Research, 60*, 265-299.

Linn, R. (2000). Assessments and accountability. *Educational Researcher, 29*(2), 4-16.

Livingston, J.A., and Gentile, J.R. (1996). Mastery learning and the decreasing variability hypothesis. *Journal of Educational Research, 90*, 67-74.

Masters, G., and Forster, M. (1996). *Progress maps. Assessment resource kit*. Victoria, Australia: Commonwealth of Australia.

Meiers, M., and Culican, S.J. (2000). Developmental assessment: A profile of DART and its use in current literacy research. *Learning Matters, 5*(3), 41-45.

Miller, M.D., and Seraphine, A.E. (1993). Can test scores remain authentic when teaching to the test? *Educational Assessment, 1*(2), 119-129.

Minstrell, J. (2000). Student thinking and related assessment: Creating a facet-based learning environment. In Committee on the Evaluation of National and State Assessments of Educational Progress. N.S. Raju, J.W. Pellegrino, M.W. Bertenthal, K.J. Mitchell, and L.R. Jones (Eds.), Commission on Behavioral and Social Sciences and Education, *Grading the nation's report card: Research from the evaluation of NAEP* (pp. 44-73). Washington, DC: National Academy Press.

Mislevy, R.J. (1996). Test theory reconceived. *Journal of Educational Measurement, 33*(4), 379-416.

Mislevy, R.J. (2000). *The challenge of context*. Presentation at the 2000 CRESST Conference. Available: <http://cresst96.cse.ucla.edu/CRESST/pages/conf2000.htm>. [December 11, 2000].

Morland, D. (1994). *Physics: Examinations and assessment. Nuffield advanced science*. Harlow, United Kingdom: Longman.

National Academy of Education. (1997). *Assessment in transition: Monitoring the nation's educational progress*. Stanford, CA: Author.

National Council of Teachers of Mathematics. (1995). *Assessment standards for school mathematics*. Reston, VA: Author.

National Research Council. (1999a). *Grading the nation's report card: Evaluating NAEP and transforming the assessment of educational progress*. Committee on the Evaluation of National and State Assessments of Educational Progress. J.W. Pellegrino, L.R. Jones, and K.J. Mitchell, (Eds.), Commission on Behavioral and Social Sciences and Education. Washington, DC: National Academy Press.

National Research Council. (1999b). *High stakes: Testing for tracking, promotion, and graduation*. Committee on Appropriate Test Use. J.P. Heubert and R.M. Hauser, (Eds.), Commission on Behavioral and Social Sciences and Education. Washington, DC: National Academy Press.

National Research Council. (1999c). *Testing, teaching, and learning.* Committee on Title I Testing and Assessment. R.F. Elmore and R.R. Rothman, (Eds.), Commission on Behavioral and Social Sciences and Education. Washington, DC: National Academy Press.

Natriello, G. (1987). The impact of evaluation processes on students. *Educational Psychologist, 22*(2), 155-175.

New Standards™. (1997a). *Performance standards: English language arts, mathematics, science, applied learning (Volume 1. Elementary School).* Washington, DC: National Center for Education Statistics and the University of Pittsburgh.

New Standards™. (1997b). *Performance standards: English language arts, mathematics, science, applied learning (Volume 2. Middle School).* Washington, DC: National Center for Education Statistics and the University of Pittsburgh.

New Standards™. (1997c). *Performance standards: English language arts, mathematics, science, applied learning (Volume 3. High School).* Washington, DC: National Center for Education Statistics and the University of Pittsburgh.

Niyogi, N.S. (1995). *The intersection of instruction and assessment: The classroom.* Princeton, NJ: Educational Testing Service.

Pellegrino, J.W., Baxter, G.P., and Glaser, R. (1999). Addressing the "two disciplines" problem: Linking theories of cognition and learning with assessment and instructional practice. In A. Iran-Nejad and P.D. Pearson (Eds.), *Review of Research in Education (Volume 24).* (pp. 307-353). Washington, DC: American Educational Research Association.

Perrenoud, P. (1998). From formative evaluation to a controlled regulation of learning processes. Towards a wider conceptual field. *Assessment in Education, 5*(1), 85-102.

Resnick, L., and Harwell, M. (1998). *High performance learning communities District 2 achievement.* High Performance Learning Communities Project. Available: <http://www.lrdc.pitt.edu/hplc/HPLC_Publications.htm>. [September 15, 2000].

Sadler, R. (1989). Formative assessment and the design of instructional systems. *Instructional Science, 18*, 119-144.

Schofield, J.W., Eurich-Fulcer, R., and Britt, C.L. (1994). Teachers, computer tutors, and teaching: The artificially intelligent tutor as an agent for classroom change. *American Educational Research Journal, 31*(3), 579-607.

Shepard, L.A. (2000). The role of assessment in a learning culture. Presidential Address presented at the annual meeting of the American Educational Research Association, New Orleans, April 26.

Siegler, R.S., and Jenkins, E. (1989). *How children discover new strategies.* Hillsdale, NJ: Lawrence Erlbaum Associates.

Snow, R.E., and Mandinach, E.B. (1991). *Integrating assessment and instruction: A research and development agenda.* Princeton, NJ: Educational Testing Service.

Stiggins, R.J. (1997). *Student-centered classroom assessment.* Old Tappan, NJ: Prentice Hall.

Stipek, D.J. (1996). Motivation and instruction. In D.C. Berliner and R.C. Calfee (Eds.), *Handbook of educational psychology* (pp. 85-113). New York: Simon and Schuster Macmillan.

Strauss, S. (1998). Cognitive development and science education: Toward a middle level model. In I.E. Sigel and K.A. Renninger (Eds.), *Child psychology in practice* (*5th Edition*) (*Volume 4*). (pp. 357-399). New York: John Wiley and Sons.

Tebbutt, M.J. (1981). Teachers' views about the Nuffield advanced physics course. *Physics Education, 16*(4), 228-233.

Vispoel, W.P., and Austin, J.R. (1995). Success and failure in junior high school: Critical incident approach to understanding students' attributional beliefs. *American Educational Research Journal, 32*(2), 377-341.

Webb, N.L. (1997). *Criteria for alignment of expectations and assessments in mathematics and science education.* National Institute for Science Education and Council of Chief State School Officers Research Monograph No. 6. Washington, DC: Council of Chief State School Officers.

Weiner, B. (1986). *An attributional theory of motivation and emotion.* New York: Springer-Verlag.

White, B.Y., and Frederiksen, J.R. (2000). Metacognitive facilitation: An approach to making scientific inquiry accessible to all. In J. Minstrell and E. van Zee, (Eds), *Inquiring into inquiry learning and teaching in science,* pp. 33-370. Washington, DC: American Association for the Advancement of Science.

Wiggins, G. (1989). Teaching to the (authentic) test. *Educational Leadership, 46*(7), 41-47.

Wiggins, G. (1998). *Educative assessment. Designing assessments to inform and improve student performance.* San Francisco: Jossey-Bass.

Wilson, M., and Sloane, K. (2000). From principles to practice: An embedded assessment system. *Applied Measurement in Education, 13*(2), 181-208.

Wolf, D., Bixby, J., Glen III, J., and Gardner, H. (1991). To use their minds well: Investigating new forms of educational assessment. *Review of Research in Education, 17*, 31-74.

CHAPTER 7

Barron, B.J.S., Vye, N., Zech, L., Schwartz, D., Bransford, J., Goldman, S., Pellegrino, J., Morris, J., Garrison, S., and Kantor, R. (1995). Creating contexts for community based problem solving: The Jasper Challenge series. In C. Hedley, P. Antonacci, and M. Rabinowitz (Eds.), *Thinking and literacy: The mind at work.* Hillsdale, NJ: Lawrence Erlbaum Associates.

Bell, P. (1997). Using argument representations to make thinking visible for individuals and groups. In R. Hall, N. Miyake, and N. Enyedy (Eds.), *Proceedings of CSCL '97: The second international conference on computer support for collaborative learning* (pp. 10-19). Toronto: University of Toronto Press.

Bennett, R.E. (1999). Using new technology to improve assessment. *Educational Measurement: Issues and Practice, 18*(3), 5-12.

Bruckman, A. (1998). Community support for constructionist learning. *Computer Supported Cooperative Work: The Journal of Collaborative Computing, 7*, 47-86.

Casillas, A., Clyman, S., Fan Y., and Stevens, R. (2000). Exploring alternative models of complex patient management with artificial neural networks. *Advances in Health Sciences Education 5*, 23-41.

Chang, H., Henriques, A., Honey, M., Light, D., Moeller, B., and Ross, M. (1998). *The union city story: Technology and education reform.* New York: Center for Children and Technology, Education Development Corporation.

Cognition and Technology Group at Vanderbilt University. (1994). From visual word problems to learning communities: Changing conceptions of cognitive research. In K. McGilly (Ed.), *Classroom lessons: Integrating cognitive theory and classroom practice* (pp. 157-200). Cambridge, MA: MIT Press/Bradford Books.

Cognition and Technology Group at Vanderbilt University. (1997). *The Jasper Project: Lessons in curriculum, instruction, assessment, and professional development.* Hillsdale, NJ: Erlbaum.

Conati, C, and VanLehn, K. (1999). *Teaching meta-cognitive skills: Implementation and evaluation of a tutoring system to guide self-explanation while learning from examples.* Proceedings of AIED Œ99, 9th World Conference of Artificial Intelligence and Education, 1999, Le Mans, France. 297-304. Winner of the Outstanding Paper Award. <http://www.cs.ubc.ca/conati/aied99.doc>. [February 9, 2001].

Dede, C. (2000). Emerging influences of information technology on school curriculum. *Journal of Curriculum Studies, 32*(2), 281-304.

Edelson, D.C. (1997). Realising authentic science learning through the adaptation of scientific practice. In K. Tobin and B. Fraser (Eds.), *International handbook of science education.* Dordrecht, Netherlands: Kluwer.

Edmondson, K.M. (2000). Assessing science understanding through concept maps. In J.J. Mintz, J.H. Wandersee, and J.D. Novak (Eds.), *Assessing science understanding: A human constructivist view* (pp. 15-40). San Diego, CA: Academic Press.

Hickey, D.T., Kindfield, A.C.H., and Horwitz, P. (1999). *Large-scale implementation and assessment of the GenScope™ learning environment: Issue, solutions, and results.* Paper presented at the meeting of the European Association for Research on Learning and Instruction, Goteborg, Sweden, August.

Horwitz, P. (1998). The inquiry dilemma: How to assess what we teach. *Concord, Winter,* 9-10.

Hunt, E., and Minstrell, J. (1994). A cognitive approach to the teaching of physics. In K. McGilly (Ed.), *Classroom lessons: Integrating cognitive theory and classroom practice* (pp. 51-74). Cambridge, MA: MIT Press.

Katz, I.R., Martinez, M.E., Sheehan, K.M., and Tatsuoka, K.K. (1993). *Extending the rule space model to a semantically-rich domain: Diagnostic assessment in architecture.* Princeton, NJ: Educational Testing Service.

Kintsch, E., Steinhart, D., Stahl, G., LSA Research Group, Matthews, C., and Lamb, R. (2000). Developing summarization skills through the use of LSA-based feedback. *Interactive Learning Environments, 8*(2), 87-109.

Koedinger, K.R., Anderson, J.R., Hadley, W.H., and Mark, M.A. (1997). Intelligent tutoring goes to school in the big city. *International Journal of Artificial Intelligence in Education, 8*, 30-43.

Landauer, T.K. (1998). Learning and representing verbal meaning: The latent semantic analyasis theory. *Current Directions in Psychological Science, 7*(5), 161-164.

Landauer, T.K., Foltz, P.W., and Laham, D. (1998). An introduction to latent semantic analysis. *Discourse processes, 25*(2-3), 259-284.

Lawton, M. (1998, October 1). Making the most of assessments. (Case study number 9.) *Education week. Technology counts '98.*

Linn, M.C., and Hsi, S. (2000). *Computers, teachers, peers: Science learning partners.* Mahwah, NJ: Lawrence Erlbaum Associates.

Minstrell, J. (2000). Student thinking and related assessment: Creating a facet-based learning environment. In Committee on the Evaluation of National and State Assessments of Educational Progress. N.S. Raju, J.W. Pellegrino, M.W. Bertenthal, K.J. Mitchell, and L.R. Jones (Eds.). Commission on Behavioral and Social Sciences and Education, *Grading the nation's report card: Research from the evaluation of NAEP* (pp. 44-73). Washington, DC: National Academy Press.

Minstrell, J., Stimpson, V., and Hunt, E. (1992). *Instructional design and tools to assist teachers in addressing students' understanding and reasoning.* Paper presented at the symposium The Role of Cognitive Science in Developing Innovative Educational Applications at the annual meeting of the American Educational Research Association, April 23, 1992.

Mislevy, R.J., Steinberg, L.S., Almond, R.G., Haertel, G.D., and Penuel, W.R. (2000). *Leverage points for improving educational assessment.* Paper prepared for the Technology Design Workshop, Stanford Research Institute, Menlo Park, CA, February 25-26.

Mislevy, R.J., Steinberg, L.S., Breyer, F.J., Almond, R.G., and Johnson, L. (1999). *A cognitive task analysis, with implications for designing a simulation-based performance assessment.* Presented at the annual meeting of the American Educational Research Association, Montreal, Canada, April 1999.

Mintzes, J., Wandersee, J.H., and Novak, J.D. (Eds.) (2000). *Assessing science understanding: A human constructivist view.* San Diego, CA: Academic.

National Council of Teachers of Mathematics. (2000). *Principles and standards for school mathematics.* Reston, VA: Author.

National Research Council. (1996). *National science education standards.* National Committee on Science Education Standards and Assessment. Coordinating Council for Education. Washington, DC: National Academy Press.

National Research Council. (1999a). *The Assessment of Science meets the science of assessment: Summary of a workshop.* Board on Testing and Assessment. Commission on Behavioral and Social Sciences and Education. Washington, DC: National Academy Press.

National Research Council. (1999b). *Being fluent with information technology.* Committee on Information Technology Literacy. Computer Science and Telecommunications Board. Commission on Physical Sciences, Mathematics, and Applications. Washington, DC: National Academy Press.

National Research Council. (1999c). *The changing nature of work: Implications for occupational analysis.* Committee on Techniques for the Enhancement of Human Performance: Occupational Analysis. Commission on Behavioral and Social Sciences and Education. Washington, DC: National Academy Press.

National Research Council. (1999d). *How people learn: Brain, mind, experience, and school.* Committee on Developments in the Science of Learning. J.D. Bransford, A.L. Brown, and R.R. Cocking, (Eds.). Commission on Behavioral and Social Sciences and Education. Washington, DC: National Academy Press.

O'Neil, H.F., and Klein, D.C.D. (1997). *Feasibility of machine scoring of concept maps.* (CSE Technical Report 460). Los Angeles, CA: Center for Research on Evaluation, Standards, and Student Testing, University of California.

Secretary's Commission on Achieving Necessary Skills (SCANS). (1991). *What work requires of schools: A SCANS report for America 2000.* Washington, DC: U.S. Department of Labor.

Shavelson, R.J., and Ruiz-Primo, M.A. (2000). On the psychometrics of assessing science understanding. In J.J. Mintz, J.H. Wandersee, and J.D. Novak (Eds.), *Assessing science understanding: A human constructivist view* (pp. 303-341). San Diego, CA: Academic Press.

Sherwood, R., Petrosino, A., Lin, X.D., and Cognition and Technology Group at Vanderbilt. (1998). Problem based macro contexts in science instruction: Design issues and applications. In B.J. Fraser and K. Tobin (Eds.), *International handbook of science education* (pp. 349-362). Dordrecht, Netherlands: Kluwer.

Vendlinski, T., and Stevens, R. (2000). The use of artificial neural nets (ANN) to help evaluate student problem solving strategies. In B. Fishman and S. O'Connor-Divelbiss (Eds.), *Proceedings of the fourth international conference of the learning sciences* (pp. 108-114). Mahwah, NJ: Erlbaum.

Vye, N.J., Schwartz, D.L., Bransford, J.D., Barron, B.J., Zech, L., and Cognition and Technology Group at Vanderbilt. (1998). SMART environments that support monitoring, reflection, and revision. In D. Hacker, J. Dunlosky, and A. Graesser (Eds.), *Metacognition in educational theory and practice* (pp. 305-346). Mahwah, NJ: Erlbaum.

White, B.Y., and Frederiksen, J.R. (1998). Inquiry, modeling, and metacognition: Making science accessible to all students. *Cognition and Instruction, 16*(1), 3-118.

White, B.Y., and Frederiksen, J.R. (2000). Metacognitive facilitation: An approach to making scientific inquiry accessible to all. In J. Minstrell and E. van Zee (Eds.), *Teaching in the inquiry-based science classroom.* Washington, DC: American Association for the Advancement of Science.

CHAPTER 8

Achieve. (2000). *Testing: Setting the record straight.* Washington, DC: Author.

Baker, E.L. (1997). Model-based performance assessment. *Theory into Practice, 36*(4), 247-254.

Carpenter, T.P., Fennema, E., and Franke, M.L. (1996). Cognitively guided instruction: A knowledge base for reform in primary mathematics instruction. *The Elementary School Journal, 97*(1), 3-20.

Cohen, D.K., and Hill, H.C. (1998). *Instructional policy and classroom performance: The mathematics reform in California.* Philadelphia, PA: Consortium for Policy Research in Education.

Cronbach, L.J., and Gleser, G.C. (1965). *Psychological tests and personnel decisions* (*Second Edition*). Urbana, IL: University of Illinois Press.

Elmore, R.F. (1996). Getting to scale with good educational practice. *Harvard Educational Review, 66*(1), 1-26.

Elmore, R.F., and Burney, D. (1998). *Continuous improvement in Community District #2, New York City.* High Performance Learning Communities Project. Available: <http://www.lrdc.pitt.edu/hplc/HPLC_Publications.html>. [September 15, 2000].

Glaser, R. (1981). The future of testing: A research agenda for cognitive psychology and psychometrics. *American Psychologist, 36*(9), 923-936.

Glaser, R., and Silver, E. (1994). Assessment, testing, and instruction: Retrospect and prospect. In L. Darling-Hammond (Ed.), *Review of research in education (Volume 20).* (pp. 393-419). Washington, DC: American Educational Research Association.

Griffin, S., and Case, R. (1997). Re-thinking the primary school math curriculum: An approach based on cognitive science. *Issues in Education, 3,* 1-65.

Hargreaves, D.H. (1999). The knowledge creating school. *British Journal of Educational Studies, 47*(2), 122-144. Oxford: Blackwell and Mott.

Herman, J.L. (1992). *Accountability and alternative assessment: Research and development issues* (CSE Technical Report 348). Los Angeles: National Center for Research on Evaluation, Standards, and Student Testing, Graduate School of Education, University of California.

Koretz, D.M., and Barron, S.I. (1998). *The validity of gains in scores on the Kentucky Instructional Results Information System (KIRIS).* Santa Monica, CA: RAND.

Messick, S. (1984). The psychology of educational measurement. *Journal of Educational Measurement, 21*(3), 215-237.

Mislevy, R.J. (1994). Evidence and inference in educational assessment. *Psychometrika, 59*(4), 439-483.

National Academy of Education. (1996). *Implications for NAEP of research on learning and cognition.* Stanford, CA: Author.

National Academy of Education. (1999). *Recommendations regarding research priorities: An advisory report to the National Educational Research Policy and Priorities Board.* New York: Author.

National Center for Education Statistics. (2001). *Digest of education statistics, 2000.* Washington, DC: U.S. Department of Education.

National Research Council. (1999a). *High stakes: Testing for tracking, promotion, and graduation.* Committee on Appropriate Test Use. J.P. Heubert and R.M. Hauser, Eds. Commission on Behavioral and Social Sciences and Education. Washington, DC: National Academy Press.

National Research Council. (1999b). *How people learn: Brain, mind, experience, and school.* Committee on Developments in the Science of Learning. J.D. Bransford, A.L. Brown, and R.R. Cocking, (Eds.). Commission on Behavioral and Social Sciences and Education. Washington, DC: National Academy Press.

National Research Council. (1999c). *How people learn: Bridging research and practice.* Committee on Learning Research and Educational Practice. M.S. Donovan, J.D. Bransford, and J.W. Pellegrino, (Eds.). Commission on Behavioral and Social Sciences and Education. Washington, DC: National Academy Press.

National Research Council. (1999d). *Testing, teaching, and learning: A guide for states and school districts.* Committee on Title I Testing and Assessment. R.F. Elmore and R.R. Rothman, (Eds.). Commission on Behavioral and Social Sciences and Education. Washington, DC: National Academy Press.

Nichols, P.D. (1994). A framework for developing cognitively diagnostic assessments. *Review of Educational Research, 64*(4), 575-603.

Pellegrino, J.W., Baxter, G.P., and Glaser, R. (1999). Addressing the "two disciplines" problem: Linking theories of cognition and learning with assessment and instructional practice. In A. Iran-Nejad and P.D. Pearson (Eds.), *Review of research in education* (*Volume 24*). (pp. 307-353). Washington, DC: American Educational Research Association.

Plake, B.S., and Impara, J.C. (1997). Teacher assessment literacy: What do teachers know about assessment. In G. Phye (Ed.), *Handbook of classroom assessment* (pp. 53-68). San Diego: Academic Press.

Snow, R.E., and Lohman, D.F. (1993). Implications of cognitive psychology for educational measurement. In R.L. Linn (Ed.), *Educational measurement* (*3rd Edition*) (pp. 263-330). Phoenix, AZ: Onyx Press.

Stigler, J.W., and Hiebert, J. (1999). *The teaching gap: Best ideas from the world's teachers for improving education in the classroom.* New York: Free Press.

Stokes, D.E. (1997). *Pasteur's quadrant: Basic science and technological innovation.* Washington, DC: Brookings Institution Press.

Wilson, M., and Adams, R.J. (1996). Evaluating progress with alternative assessments: A model for chapter 1. In M.B. Kane (Ed.), *Implementing performance assessment: Promise, problems, and challenges.* Hillsdale, NJ: Erlbaum.

Appendix

Biographical Sketches

ROBERT GLASER (*Co-chair*) is founder and former director of the Learning Research and Development Center, as well as professor in the Departments of Psychology and Education at the University of Pittsburgh. His research focuses on the development of thinking and problem-solving abilities, the assessment of subject matter learning, and the integration of cognitive science and educational measurement. His National Research Council (NRC) service has included membership on the Committee on Developments in the Science of Learning; the National Committee on Science Education Standards and Assessment; and the Committee on Research in Mathematics, Science and Technology Education. He received a Ph.D. in psychological measurement and learning theory from Indiana University.

JAMES W. PELLEGRINO (*Co-chair*) is Frank W. Mayborn Professor of Cognitive Studies at Vanderbilt University. As of September 2001 he will become Distinguished Professor of Cognitive Psychology and Education at the University of Illinois at Chicago. Previously he served as dean of Vanderbilt's Peabody College of Education and as co-director of Vanderbilt's Learning Technology Center. He has been engaged in research and development activities related to children's and adults' thinking and learning and the implications for assessment and instructional practice. His most recent work has focused on the uses of technology and media in creating meaningful learning and instructional environments. He served as chair of the NRC Committee for the Evaluation of NAEP and co-chair of the NRC Committee on Learning Research and Educational Practice, and currently is a member of the NRC Committee on Improving Learning with Information Technology. He received his Ph.D. in experimental and quantitative psychology from the University of Colorado.

EVA L. BAKER is a professor in the Divisions of Psychological Studies in Education and Social Research Methodologies, and acting dean of the Graduate School of Education and Information Studies at the University of California, Los Angeles. She is also co-director of the Center for the Study of Evaluation. Her research focuses on the integration of teaching and measurement, including the design of instructional systems and new measures of complex human performances. She served on the NRC Panel on Data Confidentiality, the Committee on Title I Testing and Assessment, and the National Academy of Sciences Panel on Education Reform. She currently chairs the NRC's Board on Testing and Assessment. She received an Ed.D. from the University of California, Los Angeles.

GAIL P. BAXTER is a research scientist in the Center for Performance Assessment of the Educational Testing Service in Princeton, New Jersey. She has also served as an assistant professor in the School of Education at the University of Michigan, Ann Arbor. Her work focuses on issues of assessment, particularly the quality and cognitive complexity of science performance assessments. Her service with the NRC includes membership on the Committee on the Evaluation of National and State Assessments of Educational Progress. She received a Ph.D. in education from the University of California, Santa Barbara.

PAUL JOSEPH BLACK is an emeritus professor of science education at King's College in London, England. He is chair of the International Commission on Physics Education and a vice-president of the International Union of Pure and Applied Physics. He was consultant to the Organization for Economic Cooperation and Development (OECD) project on innovations in science, mathematics, and technology education in OECD member countries. His NRC service has included membership on the Board on Testing and Assessment, participation in a Working Group on Science Assessment Standards, and the NRC Committee on Classroom Assessment and the *National Science Education Standards*. He received a Ph.D. in physics from Cambridge University.

NAOMI CHUDOWSKY is a senior program officer in the NRC's Board on Testing and Assessment. She has also worked for the U.S. Department of Education and the Connecticut State Department of Education on the development of student assessments. She received a Ph.D. in educational psychology from Stanford University.

CHRISTOPHER L. DEDE is Timothy E. Wirth Professor in Learning Technologies and co-director of the Technology in Education Program in the Harvard University Graduate School of Education. He has also served as a professor at George Mason University with a joint appointment in the Schools of Information Technology and Engineering and of Education. His research interests span technology forecasting and assessment, emerging technologies for learning, and leadership in educational innovation. He is currently working on developing educational environments based on virtual reality technology and innovative methods of assessing learner performance in such environments. He received an Ed.D. in science education from the University of Massachusetts.

KADRIYE ERCIKAN is an assistant professor on the Faculty of Educational and Counseling Psychology and Special Education at the University of British Columbia. She has also served as a senior research scientist at CTB/McGraw-Hill, where she designed, scaled, scored, and equated norm-referenced and criterion-referenced tests. Her research interests are in evaluation methods, psychometrics, and linking of results from different assessments. She received a Ph.D. in research and evaluation methods from Stanford University.

LOUIS M. GOMEZ is an associate professor in the School of Education and Department of Computer Science at Northwestern University. His current research interests include the support of teaching and learning with computing and networking technology, applied cognitive science, shared computer-based workspaces, and human-computer interaction. He received a Ph.D. in psychology from the University of California, Berkeley.

EARL B. HUNT is a professor in the Department of Psychology at the University of Washington. His research and teaching interests are cognition, artificial intelligence, and mathematical models and techniques in social and biological sciences. His NRC service has included serving as vice-chair of the Personnel Systems Panel of the Strategic Technologies for the Army (STAR) Project and on the Board of Army Science and Technology. He received a Ph.D. in psychology from Yale University.

DAVID KLAHR is a professor and former head of the Department of Psychology at Carnegie Mellon University. His current research focuses on cognitive development, scientific reasoning, and cognitively based instructional interventions in early science education. His earlier work addressed cognitive processes in such diverse areas as voting behavior, college admissions, consumer choice, peer review, and problem solving. He pioneered the application of information-processing analysis to questions of cognitive development and formulated the first computational models to account for children's thinking processes. He received a Ph.D. in organizations and social behavior from Carnegie Mellon University.

RICHARD LEHRER is professor of cognitive science and mathematics education at the University of Wisconsin, Madison. He is also associate director of the National Center for Improving Student Learning and Achievement in Mathematics and Science. His research focuses on children's mathematical and scientific reasoning in the context of schooling. He received a Ph.D. in educational psychology and statistics from the University of New York, Albany.

ROBERT J. MISLEVY is a professor in the Department of Measurement, Statistics, and Evaluation in the School of Education at the University of Maryland. Before joining the faculty at Maryland, he was a distinguished research scientist in the Division of Statistics and Psychometrics Research of the Educational Testing Service. His research focuses on applying recent developments in statistical methodology and cognitive research to practical problems in educational assessment. He is currently working on evidence centered designs for complex assessments, such as simulation-based tests and coached practice systems. He received a Ph.D. in methodology of behavioral research from the University of Chicago.

WILLIE PEARSON, JR., is a professor of sociology as well as an adjunct in medical education at Wake Forest University. His research has centered on the career patterns of Ph.D. scientists (particularly African-Americans), human resource issues in science and engineering, science policy, and comparative family studies. His NRC service includes membership on the Committee on Women in Science and Engineering and the Committee on Education and Training for Civilian Aviation Careers. He received a Ph.D. in sociology from Southern Illinois University, Carbondale.

EDWARD A. SILVER is a professor of mathematics education at the University of Michigan, Ann Arbor. He has also served as a professor of cognitive studies and mathematics education at the University of Pittsburgh and as a senior scientist at the Learning Research and Development Center. His research interests focus on the teaching, learning, and assessment of mathematics, particularly mathematical problem solving. His service with the NRC includes membership on the Mathematical Sciences Education Board and the Study Group on Guidelines for Mathematics Assessment. He received a Ph.D. in mathematics education from Teachers College of Columbia University.

RICHARD F. THOMPSON is a professor and director of the program in neural, informational, and behavioral sciences at the University of Southern California. His expertise is in neuroscience and psychology, particularly neurophysiology, neuroanatomy, learning and memory, and sensation and perception. He is a member on the National Academy of Sciences. His NRC service has included membership on the Commission of Behavioral and Social Sciences and Education, the Committee on Techniques for the Enhancement of Human Performance, and the Committee on National Needs for Biomedical and Behavioral Research. He currently serves on the Board on Behavioral, Cognitive, and Sensory Sciences. He received a Ph.D. in psychobiology from the University of Wisconsin.

RICHARD K. WAGNER is a professor of psychology at Florida State University. His research interests focus on theories of human intelligence and the acquisition of complex cognitive knowledge and skills. His work has addressed measurement issues and practical considerations involving assessment of constructs in the domains of language, reading, and intelligence. He served as a member of the NRC Committee on Goals 2000 and the Inclusion of Students with Disabilities. He received a Ph.D. in cognitive psychology from Yale University.

MARK R. WILSON is a professor of measurement and assessment in the Graduate School of Education at the University of California, Berkeley. His research focuses on developing new psychometric models for analyzing data from theory-rich contexts; he is also concerned with the application of current measurement theory to more practical problems of testing and evaluation. He is a convenor of the Berkeley Evaluation and Assessment Research Center and is currently advising the California State Department of Education on assessment issues as a member of the Technical Study Group. He received a Ph.D. in measurement and educational statistics from the University of Chicago.

Index